Essays on Object-Oriented Software Engineering Volume I

Edward V. Berard

Prentice Hall, Englewood Cliffs, New Jersey 07632

An Alan R. Apt Book

Library of Congress Cataloging-in-Publication Data

Berard, Edward V.
    Essays on object-oriented software engineering / by Edward
V. Berard.
        p.   cm.
    Includes bibliographical references and index.
    ISBN 0-13-288895-5 (v. 1)
    1. Object-oriented programming.   2. Software engineering.
I. Title.
QA76.64.B47   1993
005.1'1--dc20   92-29772
                                                        CIP

Publisher: Alan Apt
Production Editor: Mona Pompili
Cover Designer: Wanda Lubelska Design
Prepress Buyer: Linda Behrens
Manufacturing Buyer: Dave Dickey
Editorial Assistant: Shirley McGuire

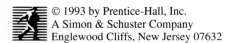 © 1993 by Prentice-Hall, Inc.
A Simon & Schuster Company
Englewood Cliffs, New Jersey 07632

The author and publisher of this book have used their best efforts in preparing this book. These efforts include the development, research, and testing of the theories and programs to determine their effectiveness. The author and publisher shall not be liable in any event for incidental or consequential damages in connection with, or arising out of, the furnishing, performance, or use of these programs.

Camera-ready copy for this book was prepared by the author on an Apple Macintosh IIfx using Aldus PageMaker 4.2 and Aldus Freehand 3.1.

Printed in the United States of America

10 9 8 7 6 5 4 3 2 1

ISBN 0-13-288895-5

ISBN 0-13-288895-5

90000

9 780132 888950

Prentice-Hall International (UK) Limited, *London*
Prentice-Hall of Australia Pty. Limited, *Sydney*
Prentice-Hall Canada, Inc., *Toronto*
Prentice-Hall Hispanoamericana, S.A., *Mexico*
Prentice-Hall of India Private Limited, *New Delhi*
Prentice-Hall of Japan, Inc., *Tokyo*
Simon & Schuster Asia Pte. Ltd, *Singapore*
Editora Prentice-Hall do Brasil, Ltda., *Rio de Janeiro*

To Margo,
my wife and my best friend

Trademark Information

Contents

Preface

The scientist takes off from the manifold observation of predecessors, and shows his intelligence, if any, by his ability to discriminate between the important and the negligible, by selecting here and there the significant steppingstones that will lead across the difficulties to new understanding. The one who places the last stone and steps across to the terra firma of accomplished discovery gets all the credit. Only the initiated know and honor those whose patient integrity and devotion to exact observation have made the last step possible.

— from As I Remember Him, *[1940] by Hans Zinsser*

I write to discover what I think.

— Daniel J. Boorstin, Librarian of Congress

Prologue

There are those who feel that "object-orientation" is just a fad — and a relatively new fad at that. These people often suspect that there is little substance to back up the concepts and claims associated with object-oriented technology (OOT). This is not the case. There are decades of research on, and well over a decade of practical applications of, OOT.

Still, even some of those who claim to be knowledgeable in things object-oriented often have problems communicating concepts and ideas. Some seem overly preoccupied with the syntax, semantics, and terminology of their pet object-oriented programming language. Others have described so-called object-oriented software development approaches (commonly referred to as "methodologies") in a manner that makes them appear little different from more conventional (e.g., structured and/or data modeling) approaches.

It seems that a good number of people want to stay in their own back yard. For those who have heard about OOT, but have not yet begun the transition, it is easy to dismiss OOT as a fad, advocated by mindless zealots and supported by only a few pieces of anecdotal evidence (at best). For practitioners of OOT, it is far easier to narrow the focus to the syntax and semantics of a particular programming language than to consider how the same concept is viewed and/or changed as it is implemented in different programming languages.

You could say that my main purpose in writing this book is to stimulate both thinking and discussion. One technique for accomplishing this goal is to cite more than one reference on each topic. When the same topic comes up in multiple places, I sometimes chose to use different references for the topic. I hope these techniques will cause two things to happen:

- Those who believe that OOT is just an unsubstantiated fad will begin to gain an appreciation of the mountains of research, technology, and experience behind many aspects of OOT.

- Those who, until now, have limited their view to one particular facet of OOT (e.g., a particular object-oriented programming language) will examine other facets and, thus, enrich their pool of ideas and views.

I used to think that I could lay out a buffet of concepts, definitions, and approaches, and that practitioners would select those that they felt would be most useful. However, my clients and fellow software engineers wanted more than just a listing of ideas. They wanted my particular recommendations — and the criteria I used to make the recommendations. Wherever possible, I have tried to make some recommendations. Still, I also do not want someone not to examine a particular option simply because Ed Berard does not recommend it.

My Background

In 1978, I became a self-employed consultant for the first time. By the end of 1979, people had found out that I could teach technical concepts, and I was tapped to develop and deliver a variety of short courses and seminars. Over the years since then, I have created seminars and short courses on over 60 different topics. However, I find teaching without practical, hands-on experience to be hollow. That is why:

- I hired a number of software engineers who helped me with the development of over one million lines of code in an object-oriented manner, and

- I provided consulting that guided my clients in making practical applications of the concepts I had covered in my training.

During the course of a normal year, I visit many different software shops, and talk with literally over 1,000 individuals about their needs and their views. My experience is not limited to the United States. For example, I have clients in Canada, the United Kingdom, France, Germany, Finland, and Belgium among others. My clients use a wide variety of programming languages, e.g., C++, Smalltalk, CLOS, Eiffel, Ada, Trellis, and others. They are at all stages of adopting object-oriented technology, and run the gamut from real-time, to management information systems (MIS), to systems programming, and even university faculty.

Naturally, each of my clients has his or her own perspective, problems, and terminology. I have spent a great deal of time sorting out what is common, and what is truly unique. For example, when a Smalltalk user speaks of "subclasses" and "superclasses," these concepts are identical to those implied by a C++ user who is talking about "derived classes" and "base classes," respectively. Parameterized classes (via genericity) on the other hand, are issues in C++ and Eiffel, but not in Smalltalk.

During the reviewing process for this book, several reviewers expressed disbelief about the state-of-the-practice as I described it. When I referred to what some felt was a particularly bad practice, I got comments such as "No one does that in this day and age." I found these comments rather provincial. While I wish that the general lack of knowledge, and some of the bad practices in general, were limited in scope, they are far more widespread than most people suspect.

Since 1979, I have visited hundreds of installations, and talked with thousands of programmers, software engineers, and their managers. In 1991 alone, I trained about 1,000 individuals, talked with a few hundred more at various conferences, and visited about two dozen sites. What I report in these articles is based on what I have heard and what I have seen.

To be fair, few technical people are afforded the luxury of researching and continually improving their software engineering practices. Far fewer have the opportunity to visit other sites with the intention of gaining perspective.

About This Book

Some of the chapters in this book are articles that I originally posted to "the net." I have updated these articles to reflect changing technology. (Most of the articles have been changed significantly.) I have also added graphics, several new articles, a set of object and class specifications (OCSs), and a glossary.

When you read these essays, keep the following in mind:

- This book is not a detailed "how to" book. It is not the intention of this book to exhaustively treat any particular branch of OOT, but rather to introduce concepts and ideas, and to stimulate discussion. (Follow on volumes will treat various topics in significantly more detail.)

- This book is a collection of essays, not a planned text where each chapter builds on the previous chapters. Although there is some thought given to the arrangement of the presentation, each chapter is meant to be self contained. You can read them in just about any order.

- Wherever possible, the discussions are programming-language-independent. I have attempted to provide a discussion in general terms that can be adapted to specific situations. For example, I tend to use the term "object" to encompass the concepts of classes, metaclasses, parameterized classes, non-class instances, and systems of objects. Some people in the object-oriented community, for example, use "object" to mean strictly an instance of a class.

- There is a vast universe of technology behind these essays. Each of them could have easily been expanded into a book (or set of books). I have tried to both limit the discussion and provide the reader with a "starter set" of references so that he or she can begin to pursue those topics that interest them the most.

- I have tried (not always successfully) to walk the line between academic research and industrial pragmatism. All of the references cited have a practical bearing on some aspect of one or more real world problems that I, or my clients, have encountered. However, academicians should find enough "research content" to make them somewhat comfortable.

Now, let me provide you with a thumbnail sketch of each essay:

- "Understanding Object-Oriented Technology" provides a brief historical introduction to object-oriented technology and a short discussion of "object-oriented programming."

- "Motivation for an Object-Oriented Approach to Software Engineering" discusses two different types of motivation: why would anyone consider using object-oriented in the first place, and considerations for using an object-oriented approach throughout the software life-cycle.

- "What Are Methodologies?" quickly describes the origins of systematic approaches to the engineering of software and describes two general influences on how we might accomplish object-oriented software engineering.

- "Life-Cycle Approaches" illustrates the fact that there are many different perspectives on software life-cycles, and the classic waterfall life-cycle approach is only one of them. The spiral life-cycle and the recursive/parallel life-cycle are briefly discussed.

- "Understanding the Recursive/Parallel Life-Cycle" is one of the few articles specifically dedicated to the recursive/parallel life-cycle. This type of life-cycle has already been successfully applied to many object-oriented projects over the past eight years.

- "Abstraction, Encapsulation, and Information Hiding" clarifies the often confused definitions of these terms.

- "Object Coupling and Object Cohesion" is the largest essay in this collection. When I attempted to survey the literature on this topic, to embellish what I have been covering in my classes and my consulting, I found very little detail, and some definite confusion. The essay will hopefully provide more detail without adding too much confusion.

- "Object and Class Specifications" describes a documentation technique for individual objects that I and others have been using for the past six years. The appendix for this book contains nine examples of OCSs.

- "Large Object-Oriented Entities" are systems of objects. These include both kits and systems of interacting objects. Both are described in this chapter.

- "Object-Oriented Domain Analysis" describes a process for systematically approaching reusability in object-oriented applications. Please note that this is at a higher level of abstraction than mere specialization hierarchies.

- "The Creation of and Conversion to Object-Oriented Requirements" serves as an introduction to the object-oriented requirements analysis (OORA) essay. It discusses the "front-end" of an OORA effort.

- "Object-Oriented Requirements Analysis" is the process that gets you from "a glimmer of an idea" to a complete object-oriented external specification for the system to be developed.

- "Object-Oriented Design" picks up where OORA leaves off. It is the process whereby a software engineer establishes the internal architecture of an object-oriented application. It mentions the difference between a software engineering view and a programming view of design.

- "Evaluating an Object-Oriented Programming Language" covers many of the favorite buzzwords used to describe so-called object-oriented programming languages. Also proposed is a three-pronged evaluation method for determining the viability of using a given programming language for an object-oriented software engineering effort.

- "Issues in Testing Object-Oriented Software" covers not only the confusion about testing terminology and testing techniques, but also some of the issues that make testing of object-oriented software different from testing non-object-oriented software.

- "Specifying Test Cases for Object-Oriented Software" provides a detailed specification mechanism for test cases for object-oriented software.

- "Readings in Object-Oriented Technology" is a starter set of reading material for object-oriented software engineering.

I hope that the content of this book will prove useful to you whatever your background — and thanks for listening.

Acknowledgments

I have received many comments on my writings over the years — far too many to list all who have contributed. However, let me try:

- Alan Apt of Prentice Hall is the one who finally coaxed me into bringing a book to fruition. Knowing my nature, this was an incredible feat.

- Ron Schultz and Jody Richardson who are members of the technical staff at Berard Software Engineering, Inc. both provided commentary on earlier drafts of the essays.

- Of course, all the students that I have had in my seminars and courses have provided innumerable insights into the material presented here.

- Other people who both reviewed the text and encouraged me to write the book include Ralph Johnson, Nancy Churchill, Scott Duncan, Paul S.R. Chisholm, and Henry A. Etlinger.

Jean Ballantyne, my administrative assistant, provided both clerical support and encouragement. Mona Pompili at Prentice Hall guided me through the final proofing and typesetting of the book.

1   **Understanding Object-Oriented Technology**

"When I use a word," Humpty Dumpty said, in a rather scornful tone, "it means just what I choose it to mean — neither more nor less."

"The question is," said Alice, "whether you can make words mean so many different things."

> — *from* Alice's Adventures in Wonderland *[1865] by Lewis Carroll (Charles Lutwidge Dodgson)*

Since its inception, and more so lately, the adjective object-oriented has been bandied about with carefree abandon with much the same reverence accorded motherhood, apple pie and structured programming.

> — *from [Bhaskar, 1983]*

What is object-oriented programming? My guess is that object-oriented programming will be in the 1980's what structured programming was in the 1970's. Everyone will be in favor of it. Every manufacturer will promote his products as supporting it. Every manager will pay lip service to it. Every programmer will practice it (differently). And no one will know just what it is.

> — *from [Rentsch, 1982]*

Prologue

In 1982, some of my clients began asking me to explain something called "object-oriented design." Although I had heard the term myself, I must admit that, at the time, I knew very little about it. Being a scientist by training, I had a plan of attack:

1. Begin a literature search, with the following goals:

    a. Find the earliest documented mention of the term (i.e., "object-oriented")

    b. Realizing that the term was technological in origin, follow the discussion (in books, articles, et cetera) with the intention of:

        i. discovering different facets of the technology. I have learned from experience that no one author, no matter how gifted, knows all things about, or expresses complete knowledge of, a given topic. Quite frankly, you have to read "a large pile of references" before you can begin to claim that you know something useful about a subject.

        ii. noticing the emergence of new facets of the technology. Most, if not all, technologies are in a constant state of flux. One aspect of this is the continual introduction of new concepts and terms.

        iii. following concepts as they mutated. In any living technology, concepts and terms take on different meanings and connotations with time. Some of these changes are subtle, others are drastic. Sometimes entire sets of ideas

1

disappear. Only if a technology exists for a prolonged period of time, do some definitions become, for all intents and purposes, "frozen." In the early stages of a technology, the mutations are often frequent and violent.

iv. identifying alternative, and possibly conflicting, interpretations of the same concept or term. Each of us sees things in a different light, and scientific debate is hardly an original concept.

v.   increasing my chances of being able to separate *concepts* from *implementations*. The job of scientists, mathematicians, and engineers is to identify valid patterns, i.e., abstractions. Low levels of abstraction tend to be implementations, while higher levels of abstraction tend to be concepts. Concepts, I have found, tend to be more "mobile" than are implementations, i.e., they can be used in more situations. (Does the word "reuse" come to mind?)

c.   Being able to justify any conclusions or recommendations I might make to my clients. I might really have an occasional good idea, but my clients felt better if, for example, they knew they were not going to be the first ones to try it out.

2.   Become comfortable enough with the technology to:

a.   explain it to all levels of personnel, e.g., from corporate management to the most technical of the techies.

b.   create and deliver organized, coherent courses and seminars on the technology — complete with very detailed "how to do it" and "how to know that you did it correctly" presentations.

c.   make specific recommendations as to how the technology could best be applied to any specific project my clients had in mind. [Notice that this implies more than just concepts. Application of technology seldom takes place in a vacuum. My clients needed commercial information (e.g., who sells the best tools?), infrastructure information (e.g., how is this going to impact our internal organization, policies, and procedures?), and political information (e.g., how is this going to impact our dealings with our customers?).]

My goal was *not* to invent any new technology. Indeed, I am a firm believer that anything I can think of has probably been thought of, and documented, by many others before me. My main purpose was, and still is, to make the technology real, i.e., to get it off of paper and into practice.

All along, my clients kept asking me questions like: "Are we the only ones doing this?", "Is this stuff going to go away?", and "Is IBM interested in object-oriented technology? It ain't real until IBM 'gives it its blessing.'" I kept assuring them that interest in things object-oriented was growing.

Well, sometime around 1985-1986, "the stuff hit the fan." All of a sudden, object-oriented technology was an "overnight sensation." I began to feel better. However, my relief was short lived.

I noticed that "object-oriented <fill-in-the-blank>" was being referred to as "the latest fad." People were claiming that object-oriented was just a buzzword, or merely old ideas in new clothing. Worse, in addition to everybody trying to get on the bandwagon, there were growing numbers of rabid object-oriented zealots who were more than happy to spread "object-oriented hype" like an oil slick over the software engineering landscape.

I would like to say that I have never seen anything like this before, but that wouldn't be true. ("It's deja vu all over again." — Yogi Berra) I have run into this problem with such items as: structured programming, relational databases, and life-cycle methodologies in general. Each time a "new" technology becomes popular, people claim it has no definition.

Let's see if we can get a handle on this object-oriented thing.

Brief History of Object-Oriented Technology

If you really dig deep, you will find a number of object-oriented concepts in the early (late 1940s, early 1950s) work in artificial intelligence. Concepts like "objects" and "attributes of objects" were indeed mentioned. However, the term "object-oriented" was not used, and there was no mention of terms such as "inheritance." The most significant contributions to object-oriented technology from the AI community have been much more recent.

The next significant "blip" to show up is Sutherland's Sketchpad ([Sutherland, 1963]). This is probably the first significant reference to "object-oriented graphics."

Many object-oriented enthusiasts like to cite the introduction of Simula ([Dahl and Nygaard, 1966]), as the first (or at least an immediate precursor to) object-oriented programming language. Kristen Nygaard and Ole-Johan Dahl introduced a number of object-oriented concepts in Simula, e.g., encapsulation at a higher lexical level than mere subprograms, and the "virtual" concept (i.e., localizing state information and operations for an object within the object itself).

(In [Wexelblat, 1981], Dahl relates an amusing story about a new grad student at the University of Norway. The student rushed into the office of the computer science department, and informed the department head that two men were arguing very loudly and forcefully in the building, and that the grad student was afraid the discussion would quickly become violent. The department head went into the hall and listened. He then returned and assured the grad student that there was no problem — it was just Nygaard and Dahl discussing Simula.)

Also during the late 1960s, Alan Kay was working at the University of Utah on FLEX. Kay wanted FLEX to be "the first personal computer to directly support a graphics and simulation-oriented language." (See [Kay, 1977].) Kay wanted the computer to be designed so that it could be used by non-expert computer users. He later said that, during the FLEX effort, he had been guided "by the central ideas of the programming language Simula...."

It is important to realize that Kay viewed object-oriented techniques as a means of *simplifying* computer usage. When you hear people say things like, "object-oriented systems more closely resemble 'real life' than do, for example, functional decomposition systems," they are echoing Kay's original intentions.

Unfortunately, Kay was frustrated by the hardware and software limitations in the late 1960s, and "although the design of FLEX was encouraging, it was not comprehensive enough to be useful to a wide variety of nonexpert users."

Around 1970, Kay went to work for Xerox at the Palo Alto Research Center (PARC). At Xerox PARC, he helped to create a hardware/software system called Dynabook. The hardware part of Dynabook later became the Xerox STAR. The software part of Dynabook was what we call Smalltalk. The first version of Smalltalk was released in 1972.

It was also around 1970, that the term "object-oriented" came into significant use. Some people credit Alan Kay as the first to use the term. He used it to describe the thinking behind Smalltalk, and many people think of Smalltalk as the first and archetypal object-oriented programming language. (See [Goldberg and Robson, 1983].)

It was not until the early- to mid-1980s that we began to see a proliferation of so-called object-oriented programming languages, e.g., Objective-C ([Cox, 1986]), C++ ([Stroustrup, 1986]), Self ([Ungar and Smith, 1987]), Eiffel ([Meyer, 1987]), Flavors ([Moon, 1986]), and Trellis/Owl ([Schaffert et al., 1986]).

(If you do any extensive reading on "object-oriented programming languages," you will find a significant amount of variation. For brevity, I will skip a series of discussions on, for example, class-based versus "classless" object-oriented languages, the importance of physical (i.e., syntactical and semantic) encapsulation, and dynamic vs. static binding.)

The late 1970s also saw the introduction of object-oriented computer hardware. Although some claim that the IBM System 38 was an object-oriented architecture, it is really more of a "capability-based" architecture. (See, e.g., [Fabry, 1974], [Levy, 1984], and [Myers, 1982].) Hardware architectures that are much more in keeping with the object-oriented spirit include the Intel iAPX 432 ([Intel, 1980] and [Organick, 1983]) and Rekursiv ([Pountain, 1988]).

Object-oriented database systems (OODBSs), which were virtually non-existent in 1980, seem to be growing in strength. The first commercial OODBSs appeared in 1985. References on the topic abound, e.g., [Atkinson et al., 1989], [Cattell, 1991], [Dittrich and Dayal, 1986], and [Zdonik and Maier, 1990].

During the 1980s, object-orientation began to have an impact on parts of the software life-cycle outside of the coding activity. In 1980, Grady Booch introduced the concept of object-oriented design (OOD) as a life-cycle process that defined the interactions and interrelationships among the software components that made up the application. See, for example, [Booch, 1981], [Booch, 1982], [Booch, 1986], and [Booch, 1991]. Others have also specified their view of what OOD should be, e.g., [Rumbaugh et al., 1991] and [Wirfs-Brock et al., 1990].

In the later part of the 1980s, the need to specify the requirements for a software product in an object-oriented manner became very evident. Attempting to use more traditional analysis methods (e.g., structured analysis) as precursors to OOD were much less than satisfactory. This led to the establishment of object-oriented analysis (OOA) and object-oriented requirements analysis (OORA) methodologies, e.g., [Coad and Yourdon, 1990] and [Shlaer and Mellor, 1988].

Today, we have discussions of object-oriented domain analysis (e.g., [Shlaer and Mellor, 1989]), testing of object-oriented software (e.g., [Smith and Robson, 1992]), and metrics for object-oriented software (e.g., [Chidamber and Kemerer, 1991]). There are even texts on the management of object-oriented software development efforts (e.g., [BSE, 1992]).

Unfortunately, one area which is badly in need of expansion is "truly object-oriented computer aided software engineering tools" (OO CASE). One of the major obstacles to OO CASE tools is the wide variety of "object-oriented" approaches that are currently in use. Some methodologists, or their organizations, have put out their own CASE tools, e.g., Rational's ROSE™ and Object International's OOATool™. Some CASE vendors have chosen to automate the approaches from several different methodologists, e.g., Mark V Systems, Ltd.'s ObjectMaker™ and Protosoft Inc.'s Paradigm Plus™. However, it will be some time before the object-oriented technology market becomes as focused as the so-called structured technology marketplace.

Those seeking more information on OO CASE tools are advised to consult [Anderson et al., 1989], [Jeffcoate and Templeton, 1991], and [Salmons and Babitsky, 1992].

To sum up: Object-oriented technology got going in the late 1960s, began to take on significant definition in the 1970s, and exploded during the mid-1980s. In the 1990s, our understanding, practice, and use of things object-oriented is still accelerating.

Two Different Cultures

To better understand object-oriented technology, it helps to understand the people who make up the so-called "object-oriented community" itself. Far from being monolithic, there is a great deal of diversity within this community. Many object-oriented people, for example, seem to focus primarily on programming language issues. They tend to cast all discussions in terms of the syntax and semantics of their chosen object-oriented programming language. These people find it impossible (for all intents and purposes) to discuss any software engineering activity (e.g., analysis, design, and testing) without direct mention of some specific implementation language.

Outside of producing executable "prototypes," people who emphasize programming languages seldom have well-defined techniques for analyzing their clients' problems or describing the overall architecture of the software product. A great deal of what they do is intuitive. If they happen to have a natural instinct/intuition for good analysis or good design, their efforts on small-to-medium, non-critical projects can result in respectable software solutions.

Programming language people use the terms "analysis" and "design" in a very loose sense. Analysis can mean listening to their customer, making some notes and sketches, thinking about both the problem and potential solutions, and even constructing a few software prototypes. Design can mean the code-level design of an individual object, the development of an inheritance (specialization) hierarchy, or the informal definition and implementation of a software product (e.g., identify all the objects, create instances of the objects, and have the instances send messages to each other).

Another sector of the object-oriented community is interested in formality and rigor. To these people, software engineering is largely very systematic, repeatable, and transferable. They view object-oriented software engineering as primarily an *engineering* process with well-defined, coordinated tasks, and well-defined deliverables. The quality of the resulting products (and the process itself) can be evaluated in a *quantitative*, as well as qualitative, manner.

For members of this second camp, "object-oriented programming" (OOP) is primarily a coding activity, and items such as "object-oriented design" (OOD) did not exist until about 1980. The programming language people, on the other hand, often lay claim to the origin of all things object-oriented, including object-oriented design. Even though a well-defined, quantifiable, transferable, and repeatable process for object-oriented design did not exist until the early 1980s, in their minds OOD has existed at least since there were object-oriented programming languages — a process many people date from 1966 when Simula was first introduced.

As you might guess, there are significant cultural differences between these two groups of object-oriented people. For example, some of those who emphasize rigor and formality view the programming language people as chaotic, overly error prone, wasteful, and largely unpredictable. On the other hand, some of the programming language people consider "formality" and "rigor" to be mere window dressing — at best adding nothing to the quality of the final product, and at worst increasing the cost of development while simultaneously delaying the delivery and lowering the quality of the resulting software product.

Even if one takes into account the widely different views described above, there are still significant variations within each of these perspectives. Consider inheritance, i.e., the process whereby an object acquires characteristics from another object. (Please note that we are using "object" in its most generic sense. Some people restrict the term "object" to mean only instances of classes.) A few object-oriented programming languages allow an object to inherit directly from only one other object (single inheritance). Other languages allow an object to inherit characteristics from more than one object (multiple inheritance). Someone who defines OOD in programming language terms may choose to include or exclude multiple inheritance from the design process based on whether or not their particular language supports the concept.

Other issues that arise in the programming language camp include the mixing of data and objects, the ability to have program elements that are not encapsulated within any object, and the use of exceptions, parameterized classes, metaclasses, and concurrency.

Within the "formality and rigor" group there is also a significant amount of diversity. Some try to portray object-oriented methods as slightly recast structured approaches (old wine in new bottles). Others advocate a more data-driven style, e.g., the extensive use of entity-relationship diagrams and other data modeling techniques. Still others seem to have successfully blended object-oriented thinking and rigorous software engineering. In effect, they have integrated the two without losing the benefits of either.

Almost everyone that advocates a formal approach views object-oriented *design* as only one part of the software development life-cycle. It may be preceded by such activities as analysis and feasibility studies and followed by the production of source code. Those accomplishing object-oriented design will be expected to interact with testing, quality assurance, and management personnel. Only if the software problem is small, and of relatively low risk, will object-oriented design be the *first* life-cycle activity, and even then it will be followed by object-oriented programming.

What Does the Word "Object" Mean?

Depending on who you ask, you will get quite a wide variety of definitions for the word "object." Those from the object-oriented programming language culture sometimes define objects in low-level implementation terms, e.g., "an object is some private memory with some associated functions" or "an object is like a 'struct' with functions in some of the fields." Those with a more software engineering bent tend to describe objects as corresponding to "real world" entities, e.g., "objects are those things that populate the universe around us."

The concept of a "**class**" is often defined as a template, description, pattern, or blueprint for a category of very similar items. (Some people define "class" as the collection or set of all things that are either created using, or matching, a specified pattern. Within the object-oriented community, this is a minority viewpoint.) Classes are used as templates or "factories" for the creation of specific items that meet the criteria defined in the class. I should also note that classes may have characteristics that they do not share with the specific items created through the use of classes.

An "**instance**" is a specific thing, item, or entity. Usually, we do not think of instances as patterns, but, rather as items created using patterns. This means that, if I wish to create instances, I will first need to define a class, and then use this class to create instances. The process of creating (manufacturing) an instance is often called "**instantiation**." (Note that "instantiation" is often used to describe both the process of creating an instance, and the instance itself.) In so-called "classless" object-oriented systems (e.g., Self), I can create an instance without first creating a class for that instance.

Many people use the term "object" to mean exclusively "an instance of a class." They would never use the term object to refer to a class. This viewpoint can be found, for example, in the Smalltalk and C++ communities.

However, things are not always that simple. A "**metaclass**" is a class whose instances are themselves classes. This means that if I use the term object to mean an instance of a class, and I allow for the existence of metaclasses, then classes can themselves be referred to as objects. In such circumstances, instances that are not classes an be referred to as "**non-class instances**."

Some object-oriented programming languages, e.g., Eiffel and C++, allow for parameterized classes. A "**parameterized class**" can be thought of as a template for a class. Those that distinguish parameterized classes from metaclasses do so by saying that metaclasses have "run-time" behavior (i.e., they have methods that can be used during program execution), whereas parameterized classes have only "compile-time" behavior. Some people refer to parameterized classes as objects.

Systems of objects (see chapter 9 of this book) are also often referred to as objects. An application created in an object-oriented manner is an example of a system of objects. A library of classes can also be thought of as a system of objects. It is occasionally useful to refer to a system of objects as if it were a single object.

So, we can see that the term object can be (and has been) used to refer to classes, instances, metaclasses, parameterized classes, and systems of objects. However, depending on who you are talking to, the term object may be restricted to mean only an instance of class. In this book, we will often use "object" in the more general sense.

What Is Object-Oriented Programming?

A flippant (and fairly inaccurate) answer to the question, "what is object-oriented programming?", would be: developing an application using an object-oriented programming language. What most of us want, however, is an answer that extracts the essence of the concept.

Peter Wegner ([Wegner, 1986]) gives us the beginnings of an answer:

> We define "object-oriented" so that it includes prototypical object-oriented languages like Smalltalk and Loops, but excludes languages like Ada, Modula, and Clu which have data abstractions but are not generally considered object-oriented. Support of data abstraction is a necessary but not sufficient condition for a language to be object-oriented. Object-oriented languages must additionally support both the management of collections of data abstractions by requiring data abstractions to have a type, and the composition of abstract data types through an inheritance mechanism:
>
> object-oriented = data abstraction + abstract data types + type inheritance.

Very often, definitions of "object-oriented anything" come off as definitions of the way Smalltalk does it. What I think is missing are the original intentions of Alan Kay. Kay wanted object-oriented to be simpler than conventional programming, and more like "real life."

Let's start with some basics. First, think of "objects" as you do in everyday (non-software-related) life. For example, if you knew nothing about computers, you would still have no problems identifying a car, a bank account, or a human being as an object. If asked, you probably would acknowledge that none of these items is only data, or only functions. You might even admit that these items are all "black boxes" in the sense that they each present an external interface to those who come into contact with them, and they all restrict access to their internal implementations.

This is probably one of the most important points about object-oriented approaches, i.e., objects are black boxes. One of the reasons that electronics engineers seem to be so much more productive than their software counterparts is that they respect and understand the value of black boxes. For example, you seldom see an engineer scraping the plastic off the top of a chip. (Yes, I know it's really a dual in-line package (dip).)

For the next concept, let's consider the implementation of a stack in a number of different programming languages. For purposes of our discussion, we will consider a stack to be a list to which we may add or delete items from one end only, i.e., a stack is a last in, first out (LIFO) structure. Now let's ask some programmers how they might implement a stack:

- A Fortran programmer might choose to implement the stack as an array.

- A C or Pascal programmer might implement the stack as a linked list.

- Someone with an Ada or Modula background might realize that a stack is more than just data. For example, there are rules which govern how this data must be handled.

They might choose to implement the stack as a package (Ada) or a module (Modula).

At this point, we have stumbled on two more aspects of objects:

1. Objects are *complete* entities. They are not "just data" or "just functions," or even "just data and functions combined." Using the capabilities of our programming language we must strive to capture the most complete abstraction possible. If our language provides exceptions and constants, for example, then we may wish to incorporate these items into our programming language abstraction of the "real world" object.

2. Objects are encapsulated concepts. If our programming language provides encapsulating mechanisms (e.g., Ada's packages, Modula's modules, Simula's classes, and Smalltalk's classes), we would be strongly advised to use these mechanisms. If our programming language lacks these mechanisms, then we will have to settle for conceptual (i.e., not physical) encapsulation.

Note that some encapsulation mechanisms allow you to both hide the underlying implementation and present a controlled interface to the outside world.

What about those other things that Wegner mentioned? Let's look at "data abstraction" first. Abstraction is the process of focusing on the essential details while ignoring the nonessential details. In functional abstraction, we may know a good deal about the interface information for a function, but very little about how the actual function is accomplished, i.e., the function is a "high level concept" (an abstraction).

Data abstraction extends functional abstraction. In data abstraction, not only is the function performed as an abstraction, but the interface data is also treated as an abstraction. For example, consider a generic sort utility. The sorting algorithm may be unknown (functional abstraction), but the items to be sorted are also treated as an abstraction.

What we really should be talking about is not data abstraction, but rather "object abstraction." For example consider a list object. If the same list object can be used for "a list of names," "a list of addresses," or "a list of stacks," then we can treat the objects which might be placed in the list as an abstraction.

Notice, once again, that real life is creeping back into the picture. In everyday life, we have few problems separating the concept of a list from those items which may be placed in the list.

What about inheritance? If I were to tell you that I had a "Frample" in the parking lot, I might get a more than one puzzled look. If I then told you that "a Frample is an automobile," some of the puzzlement would go away. You might suspect that a Frample had four wheels, was designed to carry people and other items from one location to another, and had an engine. This is an example of inheritance, i.e., the Frample has acquired (inherited) characteristics from the concept of an automobile, and, thus, shares some characteristics in common with all automobiles.

Inheritance means simply that an object acquires characteristics from one or more other objects. (A variation on this scheme is "delegation" — but that's a whole other story.) In class-based object-oriented programming languages, it is usually only the classes that can inherit from each other. (A class can be thought of as a template, a blueprint, or a pattern for a whole category of objects.)

In languages which closely follow the Smalltalk model, inheritance is a dynamic concept, but there are other schemes, e.g., static mechanisms like layers of abstraction. Each approach has its strong and weak points.

Localization

Localization is the process of placing items in close physical proximity to each other; for example, placing all the code relating to one object within the same physical file. It is the concept of localization that most clearly shows the differences between object-oriented and other forms of programming:

- functional approaches localize information around *functions,*

- data-driven approaches localize information around *data,* and

- object-oriented approaches localize information around *objects.*

Without even completely understanding the concept of just what an object is, but recognizing that objects are not functions, and that objects are not data, we can see that there will be a difference in how object-oriented software is arranged.

Summary

Object-oriented technology, far from being a "recent fad," has a history going back over two decades. One of the side effects is the diversity of views and opinions within the object-oriented community, e.g., some people staying very close to programming language issues while others cast things in terms of broader life-cycle activities.

Object-oriented programming requires that:

- information be localized around objects (i.e., not around functions, and not around data) [Remember: An object can be a specific thing, or a pattern for a whole category of things. Objects are black boxes, i.e., their internal implementations are hidden from the outside, and all interactions with an object take place through a well-defined interface.],

- objects must be complete entities, i.e., using the facilities of our programming language, we must create as complete an abstraction of the "real world" (conceptual or physical) object as possible, and

- objects must be highly independent of each other, but must be provided with some mechanism for interaction.

Bibliography

[Anderson et al., 1989]. J.A. Anderson, J. McDonald, L. Holland, and E. Scranage, "Automated Object-Oriented Requirements Analysis and Design," *Proceedings of the Sixth Washington Ada Symposium,* June 26-29, 1989, pp. 265 - 272.

[Atkinson et al., 1989]. M. Atkinson, F. Bancilhon, D. DeWitt, K. Dittrich, D. Maier, and S. Zdonik, "The Object-Oriented Database System Manifesto," (Invited Paper), *Proceedings of the First International Conference on Deductive and Object-Oriented Databases*, Kyoto, Japan, December 4-6, 1989, pp. 40 - 57.

[Bhaskar, 1983]. K.S. Bhaskar, "How Object-Oriented Is Your System," *SIGPLAN Notices*, Vol. 18, No. 10, October 1983, pp. 8 - 11.

[Bobrow et al., 1988]. D.G. Bobrow, L.G. DeMichiel, R.P. Gabriel, S.E. Keene, G. Kiczales, and D.A. Moon, "Common LISP Object System Specification X3J13 Document 88-002R," *SIGPLAN Notices*, Vol. 23, special issue, September 1988.

[Booch, 1981]. G. Booch, "Describing Software Design in Ada," *SIGPLAN Notices*, Vol. 16, No. 9, September 1981, pp. 42 - 47.

[Booch, 1982]. G. Booch, "Object Oriented Design," *Ada Letters*, Vol. I, No. 3, March-April 1982, pp. 64 - 76.

[Booch, 1986]. G. Booch, "Object Oriented Development," *IEEE Transactions on Software Engineering,* Vol. SE-12, No. 2, February 1986, pp. 211 - 221.

[Booch, 1991]. G. Booch, *Object-Oriented Design With Applications*, Benjamin/Cummings, Menlo Park, California, 1991.

[BSE, 1992]. Berard Software Engineering, Inc., *A Project Management Handbook for Object-Oriented Software Development, Volume 1*, Berard Software Engineering, Inc., Gaithersburg, Maryland, 1992.

[Cattell, 1991]. R.G.G. Cattell, *Object Data Management: Object-Oriented and Extended Relational Database Systems*, Addison-Wesley Publishing Company, Reading, Massachusetts, 1991.

[Chidamber and Kemerer, 1991]. S.R. Chidamber and C.F. Kemerer, "Towards a Metrics Suite for Object-Oriented Design," *OOPSLA '91 Conference Proceedings,* special issue of *SIGPLAN Notices*, Vol. 26, No. 11, November 1991, pp. 197 - 211.

[Coad and Yourdon, 1990]. P. Coad and E. Yourdon, *OOA — Object-Oriented Analysis*, 2nd Edition, Prentice Hall, Englewood Cliffs, New Jersey, 1990.

[Cox, 1986]. B.J. Cox, *Object Oriented Programming: An Evolutionary Approach*, Addison-Wesley, Reading, Massachusetts, 1986.

[Dittrich and Dayal, 1986]. K. Dittrich and U. Dayal, Editors, *Proceedings of the 1986 International Workshop on Object-Oriented Database Systems*, IEEE Catalog Number 86TH0161-0, IEEE Computer Society Press, Washington, D.C., 1986.

[Dahl and Nygaard, 1966]. O.J. Dahl and K. Nygaard, "SIMULA — an ALGOL-Based Simulation Language," *Communications of the ACM*, Vol. 9, No. 9, September 1966, pp. 671 - 678.

[Fabry, 1974]. R.S. Fabry, "Capability Based Addressing," *Communications of the ACM*, Vol. 17, No. 7, July 1974, pp. 403 - 412.

[Goldberg and Robson, 1983]. A. Goldberg and D. Robson, *Smalltalk-80: The Language and Its Implementation*, Addison-Wesley, Reading, Massachusetts, 1983.

[Intel, 1980]. Intel Corporation, *iAPX 432 Object Primer*, Manual 171858-001 Rev. B, Aloha, Oregon, 1980.

[Jeffcoate and Templeton, 1991]. J. Jeffcoate and A. Templeton, *Object Technology Sourcebook*, Ovum, Ltd., London, United Kingdom, 1991.

[Kay, 1977]. A.C. Kay, "Microelectronics and the Personal Computer," *Scientific American*, Vol. 237, No. 3, September 1977, pp. 230 - 244.

[Levy, 1984]. H. Levy, *Capability-Based Computer Systems*, Digital Press, Bedford, Massachusetts, 1984.

[Meyer, 1987]. B. Meyer, "Eiffel: Programming for Reusability and Extendability," *SIGPLAN Notices*, Vol. 22, No. 2, February 1987, pp. 85 - 94.

[Moon, 1986]. D.A. Moon, "Object-Oriented Programming With Flavors," *OOPSLA Conference Proceedings,* (special issue of *SIGPLAN Notices*, Vol. 21, No. 11, November 1986), Association for Computing Machinery, New York, New York, 1986, pp. 1 - 8.

[Myers, 1982]. G.J. Myers, *Advances in Computer Architecture*, Second Edition, John Wiley & Sons, New York, New York, 1982.

[Organick, 1983]. E. Organick, *A Programmer's View of the Intel 432 System*, McGraw-Hill, New York, New York, 1983.

[Pountain, 1988]. D. Pountain, "Rekursiv: An Object-Oriented CPU," *Byte*, Vol. 13, No. 11, November 1988, pp. 341 - 349.

[Rentsch, 1982]. T. Rentsch, "Object Oriented Programming," *SIGPLAN Notices*, Vol. 17, No. 9, September 1982, pp. 51 - 57.

[Rumbaugh et al., 1991]. J. Rumbaugh, M. Blaha, W. Premerlani, F. Eddy, and W. Lorensen, *Object-Oriented Modeling and Design*, Prentice Hall, Englewood Cliffs, New Jersey, 1991.

[Salmons and Babitsky, 1992]. J. Salmons and T. Babitsky, *1992 International OOP Directory*, SIGS Publications, Inc., New York, New York, 1992.

[Schaffert et al., 1986]. C. Schaffert, T. Cooper, B. Bullis, M. Killian, and C. Wilpolt, "An Introduction to Trellis/Owl," *OOPSLA '86 Conference Proceedings,* special issue of *SIGPLAN Notices*, Vol. 21, No. 11, November 1986, pp. 9 - 16.

[Shlaer and Mellor, 1988]. S. Shlaer and S.J. Mellor, *Object-Oriented Systems Analysis: Modeling the World In Data*, Yourdon Press: Prentice Hall, Englewood Cliffs, New Jersey, 1988.

[Shlaer and Mellor, 1989]. S. Shlaer and S.J. Mellor, "An Object-Oriented Approach to Domain Analysis," *Software Engineering Notes*, Vol. 14, No. 5, July 1989, pp. 66 - 77.

[Smith and Robson, 1992]. M.D. Smith and D.J. Robson, "A Framework for Testing Object-Oriented Programs," *Journal of Object-Oriented Programming*, Vol. 5, No. 3, June 1992, pp. 45 - 53.

[Stroustrup, 1986]. B. Stroustrup, "An Overview of C++," *SIGPLAN Notices*, Vol. 21, No. 10, October 1986, pp. 7 - 18.

[Sutherland, 1963]. I. Sutherland, *Sketchpad, A Man-Machine Graphical Communication System*, Ph. D. Thesis, Massachusetts Institute of Technology, January 1963.

[Ungar and Smith, 1987]. D. Ungar and R.B. Smith, "Self: The Power of Simplicity," *OOPSLA '87 Conference Proceedings,* special issue of *SIGPLAN Notices*, Vol. 22, No. 12, December 1987, pp. 227 - 242.

[Wirfs-Brock et al., 1990]. R. Wirfs-Brock, B. Wilkerson, and L. Wiener, *Designing Object-Oriented Software*, Prentice Hall, Englewood Cliffs, New Jersey, 1990.

[Wegner, 1986]. P. Wegner, "Classification in Object-Oriented Systems," *SIGPLAN Notices*, Vol. 21, No. 10, October 1986, pp. 173 - 182.

[Wexelblat, 1981]. R.L. Wexelblat, Editor, *History of Programming Languages*, Academic Press, New York, New York, 1981.

[Zdonik and Maier, 1990]. S.B. Zdonik and D. Maier, Editors, *Readings in Object-Oriented Database Systems*, Morgan Kaufmann Publishers, Inc., San Mateo, California, 1990.

2 Motivation for an Object-Oriented Approach to Software Engineering

If you must have motivation, think of your paycheck on Friday.

— *Noel Coward's advice to actors*

Prologue

Periodically, someone asks for examples of "successful (or non-successful) uses of 'fill-in-the-blank' software engineering technology." The usual reason that this question is asked is because someone is considering adopting (or preventing the adoption of) "fill-in-the-blank" technology. Experience shows that it is almost impossible to provide acceptable examples. Why? There are several reasons:

- Small examples, which are easily understood, can be (and often are) handily dismissed as "toy" (as opposed to "real") applications.

- It is difficult to justify the cost of a "large" (significant) test case (e.g., [Aron, 1969] and [Baker and Mills, 1973]). When "fill-in-the-blank" software engineering technology is used on a "real" project, accurate and detailed records are seldom kept. Thus, the results are often anecdotal. Even if accurate and detailed records are kept, it may be difficult to make any meaningful comparisons, since there may be few, if any, statistics for other "similar" projects that *did not* use "fill-in-the-blank" technology.

- The results of a large-scale use of "fill-in-the-blank" technology are seldom, if ever, all positive, or all negative. This allows different interpretations for the same information. (One of the major problems is that "success" (i.e., what must be specifically shown to declare the technology viable) is seldom defined *before* the project begins.) The all-too-regrettable, and all-too-frequent, language/technology jihads (holy wars) often result from different interpretations of the same information.

- The example is for a particular application domain, e.g., real-time embedded systems. Those with differing domains, e.g., MIS (management information systems), can assert that the example is irrelevant for their domains.

- In the case of a technology that can be implemented using a number of different programming languages, the number of problems increases dramatically, e.g.:

  - Some will observe that the example uses a programming language which they do not, cannot, or will not use, thus making the example worthless — as far as they are concerned.

- Others will state that "fill-in-the-blank" software engineering technology "cannot 'truly' be implemented in the programming language used in the example." Thus, the example is, for these people, a non-example.

- Still others will claim that the example merely demonstrates the power (or lack of power) of a particular programming language, and, therefore, the example cannot be used to justify the use (or non-use) of the general technology.

- The "metrics" used in the example may be irrelevant, incorrect, and/or incomplete. Even if the metrics are appropriate, they may not have been gathered properly. Further, the analysis and interpretation of the metrics may be faulty.

- The software engineers conducting a project may not be properly trained in "fill-in-the-blank" technology. This will make it difficult to assert that the technology was actually, or properly, used. Conversely, if well-trained, highly-skilled personnel are used, some will claim that the results are more attributable to choice of personnel, than to choice of technology.

  (This last point is particularly interesting. It is wellknown that quite a large number of factors can influence the outcome of a project. (See, e.g., [Boehm, 1981].) It is therefore not advisable for a project to pin its hopes for success *solely* on the use of a particular technology. (See [Brooks, 1987].))

There is a question which should be asked before a test project begins, i.e., "why are we looking at this technology in the first place?" It is in attempting to answer this question, that we often uncover either the motivation to attempt the technology, or the rationale for avoiding it.

The intention of this chapter is not to prove conclusively that an object-oriented approach is superior to any other approach, but rather to suggest reasons for considering such an approach.

Two Views of Motivation

The motivation for object-oriented technology can be found in the answers to two questions:

- What is the motivation for object-oriented approaches in general?

- What is the motivation for an *overall* object-oriented approach to software engineering?

The first question focuses on the intrinsic value of object-oriented software engineering, while the second question deals with maximizing the benefits (and minimizing the problems) of such an approach.

If you ask people what they hope to achieve by going to an object-oriented approach, you will receive a variety of answers. Those who have successfully made the transition cite the following benefits of adopting an object-oriented approach (in no particular order):

- Object-oriented approaches encourage the use of "modern" software engineering technology.

- Object-oriented approaches promote and facilitate software reusability.

- Object-oriented approaches facilitate interoperability.

- When done well, object-oriented approaches produce solutions which closely resemble the original problem.

- When done well, object-oriented approaches result in software that is easily modified, extended, and maintained.

- There are a number of encouraging results reported (e.g. [Boehm-Davis and Ross, 1984]) from comparisons of object-oriented technology with more-commonly-used technologies.

The benefits of object-oriented technology are enhanced if it is addressed early-on and throughout the software engineering process. Those considering object-oriented technology must assess its impact on the *entire* software engineering process. Merely employing object-oriented programming (OOP) will *not* yield the best results. Software engineers, and their managers, must consider such items as object-oriented requirements analysis (OORA), object-oriented design (OOD), object-oriented domain analysis (OODA), object-oriented database systems (OODBSs), and object-oriented computer aided software engineering (OO CASE).

We differentiate between an "overall" (or consistent) approach and a "mixed" approach. In an *overall* approach, a given technology is assumed to impact everything, and the tools and processes are adjusted accordingly. In a *mixed* approach, one approach (e.g., functional decomposition) may be used for one process (e.g. requirements analysis), and a different approach (e.g., object-oriented) may be used for a different process (e.g., design). An overall object-oriented approach appears to yield far better results than when object-oriented approaches are mixed with other approaches, e.g., functional decomposition.

Major motivations, cited by those who have successfully made the transition, for an *overall* object-oriented approach to software engineering are (in no particular order):

- Traceability improves if an overall object-oriented approach is used.

- There is a significant reduction in integration problems.

- The conceptual integrity of both the process and the product improves.

- The need for objectification and deobjectification is kept to a minimum.

Encouragement of Modern Software Engineering

"Modern software engineering" encompasses a multitude of concepts. We will focus on four, i.e.:

- information hiding,

- data abstraction,

- encapsulation above the subprogram level, and

- concurrency.

Our claim will be that an object-oriented approach either forces a software engineer to address all of these concepts, or makes the introduction of the concepts, where appropriate, much easier.

Information hiding (e.g., [Parnas, 1972] and [Ross et al., 1975]) stresses that certain (nonessential or unnecessary) details of an item be made inaccessible. By providing only essential information, we accomplish two goals:

- interactions among items are kept as simple as possible, thus reducing the chances of incorrect, or unintended, interactions, and

- we decrease the chances of unintended system corruption (e.g., "ripple effects") which may result from the introduction of changes to the hidden details. (See, for example, the discussion of "nearly-decomposable systems" in [Simon, 1981].)

Objects are "black boxes." Specifically, the details of the underlying implementation of an object are hidden to the users (consumers) of an object, and all interactions take place through a well-defined interface. Consider a bank account object. Bank customers may know that they can open an account, make deposits and withdrawals, and inquire as to the present balance of the account. Further, they should also know that they may accomplish these activities via either a "live teller" or an automatic teller machine. However, bank customers are not likely to be privy to the details of how each of these operations are accomplished.

Information hiding is key to object-oriented thinking. Objects tend to hide a great deal more information than either functions or collections of data. More importantly, well-designed objects embody more complete concepts than either functions or data alone. In effect, you could say that the "black boxes" which result from object-oriented approaches to software engineering are "blacker" (i.e., they usually hide more information) than either functions or data alone.

Abstraction, *as a process*, denotes the extracting of the essential details about an item, or a group of items, while ignoring the inessential details. Abstraction, *as an entity,* denotes a model, a view, or some other focused representation for an actual item. Abstraction is most often used as a complexity mastering technique. We often speak of "levels of abstraction." As we move to "higher" levels of abstraction, we shift our attention to the larger, and "more important," aspects of an item, e.g., "the very essence of the item," or "the definitive characteristics of the item." As we move to "lower" levels of abstraction we begin to pay attention to the smaller, and "less important," details, e.g., how the item is constructed.

For example, consider an automobile. At a high level of abstraction, the automobile is a monolithic entity, designed to transport people and other objects from one location to another. At a lower level of abstraction we see that the automobile is composed of an engine, a transmission, an electrical system, and other items. At this level we also see how these items are interconnected. At a still lower level of abstraction, we find that the engine is made up of spark plugs, pistons, a cam shaft, and other items.

Software engineering deals with many different types of abstraction. Three of the most important are: functional abstraction, data abstraction, and process abstraction. In **functional abstraction**, the function performed becomes a high-level concept. While we may know a great deal about the interface for the function, we know relatively little about how it is accomplished. For example, given a function which calculates the sine of an angle, we may know that the input is a floating-point number representing the size of an angle in radians, and that the out put will be a floating-point number between -1.0 and +1.0 inclusive. Still, we know very little about how the sine is actually calculated, i.e., the function is a high-level concept — an abstraction.

Functional abstraction is considered good because it forces us to pay attention to the concept of the function being performed — not the underlying implementation of that function, i.e., its algorithm. If done well, this makes the rest of the system less susceptible to changes in the details of the algorithm.

Data abstraction extends the concept of functional abstraction. (See, e.g., [Alexandridis, 1986].) Specifically, in **data abstraction**, the details of the underlying implementations of *both* the functions and the data are not of interest to the user. A software engineer may choose to represent some information in the form of an array or a record, for example. If he or she forces other software engineers to pay attention to this representation, then the rest of the system is overly sensitive to changes in the *form* of the information.

However, the software engineer may choose to permit access to the information only through a series of operations. In effect the information (data) is now an abstraction, and is only accessible through a well-defined interface comprised of operations (and potentially other items). These operations themselves exhibit functional abstraction.

While many definitions of data abstraction often stop at this point (e.g., [Liskov, 1988]), there is more to the story. Suppose, for example, we were to implement a list using data abstraction. We might encapsulate (package) the underlying representation for the list and provide access via a series of operations, e.g., add, delete, length, and copy. This offers the benefit of making the rest of the system relatively insensitive to changes in the underlying implementation of the list.

Assume, however, we were also interested in having several different lists, each containing a different class of item, e.g., a list of names, a list of phone numbers, and a list of addresses. We may even be interested in a list that contains a mixture of items of different classes. In these cases, we are interested in separating "the concept of a list" from "the structure of the items contained in the list." In effect, *we have two different forms of data abstraction*:

- the abstraction of the underlying structure of the list, and
- the abstraction of the items contained in the list.

The first form shields the rest of the system from both changes in the underlying structure of the data, and changes in the algorithms which manipulate that data. The second form provides for the separation of the concept of a list from the implementation(s) of its contents. There is a powerful consequence of the second form: *reusability*.

If the underlying data structure of the list, and the encapsulated algorithms, are sensitive to the structure of the items contained in the list, then, each time we wish to store a different category of items in the list, we must reimplement both the data structure of the list and the algorithms that manipulate the list. If, however, both the underlying data structure and the encapsulated algorithms treat the items stored in the list as an abstraction, we may reuse the "list abstraction" for a (potentially vast) number of lists.

At the code level, objects are implemented, in part, using data abstraction techniques. (You often hear people speak of the use of "abstract data types" (ADTs) in object-oriented programming.) Most so-called object-oriented programming languages (OOPLs) allow their users to easily encapsulate the underlying implementation of both the state information, and the algorithms which manipulate that state information. The separation of an abstraction from the underlying implementation of its state information is a more difficult issue. (Dynamic binding, sometimes called "late binding" (see, e.g., [Cox, 1986] and [Meyer, 1988]), is, at best, a partial answer.)

Process abstraction deals with how an object handles (or does not handle) itself in a parallel processing environment. In sequential processing there is only one "thread of control," i.e., one point of execution. In parallel processing there are at least two threads of control, i.e., two, or more, simultaneous points of execution. Imagine a windowing application. Suppose two, or more, concurrent processes attempted to simultaneously write to a specific window. If the window itself had a mechanism for correctly handling this situation, and the underlying details of this mechanism were of no concern, then we could say that the window object exhibits process abstraction. Specifically, how the window deals with concurrent process is a high-level concept — an abstraction.

(One of the differences between an object-oriented system and more conventional systems is in how they each handle concurrency. Many conventional systems deal with concurrency by having a "master routine" maintain order (e.g., schedule processing, prevent deadlock, and prevent starvation). In an object-oriented concurrent system, much of the responsibility for maintaining order can be shifted to the objects themselves, i.e., each object is responsible for its own protection in a concurrent environment.)

Like abstraction, the word "encapsulation" can be used to describe either a process or an entity. *As a process*, **encapsulation** means the act of enclosing one or more items within a (physical or logical) container. Encapsulation, *as an entity*, refers to a package or an enclosure that holds (contains, encloses) one or more items. It is extremely important to note that nothing is said about "the walls of the enclosure." Specifically, they may be "transparent," "translucent," or even "opaque."

Localization is the process of gathering and placing things in close physical proximity to each other. Functional decomposition approaches localize information around functions, data-driven approaches localize information around data, and object-oriented approaches localize information around objects. Since encapsulation in a given system usually reflects the localization process used, the encapsulated units that result from a functional decomposition approach will be functions, whereas the encapsulated units resulting from an object-oriented approach will be objects.

In the late 1940s and early 1950s, all that was available were lines of code. So if a system was composed of 10,000 lines of code, the programmer had to deal with 10,000 separate pieces of information. With the introduction of subroutines, programmers could encapsulate two, or more, lines of code, and treat the resulting subroutines as single units. For example, 10,000 lines of code could be grouped into 100 subroutines, with each subroutine comprising 100 lines of code. This meant that programmers had a tool (i.e., subroutines) which helped them manage the complexity of large systems.

Object-oriented programming introduced the concept of classes ([Dahl and Nygaard, 1966], and later [Goldberg and Kay, 1976]), providing programmers with a much more powerful encapsulation mechanism than subroutines. In object-oriented approaches, a class may be viewed as a template, a pattern, or even a "blueprint" for the creation of objects (instances). Programmers use classes to encapsulate many subroutines, and other items, into still larger program units called classes. (Not all object-oriented programming languages are class-based, e.g., Self ([Ungar and Smith, 1987]), but most support, at least conceptually, the concept of program units larger than subroutines.)

Consider a list object. Realizing that a list is more than just a series of storage locations, a software engineer might design a list object so that it encapsulated:

- the items actually contained in the list,

- other useful state information, e.g., the current number of items stored in the list,

- the operations for manipulating the list, e.g., add, delete, length, and copy,

- any list-related exceptions, e.g., overflow and underflow, (exceptions are mechanisms whereby an object can actively communicate "exceptional conditions" to its environment), and

- any useful exportable (from the object) constants, e.g., "empty list" and the maximum allowable number of items the list can contain.

In summary, we could say that objects allow us to deal with entities which are significantly larger than subroutines — and that this, in turn, allows us to better manage the complexity of large systems.

Many modern software systems involve at least some level of concurrency. Examples of concurrent systems include:

- an interactive management information system which allows multiple, simultaneous users,

- a heating, ventilation, and air conditioning system which controls the environment in a building, in part, by simultaneously monitoring a series of thermostats which have been place throughout the building, and

- an air traffic control system which must deal with hundreds (possibly thousands) of airplanes simultaneously.

In these "real life" examples, it is fairly easy to identify concurrent objects, e.g., the users in the management information system, the thermostats in the heating, ventilation, and air conditioning system, and the airplanes in the air traffic control system. It can be argued that it is easier to understand concurrency in terms of objects, than it is in terms of functions. For example, in the Playground system ([Fenton and Beck, 1989]), children as young as 9 and 10 years of age have constructed fairly sophisticated concurrent systems.

[We note that much of the literature on concurrent object-oriented systems (e.g., [ACM, 1989], [Agha, 1986], and [Yonezawa and Tokoro, 1987]) can seem fairly imposing. However, it can be demonstrated that an object-oriented approach to concurrent systems can greatly simplify even intensely concurrent situations, i.e., situations where concurrency is nested within concurrency. (See, for example, the discussions of "agents" in [Adams and Nabi, 1989] and [Fenton and Beck, 1989].)]

The Promotion and Facilitation of Software Reusability

When Doug McIlroy delivered his landmark article on software reusability ([McIlroy, 1969]) over twenty years ago, software reuse was not a topic which generated a great deal of interest. Since the mid 1980s, however, software reusability has become an increasingly "hot" topic.

(See, e.g., [Biggerstaff and Perlis, 1989a], [Biggerstaff and Perlis, 1989b], and [Freeman, 1987]. [Tracz, 1988] contains a reuse bibliography with over 600 references.)

Software reusability is a topic that is not well understood by the masses. For example, many software reusability discussions incorrectly limit the definition of software to source code and object code. Even within the object-oriented programming community, people seem to focus on the inheritance mechanisms of various programming languages as a mechanism for reuse. (In many OOPLs, one of the steps in creating a specialization is the setting up a "backwards pointer" to one, or more, generalizations. This allows the specialization to "reuse" the code from the generalizations.) Although reuse via inheritance is not to be dismissed, there are more powerful reuse mechanisms.

(One of the items which sparked the Industrial Revolution over two centuries ago was interchangeable parts. (See, e.g., [Brinton et al., 1964].) It is worth noting that these interchangeable parts were objects as opposed to mere functionality.)

Research into software reusability, and actual practice, have established a definite connection between overall software engineering approaches and software reusability. For example, analysis and design techniques have a very large impact on the reusability of software — *a greater impact, in fact, than programming (coding) techniques.* A literature search for software engineering approaches which appear to have a high correlation with software reusability shows a definite relationship between object-oriented approaches and software reuse, e.g., [Brown and Quanrud, 1988], [Carstensen, 1987], [Ledbetter and Cox, 1985], [Meyer, 1987], [St. Dennis et al., 1986], [Safford, 1987], [Schmucker, 1986], and [Tracz, 1987].

The Promotion and Facilitation of Interoperability

Consider a computer network with different computer hardware and software at each node. Next, instead of viewing each node as a monolithic entity, consider each node to be a collection of (hardware and software) resources. **Interoperability** is the degree to which an application running on one node in the network can make use of a (hardware or software) resource at a different node on the same network.

For example, consider a network with a Cray supercomputer, at one node, rapidly processing a simulation application, and needing to display the results on a high-resolution color monitor. If the simulation software on the Cray makes use of a color monitor on an Apple Quadra™ 900 at a different node on the same network, that is an example of interoperability. Another example would be if the Quadra 900 made use of a relational DBMS which was resident on a DEC™ VAX™ elsewhere on the network.

In effect, as the degree of interoperability goes up, the concept of the network vanishes. A user on any one node has increasingly transparent use of any resource on the network.

There are articles which attempt to document the relationship between an object-oriented approach and interoperability, e.g., [Anderson, 1987]. There are also systems which were constructed (to some degree at least) in an object-oriented manner, and seem to show a connection between object-orientation and interoperability, e.g., the X Windows System™ and Sun's NeWS™. Still, it seems that there should be a more direct way to connect object-oriented approaches and interoperability.

Polymorphism is a measure of the degree of difference in how each item in a specified collection of items must be treated at a given level of abstraction. Polymorphism is increased when any unnecessary differences, at any level of abstraction, within a collection of items are eliminated. Although polymorphism is often discussed in terms of programming languages (e.g., [Harland, 1984] and [Strachey, 1967]), it is a concept with which we are all familiar in everyday life.

For example, we use the verb "drive" in a polymorphic manner when we talk about "driving a car," "driving a truck," or "driving a bus." The concept of polymorphism is further extended when we realize that the "driving interface" to each of these vehicles includes a steering wheel, an accelerator pedal, a brake pedal, a speedometer, and a fuel gauge.

Suppose we are constructing a software system which involves a graphical user interface (GUI). Further, suppose we are using an object-oriented approach. Three of the objects we have identified are a file, an icon, and a window. We need an operation which will cause each of these items to come into existence. We could provide the same operation with a *different* name (e.g., "open" for the file, "build" for the icon, and "create" for the window) for each item. Hopefully, we will recognize that we are seeking the same general behavior for several different objects and will assign the *same* name (e.g., "create") to each operation.

It should not go unnoticed that a polymorphic approach, when done well, can significantly reduce the overall complexity of a system. This is especially important in a distributed application environment. Hence, there appears to be a very direct connection between polymorphism and enhanced interoperability.

We can make two additional observations:

- Since object-oriented approaches often stress (several different varieties of) polymorphism, it should come as no surprise that these approaches also facilitate interoperability.

- It appears that localizing information around objects (as opposed to functions) encourages software engineers to describe the same general behavior using the same names.

Object-Oriented Solutions Closely Resemble the Original Problem

One of the axioms of systems engineering is that it is a good idea to make the solution closely resemble the original problem. Thus, if we understand the original problem, we will also be better able to understand our solution. For example, if we are having difficulties with our solution, it will be relatively easy to check it against the original problem.

There is a great deal of evidence to suggest that it is easier for many people to view the "real world" in terms of objects, as opposed to functions, e.g.:

- many forms of knowledge representation, e.g., semantic networks ([Barr and Feigenbaum, 1981], page 180), discuss knowledge representation in terms of "objects,"

- the relative "user friendliness" of graphical user interfaces, and

- common wisdom, e.g., "a picture is worth a thousand words."

Unfortunately, many who have been in the software profession for more than a few years tend to view the world almost exclusively in terms of functions. These people often suffer from "object blindness," i.e., the inability to identify objects, or to view the world in terms of interacting objects. We should point out that "function" is not a dirty word in object-oriented software engineering. For example, it is quite acceptable to speak of the functionality provided by an object, or the functionality resulting from interactions among objects.

Object-Oriented Approaches Result in Software That Is Easily Modified, Extended, and Maintained

When conventional engineers (e.g., electronics engineers, mechanical engineers, and automotive engineers) design systems they follow some basic guidelines:

- They may start with the intention of designing an object (e.g., an embedded computer system, a bridge, or an automobile), or with the intention of accomplishing some function (e.g., guiding a missile, crossing a river, or transporting people from one location to another). Even if they begin with the idea of accomplishing a function, they quickly begin to quantify their intentions by specifying objects (potentially at a high level of abstraction) that will enable them to provide the desired functionality. In short order, they find themselves doing object-oriented decomposition, i.e., breaking the potential product into objects (e.g., power supplies, RAM, engines, transmissions, girders, and cables).

- They assign functionality to each of the parts (object-oriented components). For example, the function of the engine is to provide a power source for the movement of the automobile. Looking ahead (and around) to *reusing* the parts, the engineers may modify and extend the functionality of one, or more, of the parts.

- Realizing that each of the parts (objects) in their final product must interface with one, or more, other parts, they take care to create well-defined interfaces. Again, focusing on reusability, the interfaces may be modified or extended to deal with a wider range of applications.

- Once the functionality and well-defined interfaces are set in place, each of the parts may be either purchased off-the-shelf, or designed independently. In the case of complex, independently-designed parts, the engineers may repeat the above process.

- Next, the engineers identify the specific connections among the objects that will make up the final system. (These connections are themselves objects.) Finally, the engineers specify how the objects that comprise the system will interact and interrelate to provide the required characteristics of the desired system.

Without explicitly mentioning it, we have described the *information hiding* which is a normal part of conventional engineering. By describing the functionality (of each part) as an abstraction, and by providing well-defined interfaces, we foster information hiding.

However, there is also often a more powerful concept at work here. Each component not only encapsulates functionality, but also knowledge of state (even if that state is constant). This state, or the effects of this state, are accessible via the interface of the component. For example, a RAM chip stores and returns bits of information (through its pins) on command.

By carefully examining the functionality of each part, and by ensuring well-thought-out and well-defined interfaces, the engineers greatly enhance the reusability of each part. However, they also make it easier to modify and extend their original designs. New components can be swapped in for old components — provided they adhere to the previously defined interfaces *and* the functionality of the new component is harmonious with the rest of the system. Electronics engineering, for example, often uses phrases such as "plug compatibility" and "pin compatibility" to describe this phenomenon.

Conventional engineers also employ the concept of specialization. **Specialization** is the process of taking a concept and modifying (enhancing) it so that it applies to a more specific set of circumstances, i.e., it is less general. Mechanical engineers may take the concept of a bolt and fashion hundreds of different categories of bolts by varying such things as the alloys used, the diameter, the length, and the type of head. Electronics engineers create many specialized random access memory (RAM) chips by varying such things as the implementation technology (e.g., CMOS), the access time, the organization of the memory, and the packaging.

By maintaining a high degree of consistency in both the interfaces and functionality of the components, engineers can allow for specialization while still maintaining a high degree of modifiability. By identifying both the original concepts, and allowable (and worthwhile) forms of specialization, engineers can construct useful "families of components." Further, systems can be designed to readily accommodate different family members.

Object-oriented software engineering stresses such points as:

- **encapsulation** (packaging) of functionality with knowledge of state information,

- **well-defined functionality and interfaces** for all objects within a system,

- **information hiding** — particularly hiding the details of the underlying implementations of both the functionality and the state information, and

- **specialization** (using, for example, the concept of **inheritance**).

In a very real sense, object-oriented software engineering shares a great deal in common with more conventional forms of engineering. The concepts of encapsulation, well-defined functionality and interfaces, information hiding, and specialization are key to the modification and extension of most non-software systems. It should come as no surprise that, if used well, they can allow for software systems which are easily modified and extended.

The General Electric Study

There are quite a number of "paper" methodology comparisons (i.e., comparisons of methodologies made without attempting to actually use the methodologies), e.g., [Kelly, 1987] and [Loy, 1990]. (Unfortunately these papers often reveal more about the author's misconceptions and lack of expertise than they do about the intrinsic quality of a given methodology.) Other papers analyze small test cases done by others, e.g., [Boyd, 1987]. Still others relate classroom experiences, e.g., [Jamsa, 1984].

Since the late 1960s there have been a large number of "methodology contests." In a "methodology contest" the same sample problem is given to two, or more, design teams. Each design team then produces a "solution" to the problem using a different methodology. These methodology contests have been conducted by companies, local chapters of professional organizations, and software engineering research organizations, among others.

Beginning around 1984, object-oriented design (OOD) began to figure prominently in these contests. OOD was pitted against other approaches in contests run by companies, local chapters of the ACM (Association for Computing Machinery), and the Rocky Mountain Institute of Software Engineering, to name a few. In general, the test cases were slightly complicated small applications, e.g., the classic "elevator scheduler and controller" and "cruise control" problems. OOD often had favorable results in these contests.

In 1984, Debbie Boehm-Davis and Lyle Ross conducted a study ([Boehm-Davis and Ross, 1984]) for General Electric. This study compared several different development approaches for Ada software, i.e., classic Structured Analysis and Structured Design (e.g., [Page-Jones, 1980]), Object-Oriented Design (e.g., [Booch, 1983]), and Jackson System Development (e.g., [Jackson, 1983]). The results of this study indicate that, when compared to the other solutions, the object-oriented solutions:

- were simpler (in terms of control flow and numbers of operators and operands),

- were smaller (using lines of code as a metric),

- appeared to be better suited to real-time applications, and

- took less time to develop.

Similar results have been obtained from other methodology contests.

The Impact of Object-Orientation on the Software Life-Cycle

To help us get some perspective on object-oriented software engineering, it is useful to note the approximate times when various object-oriented technologies were introduced, e.g.:

- object-oriented programming: 1966 (with Simula ([Dahl and Nygaard, 1966]), although the term did not come into existence until around 1970 (many people credit Alan Kay, then at Xerox PARC, with coining the term)),

- object-oriented design: 1980 (via Grady Booch (e.g., [Booch, 1981])),

- object-oriented computer hardware: 1980 (see, e.g., [Organick, 1983] and [Pountain, 1988]),

- object-oriented databases: 1985 (See, e.g., [IEEE, 1985] and [Zdonik and Maier, 1990], although it is only recently that formal calls for standardization have appeared, e.g., [Atkinson et al., 1989]. As a side note: "semantic data modeling" (e.g., [Hammer and McLeod, 1981]) is often cited as the immediate precursor to OODBSs.),

- object-oriented requirements analysis: 1986 (this is when the first courses were available, although books did not appear until 1988 (e.g. [Shlaer and Mellor, 1988])), and

- object-oriented domain analysis: 1988 (e.g., [Cashman, 1989] and [Shlaer and Mellor, 1989])

Originally, people though of "object-orientation" only in terms of programming languages. Discussions were chiefly limited to object-oriented programming (OOP). However, during the 1980s, people found that:

- object-oriented programming alone was insufficient for large and/or critical problems, and

- object-oriented thinking was largely incompatible with traditional (e.g., functional decomposition) approaches — due chiefly to the differences in localization.

During the 1970s and early 1980s, many people believed that the various life-cycle phases (e.g., analysis, design, and coding) were largely independent. Therefore, one could supposedly use very different approaches for each phase, with only minor consequences. For example, one could consider using structured analysis with object-oriented design. This line of thinking however, was found to be largely inaccurate.

Today, we know that, if we are considering an object-oriented approach to software engineering, it is better to have an overall object-oriented approach. There are several reasons for this.

Traceability

Traceability is the degree of ease with which a concept, idea, or other item may be followed from one point in a process to either a succeeding, or preceding, point in the same process. For example, one may wish to trace a requirement through the software engineering process to identify the delivered source code which specifically addresses that requirement.

Suppose, as is often the case, that you are given a set of *functional* requirements, and you desire (or are told) that the delivered source code be object-oriented. During acceptance testing, your customer will either accept or reject your product based on how closely you have matched the original requirements. In an attempt to establish conformance with requirements (and sometimes to ensure that no "extraneous code" has been produced), your customer wishes to trace each specific requirement to the specific delivered source code which meets that requirement, and vice versa.

Unfortunately, the information contained in the requirements is localized around *functions*, and the information in the delivered source code is localized around *objects*. One functional requirement, for example, may be satisfied by many different objects, or a single object may satisfy several different requirements. Experience has shown that traceability, in situations such as this, is a very difficult process.

There are two common solutions to this problem:

- transform the original set of functional requirements into object-oriented requirements, or

- request that the original requirements be furnished in object-oriented form.

Either of these solutions will result in the requirements information which is localized around objects. This will greatly facilitate the tracing of requirements to object-oriented source code, and vice versa.

Reduction of Integration Problems

When Grady Booch presented his first-generation version of object-oriented design in the early 1980s, he emphasized that it was a "partial life-cycle methodology," i.e., it focused primarily on software design issues, secondarily on software coding issues, and largely ignored the rest of the life-cycle, e.g., it did not address early life-cycle phases, such as analysis.

One strategy that was commonly attempted was to break a large problem into a number of large functional (i.e., localized on functionality) pieces, and then to apply object-oriented design to each of the pieces. The intention was to integrate these pieces at a later point in the life-cycle, i.e., shortly before delivery. This process was not very successful. In fact, it resulted in large problems which became visible very late in the development part of the software life-cycle, i.e., during "test and integration."

As you might have guessed, the problem was again based on differing localization criteria. Suppose, for example, a large problem is functionally decomposed into four large functional partitions. Each partition is assigned to a different team, and each team attempts to apply an object-oriented approach to the design of their functional piece. All appears to be going well — until it is time to integrate the functional pieces. When the pieces attempt to communicate, they find many cases where each group has implemented "the same object" in a different manner.

What has happened? Let us assume, for example, that the first, third, and fourth groups all have identified a common object. Let's call this object X. Further, let us assume that each team identifies and implements object X based solely on the information contained in their respective functional partition. The first group identifies and implements object X as having attributes A, B, and D. The third group identifies and implements object X as having attributes C, D, and E. The fourth group identifies and implements object X as having only attribute A. Each group, therefore, has an incomplete picture of object X.

This problem may be made worse by the fact that each team may have allowed the incomplete definitions of one, or more, objects to influence their designs of both their functional partition, and the objects contained therein.

This problem could have been greatly reduced by surveying to the original *unpartitioned* set of functional requirements, and identifying both candidate objects and their characteristics. Further, the original system should have been re-partitioned along object-oriented lines, i.e., the software engineers should be using object-oriented decomposition. This knowledge should be carried forward to the design process as well.

Improvement in Conceptual Integrity

In his book *The Mythical Man Month* ([Brooks, 1975]), Fred Brooks, Jr. stresses the value of conceptual integrity. **Conceptual integrity** means being true to a concept, or, more simply, being consistent. Consistency helps to reduce complexity, and, hence, increases reliability. If a significant change in the localization strategy is made during the life-cycle of a software product, the concept of conceptual integrity is violated, and the potential for the introduction of errors is very high.

During the development part of the life-cycle, we should strive for an overall object-oriented approach. In this type of approach, each methodology, tool, documentation technique, management practice, and software engineering activity is either object-oriented or supportive of an object-oriented approach. By using an overall object-oriented approach (as opposed to a "mixed localization" approach), we should be able to eliminate a significant source of errors.

[During the maintenance phase of the software life-cycle, we have a different set of issues and problems. If we must continue to deal with a significant amount of pre-existing, non-object-oriented software (i.e., a "legacy" — see, e.g., [Dietrich et al., 1989]), there are a number of techniques we can employ. However, we will still face the problem of attempting to minimize errors which are introduced as a result of shifting localization strategies.]

Lessening the Need for Objectification and Deobjectification

Objects are not data. Data are not objects. Objects are also not merely data and functions encapsulated in the same place. However, each object-oriented application must interface with (at least some) non-object-oriented systems, i.e., systems which do not recognize objects. Two of the most common examples are:

- when objects must be persistent, e.g., when objects must persist beyond the invocation of the current application. Although an object-oriented data base system (OODBS) is called for, a satisfactory one may not be available. Conventional relational DBMSs, while they may recognize some state information, do not recognize objects. Therefore, if we desire to store an object in a non-OODBS, we must transform the object into something which can be recognized by the non-OODBS. When we wish to retrieve a stored object, we will reverse the process.

- in a distributed application, where objects must be transmitted from one node in the network to another node in the same network. Networking hardware and software is usually not object-oriented. Hence, the transmission process requires that we have some way of reducing an object to some primitive form (recognizable by the network), transmitting the primitive form, and reconstituting the object at the destination node.

Deobjectification is the process of reducing an object to a form which can be dealt with by a non-object-oriented system. **Objectification** is the process of (re)constituting an object from some more primitive form of information. Each of these processes, while necessary, has a significant potential for the introduction of errors. Our goal should be to minimize the need for these processes. An overall object-oriented approach can help to keep the need for objectification and deobjectification to a minimum.

[In truth, this is not a problem which is unique to object-oriented systems. Anytime we interface two, or more, separately developed systems, we should anticipate some conversion activity.]

Summary

We have covered the more common reasons usually cited by people for considering an object-oriented approach. Each reason was briefly explained and tied to object-oriented technology.

Bibliography

[ACM, 1989]. Association for Computing Machinery, special issue of *SIGPLAN Notices: Proceedings of the ACM SIGPLAN Workshop on Object-Based Concurrent Programming*, Vol. 24, No. 4, April 1989.

[Adams and Nabi, 1989]. S.S. Adams and A.K. Nabi, "Neural Agents — A Frame of Mind," *OOPSLA '89 Conference Proceedings,* special issue of *SIGPLAN Notices*, Vol. 24, No. 10, October 1989, pp. 139 - 150.

[Agha, 1986]. G. Agha, *ACTORS, A Model of Concurrent Computation in Distributed Systems*, MIT Press, Cambridge, Massachusetts, 1986.

[Alexandridis, 1986]. N.A. Alexandridis, "Adaptable Software and Hardware : Problems and Solutions," *Computer*, Vol. 19, No. 2, February 1986, pp. 29 - 39.

[Anderson, 1987]. J. Anderson, "Achieving Interoperability: Myth and Reality," *Infosystems*, Vol. 34, No. 7, July 1987, page 56.

[Aron, 1969]. J.D. Aron, "The Superprogrammer Project," reprinted in *Classics in Software Engineering*, E.N. Yourdon, Editor, Yourdon Press, New York, New York, 1979, pp. 37 - 39.

[Atkinson et al., 1989]. M. Atkinson, F. Bancilhon, D. DeWitt, K. Dittrich, D. Maier, and S. Zdonik, "The Object-Oriented Database System Manifesto," (Invited Paper), *Proceedings of the First International Conference on Deductive and Object-Oriented Databases*, Kyoto, Japan, December 4-6, 1989, pp. 40 - 57.

[Baker and Mills, 1973]. F.T. Baker and H.D. Mills, "Chief Programmer Teams," *Datamation*, Vol. 19, No. 12, December 1973, pp. 58 - 61.

[Barr and Feigenbaum, 1981]. A. Barr and E.A. Feigenbaum, Editors *The Handbook of Artificial Intelligence, Volume 1*, HeurisTech Press, Stanford, California, 1981.

[Biggerstaff and Perlis, 1989a]. T.J. Biggerstaff and A.J. Perlis, Editors, *Software Reusability, Volume 1: Concepts and Models*, Addison-Wesley Publishing Company, New York, New York, 1989.

[Biggerstaff and Perlis, 1989b]. T.J. Biggerstaff and A.J. Perlis, Editors, *Software Reusability, Volume 2: Applications and Experience*, Addison-Wesley Publishing Company, New York, New York, 1989.

[Boehm, 1981]. B.W. Boehm, *Software Engineering Economics*, Prentice Hall, Englewood Cliffs, New Jersey, 1981.

[Boehm-Davis and Ross, 1984]. D. Boehm-Davis and L.S. Ross, "Approaches to Structuring the Software Development Process," *General Electric Company Report Number GEC/DIS/TR-84-B1V-1*, October 1984.

[Booch, 1981]. G. Booch, "Describing Software Design in Ada," *SIGPLAN Notices*, Vol. 16, No. 9, September 1981, pp. 42 - 47.

[Booch, 1982]. G. Booch, "Object Oriented Design," *Ada Letters*, Vol. I, No. 3, March-April 1982, pp. 64 - 76.

[Booch, 1983]. G. Booch, *Software Engineering with Ada*, The Benjamin/Cummings Publishing Company, Menlo Park, California, 1983.

[Boyd, 1987]. S. Boyd, "Object-Oriented Design and PAMELA: A Comparison of Two Design Methods for Ada," *Ada Letters*, Vol. 7, No. 4, July-August 1987, pp. 68 - 78.

[Brinton et al., 1964]. C. Brinton, J.B. Christopher, and R.L. Wolff, *Civilization In the West*, Prentice Hall, Englewood Cliffs, New Jersey, 1964.

[Brooks, 1975]. F. P. Brooks, Jr., *The Mythical Man-Month*, Addison-Wesley Publishing Company, Reading, Massachusetts, 1975.

[Brooks, 1987]. F. P. Brooks, Jr., "No Silver Bullet: Essence and Accidents of Software Engineering," *IEEE Computer*, Vol. 20, No. 4, April 1987, pp. 10 - 19.

[Brown and Quanrud, 1988]. G.R. Brown and R.B. Quanrud, "The Generic Architecture Approach to Reusable Software," *Proceedings of the Sixth National Conference on Ada Technology,* March 14-18, 1988, U.S. Army Communications-Electronics Command, Fort Monmouth, New Jersey, pp. 390 - 394.

[Carstensen, 1987]. H.B. Carstensen, "A Real Example of Reusing Ada Software," *Proceedings of the Second National Conference on Software Reusability and Maintainability*, National Institute for Software Quality and Productivity, Washington, D.C., March 1987, pp. B-1 to B-19.

[Cashman, 1989]. M. Cashman, "Object-Oriented Domain Analysis," *Software Engineering Notes,* Vol. 14, No. 6, October 1989, page 67.

[Coad, 1988]. P. Coad, "Object-Oriented Requirements Analysis (OORA): A Practitioner's Crib Sheet," *Proceedings of Ada Expo 1988*, Galaxy Productions, Frederick, Maryland, 1988, 9 pages.

[Coad and Yourdon, 1989]. P. Coad and E. Yourdon, *OOA — Object-Oriented Analysis*, Prentice Hall, Englewood Cliffs, New Jersey, 1989.

[Cox, 1986]. B.J. Cox, *Object Oriented Programming: An Evolutionary Approach*, Addison-Wesley, Reading, Massachusetts, 1986.

[Dahl and Nygaard, 1966]. O.J. Dahl and K. Nygaard, "SIMULA — an ALGOL-Based Simulation Language," *Communications of the ACM*, Vol. 9, No. 9, September 1966, pp. 671 - 678.

[Dietrich et al., 1989]. W.C. Dietrich, Jr., L.R. Nackman, and F. Gracer, "Saving a Legacy With Objects," *OOPSLA '89 Conference Proceedings,* special issue of *SIGPLAN Notices*, Vol. 24, No. 10, October 1989, pp. 77 - 84.

[Fenton and Beck, 1989]. J. Fenton and K. Beck, "Playground: An Object-Oriented Simulation System With Agent Rules for Children of All Ages," *OOPSLA '89 Conference Proceedings,* special issue of *SIGPLAN Notices*, Vol. 24, No. 10, October 1989, pp. 123 - 138.

[Freeman, 1987]. P. Freeman, Editor, *Tutorial: Software Reusability*, IEEE Catalog Number EH0256-8, IEEE Computer Society Press, Washington, D.C., 1987.

[Goldberg and Kay, 1976]. A. Goldberg and A. Kay, Editors, *Smalltalk-72 Instructional Manual*, Technical Report SSL-76-6, Xerox PARC, Palo Alto, California, March 1976.

[Hammer and McLeod, 1981]. M. Hammer and D. McLeod, "Database Description with SMD: A Semantic Data Model," *ACM Transactions on Database Systems*, Vol. 6, No. 3, September 1981, pp. 351 - 386.

[Harland, 1984]. D.M. Harland, *Polymorphic Programming Languages — Design and Implementation*, Halstead Press, New York, New York, 1984.

[IEEE, 1985]. IEEE, *Special Issue on Object-Oriented Systems, IEEE Database Engineering*, Vol. 8, No. 4, December 1985.

[Jackson, 1983]. M. A. Jackson, *System Development*, Prentice Hall, Englewood Cliffs, New Jersey, 1983.

[Jamsa, 1984]. K.A. Jamsa, "Object Oriented Design vs. Structured Design — A Student's Perspective," *Software Engineering Notes*, Vol. 9. No. 1, January 1984, pp. 43 - 49.

[Kelly, 1987]. J.C. Kelly, "A Comparison of Four Design Methods for Real-Time Systems," *Proceedings of the 9th International Conference on Software Engineering*, March 30-April 2, 1987, pp. 238 - 252.

[Ledbetter and Cox, 1985]. L. Ledbetter and B. Cox, "Software ICs," *Byte*, Vol. 10, No. 6, June 1985, pp. 307 - 315.

[Liskov, 1988]. B. Liskov, "Data Abstraction and Hierarchy," *OOPSLA '87 Addendum to the Proceedings,* special issue of *SIGPLAN Notices*, Vol. 23, No. 5, May 1988, pp. 17 - 34.

[Loy, 1990]. P.H. Loy, "Comparisons of O-O and Structured Development," *Software Engineering Notes*, Vol. 15, No. 1, January 1990, pp. 44 - 48.

[McIlroy, 1969]. M.D. McIlroy, "'Mass Produced' Software Components," in *Software Engineering: A Report On a Conference Sponsored by the NATO Science Committee*, Garmisch, Germany, October 1968, P. Naur and B. Randell, Editors, pp. 138 - 155.

[Meyer, 1987]. Meyer, B., "Reusability: The Case for Object-Oriented Design," *IEEE Software*, Vol. 4, No. 2, March 1987, pp. 50-64.

[Meyer, 1988]. B. Meyer, *Object-Oriented Software Construction*, Prentice Hall, Englewood Cliffs, New Jersey, 1988.

[Organick, 1983]. E. Organick, *A Programmer's View of the Intel 432 System*, McGraw-Hill, New York, New York, 1983.

[Page-Jones, 1980]. M. Page-Jones, *The Practical Guide to Structured Systems Design*, Yourdon Press, New York, New York, 1980.

[Parnas, 1972]. D.L. Parnas, "On the Criteria To Be Used in Decomposing Systems Into Modules," *Communications of the ACM*, Vol. 5, No. 12, December 1972, pp. 1053-1058.

[Pountain, 1988]. D. Pountain, "Rekursiv: An Object-Oriented CPU," *Byte*, Vol. 13, No. 11, November 1988, pp. 341 - 349.

[Ross et al., 1975]. D.T. Ross, J.B. Goodenough, and C.A. Irvine, "Software Engineering: Process, Principles, and Goals," *IEEE Computer,* Vol. 8, No. 5, May 1975, pp. 17 - 27.

[St. Dennis et al., 1986]. R. St. Dennis, P. Stachour, E. Frankowski, and E. Onuegbe, "Measurable Characteristics of Reusable Ada Software," *Ada Letters*, Vol. VI, No. 2, March-April 1986, pp. 41 - 50.

[Safford, 1987]. H.D. Safford, "Ada Object-Oriented Design Saves Costs," *Government Computer News*, Vol. 6, No. 19, September 25, 1987, page 108.

[Shlaer and Mellor, 1988]. S. Shlaer and S.J. Mellor, *Object-Oriented Systems Analysis: Modeling the World In Data*, Yourdon Press: Prentice Hall, Englewood Cliffs, New Jersey, 1988.

[Shlaer and Mellor, 1989]. S. Shlaer and S.J. Mellor, "An Object-Oriented Approach to Domain Analysis," *Software Engineering Notes*, Vol. 14, No. 5, July 1989, pp. 66 - 77.

[Schmucker, 1986]. K.J. Schmucker, "Object Orientation," *MacWorld*, Vol. 3, No. 11, November 1986, pp. 119 - 123.

[Simon, 1981]. H.A. Simon, *The Sciences of the Artificial, Second Edition*, MIT Press, Cambridge, Massachusetts, 1981.

[Strachey, 1967]. C. Strachey, *Fundamental Concepts in Programming Languages*, Lecture Notes, International Summer School in Computer Programming, Copenhagen, August 1967.

[Tracz, 1987]. W. Tracz, "Ada Reusability Efforts: A Survey of the State of the Practice," *Proceedings of the Joint Ada Conference, Fifth National Conference on Ada Technology and Washington Ada Symposium*, U.S. Army Communications-Electronics Command, Fort Monmouth, New Jersey, pp. 35 - 44.

[Tracz, 1988]. W. Tracz, Editor, *Tutorial: Software Reuse: Emerging Technology*, IEEE Catalog Number EH0278-2, IEEE Computer Society Press, Washington, D.C., 1988.

[Ungar and Smith, 1987]. D. Ungar and R.B. Smith, "Self: The Power of Simplicity," *OOPSLA '87 Conference Proceedings,* special issue of *SIGPLAN Notices*, Vol. 22, No. 12, December 1987, pp. 227 - 242.

[Yonezawa and Tokoro, 1987]. A. Yonezawa and M. Tokoro, Editors, *Object-Oriented Concurrent Programming*, The MIT Press, Cambridge, Massachusetts, 1987.

[Zdonik and Maier, 1990]. S.B. Zdonik and D. Maier, *Readings in Object-Oriented Database Systems*, Morgan Kaufmann Publishers, Inc., San Mateo, California, 1990.

3   What Are Methodologies?

Though this be madness, yet there is method in't.

> — *from* Hamlet, Act II, *by William Shakespeare*

You know my methods, Watson.

> — *from* The Crooked Man, *by Sir Arthur Conan Doyle*

Lately, there have been a number of questions along the lines of:

- What methods (methodologies) are being used for object-oriented development efforts?

- Are approaches to object-oriented software engineering substantially different from the more traditional (e.g., functional decomposition) approaches?

- How do you define "your method/methodology of choice?"

I have spent the last fourteen years researching, teaching, consulting on, and using software engineering methodologies. For the last ten years, my main interest has been in the area of object-oriented software engineering. I feel compelled to address the questions which have been appearing of late.

Before I begin, I note that there are those who have problems with the word "methodology." Specifically, many people cite the fact that the suffix "ology" means "the study of." Therefore, the term "methodology," these people feel, is more correctly interpreted as "the study of methods." Taking this approach, most of what are commonly referred to as "methodologies" are really "methods." (Similar arguments are given for the word "paradigm." As opposed to its dictionary definition (e.g., a pattern or an example), paradigm has come to mean a way of viewing the world, or a specific approach to problem solving, e.g., [Kuhn, 1962].)

Unfortunately, for the general software engineering population the term "methodology" has come to mean an approach to some software engineering process. Further, methodologies are thought of as encompassing step-by-step methods, graphical notations, documentation techniques, quality evaluation techniques, principles, guidelines, policies, procedures, and strategies. So I beg the indulgence of those who are more comfortable with "method" — at least for the duration of this article.

General Observations

Although the success or failure of many engineering efforts may be attributed to luck, fate, or destiny, engineering, by and large, is not based on these items. Probably the most important idea behind engineering is that one can *systematically and predictably* arrive at pragmatic, cost-effective, and timely solutions to real world problems. Luck may indeed play a role in most engineering efforts, but most engineers would like to think that they have a significant amount of control over the outcome of an engineering effort.

The most worthwhile engineering techniques are those which:

- can be described quantitatively, as well as qualitatively,

- can be used repeatedly, each time achieving similar results,

- can be taught to others within a reasonable timeframe,

- can be applied by others with a reasonable level of success,

- achieve significantly, and consistently, better results than either other techniques, or an ad hoc approach, and

- are applicable in a relatively large percentage of cases.

True engineers are not magicians. If a good engineer discovers what is apparently a better way of doing things, he or she attempts to tell others about his or her method. Magicians must, by the very nature of their business, keep their techniques shrouded in mystery. A good engineer is *not* a "guru," a "wizard," or a "shaman." A good engineer may be talented, gifted, or intuitive, but in any case, a good engineer can simply and effectively communicate to others the techniques that he or she uses to achieve a high rate of success.

Engineering differs from science. Engineering uses science, mathematics, engineering disciplines (e.g., error analysis, configuration management, risk assessment, and reusability), and excellent communication skills to develop pragmatic, cost-effective, and timely solutions for real world problems. A scientist is often not an engineer. However, an engineer must have a firm grounding in science.

The Beginnings of Software Engineering Methodologies

In 1962, Edsger Dijkstra made the observation that a piece of source code was a series of essentially mathematical statements. Therefore, he supposed, one should be able to take an arbitrary program and "prove it be mathematically correct, or incorrect." His attempts at this, however, did not meet with much success. By 1965, Dijkstra, and others, were aware of one of the major obstacles, i.e., the now infamous "goto" statement (more specifically, an unconditional jump). (See [Dijkstra, 1965], [Knuth, 1974], and [Yourdon, 1975].)

By 1968, Dijkstra was so convinced that the unconditional jump was the problem, that he published his oft quoted (and satirized) "Go To Statement Considered Harmful" article ([Dijkstra, 1968a]). Dijkstra's concerns, however, were not limited to "goto" statements. Later in 1968, he published the results of his (successful) efforts at developing an operating system ([Dijkstra, 1968b]). This paper is "must reading," and describes a "layers of abstraction" approach which is so commonly used today that we seldom think of it as ever not being around.

In "Structured Programming" ([Dijkstra, 1969]), Dijkstra not only coined the term "structured programming," but also emphasized the importance of error prevention, as opposed to error cure. In this article, he posed the question:

> The leading question was if it was conceivable to increase our programming ability by an order of magnitude and what techniques (mental, organizational, or mechanical) could be applied in the process of program composition to produce this increase.

This question still concerns us today, e.g., see [Brooks, 1987].

By 1966, Böhm and Jacopini had their article on control flow constructs translated into English and published in the *Communications of the ACM* ([Böhm and Jacopini, 1966]). In 1967, the term "software engineering" was selected for a (now famous) 1968 NATO conference, whose purpose was, among other things, to help determine just what software engineering was and what it entailed.

1971 saw Niklaus Wirth's "Program Development by Stepwise Refinement" ([Wirth, 1971]). Stepwise refinement systematized the earlier work of Dijkstra and Böhm and Jacopini. David L. Parnas published his oft-cited article on "information hiding" ([Parnas, 1972]) the next year. The December 1973 issue of *Datamation* was devoted to the topic of structured programming, and contained a number of examples of the successful applications of the technique.

It was also during the late 1960s that people realized that structured programming (to a large extent, "structured *coding*"), was not sufficient. Harlan D. Mills focused his efforts on "optimizing the programmer" in the classic "superprogrammer project." The results of this work were fed into the often cited "New York Times Project" ([Baker and Mills, 1973]). It is important to realize that these large projects, and others (e.g., the Skylab effort), demonstrated not only structured programming, but also such concepts as the "chief programmer team" and early versions of "structured design."

Larry Constantine wondered if there were some dependable mechanisms for both avoiding bad designs from the start, and recognizing potential problem areas before the software got to the production stage. Constantine's first published work on the topic appeared in December of 1965, in an article titled "Towards a Theory of Program Design." By 1967, he had formulated both a graphical notation and a vocabulary for describing the structure of programs, and had written a book describing "hierarchical design" ([Constantine, 1967]).

In the late 1960s, Constantine joined IBM's Systems Research Institute (SRI). At SRI, he refined his concepts and taught quite a number of students. One of them, Glen Myers, published his view of Constantine's work (e.g., [Myers, 1973a] and [Myers, 1973b]) referring to it as "composite design." Another student, Wayne Stevens, along with Constantine and Myers, helped pull together Constantine's concepts into a landmark article ([Stevens et al., 1974]).

The 1970s — Methodologies Everywhere

By the mid to late-1970s the number of software engineering methodologies in general, and the number of software development methodologies in particular, exploded. Some examples include:

- functional decomposition approaches, e.g., Structured Design ([Yourdon and Constantine, 1979]) and Structured Analysis ([DeMarco, 1978]),

- data-driven/data-structured approaches, e.g., [Warnier, 1974] and [Jackson, 1975], and

- formal (mathematical) approaches, e.g., Vienna Development Method (VDM). See [Jones, 1980].

Probably the most commonly mentioned (*not* the same thing as "used") software methodologies were the so-called structured approaches. Tom McCabe even introduced what he called "structured testing." (See, e.g., [McCabe, 1982].)

The 1980s — Taking a Closer Look

By the beginning of the 1980s there were so many methodologies available that just tracking them was a full-time effort. There have been quite a number of "methodology surveys" published, including [Birrell and Ould, 1985], [Blank et al., 1983], [DoI, 1981], and [Freeman and Wasserman, 1982].

The U.S. Department of Defense's "Methodman" effort ([Freeman and Wasserman, 1982]) attempted to investigate 48 different methodologies, and, in the end, reported briefly on 24 of them.

The 1980s also was the decade that saw the increased importance of:

- prototyping approaches (e.g., [Boehm, 1986]),

- real-time issues (e.g., [Ward and Mellor, 1985]), and

- Computer Aided Software Engineering (CASE), to automate all these "wonderful" ideas.

Object-Oriented Methodologies

Even if you ignore the most ancient roots of object-oriented software engineering (i.e., the early work in artificial intelligence (AI)), you can still say that object-oriented techniques have existed since the late 1960s (most people cite the work of Nygaard and Dahl in Simula (e.g., [Dahl and Nygaard, 1966])). However, until the mid-1980s, much of the work in the object-oriented arena focused on "object-oriented *programming*."

While, on one hand, a good deal of "object-oriented programming" is really "object-oriented *coding*," we have to be honest and point out the following:

- Methodologies are very important if you have many small steps to accomplish, and many small items with which to deal. Objects are typically at higher levels of abstraction than are "mere data and functions." Therefore, (semi)rigorous methodologies are not as necessary in "small," non-critical, object-oriented applications as they would be in similar applications developed using more traditional tools and approaches.

- Even though the focus of many object-oriented discussions and papers tends to be highly programming language specific, many of the concepts discussed (e.g., inheritance, data abstraction, delegation, reusability, and reflection) have implications which go far beyond low levels of abstraction and simple programs.

- Until the fairly recent (within the 1980s) explosive interest in things object-oriented, object-oriented approaches were seldom used for large or critical applications. (Notice that I did *not* say "were *never* used.") Thus, the need/demand for well-formulated object-oriented methodologies was very low — until very recently.

Things are different now. The demand for object-oriented approaches is staggering. The promises of object-oriented technology are being heard in places where methodologies are the norm. Further, it is perfectly normal for someone to say: "I want to do object-oriented software engineering. How do I do it, and *more importantly* how do I know that I have done it well?"

Approaching Object-Oriented Methodologies

Imagine a "playing field" with well-defined object-oriented software engineering in the middle. We see two teams approaching the middle, from two different directions:

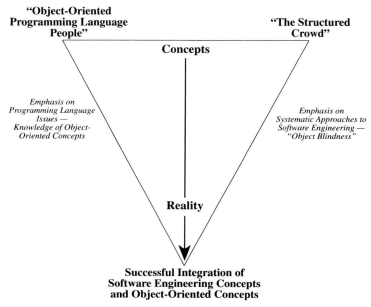

Figure 1:   **This graphic shows the all-too-common divergence between those who know about object-oriented concepts and those who know a good deal about software engineering**. Very few people have successfully merged object-oriented concepts and excellent software engineering technology into a whole that is greater than the sum of its parts.

- One team is the "object-oriented programming language people," i.e., users of programming languages/systems such as Smalltalk, C++, Eiffel, CLOS, and Self. The players on this team, despite their internal disagreements, have very few problems identifying objects. However, when asked about well-defined approaches to things like "object-oriented design," they tend either say things like "I know how to do it, but I am not sure I can tell you," or "huh?"

- The other team very much resembles Hannibal crossing the Alps. They bring a great deal of useless "baggage" with them. You guessed it, they are the "structured crowd," and their "useless baggage" consists of things like data-flow diagrams, structure charts, entity-relationship diagrams, and relational databases. When asked why they want to use these items for object-oriented software engineering, they respond with answers like: "We know how to use these, and we don't know how to solve problems without them." or "Hey, man! We just sunk a lot of money into CASE tools which support these things, and we gotta use 'em."

It should be obvious to a casual observer, that what these two teams need to do is cooperate. Unfortunately, there is very little of that going on.

Figure 1 illustrates the contributions that each group of people brings to the table. The "object-oriented programming language people" bring a detailed knowledge of object-oriented concepts, while those in the "the structured crowd" bring general software engineering knowledge and experience. Placing these two groups at opposite apexes of the inverted triangle indicates that the two forms of knowledge are largely disjoint. As the two sides interact and understand each other better, there is a gradual merging of the concepts into a reality that can be applied to real projects.

Object-Oriented Methodologies — What's Available?

From where I sit, those who are looking for well-defined, "proven" object-oriented methodologies have three choices:

1.   The beginnings of object-oriented methodologies within the object-oriented programming community. (See, for example, some of the papers presented during the "software engineering" sessions at the more recent OOPSLAs.) These come across more like helpful suggestions than they do methodologies. They appear to be heavy on object coupling, and rather wimpy when it comes to either "real time" or "object-oriented development of large systems" (OODLS).

2.   The offerings from the "newly converted structured crowd." You may get the distinct impression that these people use object-oriented terminology in a very strange, and sometimes inappropriate way. This may, in turn, make you question the appropriateness of their material.

3.   The last option is to seek out people who have been working with object-oriented methodologies for a number of years, e.g., people like Grady Booch. These people meet two criteria. First, they have been working with object-oriented technology for a number of years. Second, they have been approaching it from a methodology standpoint, not a programming standpoint.

In any event, proven highly object-oriented methodologies do exist. Unfortunately, they are few and far between. (See, e.g., chapters 10, 11, 12, 13, 15, and 16 of this book.)

Bibliography

[Abbott, 1983]. R. J. Abbott, "Program Design by Informal English Descriptions," *Communications of the ACM*, Vol. 26, No. 11, November 1983, pp. 882 - 894.

[Baker and Mills, 1973]. F.T. Baker and H.D. Mills, "Chief Programmer Teams," *Datamation*, Vol. 19, No. 12, December 1973, pp. 58 - 61.

[Birrell and Ould, 1985]. N. D. Birrell and M. A. Ould, *A Practical Handbook for Software Development*, Cambridge University Press, New York, New York, 1985.

[Blank et al., 1983]. J. Blank, M. M. H. Drummen, H. Gersteling, T. G. M. Janssen, M. J. Krijger and W. D. Pelger, *Software Engineering: Methods and Techniques*, John Wiley & Sons, New York, New York, 1983.

[Boehm, 1986]. B. W. Boehm, "A Spiral Model of Development and Enhancement," *Software Engineering Notes*, Vol. 11, No. 4, August, 1986.

[Böhm and Jacopini, 1966]. C. Böhm and G. Jacopini, "Flow Diagrams, Turing Machines and Languages with Only Two Formation Rules," *Communications of the ACM*, Vol. 9, No. 5, May 1966, pp. 366 - 371.

[Booch, 1982a]. G. Booch, "Object-Oriented Design," *Ada Letters*, Vol. I, No. 3, March/April 1982, pp. 64 - 76.

[Booch, 1986a]. G. Booch, "Object-Oriented Development," *IEEE Transactions on Software Engineering*, Vol. SE-12, No. 2, February 1986, pp. 211 - 221.

[Brooks, 1987]. F. P. Brooks, Jr., "No Silver Bullet: Essence and Accidents of Software Engineering," *IEEE Computer*, Vol. 20, No. 4, April 1987, pp. 10 - 19.

[Campos and Estrin, 1977]. I. M. Campos and G. Estrin, "Concurrent Software System Design Supported by SARA at the Age of One," *Proceedings of the Third International Conference on Software Engineering*, 1977, pp. 230 - 242.

[Constantine, 1967]. L.L. Constantine, *Concepts in Program Design*, Information and Systems Press, Cambridge, Massachusetts, 1967.

[Dahl and Nygaard, 1966]. O.J. Dahl and K. Nygaard, "SIMULA — an ALGOL-Based Simulation Language," *Communications of the ACM*, Vol. 9, No. 9, September 1966, pp. 671 - 678.

[Dahl et al., 1972]. O-J. Dahl, E.W. Dijkstra, C.A.R. Hoare, *Structured Programming*, Academic Press, New York, New York, 1972.

[De Marco, 1978]. T. De Marco, *Structured Analysis and System Specification*, Yourdon Press, New York, New York, 1978.

[Dijkstra, 1965]. E.W. Dijkstra, "Programming Considered as a Human Activity," *Proceedings of the 1965 IFIP Congress*, Amsterdam, The Netherlands, North Holland Publishing Company, 1965, pp. 213 - 217, reprinted, among other places, in [Yourdon, 1979].

[Dijkstra, 1968a]. E.W. Dijkstra, "Go To Statement Considered Harmful," *Communications of the ACM*, Vol. 11, No. 3, March 1968, pp. 147 - 148.

[Dijkstra, 1968b]. E.W. Dijkstra, "Structure of the 'THE'-Multiprogramming System," *Communications of the ACM*, Vol. 11, No. 5, May 1968, pp. 341 - 346.

[Dijkstra, 1969]. E.W. Dijkstra, "Structured Programming," originally in a report on a conference sponsored by the NATO Science Committee, Rome, Italy, October 1969, reprinted in, among other places [Yourdon, 1979].

[DoI, 1981]. *Report on the Study of an Ada-based System Development Methodology, Volume 1*, Department of Industry, London, United Kingdom, 1981.

[Freeman and Wasserman, 1982]. P. Freeman and A. I. Wasserman, *Software Development Methodologies and Ada (Methodman)*, Department of Defense Ada Joint Program Office, Arlington, Virginia, 1982.

[Hansen, 1983]. K. Hansen, *Data Structured Program Design*, Ken Orr & Associates, Inc., Topeka, Kansas, 1983.

[Jackson, 1975]. M. A. Jackson, *Principles of Program Design*, Academic Press, New York, New York, 1975.

[Jackson, 1983]. M. A. Jackson, *System Development*, Prentice Hall, Englewood Cliffs, New Jersey, 1983.

[Jones, 1980]. C. B. Jones, *Software Development A Rigorous Approach*, Prentice Hall, Englewood Cliffs, New Jersey, 1980.

[Jones, 1986]. C. B. Jones, *Systematic Software Development Using VDM*, Prentice Hall, Englewood Cliffs, New Jersey, 1986.

[Knuth, 1974]. D.E. Knuth, "Structured Programming With GOTO Statements," *ACM Computing Surveys*, Vol. 6, No. 4, December 1974, pp. 261 - 302. Reprinted in, among other places, [Yourdon, 1979].

[Kuhn, 1962]. T.S. Kuhn, *The Structure of Scientific Revolutions*, University of Chicago Press, Chicago, Illinois, 1962.

[Linger et al., 1979]. R.C. Linger, H.D. Mills, and B.I. Witt, *Structured Programming, Theory and Practice*, Addison-Wesley, Reading, Massachusetts, 1979.

[McCabe, 1982]. T.J. McCabe, Editor, *IEEE Tutorial: Structured Testing*, IEEE Computer Society Press, Silver Spring, Maryland, 1982.

[Myers, 1973a]. G.J. Myers, *Composite Design: The Design of Modular Programs*, Technical Report No. TR00.2406, IBM Corporation, Poughkeepsie, New York, January 29, 1973.

[Myers, 1973b]. G.J. Myers, "Characteristics of Composite Design," *Datamation*, Vol. 19, No. 9, September 1973, pp. 100 - 102.

[Parnas, 1972]. D. L. Parnas, "On the Criteria to be Used in Decomposing Systems into Modules," *Communications of the ACM*, Vol. 15, No. 12, December 1972, pp. 1053 - 1058.

[Stevens et al., 1974]. W.P. Stevens, G.J. Myers, and L.L. Constantine, "Structured Design," *IBM Systems Journal*, Vol. 13, No. 2, May 1974, pp. 115 - 139.

[Ward and Mellor, 1985]. P. T. Ward and S. J. Mellor, *Structured Development for Real-Time Systems*, Volumes 1, 2 and 3, Yourdon Press, New York, New York, 1985.

[Warnier, 1974]. J.-D. Warnier, *Logical Construction of Programs*, Van Nostrand Reinhold Company, New York, New York, 1974.

[Wirth, 1971]. N. Wirth, "Program Development by Stepwise Refinement," *Communications of the ACM*, Vol. 14, No. 4, April 1971, pp. 221 - 227.

[Yourdon, 1975]. E. Yourdon, *Techniques of Program Structure and Design*, Prentice Hall, Englewood Cliffs, New Jersey, 1975.

[Yourdon, 1979]. E. N. Yourdon, Editor, *Classics in Software Engineering*, Yourdon Press, New York, New York, 1979.

[Yourdon, 1982]. E. Yourdon, Editor, *Writings of the Revolution*, Yourdon Press, New York, New York, 1982.

[Yourdon and Constantine, 1979]. E. Yourdon and L.L. Constantine, *Structured Design: Fundamentals of a Discipline of Computer Program and Systems Design,* Prentice Hall, Englewood Cliffs, New Jersey, 1979.

4   Life-Cycle Approaches

My formula for living is quite simple. I get up in the morning and I go to bed at night. In between, I occupy myself as best I can.

— *Cary Grant*

Prologue

Sometimes, to an outside observer, it appears that software is developed in a process that resembles Brownian motion. Unfortunately, it is true that many software "engineering" efforts are little more than organized chaos. This may be due to ignorance, poor management, lack of training, or any one of a number of other reasons.

A professional is someone who makes his or her task look easy. From a virtual infinity of choices, a professional always seems to choose the most appropriate next step in the process at hand. There is very little wasted motion. Even "trial and error" efforts appear to progress deliberately toward an effective resolution.

Unlike the "new thinkers" in George Orwell's *1984*, professionals do not believe that "ignorance is strength." A professional knows that knowledge, methods, and discipline are not a "strait jacket," but instead amplify his or her creative capabilities.

Before we take a detailed look at object-oriented design or object-oriented requirements analysis, it might be a good idea to look at life-cycle approaches in general. If we understand how people have tackled software engineering projects in the past, we will be better able to discuss and understand the object-oriented life-cycle.

Methodologies and Life-Cycle Approaches Are Not Always Necessary

There are times when an ad hoc software creation/development process is justifiable. In fact, in some circumstances a (semi-)rigorous methodology may be worse than no methodology at all. The trick is to know when and where to consider using a methodology.

If your project is small, or non-critical, or both, a methodology may not be important. Let's look at "small" first.

A number of factors can effect the "size" of an effort. If we are only talking about less than 2,000 lines of code in just about any programming language, that may be considered small. However, if we get much above this limit, things change. Today, we know that developing very large applications is substantially different than the development of "small" applications. Further, the effort necessary to create an application does not go up linearly as the application increases in size.

We will differentiate between the development of large applications using "lines of code," and the development of large applications primarily through the (re)use of "library modules." (In 1976, F. DeRemer and H.H. Kron published an article ([DeRemer and Kron, 1976]) which gave a name to the latter concept: "programming in the large.") A well-known set of system axioms tells us that, the smaller the size of your building blocks (e.g., lines of code versus reusable modules) the lower the productivity, the more error prone the process, and the greater the need for a well-defined and disciplined development approach.

40

People had long suspected that a 100,000 lines of code project was not simply 10 times the effort of a 10,000 lines of code project. As it turns out the effort required to produce the larger project may be 50-75 times the effort required to produce the smaller project, *not* merely 10 times the effort. (See, for example, the productivity studies in [Jones, 1986a] and [Jones, 1986b].) The factors which contribute to this massive, and "unexpected" increase in effort include:

- error density increases with overall size, i.e., the rate of errors per unit of code increases with the total amount of code written. As it turns out, this problem can be mitigated by reusing software, and, thus, reducing the total amount of new code that has to be written. [Yes, software reusability, if done correctly, can have a very positive impact on reliability.]

- as the number of people assigned to a project grows, so do the number of communication paths. (The total number of communication paths is $n*(n-1)/2$, where n is the number of people involved in a project.) While communication is necessary, the more communication paths you have:

  - typically the longer it takes to get anything done, and

  - the greater is the chance that something will become corrupted in the communication process.

  (Reports from successful users of object-oriented technology indicate that fewer people are needed for an object-oriented effort when compared to implementing the same application using more traditional approaches. There are quite a few reasons for this, including an increased emphasis on reusability.)

- the probability and frequency of the "ripple effect" increase with overall systems size. (The "ripple effect" is the introduction of new errors as a result of "fixing" old errors, or "enhancing" the product.)

Size can also be impacted by the choice of programming language. What may have been a good sized project in assembly language, may be a small to medium project in Smalltalk.

Be forewarned, however, even "small" software can be critical software. Gerald Weinberg ([Weinberg, 1983]) documents an error that cost a company US $1.6 billion, and was the result of changing a single character in a line of code. Remember "small" is *not* the same thing as "non-critical."

Software is being used increasingly in applications where reliability and safety are essential. Software is important, and software errors can have serious results (see, e.g., [Neuman, 1988]).

Other factors can make the use of a methodology ill-advised, including:

- poor, or non-existent training in the methodology,

- the wrong methodology for the type of project, e.g., using classic structured technology on an object-oriented project,

- lack of professional guidance,

- a poorly defined methodology, and

- lack of management commitment to the use of the methodology.

We can conclude with these observations:

1. The need for a methodology increases in direct proportion to both the size and critical nature of the software.

2. A given methodology must *decrease* the overall complexity of the software engineering effort — thus increasing the chances of a good quality product. Improper introduction of a methodology, or the use of an inappropriate methodology, can have a negative impact on a project.

General Life-Cycle Approaches

There are three general life-cycle approaches:

- sequential,

- iterative, and

- recursive.

In a sequential approach, once one has completed a step, one never returns to that step, or to any step previous to that step. This is only practical with powerful tools (e.g., fourth generation languages) or on very small, non-critical projects.

In an iterative approach, if there is sufficient reason to do so, one may return to a previously completed step, introduce a change, and then propagate the effects of that change forward in the life-cycle. Most of the life-cycle approaches you are probably familiar with are iterative.

A recursive approach is one where the entire approach may be re-applied to the end products of the approach. All recursive life-cycle approaches are iterative, but not all iterative approaches are recursive.

Some Examples of Life-Cycle Approaches

H.A. Kinslow ([Naur and Randell, 1969], page 32), describes the "Flowchart Model":

1. Flowchart until you think you understand the problem...

2. Write code until you realize that you don't...

3. Go back and re-do the flowchart...

4. Write some more code and iterate to what you *feel* is the correct solution.

This approach is still in use today, except that people seldom draw flowcharts.

The "sequential waterfall" or "stagewise model" ([Benington, 1956] and [Boehm, 1986]) assumes that "everything is right the first time." Each step must be "signed off" and it is against the rules to go back or jump ahead.

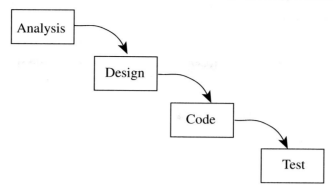

Figure 1:   **In a sequential waterfall model it is against the rules to return to some previously completed step.** This is only practical with powerful software development tools, e.g., high-end fourth-generation languages.

The most common life-cycle approach today. at least in places where they attempt "formal" life-cycles, is the "iterative waterfall" or "cascade" life-cycle. This approach requires that you complete an entire step, verify the results of the step, and then continue on to the next step. You may, however, at any time, return to some previously completed step, introduce a change, and then propagate the effects of that change.

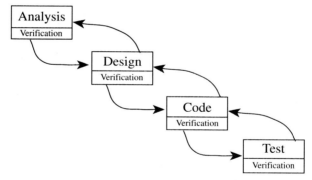

Figure 2:   **In an iterative waterfall approach, a software engineer can return to a previously completed step to introduce a necessary change.** However, this should not be taken as an invitation to be sloppy.

The waterfall life-cycle also usually implies that *all* requirements analysis is completed before going on to design, and that *all* design is completed before coding starts. In effect, once a phase is completed, the only time you return to it is *if* you wish to introduce a change.

(The waterfall life-cycle came into existence because of the grossly disorganized attempts at software development that seemed all too common. You know the story: software is late, buggy, much too expensive, and ill-suited to the user's needs. Programmers would "get an idea of what the client wanted," and then proceed to write a bunch of code. Once the coding was done, the paperwork (e.g., design) was attempted — but only until the next project started.)

Birrell and Ould ([Birrell and Ould, 1985], page 4) describe the "b-model." The b-model recognizes that the maintenance phase of the software life-cycle is seldom just fixing errors. If a software product exists for any period of time, "maintenance" almost always involves enhancements. After a while, the "maintenance phase" of a software product very closely resembles the "development phase."

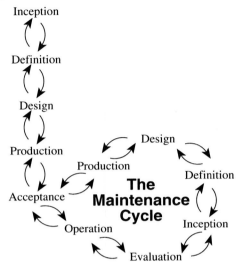

Figure 3:   **The b-model (so called because it resembles a lower case "b") is one of the few life-cycle models that extends beyond the initial delivery of the software product.** Many of the activities that were appropriate during the development of the software are also appropriate during the use and maintenance phases.

Barry Boehm has popularized the "Spiral" life-cycle ([Belz, 1986], [Boehm, 1986], [Boehm et al.,1984], [Boehm and Belz, 1986]). According to [Boehm, 1986], a "typical cycle of the spiral":

1. Begins with the identification of:

    a. the objectives of the product

    b. the alternative means of implementing this portion of the product

    c. the constraints imposed on the application of the alternatives

2. The alternatives are evaluated. The evaluation may involve "prototyping, simulation, administering user questionnaires, analytic modeling, or combination of these and other risk-resolution techniques."

3. The next step may involve "a minimal effort to specify the overall nature of the product, a plan for the next level of prototyping, and a development of a much more detailed prototype..." The next step may, however, "follow the basic waterfall approach, modified as appropriate to incorporate incremental development."

4. Each cycle is completed by a review, with go/no-go plans made for the next cycle.

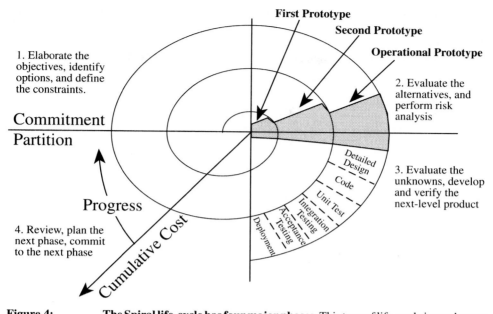

Figure 4:   **The Spiral life-cycle has four major phases.** This type of life-cycle is much more appropriate for research than it is for straight development.

As the Spiral life-cycle progresses, the overall cost of the product is determined by the radius of the spiral, and the progress is determined by "angular displacement." The "spiral" moves outward from the center.

We can make three additional observations about the Spiral life-cycle:

- The Spiral life-cycle presents an organized approach to prototyping.

- While the Spiral life-cycle does indeed involve prototyping, not every prototyping approach is an example of the Spiral life-cycle.

- The Spiral approach is most useful in a *research* project, i.e., a project where many options, requirements, and constraints are unknown at the beginning. If the effort is a *development* effort, i.e., a project where the product, options, requirements, and constraints are fairly well understood, then the Spiral life-cycle is not as appropriate as some other life-cycle approaches.

A common problem is that programmers prefer coding to almost all other life-cycle activities. Managers and clients often exacerbate this problem by continually asking when the code will be ready.

Unfortunately, many people with strong backgrounds in object-oriented programming languages have almost no background in even basic software engineering concepts and methods. (This malady is all too common when people focus on the *tools*, e.g., object-oriented programming languages, and not on the *task*, i.e., better engineered software.) Therefore, when they tackle a software problem, they go almost immediately to coding. Since coding before designing has largely fallen out of favor, these individuals have taken to calling their coding activities "prototyping." When pushed to define their methodology, they note that the Spiral approach seems to have some connection to prototyping, therefore, what they must be doing is "applying a Spiral life-cycle approach."

(Very few of the people who claim to have used a Spiral approach have actually read and understood the original definition of the Spiral life-cycle. It is no accident that those who favor formality and rigor in the software engineering process use the Spiral life-cycle much less frequently than those who emphasize object-oriented programming languages.)

A Suggestion for the Object-Oriented Life-Cycle: The Recursive/Parallel Model

The approach to object-oriented life-cycles which seems to have the most success is the "Recursive/Parallel Model." Grady Booch, and others, have caricatured this approach as: analyze a little, design a little, implement a little, and test a little.

Instead of doing "all of the analysis," followed by "all of the design," the recursive/parallel model suggests that one does analysis where it is appropriate, design where it is appropriate, et cetera.

The recursive/parallel approach was not something which was derived theoretically. It evolved from real people attempting to apply object-oriented thinking to real projects. (In truth, this approach existed long before object-oriented software engineering came along.) Anyone who has worked on a project of significant size knows that requirements are not all at the same level of abstraction. Some are broad and high-level, others are very detailed. This means that, once the entirety of the requirements are examined, some requirements may be deferred until a later time.

Likewise, some design, implementation, and testing concerns can be deferred until later. However, to make the recursive/parallel process work, several criteria have to be met:

- The entirety of the information available for a project must be examined to carefully determine which decisions can safely be left until later. Please note, that this is the recommended practice even for traditional life-cycle approaches.

- The interfaces of the system components (i.e., objects and systems of objects) must be well defined, and kept fairly constant. (Remember: Walking on water and developing software from a specification are easy if both are frozen.)

- The components of the system must be loosely coupled and highly cohesive.

- Verification and software quality assurance *must* be part of the overall process.

There are quite a number of issues which must be addressed for the recursive/parallel life-cycle. For example, since this model gives management and the client so much more control over the software development process, how is that handled effectively?

One other observation I should make, and it will confirm a lot of suspicions, is that the differences between analysis and design in an object-oriented project, are far less than in a structured project. Said another way:

Structured methods:

> *Good News*: Analysis and design use vastly different techniques, graphics, and evaluation criteria. It is fairly easy to tell when you are doing analysis, and when you are doing design.

> *Bad News*: The gap between analysis and design is very wide. For example, although there are systematic ways to convert low-level data flow diagrams into structure charts (e.g., transform analysis and transaction analysis), few people seem comfortable with these techniques.

Object-Oriented methods:

> *Good News*: The chasm between analysis and design is very narrow. Overall, object-oriented thinking is much more uniform than structured thinking.

> *Bad News*: It is more difficult to separate "analysis concerns" from "design concerns." The thinking, tools, techniques, and guidelines have much more in common, than they have differences. (This tends to be discomforting to those who felt that the stark contrasts between structured analysis and structured design provided definition (landmarks) to the software development process.)

Although we will still have life-cycles, and as much rigor (including mathematics) as necessary, in object-oriented life-cycles, we will have to change the way we view the software life-cycle. The good news is that a lot of people have already given this a great deal of thought. Further, the ideas have been tried on a good number of projects, for a few years.

Bibliography

[Belz, 1986]. F.C. Belz, "Applying the Spiral Model: Observations on Developing System Software in Ada," *Proceedings of the 1986 Annual Conference on Ada Technology*, Atlanta, Georgia, 1986, pp. 57 - 66.

[Benington, 1956]. H.D. Benington, "Production of Large Computer Programs," *Proceedings of the ONR Symposium on Advanced Program Methods for Digital Computers*, June 1956, pp. 15 - 27. Also available in *Annals of the History of Computing*, October 1983, pp. 350 - 361.

[Birrell and Ould, 1985]. N.D. Birrell and M.A. Ould, *A Practical Handbook for Software Development*, Cambridge University Press, Cambridge, United Kingdom, 1985.

[Boehm et al.,1984]. B.W. Boehm, T.L. Gray, and T. Seewaldt, "Prototyping Versus Specifying: A Multiproject Experiment," *IEEE Transactions on Software Engineering*, Vol. SE-10, No. 3, May 1984, pp. 290 - 302.

[Boehm, 1986]. B.W. Boehm, "A Spiral Model of Development and Enhancement," *Software Engineering Notes*, Vol. 11, No. 4, August, 1986.

[Boehm and Belz, 1988]. B.W. Boehm and F.C. Belz, "Applying Programming to the Spiral Model," *Proceedings of the 4th International Software Process Workshop*, May 1988, special issue of *ACM SIGSoft Software Engineering Notes*, Vol. 14, No. 4, June 1989, pp. 46 - 56.

[DeRemer and Kron, 1976]. F. DeRemer and H. H. Kron, "Programming-in-the-Large versus Programming-in-the-Small," *IEEE Transactions on Software Engineering*, Vol. SE-2, No. 2, June 1976, pp. 80 - 86. Reprinted in [Freeman and Wasserman, 1983], pp. 321 - 327.

[Freeman and Wasserman, 1983]. P. Freeman and A. I. Wasserman, Editors, *Tutorial on Software Design Techniques*, Fourth Edition, IEEE Catalog No. EHO205-5, IEEE Computer Society Press, Silver Spring, Maryland, 1983.

[Jones, 1986a]. C. Jones, *Programming Productivity*, McGraw-Hill, New York, New York, 1986.

[Jones, 1986b]. C. Jones, Editor, *Tutorial Programming Productivity: Issues for The Eighties*, Second Edition, IEEE Catalog No. EHO239-4, IEEE Computer Society Press, Washington, D.C., 1986.

[Mills, 1971]. H.D. Mills, "Top-Down Programming in Large Systems," in *Debugging Techniques in Large Systems*, R. Ruskin, Editor, Prentice Hall, Englewood Cliffs, New Jersey, 1971, pp. 41 - 55.

[Naur and Randell, 1969]. P. Naur and B. Randell, Editors, *Software Engineering: Report on a Conference Sponsored by the NATO Science Committee*, Garmisch, Germany, October 7-11, 1968.

[Neuman, 1988]. P. G. Neuman, "Letter from the Editor: Are Risks in Computer Systems Different from Those in Other Technologies," *Software Engineering Notes*, Vol. 13, No. 2, April 1988, pp. 2 - 4.

[Royce, 1970]. W.W. Royce, "Managing the Development of Large Software Systems: Concepts and Techniques," *Proceedings of WESCON*, August 1970.

[Weinberg, 1983]. G. M. Weinberg, "Kill That Code," *Infosystems*, August 1983, page 49.

5 Understanding the Recursive/Parallel Life-Cycle

[S]oftware design appears to be a collection of interleaved, iterative, loosely-ordered processes under opportunistic control ...

— [Curtis, 1989]

Prologue

In the previous chapter, I mentioned that a recursive/parallel approach is the one which is most appropriate for the object-oriented life-cycle. Many people have asked me for references on, and the details of, a recursive/parallel life-cycle. In this chapter, I will attempt to provide a better understanding of the recursive/parallel life-cycle.

In attempting to answer previous requests, I discovered that, even though this approach to the object-oriented life-cycle has been in use, and evolving, for at least 10 years, few definitive articles have been written on the topic, e.g., [Berard, 1990]. To be sure, various aspects of the recursive/parallel approach have been discussed in articles, seminars, and books. Further, it has actually been used on quite a number of real development efforts.

Simple descriptions such as "analyze a little, design a little, implement a little, and test a little," are really caricatures. Unfortunately, they are all too often incorrectly used to imply an unacceptable level of rigor in the process. In addition, there is a strong tendency to confuse the recursive/parallel life-cycle with rapid prototyping approaches (e.g., [Church et al., 1986], [Riddle and Williams, 1986], and chapter 8 of [Sage and Palmer, 1990]) and Spiral approaches (e.g., [Boehm, 1986]). This article is an attempt to reduce, if not eliminate, this confusion.

Historical Background

Chaos is a friend of mine.

— Bob Dylan (quoted in Newsweek, December 9, 1985)

Years ago, the state-of-the-practice was to "write a bunch of code, and then test and debug it into a product." Once all the code was written, and "debugged," it was often necessary to document (the so-called "design" of) the product. In short, the idea was to "code first, and think later."

To improve the quality of both the product and the process, the concept of a software life-cycle with explicit analysis and design phases emerged. The most prevalent life-cycle approach was the "iterative waterfall," or "cascade" model. This approach required that "all analysis" be completed and verified before design could begin, and that "all design" be completed and verified before coding could begin. While the waterfall life-cycle was generally an improvement over the previous chaotic attempts to develop software, it was not the final word.

When Grady Booch adopted the work of Russell J. Abbott ([Abbott, 1980]) to Ada software development (e.g., [Booch, 1981]), he referred to the process as "object-oriented design" (OOD), and demonstrated it using several simple examples. Later, when people attempted to apply Booch's method to medium-sized projects (e.g., up to, say, 30,000 lines of code), they found that the actual development effort required repeated applications of the approach. Specifically, in decomposing the problem, they found that Booch's OOD could be re-applied to some (or all) of the components uncovered via (object-oriented) decomposition.

Booch, and others, began referring to the OOD approach as "design a little, code a little." This described a process wherein some object-oriented decomposition (design) was accomplished, followed by some coding. Then, depending on the complexity of a particular component, it may have been possible to re-apply the OOD process to that component. At my former company (EVB Software Engineering, Inc.), we expanded this approach to include necessary testing, i.e., "design a little, code a little, test a little."

Later, since the word "code" seemed to cause concern among some managers (and customers), "code a little" was replaced by "implement a little." In 1986, when I and others began focusing on object-oriented requirements analysis (OORA), the phrase "analyze a little" was added.

Within the Ada community there has always been a significant effort to use Ada (a coding language) as a design language (DL). (See, e.g., [Kerner, 1982], [Masters and Kuchinski, 1983], and [Hart, 1982].) This effort encouraged the recursive/parallel approach since the "implement a little" allowed for the use of the programming language as part of the "design."

(In actuality, Ada has been used successfully for such things as a programming/process design/description language (PDL), a hardware design language (HDL), a requirements specification language (RSL), and a system design language (SDL).)

By 1985, there were already a number of reports of life-cycles being altered to reflect a more overlapping and less sequential approach, e.g., [Rajlich, 1985]. Since 1986, slightly different interpretations of recursive parallel have emerged, for example, the "fountain model" ([Henderson-Sellers and Edwards, 1990]) and Booch's "round-trip gestalt design" ([Booch, 1991]).

Many people contend, and I agree, that the recursive/parallel approach (and its closely associated variations) more accurately reflects the way software engineers really design software. In effect, the recursive/parallel approach formalizes concepts and techniques that software engineers are already using.

How We Really Design Software

Many texts and software development standards might give one the impression that software development is a strictly sequential process, and that the entirety of one phase is completed before the next phase begins. Further, to encourage a "think first, code later" approach, software engineers are often told such things as "all design must be completed before any coding can begin." However, we need to keep the following in mind:

- Any significant software engineering effort will, in reality, exhibit a great deal of iteration (i.e., returning to a previously completed step, introducing a change, and propagating the effects of that change forward) and overlap (i.e., software engineering activities at varying levels of abstraction occurring simultaneously). (See, e.g., [Curtis, 1989], [Gindre and Sada, 1989], [Malhotra et al., 1980], and [Turner, 1987].) Bill Curtis ([Curtis, 1989]) has observed that "Good designers work at multiple levels of abstraction and detail simultaneously."

(Keep in mind that what is being advocated above is *not* a "chaotic, code-driven approach." Even though good software engineers may be working "at multiple levels of abstraction and detail simultaneously," there is very often a noticeable top-down flavor to the overall approach.)

- Design is not the only software engineering activity that will cause overlapping and iteration in the software life-cycle. Often, changes require that a software engineer return to a previously completed life-cycle step, introduce the change, and, then, propagate the effects of the change forward. In effect, change traffic can cause previously completed activities to be reactivated.

(Fred Brooks, Jr. ([Brooks, 1975]) observes, "The first step is to accept the fact of change as a way of life, rather than an untoward and annoying exception.")

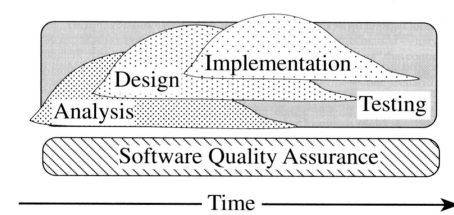

Figure 1:   **Although, traditionally the software life-cycle has often been portrayed as strictly sequential, in practice there is a great deal of overlap among the phases**. Note that "testing" and "software quality assurance" are continually on-going processes, i.e., they do not wait to begin after implementation.

- On real projects, requirements are seldom all at the same level of abstraction. Some requirements are very broad and high-level, others are very detail-oriented. Software engineers often intuitively — if not purposefully — postpone consideration of low-level requirements until "an appropriate time." You might say that a good software engineer continually surveys all of the requirements and notes which requirements must be considered for the life-cycle activity at hand, and which requirements can be safely put off.

Software engineers must continually practice cognitive dissonance (e.g., [Weinberg, 1971]). **Cognitive dissonance** can be described as the simultaneous belief in two apparently contradicting ideas. On one hand, a software engineer knows that he or she has the ability to return to some previously completed process and introduce a change or an enhancement. On the other hand, the software engineer should make a good faith effort to make each step of the software engineering process as complete as is necessary.

Engineering is not a rote discipline. By its very nature, it requires that its practitioners be aware of, and continually make trade-offs among a number of different items. While there are definite rules and guidelines in software engineering, a good software engineer will be able to inject creativity, ingenuity, and intuition into any given situation. In this sense, as well as others, software engineering is no different from other, more established forms of engineering, e.g., civil engineering, electronics engineering, and aeronautical engineering.

Let's look at some of the items that we need to consider in our life-cycle approaches.

Decomposition

Many life-cycle approaches employ some form of decomposition. The concept is simple enough:

- select a piece of the problem (initially, the whole problem),

- determine its components (using the mechanism of choice),

- show how the components interact and interrelate, and

- repeat the previous steps on each of the components until some completion criteria are met.

The most familiar example of this approach is classic functional decomposition. (For a discussion of decomposition at a very low level of abstraction (i.e., coding) see [Wirth, 1971].)

Decomposition techniques are "top down" approaches. A top down approach has the following characteristics:

- It progresses from the general to the specific, and, by induction, from "what" to "how."

- At any point in the process, we always have a complete (although possibly limited in detail) description of the system. (We often refer to the deliverable from a major step in a top down approach as a "layer," where a layer is a complete description of the system at a given uniform level of abstraction.)

- Items at higher levels of abstraction treat items at lower levels of abstraction as "black boxes."

- While items at higher levels of abstraction may be aware of items at lower levels of abstraction, items at lower levels of abstraction are unaware of items at higher levels of abstraction.

Many people often confuse "top down" with "functional decomposition" or "structured" approaches. While these approaches are indeed examples of top down thinking, they are implementations of the concept, i.e., not definitions.

(For an interesting discussion of "layers of abstraction," see [Dijkstra, 1968].)

It is possible to decompose a system in an object-oriented manner, e.g.:

- View the problem as an object or system of objects.

- Identify its major parts in terms of interacting objects.

- Show how the component parts (objects) interact to provide the characteristics of the composite object (or system of objects).

- Repeat the previous steps on each of the component objects until some completion criteria are met.

We note that object-oriented decomposition differs from functional decomposition primarily in the way information is localized, i.e., around objects versus around functions. Other examples of noticeable differences include:

- Functional decomposition components have "verb" names (e.g., "prompt the user," "determine the proper exchange rate," and "calculate trajectory"), while object-oriented components have "noun" names (e.g., "temperature sensor," "bank account," and "postal clerk").

- Objects are typically more complete abstractions than are functions.

Composition

Most conventional object-oriented programming (OOP) approaches are compositional approaches, e.g.:

- Survey the problem attempting to identify necessary components.

- Select components from an existing "library of components" and/or create new components as necessary.

- Assemble the components to form larger components.

If the larger component satisfies the complete problem, then stop; otherwise continue to assemble and merge components until the problem is (or appears to be) solved. (Obviously, in OOP, the components will be objects.)

Composition techniques are "bottom up" approaches. A bottom up approach has the following characteristics:

- It progresses from the specific to the general and, by induction, from "how" to "what."

- At any point in the process we usually do not have a complete description of the entire system (with the possible exception of the description of the original problem).

- Most often, we are building "black boxes"— not decomposing them.

A bottom up process need not be chaotic, and is most appropriate for rapid prototyping or research efforts. Further, a composition process may be entirely adequate if the problem is small, well understood, and non-critical.

Reusability and Compositional Techniques

Reusability implies that we must be using composition techniques at some point in the life-cycle. We may arrive at the composition process in one of two ways:

- We initially select reusable components and combine them to solve a problem.

- We decompose a problem to a point where we can easily and accurately identify existing reusable components, and then select these components.

(There are many issues relating to software reusability that I am not going to discuss at this point. However, suffice it to say that while an object-oriented approach facilitates software reuse, it does not guarantee reusable software.)

And Now, the Recursive/Parallel Process

In general, the recursive/parallel approach (a top down approach) stipulates that we:

- systematically decompose a problem into highly-independent components,

- re-apply the decomposition process to each of these components to decompose them further (if necessary) — this is the "recursive" part,

- accomplish this re-application of the process simultaneously on each of the components — this is the "parallel" part, and

- continue this process until some completion criteria are met.

The process that we will be applying, in whole, or in part, to each of the components is "analysis, followed by design, followed by implementation, followed by testing."

For the recursive/parallel approach to be effective, the components must be as highly independent of each other as possible. Well-designed objects tend to be much more independent of each other (in an overall system) than are well-designed functions.

At this point, we need to make several clarifications:

- Although a recursive/parallel approach may be used with functions, it is recommended that, for best results, it be used with objects.

- We will emphasize reusability in our recursive/parallel approach.

- As opposed to a "pure" top down approach, we will also use composition techniques with our recursive/parallel life-cycle:

  - The larger the product (or component) the more "top down" (and decompositional) will be our approach.

  - The smaller the product (or component) the more likely it will be that we use compositional techniques.

(An interesting observation that I have made is that software practitioners tend to re-cast the recursive/parallel approach based on their specific backgrounds. For example, those who are most comfortable with coding tend to "design a little, code a lot." Those who have a great deal of reverence for analysis and design tend to "analyze a lot, design a lot, and code much later.")

Occasionally, when people first see "analyze a little," they think that this implies a "sloppy" (or an inappropriate amount of) analysis. This is not true. As with any other life-cycle approach, some decision must be made at the beginning of the project as to which details must be considered first, and which can be considered later. The recursive/parallel life-cycle is no different. "Analyze a little" means that one must identify the details which are appropriate to the current level of abstraction. Further, the analyst must make sure that details which are left for later can truly be ignored until later.

Most people recognize that, for any given project, all requirements are seldom, if ever, at a uniform level of abstraction. For example, there may be very high-level requirements relating to efficiency and user-friendliness, and at the same time, very low-level requirements relating to bit patterns in memory. During just about any software development effort, the analysts and the designers make an almost unconscious determination as to which requirements can be left for later parts of the development process. The recursive/parallel process formally recognizes this line of thought.

We do not necessarily have to perform an entire "analyze a little, design a little, implement a little, test a little" process with each new component. For example, if the size of the component is "small," we may not need to perform analysis or design. We may recognize a component as being one which is already in our reuse library, or is a relatively simple modification of a pre-existing component. In this case, we may simply reuse (or slightly modify) the pre-existing component.

The Size and Critical Nature of a Software Product

If a software product (or component) is small enough (e.g., ≤ 2,000 lines of code), then all that may be needed is "implement a little, test a little." However, size alone is not a determining factor. (See, e.g., [Weinberg, 1983].)

Even if a software product (or component) is relatively small (e.g., ≤ 2,000 lines of code), it may be a highly critical application, e.g., the kernel of an operating system or an embedded flight control application in a commercial aircraft. For critical applications, some serious analysis and/or design is often mandatory, i.e., we will be required to "analyze a little, design a little, implement a little, and test a little" even if the product is "only a few hundred lines of code."

(There are many different definitions for "critical software." Most people have no problem with calling "life-sustaining" and "life-threatening" applications critical. Still, depending on how important a particular application is to you, critical can also be applied to such things as software applications that significantly impact the financial well-being of persons or organizations, for example.)

Accomplishing the Recursive/Parallel Approach

It is useful to establish some general guidelines for what we mean by each part of "analyze a little, design a little, implement a little, and test a little."

The "analyze a little" step requires that we:

- understand the requirements for the product (or component),

- propose a "high level" solution for these requirements which involves identification of the major components (or subcomponents), and

- demonstrate that the proposed solution meets the "client's" needs.

The "design a little" step requires that we:

- precisely define the interfaces to the components (or subcomponents),

- make decisions about how each component (or subcomponent) will be implemented in the selected programming language,

- identify any necessary additional program units, and

- describe any necessary programming language relationships, e.g., nesting and dependency.

The "implement a little" step requires that we:

- implement the programming language *interfaces* for each of the components (or subcomponents) [Note that this substep, and the next one, allow one to use a programming language in the form of a design language.],

- implement the algorithm which describes the interactions among the components (or subcomponents), and

- implement the internals of those components that will not be further decomposed.

(It is usually either in the "design a little" step or the "implement a little" step that we may identify (select) a previously-existing component for the implementation. There are many issues which must be addressed here. However, we will sidestep them for the moment. (See, also, the discussion of object-oriented domain analysis in Chapter 10.))

The "test a little" step requires that we:

- compile any code produced (or selected) as a result of the "implement a little" step (This should check things like syntax, some semantics, and some interfaces.),

- carry out any dynamic testing (machine-executable testing) which is possible, and

- perform any necessary (or required) static testing.

Of course, regardless of where we are in the recursive/parallel life-cycle, we must take care to ensure the quality of the product. Software quality assurance (SQA) is a continually on-going effort.

"Analysis Objects," "Design Objects," "Interface Objects," and "Commuting Objects"

Object-Oriented Requirements Analysis (OORA) stops at the ("user") interface to a (potential collection of) system(s) of objects. It is the job of object-oriented design (OOD) to precisely define the interface for each system of objects, and to define the internal structure (architecture) of each system of objects.

It is very likely that some objects were identified during analysis that will not become code software. We refer to these objects as "analysis objects." (Note: These objects may already be in the form of code software.)

It is also very probable that we will identify objects during design which were not addressed in analysis. We refer to these objects as "design objects." Most of these objects will indeed become code software.

One, or more, objects may lie on the "user" interface to the system of objects, i.e., taken in combination with other such objects, they *are* the (user) interface for the system of objects. We refer to these objects as "interface objects." (Note: A "user" may be another piece of software, a piece of hardware, or even a human being.)

There will be objects which were mentioned in analysis, *and* are needed for the proper behavior of the system of objects. In effect, these objects are inputs to the system of objects, outputs from the system of objects, or both. We refer to these as "commuting objects."

A Simple Example

Let us now consider s simple example. We have been tasked with the creation of a simple "electronic message system" (EMS). What are some example scenarios for the object-oriented development of such a system?

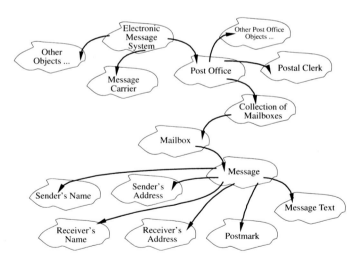

Figure 2: **A graphical representation of a partial object-oriented decomposition of a simple electronic message system shows several levels of abstraction**. This "cloud diagram" is similar to the "exploding diagrams" used to show the composition and component relationships for mechanical hardware.

One scenario might be to say that:

- The EMS is composed of:

    - a post office,

- a message carrier,

- and other EMS objects ...

- The post office is in turn composed of:

  - a postal clerk,

  - a collection of mailboxes,

  - and other post office objects ...

- One of the components of a collection of mailboxes is an individual mailbox.

- One of the components of an individual mailbox would be an individual message.

- The components of a message could be:

  - the sender's name,

  - the sender's address,

  - the receiver's name,

  - the receiver's address,

  - the postmark (i.e., the date and time the message was sent),

  - and the actual text of the message.

Given the previously (partially) described electronic message system (EMS):

- The first pass at OORA would:

  - identify the post office, message carrier, and "other objects" as being the major, top-level components of the EMS,

  - describe the environment in which the EMS will be used, and

  - describe the conceptual interfaces of the EMS, post office, message carrier, and "other objects."

- The first pass at OOD would:

  - detail the precise programming language interfaces for the EMS, post office, message carrier, and "other objects."

  - create the programming language algorithm for the internal structure of the EMS at the top level, i.e., how the EMS will manipulate the post office, message carrier, and "other objects."

  Remember, that many object-oriented systems do not have "tops" in the same sense as functionally decomposed systems. Object-oriented systems often do not exhibit the same invocation hierarchy found in more conventional systems.

- Assuming that the message carrier is fairly simple, the first pass at OOP would create the entirety of the source code for the message carrier (and any other very simple objects at that level).

- Assuming a certain level of complexity, one of the second passes at OORA would identify the collection of mailboxes, postal clerk, and "other post office objects" as being components of the post office.

- The pass at OOD for the post office would:

  - detail the precise programming language interfaces for the collection of mailboxes, the postal clerk, and the "other post office objects."

  - create the programming language algorithm for the internal structure of the post office at the top level, i.e., how the post office will manipulate the collection of mailboxes, the postal clerk, and the "other post office objects."

- Assuming that the postal clerk is a fairly simple object with life, OOP would create the entirety of the source code for the postal clerk.

Returning to the top level of abstraction (i.e., the EMS):

- The users of the EMS and other systems with which the EMS must interface would be considered "analysis objects" with respect to the EMS.

- The post office, message carrier, and "other objects" would be the "design objects" for the EMS.

- With respect to the post office, the collection of mailboxes, the postal clerk, and the "other post office objects" are "design objects."

- The post office, message carrier, and "other objects" are the "interface objects" with respect to the EMS and the rest of the EMS system.

- Message objects are "commuting objects" with respect to the top-level EMS and the post office.

When to Use OORA, When Not to Use OORA, and When to Stop Using OORA

Often, OOD and OOP are all that are necessary for a product. However there are times when OORA is justified, e.g.:

- when the overall size of the project is very large, e.g., significantly larger than, say, 2,000 lines of code,

- when the software product being developed is critically important, or

- when the customer, or management, dictates that a conventional, waterfall life-cycle must be followed — even though this is inappropriate for an object-oriented approach.

Given a recursive/parallel approach, a large (or critical) project, and the fact that OORA was used at least at the start of the effort, a software engineer, would want to know when to stop using OORA on the project. The following are situations where one can consider not using OORA:

- if the component (or subcomponent) is small (e.g., ≤2,000 lines of code),

- if the component is slightly larger than, say 2,000 lines of code, and the component is non-critical,

- if the component (or subcomponent) is recognized as a pre-existing library component, or

- if the component (or subcomponent) is a relatively simple variation on a pre-existing library component.

Consistency in the Object-Oriented Life-Cycle

Object-oriented thinking is more consistent than traditional structured thinking. This both simplifies and complicates matters, i.e.:

- *Good News*: Since they are more consistent in thinking, the "gap" between OORA and OOD is very narrow, when compared to the "gap" between structured analysis and structured design.

- *Bad News*: This high level of conceptual integrity makes it harder to distinguish between OOD and OORA. (This may be confusing to those who require stark contrasts and well-defined landmarks.)

Differences between OORA and OOD

Even though I mentioned some of the differences between OORA and OOD in the previous chapter, it might be useful to repeat them here:

- Although they share many graphical techniques in common, there are differences. For example, OOD uses program unit graphics, whereas OORA does not.

- Programming language issues are much more prevalent in OOD than in OORA. Client visibility is higher in OORA than in OOD.

- Not all objects identified during OORA will become code software, whereas many (if not all) of the objects identified during OOD will become code software.

- OORA does not identify all of the objects in a system. Additional objects will be introduced during the OOD process.

- The larger the overall project, the higher the ratio of design objects to analysis objects.

Summary

Some software development approaches are presented as if they were strictly linear. The recursive/parallel approach, on the other hand, allows for a more natural partitioning of development activities. Items that are important can be addressed early on, while less important items can be addressed later. This has the added side effect of keeping overall complexity to a minimum.

Bibliography

[Abbott, 1980]. R.J. Abbott, "Report on Teaching Ada," *Technical Report SAI-81-313-WA*, Science Applications, Inc., McLean, Virginia, 1980.

[Abbott, 1983]. R.J. Abbott, "Program Design by Informal English Descriptions," *Communications of the ACM*, Vol. 26, No. 11, November 1983, pp. 882 - 894.

[Arthur, 1992]. L.J. Arthur, *Rapid Evolutionary Prototyping and Development*, John Wiley and Sons, New York, New York, 1992.

[Berard, 1990]. E.V. Berard, "Understanding the Recursive/Parallel Life-Cycle," *Hotline On Object-Oriented Technology*, Vol. 1, No. 7, May 1990, pp. 10 - 13.

[Boehm, 1986]. B.W. Boehm, "A Spiral Model of Development and Enhancement," *Software Engineering Notes*, Vol. 11, No. 4, August, 1986.

[Booch, 1981]. G. Booch, "Describing Software Design in Ada," *SIGPLAN Notices*, Vol. 16, No. 9, September 1981, pp. 42 - 47.

[Booch, 1991]. G. Booch, *Object-Oriented Design With Applications*, Benjamin/Cummings, Menlo Park, California, 1991.

[Brooks, 1975]. F. P. Brooks, Jr., *The Mythical Man-Month*, Addison-Wesley Publishing Company, Reading, Massachusetts, 1975.

[Church et al., 1986]. V.E. Church, D.N. Card, W.W. Agresti, and Q.L. Jordan, "An Approach for Assessing Software Prototypes," *Software Engineering Notes*, Vol. 11, No. 3, July 1986, pp. 65 - 76.

[Curtis, 1989]. B. Curtis, *... But Your Have to Understand. This Isn't the Way We Develop Software At Our Company*, MCC Technical Report No. STP-203-89, Microelectronics and Computer Technology Corporation, Austin, Texas, 1989.

[Dijkstra, 1968]. E.W. Dijkstra, "Structure of the 'THE'-Multiprogramming System," *Communications of the ACM*, Vol. 11, No. 5, May 1968, pp. 341 - 346.

[Gindre and Sada, 1989]. C. Gindre and F. Sada, "A Development in Eiffel: Design and Implementation of a Network Simulator," *Journal of Object-Oriented Programming*, Vol. 2, No. 1, May/June 1989, pp. 27 - 33.

[Hart, 1982]. H. Hart, "Ada for Design: An Approach for Transitioning Industry Software Developers," *Ada Letters*, Vol. II, No. 1, July/August 1982, pp. 50 - 57.

[Henderson-Sellers and Edwards, 1990]. B. Henderson-Sellers and J.M. Edwards, "The Object-Oriented Systems Life-Cycle," *Communications of the ACM*, Vol. 33, No. 9, September 1990, pp. 145 - 159.

[Kerner, 1982]. J. S. Kerner, "Should PDL/Ada Be Compilable?," *Ada Letters*, Vol. II, No. 2, September/October 1982, pp. 49 - 50.

[Malhotra et al., 1980]. A. Malhotra, J.C. Thomas, J.M. Carroll, and L. Miller, "Cognitive Processes in Design," *International Journal of Man-Machine Studies*, Vol. 12, No. 2, February 1980, pp. 119 - 140.

[Masters and Kuchinski, 1983]. M. W. Masters and M. J. Kuchinski, "Software Design Prototyping Using Ada," *Ada Letters*, Vol. II, No. 4, January/February 1983, pp. 68 - 75.

[Rajlich, 1985]. V. Rajlich, "Paradigms for Design and Implementation in Ada," *Communications of the ACM*, Vol. 28, No. 7, July 1985, pp. 718 - 727.

[Riddle and Williams, 1986]. W. Riddle and L.G. Williams, "Software Engineering Workshop Report," *Software Engineering Notes*, Vol. 11, No. 1, January 1986, pp. 73 - 102.

[Sage and Palmer, 1990]. A.P. Sage and J.D. Palmer, *Software Systems Engineering*, John Wiley & Sons, New York, New York, 1990.

[Turner, 1987]. J.A. Turner, "Understanding the Elements of System Design," in *Critical Issues in Information Systems Research*, Edited by R.J. Boland, Jr. and R.A. Hirschheim, John Wiley & Sons, Chichester, U.K., 1987, pp. 97 - 111.

[Weinberg, 1971]. G. M. Weinberg, *The Psychology of Computer Programming*, Van Nostrand Reinhold Company, New York, New York, 1971.

[Weinberg, 1983]. G. M. Weinberg, "Kill That Code," *Infosystems*, August 1983, page 49.

[Wirth, 1971]. N. Wirth, "Program Development by Stepwise Refinement," *Communications of the ACM*, Vol. 14, No. 4, April 1971.(Reprinted in *Communications of the ACM*, Vol. 26, No. 1, January 1983, pp. 70 - 73).

6   Abstraction, Encapsulation, and Information Hiding

> *A powerful agent is the right word. Whenever we come upon one of those intensely right words in a book or a newspaper the resulting effect is physical as well as spiritual, and electrically prompt.*
>
>   — *Mark Twain (Samuel Langhorne Clemens),* Essay on William Dean Howells, *1906*

Prologue

I recently read a magazine article that said, "Encapsulation is just a fancy name for information hiding." Since the writer was non-technical, I just assumed that he was attempting to show that he really did not understand technical matters. However, the passage reminded me of several situations in which other authors — both technical and non-technical — had confused encapsulation and information hiding.

Information hiding is not only confused with encapsulation; it is also often confused with abstraction. For example, in a class I was teaching recently, one of the students remarked that my definition of information hiding was remarkably close to my definition of abstraction. Since I had taken both definitions from different sources at different times, I had not thought of comparing them side-by-side. When I did, I was startled at how close the definitions were.

This led to some fanciful speculation on my part. "If encapsulation could be confused with information hiding," I reasoned, "and information hiding could also be confused with abstraction, then could someone argue that abstraction and encapsulation were the same thing?" Of course, when I said it this way, the argument sounded absurd.

Still, I was curious. I decided to gather a number of different definitions for abstraction, information hiding, and encapsulation, and to compare them. This essay details what I found.

Abstraction

A view of a problem that extracts the essential information relevant to a particular purpose and ignores the remainder of the information.

   — *[IEEE, 1983]*

The essence of abstraction is to extract essential properties while omitting inessential details.

   — *[Ross et al., 1975]*

Abstraction is a process whereby we identify the important aspects of a phenomenon and ignore its details.

   — *[Ghezzi et al., 1991]*

> Abstraction is generally defined as "the process of formulating generalised concepts by extracting common qualities from specific examples."
>
> — *[Blair et al., 1991]*

> Abstraction is the selective examination of certain aspects of a problem. The goal of abstraction is to isolate those aspects that are important for some purpose and suppress those aspects that are unimportant.
>
> — *[Rumbaugh et al., 1991]*

> The meaning [of abstraction] given by the *Oxford English Dictionary* (OED) closest to the meaning intended here is 'The act of separating in thought'. A better definition might be "Representing the essential features of something without including background or inessential detail."
>
> — *[Graham, 1991]*

> [A] simplified description, or specification, of a system that emphasizes some of the system's details or properties while suppressing others. A good abstraction is one that emphasizes details that are significant to the reader or user and suppress details that are, at least for the moment, immaterial or diversionary.
>
> — *[Shaw, 1984]*

> An abstraction denotes the essential characteristics of an object that distinguish it from all other kinds of object and thus provide crisply defined conceptual boundaries, relative to the perspective of the viewer.
>
> — *[Booch, 1991]*

One point of confusion regarding abstraction is its use as both a process and an entity. Abstraction, *as a process*, denotes the extracting of the essential details about an item, or a group of items, while ignoring the inessential details. Abstraction, *as an entity*, denotes a model, a view, or some other focused representation for an actual item. Abstraction is most often used as a complexity mastering technique. For example, we often hear people say such things as: "just give me the highlights" or "just the facts, please." What these people are asking for are abstractions.

We can have varying degrees of abstraction, although these "degrees" are more commonly referred to as "levels." As we move to higher levels of abstraction, we focus on the larger and more important pieces of information (using our chosen selection criteria). Another common observation is that as we move to higher levels of abstraction, we tend to concern ourselves with progressively smaller volumes of information, and fewer overall items. As we move to lower levels of abstraction, we reveal more detail, typically encounter more individual items, and increase the volume of information with which we must deal.

A number of sources (i.e., [IEEE, 1983], [Ross et al., 1975], [Ghezzi et al., 1991], [Blair et al., 1991], [Rumbaugh et al., 1991], and [Graham, 1991]) all appear to view abstraction as a process. (Note that the [Blair et al., 1991] definition is somewhat different from the others in that it suggests examining a number of "specific examples" — as opposed to examining a single item.) [Shaw, 1984] and [Booch, 1991] describe abstraction as an entity. Both views are equally valid, and in fact, necessary.

We also note that there are many different types of abstraction, e.g., functional abstraction, data abstraction, process abstraction, and even object abstraction. (See, for example, the following references: [Alexandridis, 1986], [Guttag, 1977], [Liskov and Guttag, 1986],

[Park, 1991], [Shaw, 1984], and [Zimmer, 1985].) Each of the above definitions, because they are *general* definitions of abstraction, correctly avoids describing which *specific* categories of information are emphasized or de-emphasized.

Usually, abstraction is not defined in terms of information hiding, e.g., note the use of words such as "ignore" and "extracting." However, we should also note the use of the words "suppress" and "suppressing" in some of the above examples. In short, you might say that abstraction dictates that some information is more important than other information, but (correctly) does not specify a specific mechanism for handling the unimportant information.

Information Hiding

The second decomposition was made using "information hiding" … as a criterion. The modules no longer correspond to steps in the processing. … Every module in the second decomposition is characterized by its knowledge of a design decision which it hides from all others. Its interface or definition was chosen to reveal as little as possible about its inner workings.

> — *[Parnas, 1972b]*

… the purpose of hiding is to make inaccessible certain details that should not affect other parts of a system.

> — *[Ross et al., 1975]*

… [I]nformation hiding: a module is characterized by the information it hides from other modules, which are called its clients. The hidden information remains a secret to the client modules.

> — *[Ghezzi et al., 1991]*

[Information hiding is] the principle that users of a software component (such as a class) need to know only the essential details of how to initialize and access the component, and do not need to know the details of the implementation.

> — *[Budd, 1991]*

The technique of encapsulating software design decisions in modules in such a way that the module's interfaces reveal as little as possible about the module's inner workings; thus each module is a "black box" to the other modules in the system.

> — *[IEEE, 1983]*

The process of hiding all the details of an object that do not contribute to its essential characteristics; typically, the structure of an object is hidden, as well as the implementation of its methods. The terms information hiding and encapsulation are usually interchangeable.

> — *[Booch, 1991]*

The principle of information hiding is central. It says that modules are used via their specifications, not their implementations. All information about a module, whether concerning data or function, is encapsulated with it and, unless specifically declared public, hidden from other modules.

> — *[Graham, 1991]*

In his classic 1972 article ([Parnas, 1972b]), D.L. Parnas describes two different implementation scenarios for a simple key word in context (KWIC) application. One is decomposed and modularized based on the steps one might take in accomplishing the purpose of the application. (Parnas speculates that this approach would be taken by someone who is basing their design on a flowchart.)

The second (and better) scenario is modularized based on "design decisions." Parnas observes, "We propose instead that one begins with a list of difficult design decisions or design decisions which are likely to change. Each module is then designed to hide such a decision from the others." Like Dijkstra ([Dijkstra, 1968]), Parnas advocates that the details of these difficult and likely-to-change decisions be hidden from the rest of the system. Further, the rest of the system will have access to these design decisions only through well-defined, and (to a large degree) unchanging interfaces. (See also [Parnas, 1972a].)

In truth, both of the scenarios presented by Parnas involve "information hiding." In his first scenario, the hidden information involves the details of the procedural steps necessary to accomplish the application. (By 1971, when Parnas first published his work in a university technical report, programmers had known for almost 20 years of the usefulness of subroutines in mastering complexity.) The second, and (very arguably) superior, scenario requires that the hidden information be the details of difficult and/or likely-to-change design decisions.

"Hiding information," in and of itself, was not new. For that matter, the isolation of difficult and/or likely-to-change design decisions in modules was also not new. (Dijkstra had done this earlier in his implementation of the "THE"-Multiprogramming System.) The significance of Parnas's 1972 article on software module specification lay in two areas:

- His avocation and specification of the (then innovative) technique of basing system modularization on design decisions. (You would have to say that the article presented a significantly different view of Dijkstra's "levels of abstraction" approach.)

- His use of the term "information hiding." Virtually every article which mentions the topic traces its origin to [Parnas, 1972b].

Obviously, Parnas did *not* say all information hiding is good, nor did he say that all information hiding techniques are equally useful. He was identifying a particularly pragmatic approach to information hiding.

Just as with abstraction, there are degrees of information hiding. For example, at the programming language level, C++ provides for public, private, and protected members ([Ellis and Stroustrup, 1990]), and Ada has both private and limited private types ([ARM, 1983]).

We can now identify some of the sources of confusion about the differences between information hiding and abstraction, i.e.:

- Abstraction can be (and often is) used as a technique for identifying which information should be hidden. For example, in functional abstraction we might say that it is important to be able to add items to a list, but the details of how that is accomplished are not of interest and should be hidden. Using data abstraction, we would say that a list is a place where we can store information, but how the list is actually implemented (e.g., as an array or as a series of linked locations) is unimportant and should be hidden.

Confusion can occur when people fail to distinguish between the hiding of information, and a technique (e.g., abstraction) that is used to help identify which information is to be hidden.

- Some of the definitions for abstraction can also be sources of confusion. For example, words like "ignore," "omit," "extract," and "without including" are rather passive, and would not necessarily imply the deliberate hiding of any information, e.g., "the information is there, and accessible, but we just ignore it." However, words like "suppress" and "suppressing" present a somewhat different image — quite possibly the active and deliberate hiding of information.

Now, let's look at the other definitions for information hiding:

- The [Ross et al., 1975] definition somewhat generalizes Parnas's definition, but still stipulates that the information that should be hidden are those "details that should not affect other parts of a system."

- The [Ghezzi et al., 1991] definition also presents a somewhat generalized view of Parnas's view on information hiding.

- The [Budd, 1991] and [Booch, 1991] definitions are specialized to an object-oriented view of the world.

- Note the use of the words "encapsulating" and "encapsulated" in [IEEE, 1983] and [Graham, 1991], respectively. As we shall see in the next section, there is a significant difference between information hiding and encapsulation. However, some people might attempt to infer incorrectly from the [IEEE, 1983] and [Graham, 1991] definitions for information hiding that encapsulation and information hiding are the same thing.

It is all too common to confuse a concept with a strategy of accomplishing that concept. Information hiding, as we have just seen, is the process of making certain pieces of information inaccessible. However, this raises the questions:

- What is the purpose for hiding information?

- Are there any strategies for hiding information?

Abstraction is the most important answer for the first question, and encapsulation is probably the most important answer for the second question.

Encapsulation

1. to enclose in or as if in a capsule

— *[Mish, 1988]*

The concept of encapsulation as used in an object-oriented context is not essentially different from its dictionary definition. It still refers to building a capsule, in this case a conceptual barrier, around some collection of things.

— *[Wirfs-Brock et al., 1990]*

It is a simple, yet reasonable effective, system-building tool. It allows suppliers to present cleanly specified interfaces around the services they provide. A consumer has full visibility to the procedures offered by an object, and no visibility to its data. From a consumer's point of view, an object is a seamless capsule that offers a

number of services, with no visibility as to how these services are implemented ...
The technical term for this is encapsulation.

— *[Cox, 1986]*

Encapsulation or equivalently information hiding refers to the practice of including within an object everything it needs, and furthermore doing this in such a way
that no other object need ever be aware of this internal structure.

— *[Graham, 1991]*

We say that the changeable, hidden information becomes the secret of the module;
also, according to a widely used jargon, we say that such information is encapsulated within the implementation.

— *[Ghezzi et al., 1991]*

Data hiding is sometimes called encapsulation because the data and its code are put
together in a package or "capsule."

— *[Smith, 1991]*

Encapsulation is used as a generic term for techniques which realize data abstraction. Encapsulation therefore implies the provision of mechanisms to support both
modularity and information hiding. There is therefore a one to one correspondence
in this case between the technique of encapsulation and the principle of data
abstraction.

— *[Blair et al., 1991]*

Encapsulation (also information hiding) consists of separating the external aspects
of an object which are accessible to other objects, from the internal implementation
details of the object, which are hidden from other objects.

— *[Rumbaugh et al., 1991]*

[E]ncapsulation — also known as information hiding — prevents clients from
seeing its inside view, where the behavior of the abstraction is implemented.

— *[Booch, 1991]*

Like abstraction, the word "encapsulation" can be used to describe either a process or an
entity. *As a process*, encapsulation means the act of enclosing one or more items within a
(physical or logical) container. Encapsulation, *as an entity*, refers to a package or an enclosure
that holds (contains, encloses) one or more items. It is extremely important to note that
nothing is said about "the walls of the enclosure." Specifically, they may be "transparent,"
"translucent," or even "opaque."

Programming languages have long supported encapsulation. For example, subprograms
(e.g., procedures, functions, and subroutines), arrays, and record structures are common
examples of encapsulation mechanisms supported by most programming languages. Newer
programming languages support larger encapsulation mechanisms, e.g., "classes" in Simula
([Birtwistle et al. 1973]), Smalltalk ([Goldberg and Robson, 1983]), and C++, "modules" in
Modula ([Wirth, 1983]), and "packages" in Ada.

If encapsulation were "the same thing as information hiding," then one might make the
argument that "everything that was encapsulated was also hidden." This is obviously not true.
For example, even though information may be encapsulated within record structures and
arrays, this information is usually not hidden (unless hidden via some other mechanism).

Another example of encapsulated, but not hidden, information is the (highly undesirable) "block of global information" technique reminiscent of Fortran's common blocks. Unfortunately, it is quite easy in some object-oriented languages to create blocks of global data in the form of classes. Specifically, it is possible to create classes with nothing but constants and variables in their public interfaces, i.e., there are no operations in the interface. (For reasons why this is undesirable, see discussions of "module coupling," e.g., [Myers, 1978] and [Yourdon and Constantine, 1979].)

It is indeed true that encapsulation mechanisms such as classes allow some information to be hidden. However, these same encapsulation mechanisms also allow some information to be visible. Some even allow varying degrees of visibility, e.g., C++'s public, protected, and private members.

Even arguing that encapsulation is necessary for information hiding is not as simple as one might suspect. Of course, one could very loosely define encapsulation such that any hidden information is (logically or physically) encapsulated in something.

Examining the cited definitions for encapsulation above, we make the following observations:

- [Wirfs-Brock et al., 1990] comes closest to a simple, straightforward definition for encapsulation.

- Brad Cox's definition ([Cox, 1986]) allows for encapsulation to reveal some information ("full visibility to the procedures offered by an object"), while hiding other information ("no visibility to its data").

- Although not as clean as it could be, the definition supplied by [Blair et al., 1991] presents an accurate view of the relationship among abstraction, information hiding, and encapsulation.

- [Ghezzi et al., 1991] at least acknowledges the confusion associated with information hiding and encapsulation, i.e., "widely used jargon."

- [Booch, 1991], [Graham, 1991], [Rumbaugh et al., 1991], and [Smith, 1991] make no (or very little) distinction between "information hiding" and "encapsulation."

Conclusions

Abstraction, information hiding, and encapsulation are very different, but highly related, concepts. Abstraction is a technique that helps us identify which specific information should be visible, and which information should be hidden. Encapsulation is the technique used to package the information in such a way as to hide what should be hidden, and make visible what is intended to be visible.

It is not hard to see how abstraction, information hiding, and encapsulation became confused with one another. Further, one could argue that, regardless of their "dictionary definitions," these terms have evolved new meanings in the context of software engineering, e.g., in much the same way as "paradigm" has. (See, e.g., [Kuhn, 1962].) However, a stronger argument can be made for keeping the concepts, and thus the terms, distinct.

Bibliography

[Alexandridis, 1986]. N.A. Alexandridis, "Adaptable Software and Hardware: Problems and Solutions," *IEEE Computer*, Vol. 19, No. 2, February 1986, pp. 29 - 39.

[ARM, 1983]. *Reference Manual for the Ada Programming Language, ANSI/MIL-STD 1815A (1983)*, United States Department of Defense, February 1983.

[Birtwistle et al. 1973]. G. Birtwistle, O. Dahl, B. Myhrtag and K. Nygaard, *Simula Begin*, Auerbach Press, Philadelphia, 1973.

[Blair et al., 1991]. G. Blair, J. Gallagher, D. Hutchison, and D. Sheperd, *Object-Oriented Languages, Systems and Applications*, Halsted Press, New York, New York, 1991.

[Booch, 1991]. G. Booch, *Object-Oriented Design With Applications*, Benjamin/Cummings, Menlo Park, California, 1991.

[Budd, 1991]. T. Budd, *An Introduction to Object-Oriented Programming*, Addison-Wesley, Reading, Massachusetts, 1991.

[Cox, 1986]. B.J. Cox, *Object Oriented Programming: An Evolutionary Approach*, Addison-Wesley, Reading, Massachusetts, 1986.

[Dijkstra, 1968]. E.W. Dijkstra, "Structure of the 'THE'-Multiprogramming System," *Communications of the ACM*, Vol. 11, No. 5, May 1968, pp. 341-346.

[Ellis and Stroustrup, 1990]. M.A. Ellis and B. Stroustrup, *The Annotated C++ Reference Manual*, Addison-Wesley, Reading, Massachusetts, 1990.

[Ghezzi et al., 1991]. C. Ghezzi, M. Jazayeri, and D. Mandrioli, *Fundamentals of Software Engineering*, Prentice Hall, Englewood Cliffs, New Jersey, 1991.

[Goldberg and Robson, 1983]. A. Goldberg and D. Robson, *Smalltalk-80: The Language and Its Implementation*, Addison-Wesley, Reading, Massachusetts, 1983.

[Graham, 1991]. I. Graham, *Object-Oriented Methods*, Addison-Wesley, Reading, Massachusetts, 1991.

[Guttag, 1977]. J. Guttag, "Abstract Data Types and the Development of Data Structures," *Communications of the ACM*, Vol. 20, No. 6, June 1977, pp. 396 - 404.

[IEEE, 1983]. IEEE, *IEEE Standard Glossary of Software Engineering Terminology*, The Institute of Electrical and Electronic Engineers, New York, New York, 1983.

[Kuhn, 1962]. T.S. Kuhn, *The Structure of Scientific Revolutions*, University of Chicago Press, Chicago, Illinois, 1962.

[Liskov and Guttag, 1986]. B. Liskov and J. Guttag, *Abstraction and Specification in Program Development*, The MIT Press, Cambridge, Massachusetts, 1986.

[Mish, 1988]. F.C. Mish, Editor in Chief, *Webster's Ninth New Collegiate Dictionary*, Merriam-Webster Inc., Springfield, Massachusetts, 1988.

[Myers, 1978]. G.J. Myers, *Composite/Structured Design*, Van Nostrand Reinhold, New York, New York, 1978.

[Park, 1991]. H.-S. Park, "Abstract Object Types = Abstract Knowledge Types + Abstract Data Types + Abstract Connector Types," *Journal of Object-Oriented Programming*, Vol. 4, No. 3, June 1991, pp. 37 - 39, 42 - 44, 46 - 48, 51 - 52.

[Parnas, 1971]. D.L. Parnas, *Information Distribution Aspects of Design Methodology*, Technical Report, Department of Computer Science, Carnegie-Mellon University, Pittsburgh, Pennsylvania, February 1971.

[Parnas, 1972a]. D.L. Parnas, "A Technique for Software Module Specification With Examples," *Communications of the ACM*, Vol. 15, No. 5, May 1972, pp. 330 - 336.

[Parnas, 1972b]. D.L. Parnas, "On the Criteria To Be Used in Decomposing Systems Into Modules," *Communications of the ACM*, Vol. 5, No. 12, December 1972, pp. 1053-1058.

[Ross et al., 1975]. D.T. Ross, J.B. Goodenough, and C.A. Irvine, "Software Engineering: Process, Principles, and Goals," *IEEE Computer,* Vol. 8, No. 5, May 1975, pp. 17 - 27.

[Rumbaugh et al., 1991]. J. Rumbaugh, M. Blaha, W. Premerlani, F. Eddy, and W. Lorensen, *Object-Oriented Modeling and Design*, Prentice Hall, Englewood Cliffs, New Jersey, 1991.

[Shaw, 1984]. M. Shaw, "Abstraction Techniques in Modern Programming Languages," *IEEE Software*, Vol. 1, No. 4, October 1984, pp. 10 - 26.

[Smith, 1991]. D.N. Smith, *Concepts of Object-Oriented Programming*, McGraw-Hill, New York, New York, 1991.

[Wirfs-Brock et al., 1990]. R. Wirfs-Brock, B. Wilkerson, and L. Wiener, *Designing Object-Oriented Software*, Prentice Hall, Englewood Cliffs, New Jersey, 1990.

[Wirth, 1983]. N. Wirth, *Programming In Modula-2,* Second Edition, Springer-Verlag, New York, New York, 1983.

[Yourdon and Constantine, 1979]. E. Yourdon and L.L. Constantine, *Structured Design: Fundamentals of a Discipline of Computer Program and Systems Design,* Prentice Hall, Englewood Cliffs, New Jersey, 1979.

[Zimmer, 1985]. J.A. Zimmer, *Abstraction for Programmers*, McGraw-Hill, New York, New York, 1985.

7   Object Coupling and Object Cohesion

> We build systems like the Wright brothers built airplanes — build the whole thing, push it off a cliff, let it crash, and start over again.
>
> — *Professor R.M. Graham (in [Naur and Randell, 1969])*

> A more detailed study ... reveals that the error is proportional to the degree of coupling between subsystems, and inversely proportional to the 'undecomposability' of each subsystem.
>
> — *P.J. Courtois ([Courtois, 1985])*

> Neither SA nor SD as currently practiced have proved to be very good routes to actually deriving a sound OO design, but nearly all of the basic principles still apply: problem partitioning, component integrity (cohesion), independence (coupling), etc. All science and engineering builds on what has gone before. It is silly to think that OO in our field would be an exception.
>
> — *Larry Constantine ([Constantine, 1991])*

> Coupling tells us to reduce the knowledge one class has of others, so when one class changes, it is less likely to change the others. Cohesion tells us to make sure all the member variables and methods of a class make sense as part of the class. Coupling and cohesion help the designer determine how to apply the basic object-oriented design concepts of classification, encapsulation, and inheritance.
>
> — *David K. Taylor and Alan Hecht ([Taylor and Hecht, 1990])*

Prologue

Technology, as we know it, is continually evolving — and hopefully, continually improving. Still, there is a significant difference between the way we view computer *hardware* technology and the way we view computer *software* technology. On one hand, we have come to expect computer hardware technology to rapidly evolve and improve. On the other hand, many people think of software engineering technology as little different than it was a decade ago. In general, our expectations for software engineering are much lower than are our expectations for computer hardware engineering.

Some people seem to be searching for "the pinnacle of software engineering technologies." For example, "if it is not 'structured,' maybe it is 'object-oriented,'" or, "if it is not character-based, surely it must be graphical." Personal experience, if not the whole of technological history, should tell us that, just about the time that we become comfortable with a "new" technology, a better one is already beginning to establish itself.

In truth, technological evolution has more to do with "plateaus" than it does with "pinnacles." For example, in the 1950s and 1960s software development seemed to be governed by few guidelines, and even fewer formal procedures. In the 1970s, we saw the introduction of structured programming, structured design, structured testing, and structured analysis. In the 1980s, object-oriented concepts began to show promise of being a significant improvement over more traditional (e.g., structured) approaches.

If we step back, we see that, from the perspective of the chaos of the 1960s, structured approaches appeared to be a pinnacle. When we began using structured techniques, we did indeed find them to be improvements to the state-of-the-practice. However, after using structured techniques for a while, we noticed a new pinnacle, i.e., "object-oriented techniques." Some of us have migrated upward from the "structured plateau," to object-oriented technologies. However, we should be under no delusion that object-oriented software engineering is a pinnacle. Like structured technologies, object-oriented technologies represent a useful plateau, and will likely be replaced by something better in the future.

Plateaus are a necessary part of technology. They allow us to rest, collect our thoughts, further discover and study the concepts that make up the technology, and achieve some tangible benefits from the plateau technology. In software engineering approaches, these plateaus appear to be typically 10-14 years in duration.

When we are ready to go to the next plateau, we must decide which concepts can be used unchanged with the new technology, which will be left behind, and which can be used with modifications. Since the major thrust of this article concerns topics that originated in what is generally called "structured design," let's draw some examples from that area. (See, e.g., Chapter 6 of [Myers, 1978] and Chapter 9 of [Yourdon and Constantine, 1979].)

In the process of creating the software architecture for a system, structured design dictates that we must avoid "**decision splitting**," i.e., we should keep the actions taken based on a decision as close as possible to the point where the decision was made. (Of course, there still are a very few situations in both structured and object-oriented systems where it is advisable to delay acting on a decision until some later point in time.) This is a concept that can be moved unchanged from structured to object-oriented approaches.

The concept of "**system shape**," on the other hand, does not translate at all into an object-oriented point of view. Evaluating the system shape, in systems developed using structured techniques, allowed a designer to determine if a proposed system was "input driven," "output driven," or "balanced," with "balanced" being the most desirable. This was based on an overall input-processing-output view of a software system. While object-oriented systems do indeed take in "input," and produce "output," they tend to much more closely model the real world, and hence their structure is not dictated strictly by an input-processing-output model.

Other concepts require slight modifications. For example, the concept of a "module" must move from meaning a subprogram (e.g., a procedure, function, subroutine, or paragraph) to encompass the idea of objects (e.g., classes, metaclasses, parameterized classes, and their instances). Consider the following:

- Small module size is still important. However, it has slightly different interpretations. The number of lines of source code for well-designed encapsulated methods, for example, are usually very small in number. Further, the number of encapsulated methods in the public interface for any given object should be kept to a manageable number. (See also [Card and Glass, 1990].)

- The public interface for an item should still be consistent with the overall concept embodied by the item. By "item," we mean both objects, and methods encapsulated within objects.

- The concepts behind "fan in" and "fan out" still hold. Specifically, the more system components that make use of a particular object, i.e., the higher the particular object's "fan in," usually the better is the design of the overall system. The larger the number of other distinct system components with which an object must deal directly, i.e., the higher the "fan out" of an object, usually the poorer is the design of the overall system.

- The characteristics of the public interface of an object and its overall characteristics should still not be overly restrictive. Software engineers will still have to strike a balance between making an object very general to increase its reusability, the increased costs of doing so, and making an object so specialized that it cannot be easily reused, and is subject to frequent changes.

- Unless intentionally designed otherwise, an object's characteristics (e.g., its behavior, its capacities, and its allowed states) should still be generally predictable. We note that it is almost always in bad form to design functional modules with a "memory," i.e., a module's behavior should not be different depending on when it is invoked. However, since all objects have state, it is normal (in fact, required) for objects to have a memory, and to behave somewhat differently based on their current states.

As with any engineering discipline, there is usually no one single criterion for evaluating the quality of a design. Each of the applicable items above must be traded off against other criteria. The software engineer must consider minimizing the impact of change, reliability, reusability, and efficiency among other design goals.

History of Coupling and Cohesion

Many of us have had the experience of having a piece of code compile cleanly (i.e., without errors) the first time the source code was submitted to the compiler. A few of us have even had a program execute properly the first time it was submitted for execution. Some may have attributed these occurrences to luck, or to fate, but others have speculated that these and other positive software engineering situations could be made to happen deliberately. The only question was, "How?" In 1969, E.W. Dijkstra ([Dijkstra, 1969]) phrased it as follows:

> The leading question was if it was conceivable to increase our programming ability by an order of magnitude and what techniques (mental, organizational or mechanical) could be applied in the process of program composition to achieve this increase.

During the late 1960s and early 1970s, work focused on a number of areas, including optimization of programming personnel (e.g., [Aron, 1968]), [Baker, 1972], [Baker and Mills, 1973], and Chapter 2 of [Yourdon, 1975]) and module and system design techniques (e.g., [Parnas, 1972] and [Stevens et al., 1974], respectively). One of the first system design techniques to gain widespread popularity was what is commonly referred to as "structured design."

Structured design was more than a process for producing software designs. It also encompassed techniques for the evaluation of the quality of the resulting designs. Two very important quality evaluating concepts from structured design are "module coupling" and "module cohesion." The overall goal is to create systems in which all the modules are as independent of each other as possible. This can be accomplished if the interconnections and interrelationships among the modules are as tenuous as possible (i.e., they are loosely coupled), *and* if each module's components are tightly bound to each other (i.e., individual modules are highly cohesive).

The originating, and most significant, work in the area of "structured design" was accomplished by Larry Constantine. In the preface to [Yourdon and Constantine, 1979], he traces his earliest thoughts on the subject to 1963. Constantine's first published work on the topic appeared in December of 1965, in an article titled "Towards a Theory of Program Design." By 1967, he had formulated both a graphical notation and a vocabulary for describing the structure of programs, and had written a book describing "hierarchical design" ([Constantine, 1967]).

In the late 1960s, Constantine joined IBM's Systems Research Institute (SRI). At SRI, he refined his concepts and taught quite a number of students. One of them, Glen Myers, published his view of Constantine's work (e.g., [Myers, 1973a] and [Myers, 1973b]) referring to it as "composite design." Another student, Wayne Stevens, along with Constantine and Myers, helped pull together Constantine's concepts into a landmark article ([Stevens et al., 1974]).

All of the authors of [Stevens et al., 1974] have gone on to write books on the topic, e.g., Myers's [Myers, 1975] and [Myers, 1978], Stevens's [Stevens, 1981], and, of course, Constantine's now famous collaboration with Ed Yourdon, i.e., [Yourdon and Constantine, 1979]. (Other discussions of structured design can be found, for example, in [Bergland, 1981], [Myers, 1976], and [Page-Jones, 1988]. We should also point out that there are a fair number of variations on Constantine's original view of structured design. Most of these are in the area of real-time systems design, e.g., [Gomaa, 1984], [Hatley and Pirbhai, 1987], and [Ward and Mellor, 1985].)

Module coupling and module cohesion have applications outside of structured design. For example, by 1985 they were being discussed in the context of object-oriented design (e.g., [Berard, 1985]). In 1986, the concept of coupling had been extended to address "object coupling" (e.g., [Berard, 1986]). Lately, discussions of object coupling are becoming more commonplace. (See, e.g., [Blair et al., 1991], [Booch, 1991], [Budd, 1991], [Liberherr and Riel, 1988a], [Wild, 1991], and [Wirfs-Brock et al., 1990].) Discussions of "object cohesion" are somewhat less common, but do occur. (See, e.g., [Blair et al., 1991] and [Budd, 1991].)

General Concepts Behind Coupling and Cohesion

Scientists and engineers have been studying systems (literally) for centuries. Although much of the work has involved the study of specific systems (e.g., mechanical systems, chemical systems, and biological systems), there has been a fair amount of work devoted to the study of systems in general. In this article I will first focus primarily on the contributions made by Herbert A. Simon and P.-J. Courtois to general systems science. Further, I will relate this work to the concepts of coupling and cohesion.

I must first define the much-used term "system." A **system** is a collection of two or more interacting or interrelated items. (Mathematical purists will point out that I can have a completely empty system, as well as a system containing only one item, but we need not consider these situations for the present.) We further stipulate that the components of a system can be bound together in a logical manner, a physical manner, or both.

Systems can, in turn, be composed of smaller systems. A system which is itself part of a larger system is referred to as a "subsystem" of the larger system.

In 1961, H. Simon and A. Ando observed ([Simon and Ando, 1961]):

- Most often, complex systems can be shown to be hierarchies of interrelated or interacting subsystems. These subsystems can, in turn, be further decomposed into smaller subsystems. This decomposition process can continue until all that is left are the most elementary (primitive) components.

- In general, interactions and interrelationships inside subsystems are stronger than are the interactions and interrelationships between and among subsystems.

We note that the second point, although not phrased in terms of, nor restricted to, software systems, is a statement about coupling and cohesion. We can separate the ideas by saying that the forces that hold together an individual subsystem (cohesion) are stronger than the forces that bind individual subsystems together into a larger system (coupling).

The first of Simon and Ando's observations is also intriguing. In his 1962 article, "The Architecture of Complexity" ([Simon, 1962], reprinted in [Simon, 1981]), Simon states:

> "We have shown thus far that complex systems will evolve from simple systems much more rapidly if there are stable intermediate forms than if there are not. The resulting complex forms in the former case will be hierarchic."

Earlier, in the same article, Simon illustrates this point with a parable about two watchmakers (Hora and Tempus). Both watchmakers build fine watches from about 1,000 separate parts. However, one watchmaker (Hora) produces subassemblies of about 10 components each, while the other (Tempus) uses no subassemblies. Each watchmaker is successful enough so that they are constantly interrupted by phone calls. The watchmaker using subassemblies, however, is more likely to finish a subassembly before the phone rings than the other watchmaker is likely to finish a complete watch. As a consequence, Hora prospers while Tempus has difficulty assembling even one watch. (Simon even includes a strong mathematical demonstration as to why the watchmaker using subassemblies is better off.)

The implications of this argument for software are most interesting. We know, almost intuitively, that dealing with 100 subprograms, each 100 lines of code in length, is easier than is dealing with 10,000 separate lines of source code. We also know that there are limits to the complexity that any one human mind can deal with effectively, e.g., [Miller, 1956]. One could argue, almost without proof, that building software from subassemblies, will not only be much faster, but also less error prone, than constructing software on a strictly line-by-line basis.

We can say that subprograms (e.g., functions, procedures, subroutines, and paragraphs) provide this "intermediate form" between individual lines of code and a completed program. We might also say that objects (e.g., classes, metaclasses, and their instances) provide another intermediate form, but at a higher level, i.e., between subprograms and a completed program. Following the logic described by Simon, one could argue that it will be easier, faster, and less error prone to construct a system from object-oriented components than it would be to construct the same system from (smaller) subprogram units.

Of course, the strength of this argument depends largely on both how well the individual objects are designed, and on how well the overall system is designed. We can say that if a software engineer examining an individual object in isolation observes that the components of the object very much logically belong together, then the individual object has met one of the criteria for a well-designed object. We can further state that the less each object in the system knows, or needs to know, about any other object in the same system then the better the overall design, since a change to one object need not require a corresponding change in one or more other objects.

Later, in [Simon, 1962], Simon discusses "decomposable systems" and "nearly decomposable systems." If one or more of the components of a system have no interactions or other interrelationships with any of the other components at the same level of abstraction within the same system, then we call such a system a **decomposable system**. Specifically, the system can easily be decomposed into two or more smaller systems, one containing the components that have no interactions or interrelationships with the rest of the original system, and another containing only those components of the original system that have established interactions or other interrelationships. This process can then be repeated using the system containing components that had no interactions or interrelationships with the rest of the original system, until all that we are left with are systems which cannot be decomposed in this manner.

A **nearly decomposable system**, on the other hand, is a system in which:

- every component of the system has a direct or indirect interaction or other interrelationship with every other component at the same level of abstraction within the same system, and

- the interaction or other interrelationship between any two components at the same level of abstraction within the system is as weak (tenuous) as possible, i.e., if it were any weaker, the system would be a decomposable system.

The components of a well-designed software system always have (logical or physical) interactions or other interrelationships with at least one other component of the same system. Further, we stipulate that in well-designed software systems there is a (logical or physical) direct or indirect connection (interrelationship) between any two components at the same level of abstraction within the system. As we have said, we want these connections to be as weak as possible so that a change to one component need not require a corresponding change in one or more other components. Said another way, well-designed software systems are nearly decomposable systems.

P.-J. Courtois, in [Courtois, 1985], expands on Simon's ideas. He makes a number of interesting observations, e.g.:

- "Usually, but not always, events that take place at quite different scales [of time and size] have a negligible influence on each other." For example, if a system is well designed, one can study and understand the system at a given level of abstraction by considering only the components at that level of abstraction — without regard to the details of the lower-level implementations.

- "[W]hen interrelated events take place within a system at various size or time scales not far apart from each other, the choice of an appropriate level of analysis and the assessment of the influence of other levels not directly taken into account on the validity of the analysis can be difficult." Said another way, system decomposition (functional, object-oriented, or otherwise) in which the components do not differ significantly in scales of time and size is not always straightforward. One could even say that software engineers should make an assessment of the differences in the time and/or size scales between one level of decomposition and the level immediately above that level. If the differences are "small," then the results of the decomposition process deserve a closer scrutiny than if the differences were "large."

- "It is not easy ... to predict the macroscopic properties of a system from known microscopic properties." One can optimize a particular low-level system compo- nent, for example, but one cannot guarantee the effects of this optimization without knowledge of the overall system.

- Usually small changes in parts of a large system have a small effect on the overall system. However, through a series of small changes, systems can find themselves in a state where one very small (previously insignificant) change can result in a very large change to the entire system. (This is a variation on "the straw that broke the camel's back.") System engineers must be mindful of the contributions that many small changes can make to a large system over time.

- "A first design principle, suggested by the space-time separation studied here, is that distributed control, which relies on local state information, should primarily pertain to fast transient changes, and centralized control to the slow and long-term evolution of the system." In effect, as we move to lower levels of abstraction in a system, we should expect events to occur at a much faster pace.

We can summarize the work of both Simon and Courtois by saying that in designing any system (software, hardware, social, biological, or otherwise), we should:

- make sure that the components of the system (i.e., the subsystems) are comprised of parts that are all highly logically related, i.e., each individual component is very cohesive,

- ensure that the relationships among the components of the system are as tenuous as possible, i.e., that the coupling is kept to a minimum,

- carefully examine our decomposition, paying closest attention to those parts where there are relatively "small" differences in the scales of time and/or size between a decomposed item and its components, and

- keep in mind that, even in nearly decomposable systems, the contribution of many small interactions (or other interrelationships) over time can lead not only to significant changes, but also to the possibility of a "large" change as a result of a (previously) insignificant interaction.

David L. Parnas has also indirectly addressed the concepts of module coupling and cohesion. In [Parnas et al., 1983], for example, he, and his co-authors, observe:

> The primary goal of the decomposition into modules is reduction of software cost by allowing modules to be designed and revised independently. Specific goals of module decomposition are:
>
> (a) each module's structure should be simple enough that it can be understood fully;

One could view this point in terms of a module's cohesion. The more any one module represents a single, coherent concept, at a uniform level of abstraction, the easier it will be to understand that module. In the case of object-oriented software engineering, we can interpret "module" to mean an individual object, a system of interacting or interrelated objects, or an unencapsulated operation.

[Parnas et al., 1983] continues:

> (b) it should be possible to change the implementation of one module without knowledge of the implementation of other modules and without affecting the behavior of other modules;

This statement is, of course, directly related to coupling. In a totally uncoupled system, a change can be made to any one component without any impact on any other component. In a loosely coupled (nearly decomposable) system, as long as the components of that system continue to represent (to the outside world) their original abstractions, and maintain their original interfaces, changes to the underlying implementation of any one component should not adversely impact any other component, or the overall system. (See also the discussion of "coupling" in Chapter 8 of [Coad and Yourdon, 1991].)

The next point [Parnas et al., 1983] brings up is:

> (c) the ease of making a change in the design should bear a reasonable relationship to the likelihood of the change being needed; it should be possible to make likely changes without changing any module interfaces; less likely changes may involve interface changes, but only for modules that are small and not widely used. Only very unlikely changes should require changes in the interfaces of widely used modules;

This point relates to the cohesiveness of an individual system component. If a software component accurately represents a single coherent "real world" item or concept, then it is only likely to change if its real world counterpart changes. On the other hand, if a component contains information about things not directly related to the main item or concept, then the whole software component is more vulnerable to change.

The next two points mentioned in [Parnas et al., 1983] address both coupling and cohesion, i.e.:

> (d) it should be possible to make a major software change as a set of independent changes to individual modules, i.e., except for interface changes, programmers changing the individual modules should not need to communicate. If the interfaces of the modules are not revised, it should be possible to run and test any combination of old and new module variations.
>
> ... (e) A software engineer should be able to understand the responsibility of a module without understanding the module's internal design.

Specifically, the more loosely coupled the components are, and the more cohesive each component is (i.e., the more that each component represents a single coherent item or concept), then the easier it will be to both introduce changes and understand individual components.

Lastly, for a more rigorous attempt at defining "module coupling," see [Wand and Weber, 1990].

Module Coupling and Module Cohesion in an Object-Oriented Context

We now turn to a discussion of module coupling and, then, module cohesion. Our discussions will chiefly center around encapsulated methods in the public interfaces of objects. We will show that an understanding of classic module coupling and module cohesion can improve the quality of our object-oriented designs.

[Several authors have suggested that a discussion of "object coupling and cohesion" should begin with an examination of the more classical "module coupling and cohesion." See, for example, [Bulman, 1989], [Loy, 1990], and [Taylor and Hecht, 1990].]

In non-object-oriented systems, it is common to talk about invoking a subprogram, potentially passing it one or more input parameters, and having the invoked routine potentially return one or more output parameters. In addition to the normal concepts of programming-language-defined transfer of control between modules, we can also think of modules as passing control via input and/or output parameters. As a consequence of this, in non-object-oriented systems, we can think of input and output parameters as representing either data or control.

For simplicity, during our discussion of module coupling and module cohesion in an object-oriented context, we will use the terms "invoking a method" and "sending a message" as if they were interchangeable. We must also allow the encapsulated methods to have return parameters. While we will stipulate that these return parameters are indeed returned to the original message sender (method invoker), we will generally not be concerned with the actual mechanism(s) by which this might take place. As in non-object-oriented systems, we allow for both programming-language-defined transfer of control and passing control via input and/or output parameters.

Finally, in our object-oriented systems, we will generally consider both input and output parameters to be objects (i.e., not data).

Module Coupling

[Coupling is] a measure of the interdependence among modules in a computer program.

— *[IEEE, 1983]*

Coupling is related to cohesion — it is an indication of the strength of interconnections between program units. Highly coupled systems have strong interconnections, with program units dependent on each other, whereas loosely coupled systems are made up of units which are independent or almost independent.

— *[Sommerville, 1989]*

The strength of coupling between two modules is influenced by the complexity of the interface, the type of connection, and the type of communications. Obvious relationships result in less complexity than obscure or inferred ones.

— *[Fairley, 1985]*

The subject of module coupling is entirely concerned with intermodule relationships. Minimizing module coupling is a process of both eliminating unnecessary relationships among modules and minimizing the tightness of those relationships that are necessary.

— *[Myers, 1978]*

Coupling as an abstract concept — the degree of interdependence between modules — may be operationalized as the probability that in coding, debugging, or modifying one module, a programmer will have to take into account something about another module. If two modules are tightly coupled, then there is a high probability that a programmer trying to modify one of them will have to make a change to the other. Clearly, total systems cost will be strongly influenced by the degree of coupling between modules.

— [Yourdon and Constantine, 1979]

There is much that has been written about module coupling. However, we will take our discussion from two primary sources, i.e., Chapter 6 of [Yourdon and Constantine, 1979] and Chapter 5 of [Myers, 1978]. (Discussions on module coupling can also be found in [Bergland, 1981], [Fairley, 1985], [Myers, 1975], [Myers, 1976], [Page-Jones, 1988], [Sage and Palmer, 1990], [Sommerville, 1989], and [Stevens, 1981] among others.) We will structure our plan of attack as follows:

- Our discussion will loosely follow the ranking (best to worst) of module coupling as described in [Myers, 1978].

- We will compare and contrast each source's view on each form of coupling.

- We will describe how each type of module coupling relates to object-oriented software.

Please note that there may be more than one type of coupling between two modules. In such cases, we refer to the type of coupling as the strongest (worst) form of coupling.

Outside of no coupling at all, the weakest form of coupling between any two modules is **data coupling**:

- [Yourdon and Constantine, 1979] describes data coupling by stating that "a connection [between modules] establishes input-output coupling, or data coupling, if it provides output data from one module that serves as input data to the other."

- [Myers, 1978] breaks input-output coupling into two categories, data coupling (better) and stamp coupling (worse).

  - "Two modules are defined as being **data coupled** 1) [if they exhibit no other form of coupling], 2) if the modules directly communicate with one another (e.g., one module calls the other module), and 3) if all interface data (e.g., input and output arguments) between the modules are homogeneous data items." The data items must be conceptually, as well as physically, homogeneous.

  - "Two modules are **stamp coupled** if they are [not coupled otherwise], and if they reference the same nonglobal data structure." Said another way, if one module passes a *heterogeneous* data structure as an argument to another module, then the two modules are stamp coupled. A "homogeneous data structure" that contains elements which are conceptually and/or physically different is considered to be a heterogeneous data structure.

In object-oriented systems, if one object sends a message to another object, and that message contains one or more other objects necessary to accomplish the request, then we very likely have a case of data or stamp coupling (using Myers's definitions). Please note that it is best for the object receiving the message to treat the supplied object(s) as a monolithic entity (or series of monolithic entities). If the object receiving the message is handed a composite object, and knows how to extract the needed component object(s) from that composite object, then we have a major problem. Specifically, if the composition, or the public interface, of the composite object changes, then the receiving object must know of this change.

The impact of this problem can be mitigated, at least partially, through the specification of what Booch refers to as "required operations" ([Booch, 1986]), i.e., the operations that the receiving object *requires* to handle the composite object contained in the message. These required operations are best handled by such things as templates in C++ ([Stroustrup, 1991]) and genericity in Eiffel ([Meyer, 1992]).

The idea of parameterizing a class with methods that are used by the methods internal to the class is, unfortunately, foreign to many. Consider the following example. Suppose that I am attempting to create an ordered list. Specifically, when an item is added to the list, it must be added in its proper, order-determined location. The method for the "add operation" maintains order by sending a "<" (less than) message (using a Smalltalk-like terminology) containing the item to be added to various list locations until it finds the appropriate location to insert the item.

Notice the assumptions that are made. First, that the object receiving the message will understand what "<" means. Second, if there are multiple "<", then the appropriate "<" will be selected.

Next, assume that we wish to create a general ordered list, i.e., an ordered list that can be used to store many different kinds of objects, although at any one time, all the objects contained in a list would all be of the same kind. If we "hard code" into our add operation the "<" operator, we are making some assumptions about the kinds of object that we wish to place in the ordered list. The most specific assumption is that the objects to be placed in the list will all understand the "<" operator. But what about the following situations?:

- The objects to be placed in the list have a "lessThan" method selector (again, I am using Smalltalk-like terminology), but not a "<".

- The objects to be placed in the list have a ">" (greater than) operator and a "=" (test for equality) operator from which can be fashioned a "<" (less than) operator, but they have no specific "<".

If we allow a class to be parameterized (allow a template to be created) with a user-supplied "<" method, we can stipulate (at the time the template is instantiated) how the objects to be placed in the list are to be compared. Notice that there is a great deal of flexibility in this approach. For example, I can invert the sorting order by simply instantiating the list template with a ">" operation, or, if I am dealing with composite objects, I can select which component objects, in which order, I wish to use in determining the ordering.

Both Constantine and Myers talk about **control coupling**:

- [Yourdon and Constantine, 1979] states that, "Control-coupling covers all forms of connection that communicate elements of control. This may involve actual transfer of control (e.g., activation of modules), or it may involve the passing of data that change, regulate, or synchronize the target module (or serve to do the same for the originating module)."

- [Myers, 1978] states, "Two modules are control coupled if they are not [coupled otherwise], and if one module explicitly controls the logic of the other, that is, one module passes an explicit element of control to the other module."

In object-oriented systems, control coupling usually occurs under one of the following situations:

- One object sends a message to another object, and the method in the receiving object that responds to the message will do different things based on "control information" contained in the message. For example, a lamp object may be designed with only one "set" method, and the lamp is turned on, turned off, or set to flashing based on the value of a control parameter passed to this "set" method. (It would be better, for example, to break out this method into three separate methods.)

- In the process of responding to a message, a method returns "control information" to the object that originally sent the message. The most common example of this is an "error code" returned by the method that handled the original message, e.g., if the error code has a zero value, no errors occurred in handling the original request. (This type of coupling can be loosened through the proper use of exceptions. See e.g., [Borgida, 1985], [Borgida, 1986], [Dony, 1988], [Dony, 1988], [Goodenough, 1975], and [Koenig and Stroustrup, 1990].)

It is very easy to avoid the first situation described above. However, in programming languages which do not support exceptions, it is difficult to avoid the second scenario and still maintain an acceptable level of system reliability.

Unprotected global information introduces its own set of coupling problems. By "unprotected" we mean information whose underlying structure and/or implementation is *not* hidden. Two of the most common examples of such global information are the use of COMMON in Fortran, and the entire Data Division in a Cobol program.:

- [Yourdon and Constantine, 1979] describes **common-environment coupling** as follows, "Whenever two or more modules interact with a common data environment, these modules are said to be common-environment coupled. Each pair of modules which interacts with the common environment is coupled — regardless of the direction of communication or the form of reference. ... Common-environment coupling is a second-order, rather than a first-order, effect. Modules A and B are common environment by virtue of their references to a third entity, the common environment." ([Yourdon and Constantine, 1979] stipulates that common-environment coupling can also occur even when two modules reference the same non-global common environment, e.g., two modules reference the same file.)

- [Myers, 1978] both restricts its definition of this type of module coupling to unprotected global information, and breaks into two separate forms of coupling:

  - "A group of modules are **externally coupled** if they are not [coupled otherwise] and if they reference a homogeneous global data item."

- "**Common coupling** ... occurs among a group of modules that reference a global data structure."

One can think of module coupling as the sharing of knowledge among a group of modules. The more one module knows about other modules (directly or indirectly), the tighter is the coupling between the two modules. In the type of coupling we are describing here, modules share a knowledge of the existence of a "common environment," and, in the case of unprotected information, they also share a knowledge of the structure and/or implementation of that information. If the common environment is removed, or if the structure and/or implementation of the unprotected information is changed, then all modules which reference this common environment will very likely have to be altered in some manner, shape, or form.

It should be obvious that references to an external entity, without referencing its underlying implementation, are a looser form of coupling than are references which depend on knowledge of the structure and/or implementation of the same external entity. (This is why, for example, Myers makes the distinction between "external coupling" and "common coupling.")

In object-oriented systems, this type of coupling can occur in the following situations — organized in progressively tighter couplings:

- A method in one object makes a specific reference to a specific external object. (This type of coupling can be removed by making the reference generic (non-specific), e.g., through the use of templates in C++.)

- A method in one object makes a specific reference to a specific external object, and to one or more specific methods in the interface to that external object. (Again, by making the references generic (non-specific), we can minimize the impact of this coupling.)

- A component of an object-oriented system has a public interface which consists partially, or entirely, of items whose values remain constant throughout execution, and whose underlying structures/implementations are hidden.

- A component of an object-oriented system has a public interface which consists partially, or entirely, of items whose values remain constant throughout execution, and whose underlying structures/implementations are *not* hidden.

- A component of an object-oriented system has a public interface which consists partially, or entirely, of items whose values *do not* remain constant throughout execution, and whose underlying structures/implementations are hidden.

- A component of an object-oriented system has a public interface which consists partially, or entirely, of items whose values *do not* remain constant throughout execution, and whose underlying structures/implementations are *not* hidden.

It is sometimes useful, and occasionally even necessary, for objects to include items other than methods in their public interfaces. The general guideline, however, is that constants in the public interface of an object are much more tolerable than are variables in the public interface of an object. In fact, the use of variables in the public interfaces of objects should be allowed only with the strongest of justifications.

"Self-modifying code" is an aspect of what Myers refers to as the tightest form of module coupling. Constantine and Myers both describe this type of coupling, but give it different names:

- [Yourdon and Constantine, 1979] defines **hybrid coupling** as follows, "When one module modifies the procedural contents of anther module, we have hybrid-coupling. Hybrid-coupling is simply intermodular statement modification. To the target (modified) module, the connection functions as control; to the modifying module, it functions as data."

- Glen Myers ([Myers, 1978]) defines the same phenomenon as part of what he calls **content coupling**, "Two modules are content coupled if one directly references the insides of the other or if the normal linkage conventions between the modules are bypassed (e.g., a module branches to, rather than calls, the other module). The word 'directly' describes a relationship that is not resolved by some other binding program or mechanism, such as a linkage editor."

(To be totally accurate, Myers extends the definition suggested by Yourdon and Constantine. He does this by including modules where "the normal linkage conventions between the modules are bypassed (e.g., a module branches to, rather than calls, the other module).")

Understanding and debugging programs in which the structure remains consistent during execution is difficult enough. Dealing effectively with programs that modify their own executable code during execution, or which use language/implementation "tricks" to bypass normal transfer of control among modules is nearly impossible. Fortunately, most commonly-used object-oriented programming languages make such concepts relatively difficult to implement.

We must point out, however, that in some programming languages, self-modification during execution is considered quite normal — in fact expected. The most common examples of such languages are the derivatives of Lisp, e.g., Flavors ([Moon, 1986]) and CLOS ([Keene, 1989] and [Lawless and Miller, 1991]). These languages usually allow not only the run-time modification of individual methods, but also the run-time modification of the entire structure of individual objects. While the capabilities of such languages are powerful, and sometimes useful, software engineers must still take extra care to avoid potentially erroneous and unreliable situations during program execution.

[Yourdon and Constantine, 1979] discusses one form of module coupling that is not discussed in [Myers, 1978], i.e., what [Yourdon and Constantine, 1979] refers to as "content-coupling":

> "Content coupling occurs when some or all of the contents of one module are included in the contents of another."

[Yourdon and Constantine, 1979] further breaks content coupling down into three categories:

- "**Lexical inclusion** of one module inside another, by itself, is a fairly mild form of coupling. While neither the lexical superordinate nor its subordinate can be used without the other in some form, the process of separating the two into lexically independent units is generally straightforward, unless the lexical subordinate is activated in-line (by 'falling into' the code) in some circumstances."

- "**Partial content overlap** is a more extreme form of lexical content-coupling." In this situation, one module begins "in the middle" of another module and ends outside of that other module.

- "A **multiple-entry module** is an example of content-coupling, and represents a special case of lexical inclusion in which the identity interface of several modules (the alternative functions) are defined at the same lexical level. It is usually difficult to maintain or modify the various functions of a multiple entry module independently."

Of course, C and C++ programmers will recognize this form of coupling. It would be extremely unusual to find a C or C++ program which did not include at least one "header file." The "proper" use of *C++* header files is to provide class interface specifications — not to serve as a means of lexically including program items. Unfortunately, some C++ programmers choose to include items over and above class interface specifications, e.g., constants. In general, the information in a C++ header file should be kept to the minimum information needed by the compiler to successfully compile the item that is included the header file.

We end our discussion of module coupling by pointing out that there have been a fair number of attempts to measure (both qualitatively and quantitatively) module coupling. For examples of module coupling metrics, see [Beane et al., 1984], [Card et al., 1986], [Card and Glass, 1990], [Conte et al., 1986], [Ejiogu, 1991], [Lohse and Zweben, 1984], [Myers, 1975], and [Troy and Zweben, 1981].

Module Cohesion

[Cohesion is] the degree to which the tasks performed by a single program module are functionally related.

> — *[IEEE, 1983]*

Cohesion is the 'glue' that holds a module together. It can be thought of as the type of association among the component elements of a module. Generally, one wants the highest level of cohesion possible.

> — *[Bergland, 1981]*

A software component is said to exhibit a high degree of cohesion if the elements in that unit exhibit a high degree of functional relatedness. This means that each element in the program unit should be essential for that unit to achieve its purpose.

> — *[Sommerville, 1989]*

"Intramodular functional relatedness" is a clumsy term. What we are considering is the cohesion of each module in isolation — how tightly bound or related its internal elements are to one another. Other terms sometimes used to note the same concept are "modular strength," "binding," and "functionality."

> — *[Yourdon and Constantine, 1979]*

In our discussion of module cohesion, we will again focus on two sources, i.e., Chapter 7 of [Yourdon and Constantine, 1979] and Chapter 4 of [Myers, 1978]. (Additional discussions on module cohesion can be found, for example, in Bergland, 1981], [Fairley, 1985], [Myers, 1975], [Myers, 1976], [Page-Jones, 1988], [Sage and Palmer, 1990], [Sommerville, 1989], and [Stevens, 1981] among others.) Further, although Myers refers to module cohesion as "module strength," we will primarily use the term "module cohesion."

As with module coupling, we will have a three-part plan of attack, i.e.:

- Our discussion will loosely follow the ranking (worst to best) of cohesion as described in [Yourdon and Constantine, 1979].

- We will compare and contrast each source's view on each form of cohesion.

- We will describe how each type of module cohesion relates to object-oriented software.

Glen Myers's definitions of module cohesion, to this reader, appear to be more focused (yes, more cohesive) than are Larry Constantine's definitions of module cohesion. In addition, their concepts do not totally overlap, e.g., Constantine's definition for communicational strength does not correspond directly to any of Myers's definitions.

In studying cohesion, Larry Constantine noted that the components of a module that were connected via data relationships (e.g., a component passed data to, or accepted data from another component) were more strongly bound together (i.e., more cohesive) than were the components of a module that were associated based primarily on control flow. We can generalize this to say that the greater the degree of interactions among the components of a module, then the higher will be the degree of cohesion for that module.

Both Constantine and Myers discuss **coincidental cohesion**:

- [Yourdon and Constantine, 1979] defines coincidental cohesion by saying that, "Coincidental cohesion occurs when there is little or no constructive relationship among the elements of a module; one is tempted to refer to such a situation as a 'random module.'"

- [Myers, 1978] says, "A coincidental strength module is a module that meets either of the following criteria: 1) its function cannot be defined (i.e., the only way of describing the module is by describing its logic), or 2) it performs multiple, completely unrelated functions."

Coincidentally cohesive modules are usually the result of partitioning a system based primarily on the criterion of module size, e.g., every 50 lines of code will be a module. Another manner in which coincidentally cohesive modules are generated is the isolation of common code from two or more modules, and this common code represents no single, coherent abstraction, e.g., it is neither a single function, nor a single object-oriented concept.

Coincidental cohesion can show up in a number of places in object-oriented systems, e.g.:

- an encapsulated method meets either of the two stated criteria in [Myers, 1978]. This should be exceedingly rare — it is indicative of very poor design skills.

- an "object" is defined in such a way that it does not represent any single, coherent *object-oriented* concept. For example, the public interface for the object resembles a collection of "common routines," e.g., a "math object."

- in a multiple inheritance scheme, a collection of commonly used source code, representing no coherent object-oriented concept, is collected into a "class," and is provided to other objects via inheritance. If such a "class" was viewed in isolation, it would be very difficult to describe what object, or object-oriented concept that it represented.

Coincidentally cohesive components (objects, encapsulated methods, or unencapsulated methods) are the direct result of poor design, or poor maintenance, practices. Their removal will require a comprehensive review, and at least some redesign, of the system containing the components.

While both Constantine and Myers describe **logical cohesion**, Myers is much more direct and focused in his definition.:

- [Yourdon and Constantine, 1979] says that "the elements of a module are logically associated if one can think of them as falling into the same logical class of similar or related functions — that is, ones that would logically be thought of together." (Constantine only very indirectly indicates that one of these elements (functions) can be selected in some manner, e.g., via an input parameter.)

- On the other hand, [Myers, 1978] says that, "A logical strength module is one that performs a set of related functions, one of which is explicitly selected by the calling module. In other words, the interface to a logical-strength module includes some type of function code argument; this argument is used to dynamically select a function to be performed."

As you might guess, logical cohesion is related to control coupling. Specifically, if one module controls the behavior (selects the function performed) by passing it a control parameter (sometimes referred to as a "flag"), then the two modules are control coupled, and the module being controlled exhibits logical cohesion. We also note that functions performed by a module with logical cohesion must be logically related, e.g., they must all be input functions. If they are not logically related, then we say that the module exhibits coincidental cohesion.

Examples of logical cohesion in object-oriented systems include:

- an encapsulated method that performs multiple related functions, one of which is selected by a control parameter, and

- an encapsulated method that can be "toggled," i.e., the basic function performed by the encapsulated method varies depending on how many times it has been invoked (received messages).

The simplest method for removal of logical cohesion is to isolate each separate function in its own method.

Temporal cohesion, described by Constantine, is a narrow subset of what Myers refers to as classical strength.:

- [Yourdon and Constantine, 1979] observes that, "**Temporal cohesion** means that all occurrences of all elements of processing in a collection occur within the same limited period of time during the execution of the system. Because the processing is required or permitted to take place in a limited time period, temporally associated elements of processing may be combined into a module that executes them all at once."

- The rough equivalent to temporal cohesion in Myers's scheme ([Myers, 1978]) is classical strength, i.e., "A **classical-strength** module performs multiple sequential functions where there is a weak, but non-zero relationship among all of the functions."

Both definitions speak of sequentially processing a group of related functions. However, Constantine stipulates that the only criterion for grouping the functions into one module is their time of processing relationship, e.g., the classic "initialization" and "end of job processing" modules. Myers's definition allows that the multiple functions in a classical strength module will also be related in that they are all processed in the same limited time period. However, Myers stipulates that there may be other, non-time-related, "weak, but non-zero" relationships that bind the functions together.

There are obvious problems with theses types of modules. For example, suppose a change necessitates the reordering of events (functions) within a temporally cohesive module. This will necessitate the editing of the temporally cohesive module. As another example, consider the lowered possibilities of reusing only one, or a few, of the grouped functions. Of course, if all the functions were in their own respective modules, then both changes and reusability would be significantly easier.

Unfortunately, temporal cohesion (and classical strength) are all too common in object-oriented systems. Many object-oriented programming language texts show examples of "initialization" methods that provide default values for objects, or set up the initial conditions for an application, or parts of an application.

A simple method of removing this form of cohesion is to ensure that each function is isolated to a single method. Further, these separate functions can be assembled into unencapsulated composite methods that perform single, cohesive functions.

Myers and Constantine have slightly differing interpretations of what we call **procedural cohesion**.:

- [Yourdon and Constantine, 1979] provides a definition that mentions the mechanics of the grouping method, i.e., "Procedural cohesion associates processing elements on the basis of their procedural or algorithmic relationships. Although this level of cohesion can result from many practices that emphasize sequence, method, and efficiency, it commonly results when modular structure is derived from flowcharts or other models of procedure such as Nassi-Shneiderman charts (sometimes referred to as 'Chapin Charts')."

- According to [Myers, 1978], "A procedural-strength module ... is a module that performs multiple sequential functions, where the sequential relationship among all of the functions is implied by the problem or application statement."

Taken in context, procedurally cohesive modules seem quite natural. However, taken in isolation, they often seem very strange, and incoherent. In effect, they are sequences of functions that are to be performed when some condition is met. To fully understand these modules, a software engineer must know something about the overall program from which the procedurally cohesive modules were taken, and something about the conditions that will cause them to be executed. Without an adequate understanding of both these points, modification of procedurally cohesive modules is likely to be error prone. In addition, procedurally cohesive modules are seldom reusable.

Procedurally cohesive modules show up in object-oriented applications where the objects were designed specifically for the application, i.e., reusability of the objects was not a major consideration. Some of the methods within some of these objects tend to be procedurally cohesive. If an encapsulated method appears more like a sequence of functions to be performed when a condition is met than like a single function commonly and closely associated with its encapsulating object, then it is likely that that method is procedurally cohesive.

It is generally bad form to have such encapsulated methods, both because of diminished reusability of the entire object, and because of the higher probability or error introduction when modifying these methods. If the software engineer still thinks that these methods are necessary, they should be removed from their encapsulating object, and, if the implementation language allows it, placed in **unencapsulated composite operations**, i.e., methods not physically encapsulated in any object, other than the overall application.

We generally improve the situation by doing this, e.g., the reusability and reliability of the object have been enhanced. However, we are still left with a procedurally cohesive unencapsulated composite operation. This may be the best solution for the immediate application, but the software engineer should still consider improving the cohesion situation.

Although he uses a term also used by Myers, Constantine ([Yourdon and Constantine, 1979]) describes a type of cohesion not described by Myers, i.e., **communicational cohesion.**:

> To say that a set of processing elements is communicationally associated means that all of the elements operate upon the same input data set and/or produce the same output data.

There appears to be more of a logical reason for binding the components of a communicationally cohesive module, i.e., the components all operate on, or produce, the same data. However, if we should notice several problems with such modules, e.g.:

- If we insist on grouping all components that operate on, or produce, the same data in a single module, then these modules could grow very large. Large modules are difficult to understand, and are, hence, error prone. If we later decide to break such modules into smaller such modules, what would be our criteria?

- The reusability of such modules is less than it could be, e.g., a new system might not need all the capabilities, and hence all the code, provided by such modules. Rather than representing a single abstraction, such modules represent a collection of functions necessary for a specific application.

- Software reliability is lowered as the size of the module is increased, i.e., there are more parts, raising the complexity.

Improving on this form of cohesion is relatively easy. The software engineer simply isolates each element into its own module. This allows for more flexibility in the design, and greater reusability, to say nothing of the increased reliability.

Fortunately, this form of cohesion is relatively rare in object oriented systems. One reason is that many object-oriented approaches and many object-oriented programming languages stress polymorphism.

Polymorphism is a measure of the degree of difference in how each item in a specified collection of items must be treated at a given level of abstraction. Polymorphism is increased when any unnecessary differences, at any level of abstraction, within a collection of items are eliminated. (See [Gabriel, 1989], [Harland, 1984], [Milner, 1978] and [Milner, 1984].)

One type of polymorphism, ad hoc polymorphism (often referred to as "overloading"), in effect, allows for one module to handle many different types of input information. One could say that ad hoc polymorphism is exactly the inverse of communicational cohesion.

Although they use different names for it, Constantine and Myers both deal with **sequential cohesion**.:

- [Yourdon and Constantine, 1979] states that "sequential association [is the type of association] in which the output data (or results) from one processing element serve as input data for the next processing element."

- [Myers, 1978] describes the same phenomenon, calling it communicational strength, i.e., "A communicational-strength module is one that performs multiple sequential functions, where the sequential relationship among all of the functions is implied by the problem or application statement, and where there is a data relationship among all of the functions."

While the components of a sequentially cohesive module are indeed more tightly bound than are the components of either a procedurally cohesive, or (using Constantine's definition) a communicationally cohesive module, they still suffer the problems of both of these types of cohesion. Specifically they tend to be large (decreasing both their reusability and reliability), and it is difficult to reuse a component of such modules even in the same application. It is fortunate that modules exhibiting this type of cohesion are relatively easy to decompose into smaller modules, each performing a single specific function.

The discussion of sequentially cohesive modules in an object-oriented system exactly parallels that of procedural cohesion in an object-oriented system.

The highest (best) form of module cohesion is **functional cohesion**:

- [Yourdon and Constantine, 1979] describes functional cohesion by observing that, "in a completely functional module, every element is an integral part of, and is essential to, the performance of a single function."

- [Myers, 1978] defines a functionally cohesive module in much the same manner, i.e., "a functional-strength module is defined as a module that performs a single specific function."

Myers ([Myers, 1978]) provides some additional advice, "If a set of functions can be collectively described as a single specific function in a coherent way, then the module performing these functions has functional strength [cohesion]; if not, it has a lower type of strength [cohesion]." Another way of saying this is that if we can coherently and completely describe the function of a module without the use of the words "and" or "or," then it is likely that the module is functionally cohesive.

In object-oriented systems, it is very desirable for the methods in the public interfaces of the objects to be functionally cohesive, i.e., each should perform a single specific function. We can also introduce a variation on this theme by also requesting that each object in an object-oriented system represent a single cohesive concept.

Glen Myers (in [Myers, 1978]) includes one form of cohesion that Constantine does not, i.e., informational strength. The following definition should sound familiar to practitioners of object-oriented software engineering. "The purpose of an informational-strength module is to hide some concept, data structure, or resource within a single module. An **informational strength** module has the following definition:

"1. It contains multiple entry points.

"2. Each entry point performs a single specific function.

"3. All of the functions are related by a concept, data structure, or resource that is hidden within the module."

One might even say that this is the first (partial) attempt at defining "object cohesion." (See, e.g., [Bulman, 1989].)

As we did with module coupling, we end our discussion of module cohesion by citing a few of the attempts to measure (both qualitatively and quantitatively) module cohesion. For examples of module cohesion metrics see [Card et al., 1985], [Card et al., 1986], [Card and Glass, 1990], [Conte et al., 1986], [Lohse and Zweben, 1984], [Myers, 1975], [Troy and Zweben, 1981], and [Yourdon and Constantine, 1979].

Object Coupling

The coupling between two classes is a measure of how much they depend upon each other.

— *[Wirfs-Brock et al., 1990]*

[C]oupling is the level to which one module in the system is dependent on other modules. Obviously the greater the amount of coupling between modules, the more complex the design and therefore the harder it will be to understand and maintain.

— *[Blair et al., 1991]*

"Coupling" describes the degree of interdependence between people; in OOD, it is the "interconnectedness" between pieces of an OOD.

— *[Coad and Yourdon, 1991]*

A class and its clients are connected through a Use relationship. Objects related in this manner are referred to as being interface coupled. ... Interface coupling is the lowest form of coupling between objects.

— *[Wild, 1991]*

Coupling with regard to modules is still applicable to object-oriented development, but coupling with regard to classes and objects is equally important. However, there is tension between the concepts of coupling and inheritance. On one hand, weakly coupled classes are desirable; on the other hand, inheritance — which tightly couples superclasses and their subclasses — helps us to exploit the commonality among abstractions.

— *[Booch, 1991]*

In reading about object coupling, one can get the mistaken impression that any object coupling, under any circumstances, is undesirable. Therefore, we need to distinguish between two different categories of object coupling: necessary and unnecessary. Most, if not all, object-oriented applications may be viewed as systems of interacting objects. In such systems it is required (i.e., necessary) that objects be coupled — otherwise no interactions can take place. However, when we design an individual object in isolation, we must minimize the knowledge that this object has about, or requires of, any other object, i.e., the object must be highly decoupled with respect to all other objects.

As a general guideline, the coupling of objects should take place only on an application-by-application basis. Further, even in these situations, care should be taken to minimize the coupling between objects. Finally, we allow for the fact that highly useful collections of interacting (coupled) objects can be created and treated as coherent, cohesive, and useful reusable units (subassemblies).

(A good deal of work has been done — and is still going on — to ensure that objects can interact (become coupled) in an appropriate and correct manner when necessary. See, for example, [Berlin, 1990] and [Helm et al., 1990].)

Unnecessary (premature) coupling of objects should be avoided because:

- *Unnecessary object coupling needlessly decreases the reusability of the coupled objects.* Specifically, the larger and/or more specialized an object (or system of objects) is, the lower will be the probability that that object (or system of objects) can be reused.

- *Unnecessary object coupling also increases the chances of system corruption when changes are made to one or more of the coupled objects.* Since coupled objects make assumptions about the objects to which they are coupled, changes in these objects can result in unpredictable and undesirable changes in overall system characteristics, e.g., behavior.

To date, even the more involved discussions of object coupling (e.g., [Budd, 1991], [Coad and Yourdon, 1991], and [Korson and McGregor, 1990]) seldom contain more than a few paragraphs of text. Frederic Wild ([Wild, 1991]) has presented probably the most detailed discussion on the topic and we will loosely base our presentation on his thoughts.

Object coupling is influenced by two major concepts, i.e.:

- the coupling that takes place between an object and all objects external to that object, and

- the coupling among the items that make up an individual object, e.g., methods, state information, and, in the case of composite objects, component objects.

The coupling among the individual items that make up a given object is sometimes confused with the cohesion for that object. Coupling is a measure of the strength of the *physical* relationships among the items that comprise the object, whereas cohesion is a measure of the *logical* relationships among those same components. A well-designed object has parts that are tightly related in a logical sense, while at the same time are loosely connected in a physical sense.

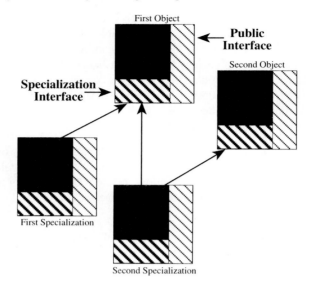

Figure 1:   **To better understand both object coupling and object cohesion, we must understand that many objects present two distinct interfaces to the outside world, i.e., a public interface that is accessible by all other objects, and a specialization interface that is available only to specializations of the object.** In class-based object-oriented programming languages, specializations are referred to by such names as "subclasses," "derived classes," and "child classes." In so-called "classless" object-oriented programming languages, specializations are sometimes referred to as "extensions."

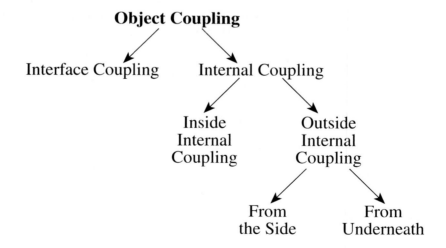

Figure 2:   **The taxonomy for object coupling shows the impact of public interface versus specialization interface issues.** The other major component of object coupling is the relationships among the items (e.g., methods and state information) that make up individual objects.

Interface Coupling

[Wild, 1991] identifies two broad categories of object coupling: interface coupling and internal coupling. **Interface coupling** occurs when one object refers to another *specific* object, and the original object makes direct references to one or more items contained in the specific object's public interface. We further stipulate that items other than operations (method selectors), e.g., constants, variables, exportable definitions, and exceptions, may be found in the public interface of an object. Of course, the exact form and nature of any items that may be present in an object's public interface are dictated by the syntax and semantics of the implementation language.

[Wild, 1991] stipulates that interface coupling may vary in strength, and is the lowest (loosest) form of object coupling. Almost all of our previous discussion on "module coupling," *and specifically on its relation to object-oriented software*, dealt with various forms of interface coupling. In addition, the ranking of the module coupling (best to worst) serves as a good first approximation for the ranking of various forms of interface coupling. (For example, both [Budd, 1991] and [Wild, 1991] make this observation.)

As examples of a fairly loose form of interface coupling, consider three unordered lists, i.e., a "list of names," a "list of phone numbers," and a "list of addresses." We make the following observations regarding these lists:

- Apart from the type of item stored in each list, the implementation of each individual list should be highly consistent with the implementations of the other lists.

- To implement the method for adding an item to a list, we will require that we have access to a method that will "copy" the value of an item to another instance of the same item, i.e., we will need to copy the value of an item into a node in the list. For purposes of this discussion, we are not interested in the details of how the copying occurs (e.g., by passing a pointer or by actually reproducing the values). This "copy method" could, of course, be used by other methods within the list.

  In addition, for purposes of this discussion, we will assume that the needed "copy method" is accessible via the public interface of the items being placed in each respective list. For example, the "list of names object" will make use of a copy method encapsulated within the "name object," and made available via a method selector in the public interface.

- Over and above this "copy operation," we will assume that the lists require no additional information about the items they contain.

As we have described it, each list object is coupled (very loosely) to the objects it contains, e.g., the list of names object is coupled to the name objects within it. If, for example, the copy method or its corresponding method selector were to be deleted from the name object, then the list of names object could no longer add name objects to itself. Other, more subtle, changes could also cause problems, e.g., if the name of the copy method selector changed, or if the number or ordering of parameters for the copy method changed.

With the exception of the requirement for an appropriate copy method, each of the list objects makes no assumptions about the objects it contains. You might even say that each list object treats its components as (almost perfectly) black boxes. Yet, as loose as this coupling appears to be, we still have one conceptual problem and one ease of implementation problem.

The conceptual problem involves the separation of the concept of a list from the items contained in a specific list. Specifically, we would like to separate the characteristics of a list from the characteristics that are specific to the items contained in the list. In effect, we would like to identify a set of characteristics that are common to all lists, or, at least, common to lists of names, lists of phone numbers, and lists of addresses in our example.

The ease of implementation problem has two dimensions:

- First, we would like a simple, automatic means of creating new list objects. For example, if we needed a list of computers, we should not have to make a copy of an existing list, and then physically edit that copy to accommodate the necessary changes.

- The second dimension is the specification of the assumptions that the list object makes about its component objects. For example, what specific methods does the list object require from its component objects, and what specific information do these methods require?

The solution to our problem is to have one object (in our example, the list) treat the other objects (in our examples, names, addresses, phone numbers, and computers) as abstractions. Specifically, we will create a "generic list" object, that can, in turn, be instantiated with the necessary information (i.e., the class of objects to be placed in the list, along with an appropriate "copy" operation) to create any desired lists, e.g., lists of names, addresses, phone numbers, or computers. (Many programming languages already provide this capability. For example, C++ provides templates, Eiffel has generic classes, and Ada supports generics.)

This solution is attractive for several reasons, i.e.:

- It clearly and cleanly separates concepts. In our examples, we can separate the concept of a list from the concepts embodied by the items that can be contained in lists (e.g., names, addresses, phone numbers, and computers).

- It allows one object to *explicitly* state — via parameters — the assumptions that it makes about other objects.

- It simplifies the creation of new categories of objects. Specifically, the instantiation of a template or generic object is usually easier, and far less error prone, than the physical editing of an object.

We refer to this type of object decoupling, i.e., where the assumptions that one object makes about a category of other objects are isolated and used as parameters to instantiate (a template or a generic version of) the original object, as **object abstraction decoupling**.

Now, consider a different example. Imagine a counter object, i.e., an object which is used to count things. The public interface for the counter object contains the following operations: zero (the value of the counter), increment (the current value of the counter), and display (the current value of the counter). The first two operations, i.e., zero and increment, clearly involve only the counter object itself.

The display operation, however, requires access to some form of "output object." In fact, depending on the complexity of the display operation, several other different objects may be involved in displaying the current value of a counter. This operation *tightly* couples the counter object with the output object, and thus, presents a number of problems, i.e.:

- The assumptions that the counter object makes about the output object (and any other objects involved in the displaying process) can only be determined by explicitly examining the source code for the display method. These assumptions can include:

    - the name of the output object,

    - the specific operations in the public interface for the output object that the display method will use to display the value of the counter,

    - the number and forms of the parameters for these specific operations,

    - the intended behavior of these specific operations,

    - the use of any exceptions, constants, variables, and/or other non-operation items contained in the public interface for the output object, and

    - what other objects (besides the output object and the counter object) may be involved in the displaying process, and the assumptions that are made about these objects.

    Even with concepts such as late (dynamic) binding, software engineers need to know what these assumptions are so that they can make informed choices when making system modifications, e.g., substituting alternate output objects.

- Any changes made to objects involved in the display method (other than to the counter object itself) may make these objects incompatible with the counter object's display method. The consequences of this very severe. For example, imagine a system where any change to any object may adversely impact the overall system. This means that any time that any object within the system is modified or deleted, the entire system (including the source code for all methods encapsulated in all system objects) must be examined to determine the impact of the change.

- A new system may require the counter object, but may not require that the values of the counter be displayed. A software engineer may elect to create an entirely new counter object rather than modify the existing counter object. If the specific output object (or category of output objects) necessary for the display operation is not present in the new application, reuse of the counter object without changing or deleting the display method is risky.

- When attempting to represent the value of any object to those outside of the object, we must consider the most appropriate form for the representation. For example, will it be textual or numeric, what style will be used (e.g., plain, bold, italic, or underlined), and will the representation take advantage of the media, e.g., one might display information differently depending on the output media — paper, voice, screen, or some other media? The display method must make many assumptions about both the form of the output and the characteristics of the output media. The value will very likely be "displayed" differently depending on the choice of media. Even using the same media (e.g., a color screen), there are many different ways to represent the information.

Decoupling the counter object from the output object (and any other objects necessary for the display method) will not be as simple as decoupling the list object and its components in our earlier examples. The primary reason for this is that while the "add" operation can be viewed as an intrinsic property of a list, the "display" operation is not an intrinsic property of counter objects. The concept of a counter can be sufficiently and completely defined without ever mentioning the fact that the value of a counter may be displayed. Another way of saying this is that while the zero and increment operations are "object-specific," the display operation is "application-specific."

Probably the simplest way to decouple the counter object from the output object (and any other objects involved in the display method) is to replace the display method with an operation that returns the current value of the counter, e.g., a value_of method. In this solution, the counter object is no longer vulnerable to changes in the output object. However, there is a much more important advantage. Software engineers are now free to design applications involving the counter where any of an infinity of things can be done with the counter's values, e.g., they may be used in calculations, stored in databases, or used as components of larger objects.

What we have done specifically is to replace a composite method such as display, with a primitive operation, e.g., value_of. A **primitive method** is any method that cannot be implemented simply, efficiently, and reliably without knowledge of the underlying implementation of the object in which it is encapsulated. A **composite method** is any method constructed from two or more primitive methods — sometimes from different objects.

(We should also note that primitive methods have some additional defining characteristics, e.g.:

- they are functionally cohesive, i.e., they each perform a single specific function, and

- they are "small," e.g., when implemented in terms of source code they seldom exceed about five "lines of code.")

We can identify three broad categories of primitive operations, i.e., selectors, constructors, and iterators. The terms "selector" and "constructor" to describe different categories of operations can be traced to the work of Barbara Liskov (e.g., [Liskov and Zilles, 1975]). The concept of an "iterator" had its formal origins in the programming language Alphard ([Shaw, 1981]), and has been discussed frequently in the literature, e.g., [Cameron, 1989], [Eckart, 1987], [Lamb, 1990], [Ross, 1989], and [Shaw et al., 1981].

Selectors are encapsulated operations which return state information about their encapsulating object, and cannot, by definition, alter the state of the object in which they are encapsulated. (Note that this is a general software engineering definition, and is not to be confused with the concept of a "method selector," e.g., as in Smalltalk.) Selectors are discussed in, e.g., [Bauer and Wossner, 1982], [Booch, 1986], [Booch, 1987], and [Booch, 1991].

The "value_of" operation in the counter object is an example of a selector operation. Replacing the display method with the value_of method is an example of selector decoupling. **Selector decoupling** is the process of replacing an encapsulated composite method with a primitive selector operation with the intended and actual result of decoupling the encapsulating object from other objects.

Next, consider a month object, i.e., an object that represents a month in a Gregorian date (e.g., January … December). Suppose one of the operations in the public interface for the month object is "get_month." When we ask the question "from where or what?", we will probably find that the get_month operation couples the month object with at least an "input object," and probably a variety of other objects. This object coupling suffers from all of the problems we mentioned earlier for the display operation in the interface to the counter object.

As before, we will replace the composite method (get_month) with a primitive operation. However, a selector operation will not be appropriate. We will need a constructor operation. **Constructors** are operations which can (and often do) change the state of their encapsulating object to accomplish their function. We can think of constructors as operations which "construct a new, or altered, version of an object." Constructors are discussed in [Bauer and Wossner, 1982], [Booch, 1986], and [Booch, 1987].

In our example, we will replace the get_month method with a "from_string" method. The from_string method is a constructor. (It will cause a month object to come into existence whose initial value will be derived from a string value.) The from_string method effectively decouples the month object from the input object and any other objects that might have been involved in the get_month method. (Said another way, the month object no longer requires direct knowledge of the input object.)

Replacing the get_month method with a from_string method is an example of constructor decoupling. **Constructor decoupling** is the process of replacing an encapsulated composite method with a primitive constructor operation with the intended and actual result of decoupling the encapsulating object from other objects.

At this point, someone might observe that the value_of method in the counter object probably returns an integer object, and the from_string method in the month object requires a string object as input. Does this mean that the counter object is coupled to an integer object and that the month object is coupled to a string object? The answer is "no," and the reason is that both integers and strings are primitive objects.

Primitive objects are objects that are:

- *defined in the standard for the implementation language* (note that the standard may encompass more than just the syntax and semantics for the language, e.g., it may include standard libraries of objects and a standard environment), and

- *globally known*, i.e., these are objects that are known (and whose characteristics are known) in any part of any application created using the implementation language.

Please note that primitive objects may be quite complex in nature. We are using the word "primitive" in the "basic building block" sense rather than in the "simplest of all forms" sense.

An object that refers only to itself and to primitive objects is considered, for all intents and purposes, totally decoupled from other objects.

For our next example, consider a "list of names" object. Suppose someone included a "display" operation in the public interface for this list of names object. We would, of course, have all the problems that we previously mentioned for the display operation in the interface for the counter object. However, our problems would be compounded with two additional problems, i.e.:

- The problems of representation form and output media are more complex with objects having composite state than they are with objects having states that can be represented using single monolithic values. For example, will there be multiple columns, will all components be displayed in the same manner, will there be labels and headings, and how will the output be ordered? Displaying a list of names is a much more involved process than displaying an integer representing the current value of a counter.

- Suppose that, instead of displaying all the names in the list, we wish to delete all the names that begin with "N" or change each occurrence of "Hendricks" with "Hendrix"? While each of these methods requires that we iterate over (loop through) the object, the specific tasks to be performed at each node in the list vary. It seems that we should be able to "factor out" or separate the iteration capability from the specific tasks we must accomplish.

A **composite object** is an object which is *conceptually* composed of two, or more, other objects. The objects which make up the composite object are referred to as **component objects**. A **heterogeneous composite object** is an object that is *conceptually* composed from objects which are not all *conceptually* the same. A **homogeneous composite object** is a composite object that is *conceptually* composed of component objects which are all *conceptually* the same.

A Gregorian date is an example of a heterogeneous composite object. Specifically, it is comprised of three different types of objects, i.e., a month, a day, and a year. Even if each of these component objects is implemented as, for example, an integer, they still remain conceptually different. A "list of names" is an example of a homogeneous composite object, i.e., it is comprised of multiple instances of a "name class." Even though the value of each name may differ from all other names in the same list, each name is a member of the same general category of object, i.e., a name.

If we are dealing with a homogeneous composite object, we can consider the inclusion of an iterator capability in its interface. An **iterator capability** (often simply referred to as an **iterator**) allows its users to systematically visit all the nodes in a homogeneous composite object and to perform some user-supplied operation at each node. (There is a great deal of technology associated with iterators. For example see chapter 7 of [Booch, 1987] for a discussion of active (open) iterators versus passive (closed) iterators.)

Returning to our "list of names" object, if we replace the display method with an iterator capability, we will have decoupled the list of names object from the output object. Specifically, the list of names object will offer an iterator capability, and those wishing to display the names on the list will "instantiate" the iterator capability with the operation(s) necessary to display the names contained in the list. This is an example of iterator decoupling. **Iterator decoupling** is the process of replacing an encapsulated composite method with an iterator capability with the intended and actual result of decoupling the encapsulating object from other objects.

Interface coupling occurs when an object references the items in the public interface of another object. Up to this point, our discussion has focused almost exclusively on the coupling related to the *operations* (method selectors) in the public interface. We must also consider any stand-alone constants and variables that may be in the interface. We have already discussed this problem somewhat when we covered common-environment coupling ([Yourdon and Constantine, 1979]), and common and external coupling ([Myers, 1978]). However, we will add the following items to our discussion:

- Even if our programming language allows for both data and objects (e.g., C++), we should avoid the use of data (in the form of either variables or constants) in the public interface for an object. The concept of an object both protects others from changes in the underlying implementation for some information and embodies (via a set of operations and their corresponding methods) a set of rules regarding the examination and manipulation of that information. Data offers no such protection.

- Except in unusual circumstances, it is far better to have constants in the public interface for an object than it is to have variables. Attempting to determine who changed globally available information, let alone attempting to understand the overall application, is difficult at best. Further, system components that communicate via global information are often difficult to modify and to reuse.

- Even if information is made available in the form of constants in the public interface for an object, it is far better that this information be in the form of discrete scalar items or homogeneous structures, i.e., not in the form of a heterogeneous structure. Objects that have access to these global structures are sensitive to changes in the structure. Further, they may also have access to information that they do not need. (Specifically, they may need only part of the information provided in a heterogeneous item; however, nothing prevents them from accessing other information in the heterogeneous structure.)

Internal Object Coupling

We now shift our attention to internal coupling. **Internal object coupling** is present in two situations:

- **Inside internal object coupling** which is a normal by-product of object design, and occurs when:

  - the methods for an object are coupled to the encapsulated state information for the object, and/or

  - the component objects that make up a composite object are coupled with the overall composite object and/or with each other.

  All objects will exhibit one or both of these forms of inside internal object coupling. However, there are varying degrees of tightness for this form of coupling, and software engineers should strive to keep this variety of coupling as loose as possible.

- **Outside internal object coupling** occurs if an object external to another object has access to, or knowledge of, the underlying implementation of the other object, i.e., that part of an object that we normally consider hidden to those outside of the object.

Overall, internal coupling is generally much tighter (i.e., much worse) than is interface coupling. In addition, *outside* internal object coupling is almost always tighter (worse) than *inside* internal object coupling. While there are indeed some situations where tight internal object coupling could be justified, these situations are very rare.

Inside Internal Object Coupling

All objects have state. (See, e.g., [Booch, 1991].) State information is often physically stored inside an object. Many object-oriented programming languages, for example, provide "class variables" and "instance variables" expressly for the purpose of storing state information for objects. (See, e.g., [Goldberg and Robson, 1983], [Meyer, 1992], and [Stroustrup, 1991].) We also allow that some state information can be derived when needed, i.e., it is derived from other physically stored state information.

The internal algorithms (i.e., the methods) by which an object accomplishes its operations must know something about this internally stored information. Specifically, they must know what information exists, and how to access (and possibly convert) the information they need.

Suppose, for example, that the state information for a given object is stored in the form of a data structure (e.g., an array or a record). All the internal methods for that object can be, and probably are, aware of this structure. If this data structure is modified, or if a new data structure is added, the internal methods for the object may have to be modified to accommodate the change.

Good software engineering dictates that we hide (isolate the details of) design/implementation decisions (e.g., [Parnas, 1972], [Parnas, 1979], and [Parnas et al., 1983]). This idea is one of the cornerstones of an object-oriented approach, and it need not be ignored simply because we are inside (as opposed to outside) of an object. For example, [Wirfs-Brock and Wilkerson, 1989] and others have suggested that all access to state information by the internal methods for an object be via "access methods." This approach:

- isolates the internal methods from changes in the form of the internally stored state information, and

- makes the incremental modification/extension of objects (e.g., the subclassing of methods) easier.

(Others (e.g., [Taenzer et al., 1989]) have extended the advice of [Wirfs-Brock and Wilkerson, 1989] to encompass the accessing of inherited (as opposed to locally defined) instance variables as well, viz., "We have also adopted a coding style of not directly accessing inherited instance variables, but instead using messaging to access them.")

[Wirfs-Brock and Wilkerson, 1989] provides the following guidelines to both minimize inside internal object coupling and make the creation of more specialized objects (subclassing) easier:

- "For each variable defined by a class, define two accessing methods: one to set the value of the variable, and one to retrieve the value of the variable.

- "Variables should only be accessed or modified [through the sending of messages to, or the invoking of] the accessing methods.

- "An accessing method should only store or retrieve the value of its associated variable. It should perform no other computations.

- "Because variable accessing methods reflect the internal representation of the object, they should be considered private methods."

Korson and McGregor ([Korson and McGregor, 1990]) cite the coupling of a composite object with its components. For example, suppose that we have a date object which is, in turn, composed of a month, a day, and a year object. Further suppose that our intention is to have the date object act merely as "a box into which we place a month, a day, and a year," i.e., the date object itself does no verification as to the validity of any given date. Even with this simple form for a date object, we are already making assumptions about the objects involved, e.g., we will have mechanisms for copying the values of day objects, month objects, and year objects into and out of date objects.

To minimize the coupling between a date and its component objects, and to more clearly specify the assumptions that the date object makes about its component objects, we can use *object abstraction decoupling* in much the same way we did in our list object example. The chief difference will be that instead of worrying about only one category of object, we will specify three categories of objects as abstractions, i.e., days, months, and years.

Next, suppose that we were interested in a "smart date" object, i.e., one that would not permit date objects with invalid values, e.g., "February 31, 1991." We could still use object abstraction decoupling, but we would have to specify more requirements. For example, we could require that each component object of a date object supply an operation that would return an integer value representing the current value of that component, e.g., "5" for a month whose value was "May."

Notice that this last example points to a conflict between coupling and the complexity of object implementation. To maintain loose coupling, and at the same time create more complex composite objects, requires that our templates (generics) become more complex. Further, more complex interrelationships between a composite object and its component objects may require such things as selector, constructor, or iterator decoupling as well.

Outside Internal Object Coupling

Outside internal object coupling is the tightest (worst) form of all object coupling. It has two major forms:

- **"coupling from the side"** in which an object that is *not* a specialization of another object has access to the underlying implementation of that other object (for example, the first object is not a subclass, a derived class, nor an extension of the other object), and

- **"coupling from underneath"** in which an object that is a specialization of another object (e.g., the object is a subclass, a derived class, or an extension of the other object) has access to the underlying implementation(s) of one or more of its less specialized predecessors (e.g., its superclasses, base classes, or prototypes).

("From the side" and "from underneath" have their origins in how object relationships are often shown graphically. Specifically, in a top-to-bottom orientation, specializations are most often shown *underneath* their corresponding generalizations. "From the side" implies that an object gains access through an interface other than the specialization interface, i.e., from the side.)

We refer to outside internal coupling as the tightest form of coupling because it requires one object to know something about the underlying implementation of another object. This violates one of the most fundamental concepts of object-orientation, i.e., information hiding. Normally, if a software engineer modifies the underlying implementation of an object, but does not alter that object's public interface and preserves the object's outwardly observable characteristics, then other objects will not have to take these changes into account. Unfortunately, if outside internal object coupling is present, this is not true.

Coupling from the Side

Let us first focus on "coupling from the side." In this form of outside internal coupling, the coupled objects need not have any relationship with each other — other than the fact that they are coupled — yet one object has direct access to the underlying implementation of the other. This type of coupling usually occurs under one of the following conditions:

- The implementation language does *not* directly (syntactically and semantically) support information hiding with respect to objects. This means that there is no effective way to "erect a barrier" between all aspects of the underlying implementation for an object and the outside world. This problem shows up when software engineers attempt to use more conventional (i.e., "non-object-oriented") programming languages (e.g., C, Pascal, and assembly languages) to create object-oriented applications.

  We should note, however, that just because a programming language is not considered "truly object-oriented," does not dictate that we must have this problem. For example, Ada's packages and private types ([Ammirati and Gerhardt, 1990], [ARM, 1983], [Bach, 1988], and [Cohen, 1986]), and Modula's modules and opaque types ([Bergin and Greenfield, 1988], [Wegmann, 1986], and [Wirth 1983]), provide the elements necessary to encapsulate and hide the underlying implementation of an object.

- The programming language does indeed provide direct support (syntactically and semantically) for information hiding with respect to object, but the information hiding for one or more objects has been violated (unintentionally or intentionally) by objects that are not specializations of the objects. This violation may even have occurred through the use of "programming language tricks," i.e., little known, little used, and hard-to-understand aspects of the programming language.

- The programming language is considered "object-oriented," but directly (syntactically and semantically) allows objects to access fully or partially the underlying implementations of other objects. The classic example of this is "friends" in C++. (See, e.g., pages 161-163 in [Stroustrup, 1991].) This is often presented as a "feature" of the programming language, and arguments in favor of its use are often based on (both real and imaginary) efficiency concerns. (In situations such as this, it is best to remember the advice of Donald E. Knuth ([Knuth, 1974]), who advised us to first create a solution using excellent software engineering techniques, and, then, only if necessary, introduce *small* violations of good software engineering for efficiency's sake.)

We can provide some general guidelines regarding coupling from the side, i.e.:

- If you are attempting to implement an application in an object-oriented manner, avoid the use of languages that do not directly support (syntactically and semantically) information hiding with respect to objects. Use programming languages that are at least "object-based," i.e., languages that support objects as a language primitive. (See, e.g., [Wegner, 1990].)

- If you must use a programming language that does not support information hiding with respect to objects, make every effort to *logically* enforce the information hiding associated with objects.

- If you are using a programming language that is "object-based" or "class-based," implement objects in a manner that maximizes and enforces information hiding. ([Wegner, 1990] defines a "class-based programming language" as one that requires the definition of classes before instances can be created, e.g., CLU ([Liskov et al., 1977] and [Liskov et al., 1981]), but lacking inheritance.) For example, if you are using Ada, use both packages and limited private types, or, at the least, private types.

- If you are using a programming language that is object-oriented, or at least supports objects as a primitive, keep the details of the form and structure of the underlying implementation of objects hidden. Users should be able to query or change the state of objects only through encapsulated methods. A change in the form and/or structure of the underlying implementation for an object that does not require a change in the public interface, nor a change in the outwardly observable characteristics for that object, should *not* necessitate a change in other objects in the same system.

- Programming language features (e.g., "friends" in C++) that allow objects that are not specializations of an object to access the underlying implementation of that object should be avoided. Specifically, the use of such features should require extensive justification.

- Some object-oriented programming languages (e.g., CLOS and Flavors) provide their users with the power to not only access the underlying implementation of an object, but also to create or alter such implementations during the execution of a program. Arguments for such capabilities are often based on flexibility. The use of these capabilities places the responsibility of well-engineered software very much on the shoulders of the software engineer, i.e., the programming language will do little to prevent unsound practices.

  In situations where such powerful programming languages are used, a good deal of thought must be given to when and where to access/create/modify the underlying implementation of any object during the execution of the software. (As more than one person has observed, "With great power comes great responsibility.")

Coupling from Underneath

Now let's shift our attention to "coupling from underneath." Coupling from underneath is a fairly complex issue that is primarily tied to the syntax and semantics of inheritance. Inheritance directly impacts the strength of the coupling both between an object and its specializations, and between the objects in a specialization hierarchy and other objects.

Inheritance is the means by which an object acquires characteristics from one or more other objects. In this context, we take "characteristics" to mean such things as methods, state information representation mechanisms (e.g., instance variables), exceptions, constants, variables, and any other items that are "inheritable." Markku Sakkinen ([Sakkinen, 1989]) has described two major varieties of inheritance, i.e.:

- *"essential inheritance"* which emphasizes the inheritance of behavior and other outwardly observable characteristics of an object, and

- *"incidental inheritance"* which emphasizes the inheritance of all or part of the underlying implementation of the more general object.

Essential inheritance is more commonly referred to as "inheritance of *specification*," and incidental inheritance is more commonly referred to as "inheritance of *implementation*."

These two views of inheritance correspond to the two most prevalent interpretations as to the purpose of inheritance:

- Some people characterize inheritance as a mechanism for mapping "real world" specialization-generalization hierarchies into software. For example, "vehicle" is a more generalized concept than either "automobile" or "motorcycle," and "military aircraft" is a more specialized concept than is "aircraft." The way that this is accomplished in a given programming language is of secondary interest.

- Others view inheritance primarily as a "code sharing/code reusing" mechanism.

Subtyping is a term that is often used inconsistently with regard to inheritance. For example, Pierre America ([America, 1987]) states that "inheritance is concerned with the implementation of the classes, while the subtyping hierarchy is based on the behaviour of the instances (as seen from the outside, by other objects)." In other words, what Sakkinen and others refer to as "inheritance of specification," America calls "subtyping." On the other hand Alan Snyder ([Snyder, 1986]) describes subtyping as something completely apart from inheritance, i.e., "[subtyping is] the rules by which objects of one type (class) are determined to be acceptable in contexts expecting another type (class)." In fact, [Snyder, 1986] discusses the separation of the "inheritance hierarchy" from the "type hierarchy."

[Although we will not discuss it in detail, "delegation" is a concept that is very similar to inheritance, and shows up in systems that use "prototypes" (sometimes referred to as "exemplars," e.g., [LaLonde et al., 1986]) instead of classes. (See, e.g., [Borning, 1986] and [Liberman, 1986].) Inheritance and delegation are often contrasted with each other. (See, for example, the discussions in [Liberman et al., 1988] and [Stein, 1987].) Languages such as Self ([Chambers and Ungar, 1989], [Chambers et al., 1989], and [Ungar and Smith, 1987]) and most actor languages ([Agha, 1986]) use prototypes and delegation instead of classes and inheritance.

Gul Agha and Carl Hewitt ([Agha and Hewitt, 1987]) have observed that, "Delegation does not help organize knowledge in terms of a taxonomy, but provides a mechanism for code sharing whereby control is passed to an independent actor. The independent actor is created dynamically and has access to data internal to the actor that created it." Using this definition, delegation appears very close to incidental inheritance (inheritance of implementation).]

Another dimension of inheritance is single inheritance versus multiple inheritance. In **single inheritance** an object can acquire characteristics directly from only one other object, e.g., its immediate superclass. In a **multiple inheritance** scheme, an object can inherit (acquire) characteristics directly from *more than one* object. This sometimes leads to problems. For example, what happens if an object attempts to inherit two or more different characteristics with the same name, each provided by a different parent. All situations that allow for multiple inheritance must also provide some systematic means of resolving such conflicts. As we shall see, multiple inheritance significantly complicates the problems associated with "coupling from underneath."

To fully understand "coupling from underneath," we must realize that objects that are used as templates to create other objects (e.g., classes) have two distinct interfaces:

- an "inheritance interface" that they present only to their specializations (e.g., subclasses, derived classes), and

- a "public interface" to which all other objects (including the specializations of the object) have access.

(See, for example, the discussion in Section 3.3 of [America, 1987].)

We can divide our discussion of coupling from underneath into two areas: an internal form and an external form. The internal form is based on how specializations interact with inherited state representation mechanisms (e.g., instance variables). The external form is concerned with the visibility of inheritance in the public interface of an object. Specifically, we are interested in the degree to which objects that are outside of the inheritance hierarchy for a given object are sensitive to changes in that inheritance hierarchy.

[Wirfs-Brock and Wilkerson, 1989] discussed the potential problems of allowing encapsulated methods for an object to have direct access to the underlying implementations of the encapsulated state information for the same object. [Taenzer et al., 1989] went further, commenting on the problems of inherited state information, i.e., "We have also adopted a coding style of not directly using inherited instance variables, but instead using messaging to access them."

The concept of inheritance alone implies (at lease a loose) coupling among the objects within a given inheritance hierarchy. However, the actual implementation mechanisms for inheritance (i.e., the semantics of inheritance) in most object-oriented programming languages can introduce undesirable side effects.

The most obvious problem is the sensitivity to change in the underlying implementation (structure) of inheritable state information. Suppose, for example, that a specialization (e.g., subclass, derived class, or child) knows the structure of an inherited instance variable, and takes advantage of (depends on) this structure. Changes in the generalization (e.g., superclass, base class, or parent) that involve changes in the structure of an inheritable instance variable will invalidate methods in the specialization that depend on the structure of that variable. Removal of inheritable instance variables will obviously also cause problems for specializations that attempt to use these variables.

Alan Snyder, in [Snyder, 1986], cites a number of other problems that can occur as a result of the coupling between an object and the objects that inherit state information from that object, e.g.:

- If an inheriting object can only access inherited state information via methods, and a sufficient (minimum necessary) set of methods for this access are not provided, then the designers of the inheriting object must negotiate with the designers of the object providing the inheritable characteristics for the needed methods.

- Some of the operations that make up a sufficient (minimum necessary) set of methods for the inheritable information may not be appropriate for those who are not specializations of the object providing the inheritable information. In other words, if access to inherited state information is only allowed via methods, we would like the option to provide some or all of these methods via the inheritance interface, and not via the public interface of the object providing the inheritable information. Languages such as Trellis ([Kilian, 1990], [Moss and Kohler, 1987], [O'Brien et al., 1987], and [Schaffert et al., 1986]) allow a software engineer to stipulate that some specific methods are only available to specializations of an object, i.e., the objects that inherit the state information representation mechanisms. (C++ also provides such a mechanism via its "protected" members. See, e.g., section 6.6.1 of [Stroustrup, 1991].)

- Some programming languages (e.g., Flavors) stipulate, for example, that inherited instance variables will be "merged with" locally defined instance variables. ("If several components define instance variables with the same name, they are combined into one instance variable." ([Moon, 1986])) Snyder observes that "if a local instance variable and an inherited instance variable with the same name wind up as a single instance variable, then changing the name of the instance variable in the parent is likely to change the behavior of the child class." Smalltalk ([Goldberg and Robson, 1983]) views this as a problem, and attempts to correct it, e.g., attempting to define an instance variable in a subclass with the same name as an instance variable in the corresponding superclass will cause an error to be signaled.

We have just discussed one aspect of the coupling between an object and those objects that inherit characteristics from that object. Specifically, we have observed that knowledge of the underlying implementation of, or sensitivity to changes in, inheritable state information can result in undesirable and/or unintended side effects. However, this does not mean that we should not allow state information to be inheritable.

Grady Booch has observed ([Booch, 1991]) that "there is tension between the concepts of coupling and inheritance. On one hand, weakly coupled classes are desirable; on the other hand, inheritance — which tightly couples superclasses and their subclasses — helps us to exploit the commonality among abstractions." We know that there are a number of things that we can do to minimize the tightness of this form of internal object coupling, i.e.:

- Whenever possible (and practical), allow access to inherited state information only via methods. Specifically, objects that inherit state information should have little, if any, knowledge of the underlying implementation of this state information.

- If one or more of the methods allowing access to the inherited state information is inconsistent with (does not make sense in) the public interface of the object providing the inheritable state information, seek out mechanisms that will restrict access to these methods to the objects inheriting the information, e.g., "protected" members in C++.

- An inheriting object does not necessarily need all possible inheritable state information. Just because an object *can* inherit some information does not mean that it *should* inherit that information. Avoid situations where you have no, or little, control over what state information can be inherited. *Said another way, inheritance should be selective.*

Up to this point, we have discussed "internal object coupling from underneath" from the viewpoint of internal state information representations. However, the coupling between an object and those objects that inherit information from the object can also impact the outside (public interface) of the objects involved in an inheritance relationship. Alan Snyder ([Snyder, 1986]) states the problem in the following manner:

> A deeper issue raised by inheritance is whether or not the use of inheritance itself should be part of the external interface (of the class or the objects). In other words, should the clients of a class (necessarily) be able to tell whether or not a class is defined using inheritance?

Suppose, for example, that we are working in an environment where inheritance is not selective. This means that anything that has the possibility of being inherited will be inherited. Imagine that a particular object has 5 separate specializations (e.g., subclasses, derived classes, or child classes). Imagine further that 4 of these specializations require a specific message, but the fifth specialization has no need of that specific message. If we place this message in the original object, then it can be inherited by all 5 of its specializations.

If inheritance is not selective, i.e., we must inherit everything (even if some items do not make sense), then the interface of the inheriting object that did not need the message contains an unnecessary message. This leads to a number of problems, e.g.:

- The complexity of the object inheriting the unnecessary operation/message has been increased, thus decreasing the inheriting object's reliability. (There may also be a decrease in the efficiency of the inheriting object, but this is usually inconsequential.)

- The inclusion of the unnecessary operation/message makes the inheriting object more difficult to understand. Software engineers must remember which methods are necessary, and which methods are there only because inheritance is not selective. This will make systems that use the inheriting object more error prone.

- If, for some reason, an application chooses to use the unnecessary method, then software engineers are no longer free to make (seemingly inconsequential) changes to the inheritance hierarchy for the inheriting object. For example, if they modify (or remove) the unnecessary operation/message in the object that provided the method originally, this will have unpredictable (and very likely undesirable) side effects.

Types and Inheritance

The concept of "types" is often confused with the concept of "classes." A **type** is often defined as "a set of values, and a set of operations applicable to those values." (See, e.g., [IEEE, 1983].) In modern software engineering, types are usually used to dictate which items may participate in the same operation. If we say that a language is **strongly typed**, we mean that, with very few exceptions, only items of the same type may participate in the same operation. For example, we may not be allowed to divide an integer by a floating point number until we first convert the type of the integer value to the proper floating point type, or until we convert the type of the floating point value to the proper integer type. In **weakly typed** (and untyped) languages items of different types are allowed to participate in the same operation, even if the result will be nonsensical.

In strongly typed programming languages we often allow software engineers to define types that encompass a subset of the values for a given type. We refer to such types as **subtypes** of the original type. As a general rule, items of the subtype of a specific type may participate in the same operations with items of the original type (i.e., the type from which the subtype was derived). The type-subtype relationship is usually unbounded, i.e., any type, including subtypes, can have a subtype. Typed languages (i.e., languages in which there are two or more types) define, and often allow software engineers to embellish upon, type hierarchies, i.e., relationships among types and their corresponding subtypes.

Software engineers also use the terms "statically typed languages" and "dynamically typed languages." In **statically typed languages**, the type of an item is often determined early on (e.g., at compile or link time) and does not change. (Note, however, that static typing does not necessarily imply static binding.) This allows a software engineer (and, for that matter, the compiler) to determine the legality of both an individual operation and the overall program through a static analysis, i.e., without having to execute the program. **Dynamically typed languages**, on the other hand, allow the type of some items to change during the execution of a program. The type of an item is usually determined based on the context of the operation in which it is participating.

Classes, on the other hand, define structures, e.g., methods, internal state information representation, and exportable constants and exceptions, for objects. Specifically, it is possible to have a programming language that supports classes, but not types, e.g., Smalltalk. It is also possible to have an object-oriented programming language that supports both classes and types, e.g., C++. Eiffel is an example of an object-oriented programming language that is strongly typed and supports classes.

We can see that it is possible to have a programming language that supports both an inheritance hierarchy and a type hierarchy. Very often the type hierarchy is tightly coupled to the inheritance hierarchy. This can lead to problems. (See, e.g., [Cook et al., 1989], [Madsen et al., 1990], and [Porter, 1992].)

Suppose that we are working with a system in which the typing hierarchy is closely tied to the inheritance hierarchy. Specifically, a situation in which a specialization of a class is also a subtype of the original class. Therefore, if A is a specialization of B, and B is a specialization of C, then, by induction, A is also a subtype of C. Now, further suppose that we are in a somewhat strongly typed system, and that it is important for A to be a subtype of C. If we decide to redesign B so that it is no longer a specialization of C, then instances of A are no longer subtypes of C. This will make previously legal operations involving A illegal. In a very real sense A is closely coupled with C, and is sensitive to changes in both B and C. (This example is closely based on one that appears in [Snyder, 1986].)

One way to prevent such problems is to allow for a clear separation of the inheritance hierarchy and the type hierarchy. Unfortunately, the semantics of most commonly used object-oriented programming languages (e.g., C++) do not easily allow for this, if they allow for it at all.

Multiple inheritance both complicates the previously existing problems, and introduces a few new problems. Most object-oriented programming languages that allow for multiple inheritance, also provide some systematic conflict resolution mechanism. Suppose, for example, that object A directly inherits characteristics from objects B and C. Further suppose that both B and C provide an inheritable operation called "set." Assume that the conflict resolution mechanism dictates that the method for "set" in object A will be that found in object C. Next, suppose the designer of object C changes C so that it no longer provides a "set" operation. This means that the method for the "set" operation in object A will change, i.e., it will be based on the "set" operation provided in object B. (Of course, the changes made to object C might cause changes in the implementation of the methods in object A by displacing methods previously supplied by object B.)

In a multiple inheritance scheme, an object that inherits from multiple parents is tightly coupled to these parents. Depending on both the items being inherited, and the conflict resolution mechanism, changes to any of the parents can cause significant changes to the object inheriting the characteristics.

Multiple inheritance is a useful concept and can be used both to accurately reflect the "real world," and to reduce the total amount of source code required for a particular application. However, as we have seen above, there can be problems (and these are not the only problems). When we are designing object-oriented systems (e.g., libraries or applications) we should take care when using inheritance, single or multiple. (See, e.g., [Coggins, 1990].)

Lastly, we should mention that there are a number of metrics available to measure various aspects of object coupling, e.g., [Chidamber and Kemerer, 1991], [Liberherr and Holland, 1989], [Liberherr and Riel, 1988a], [Liberherr and Riel, 1988b], [Liberherr and Riel, 1989], and [Liberherr et al., 1988].

Object Cohesion

Simply stated, cohesion measures the degree of connectivity among the elements of a single module (and for object-oriented design, a single class or object).

— *[Booch, 1991]*

Designs in which the modules (in the case of object-oriented design, objects or classes) exhibit high cohesion are those in which the modules group together parts of the system which are closely related.

— *[Blair et al., 1991]*

> [Cohesion is] the degree to which components of a single software system (such as members of a single class) are tied together.
>
> *— [Budd, 1991]*

> ... [C]ohesion is: the degree to which the elements of a portion of a design contribute to the carrying out of a single, well-defined purpose.
>
> *— [Coad and Yourdon, 1991]*

A good deal of the discussion regarding object coupling focuses on relationships among different objects. Object cohesion, on the other hand, is based on the logical and physical relationships that bind an individual object together. The more cohesive an object is, the less susceptible it is to change, i.e., the more stable the object is. The introduction of changes into any individual object usually results in undesirable "ripple effects" (i.e., the propagation of change requirements) in the systems that contain that object. Highly cohesive objects usually require very few, if any, changes.

Object cohesion is an externally discernible concept. Specifically, when we discuss the cohesion of an object, we are *not* referring to its underlying implementation, but rather to the interface it presents to the outside world. The underlying implementation of a given object may indeed be chaotic or incoherent, but this does not affect our assessment of the cohesiveness of that object. (There are other concepts and metrics for dealing with the actual underlying implementation of an object.)

Very little has been written about object cohesion. Even the most detailed presentations do not offer more than two to three pages of discussion on the topic. This is not because the topic is not important, but rather because it is more difficult to describe and quantify. For example, given a Gregorian date (i.e., a date composed of a month, a day, and a year) and an "electronic mail message header" (containing information about the sender, the receiver, the passage of the message through the electronic mail system, and the message itself), it might be "intuitively obvious" that the Gregorian date is more cohesive than the "electronic mail message header," but why?

Timothy Budd ([Budd, 1991]) uses [Yourdon and Constantine, 1979] as the basis for his discussion of object cohesion, but provides very few insights into the topic. Peter Coad ([Coad and Yourdon, 1991]) stipulates that "services" (methods) should be functionally cohesive, there should be no extra "services" or "attributes" (state information), all "services" and "attributes" should be descriptive of the object in which they are encapsulated, and specializations of general concepts should be true specializations — not incoherent extensions.

Korson and McGregor ([Korson and McGregor, 1990]) suggest that encapsulated methods must query or modify state information, inherited characteristics should naturally blend with the additional characteristics in the inheriting object, and that "the ultimate test of cohesion is met by the fact that all these pieces are brought together to represent one concept." [Taylor and Hecht, 1990] advise us that, "Cohesion tells us to make sure all the member variables and methods of a class make sense as part of the class." Finally, Grady Booch [Booch, 1991] observes (borrowing terminology from structured design), "The most desirable form of cohesion is functional cohesion, in which the elements of a class or module all work together to provide some well-bounded behavior."

Because there is so little written down (as opposed to known) about object cohesion, the discussion presented here will be based on my personal experience in guiding the development of over one million lines of object-oriented software, experiences of my consulting clients (some of whom have developed object-oriented software systems that exceed two million lines of code), a basic knowledge of software engineering, and hints provided by some of the previously mentioned authors. What I am about to present is more than an attempt to qualify and quantify object cohesion. It is also an attempt to make the diagnosis and enhancement of object cohesion a teachable, transferable, and repeatable process.

Why is cohesion in general a more difficult concept to grasp than coupling? The answer is fairly simple. Since coupling requires some form of physical or logical linkage between two items, once we have identified that linkage, we have identified a form of coupling. Removing the linkage removes the coupling, and avoiding the establishment of linkages prevents the establishment of coupling.

If one has a reading knowledge of the syntax and semantics of a given programming language, one can identify many types of linkages. This thinking carries over to textual descriptions and graphical models as well. In fact, regardless of the representation mechanism, if one understands the semantics of that representation mechanism, one can identify (at least some forms of) coupling.

The difficult aspects of coupling are:

- identifying some of the more subtle (less blatant) forms of coupling,

- ranking (ordering) different forms of coupling,

- unambiguously specifying the particular attributes of a particular form of coupling (so as to both know when we have that form of coupling, and to differentiate it from other forms of coupling),

- identifying mechanisms to prevent coupling from occurring, and

- removing coupling once it is in place.

Cohesion, on the other hand, requires that we examine an item in isolation, i.e., apart from any other item, and any application that might use the item. When we hear the phrase "logically-related components," this implies that there is some mechanism for knowing which, if any, of the components are logically related. In addition, we must understand degrees of "logical relatedness," i.e., saying that one item is more cohesive than another item implies that we have some means of assessing how closely related the components of an item are to each other.

The earlier example of the Gregorian date and the "electronic mail message header" gives us a clue. Most of us are much more familiar with dates composed of months, days, and years, than we are with "electronic mail message headers." If we think about it, knowing whether or not a specific type of "electronic mail message header" was cohesive depends on our knowledge and experience with such things. While it would be extremely difficult to reach the age of even 6 years without encountering the concept of a date, many people live their entire lives without having to know about "electronic mail message headers."

In a very real sense, understanding cohesion requires many of the same skills necessary to understand reusability, i.e., to both assess the cohesiveness of an item, and to understand the reusability of that same item, we must have:

- technical knowledge of the application domain(s) in which the item will be used,

- at least some limited amount of experience in constructing, modifying, maintaining, testing, and managing applications in the appropriate application domain(s),

- technical knowledge and experience in the types of items found, created, and modified in the application domain(s), i.e., if we are dealing with object-oriented items, we need to know about, and have experience with, objects, and

- a good technical background in and experience with reusability, and in particular, software reusability.

Those involved with the creation of telephone switching systems will very likely need to know about such items as "trunk groups" and "trouble tickets" to assess the cohesiveness (or lack thereof) in these items. Software engineers developing banking applications will be required to recognize that "annual percentage rates" and "loan amounts" are objects. Embedded systems builders will have to know that items such as switches, lamps, and ports are objects that can be used across a wide variety of embedded applications.

In assessing the cohesiveness of any object (or system of objects), we should be asking questions such as:

- Overall, does the object represent a complete and coherent concept, or does it more closely resemble a partial concept, or a random collection of information? (This will be difficult without the skills mentioned above.)

- Does the object directly correspond to a "real world entity," physical (e.g., a post office, phone number, or insurance policy) or "logical entity" (e.g., a queue, a rule, or a unit of time)?

- Is the "object" characterized in very non-specific terms, e.g., as a collection of "data," "information," "statistics," or "metrics"?

- Do each of the methods in the public interface for the object perform a single coherent function?

- If the object is really a "system of objects," does the overall system of objects truly represent an object-oriented concept, e.g., as opposed to a functional concept?

- If we are dealing with a system of objects, do all of the component objects directly support, or directly contribute to the support of, the object-oriented concept that the system represents?

- If we are dealing with a system of objects, are there any missing objects?

- If a system of objects presents multiple interfaces to the outside world, does each of the interfaces represent a complete and coherent object-oriented concept, or a coherent, object-oriented view of the system of objects?

- If the object (or system of objects) is removed from the context of the immediate application, does the object, in isolation, still represent a coherent and complete object-oriented concept?

There are two dimensions of object cohesion, i.e.:

- the cohesiveness of the object in isolation, and

- if the object is part of a specialization hierarchy, how cohesive is the specialization interface (if present) for the object, and does the object represent a coherent and proper specialization with respect to the rest of the specialization hierarchy?

Objects in Isolation

We begin our discussion by first focusing on objects in isolation, i.e., apart from any specialization hierarchy.

We will first eliminate "non-objects" (sometimes called "pseudo-objects") from our discussion. Most object-oriented (and object-based) programming languages supply a physical encapsulation mechanism, e.g., classes in C++ and Smalltalk, packages in Ada, and modules in Modula-3. Sometimes these encapsulation mechanisms are used to package non-object-oriented concepts, i.e.:

- *an "object" containing only functions*, i.e., an "object" with no state information. Since these items embody only behavior — and no state information — they are not objects. A common example of this is a "math object," an "object" that contains only mathematical functions. This may be cohesive in a functional sense, but it is not cohesive in an object-oriented sense.

- *an "object" containing only data*, i.e., an "object" that allows direct access to its encapsulated state information. Since these items do not embody any behavior — only directly accessible constants and variables — they are not objects. A common example of this is the "universal constants object." Again, these items may be cohesive in a data-oriented sense, but they are not at all cohesive in an object-oriented sense.

Even though both of the above can be created using the object-packaging mechanism of our chosen implementation language, we do not consider either of them to be objects, and, hence, they fall outside of our discussion of object cohesion.

We will divide our discussion of object cohesion into two parts. One part will focus on individual objects; the other part will be dedicated to systems of objects.

Individual Objects

When we speak of "individual objects" we are referring to objects as they are defined in most common object-oriented programming languages, e.g classes, metaclasses, parameterized classes, and their instances. Individual objects are definable using the syntax and semantics of object-oriented (and object-based) programming languages. We include language-definable aggregations of objects (what we have been calling "composite objects") in our definition of "individual objects."

In our discussion of individual objects we will first turn our attention to the methods in the public interfaces of these objects. (Virtually all of the arguments we will make apply equally well to inheritance interfaces.)

Earlier we said that a primitive method is any method that cannot be implemented simply, efficiently, and reliably without knowledge of the underlying implementation of the object in which it is encapsulated. We also defined a composite method as any method constructed from two or more primitive methods — sometimes from different objects.

We now extend our discussion to include "sufficient sets of primitive methods" and "complete sets of primitive methods." For a given object, a **sufficient set of primitive methods** is a minimum set of primitive methods necessary to accomplish all necessary work with the object in which they are encapsulated. Please note that this is not necessarily the set of all primitive methods for the given object, and that, for any given object, there is usually more than one sufficient set of primitive methods.

While a sufficient set of primitive methods allows us to accomplish all necessary work for the object in which they are encapsulated, such sets of methods often suffer from two major problems, i.e.:

- Attempting to accomplish some tasks with only a sufficient set of primitive methods may be awkward and/or difficult.

- A sufficient set of primitive methods may not allow us to fully capture the abstraction represented by the object.

Therefore, we often extend a sufficient set of primitive methods for an object with additional primitive methods. A **complete set of primitive methods** for a given object is that set of primitive methods that both allows us to easily work with the object, and fully captures the abstraction represented by the object. Complete sets of primitive methods are at least equal in size, and are almost always larger, than sufficient sets of primitive methods for the same object.

If we examine the set of methods in the public interface for an object and find that the set of methods in the object's public interface contains:

- only primitive methods, but does not represent at least a sufficient set of primitive methods for the encapsulating object,

- primitive methods, but there is not a sufficient set of primitive methods, and there are also composite methods present,

- a sufficient set of primitive methods, but it also contains additional composite methods, or

- no primitive methods, i.e., all methods in the object's public interface are composite methods,

then the object is not as cohesive as it could be. Specifically, well-designed objects should contain only primitive methods in their public interface, and there should be at least a sufficient set of primitive methods— and preferably a well-thought-out complete set of methods.

We should keep the following items in mind:

- Objects that have at least a sufficient set of primitive methods in their public interfaces, but also some composite operations, are typically much more cohesive than objects that do not contain at least a sufficient set of primitive methods in their public interfaces.

- Primitive or composite, all methods in the public interface for a given object must directly support the abstraction represented by the object. Further, the encapsulated methods must make sense even when we consider the object in isolation. Specifically, all encapsulated methods should be application-independent. If the only reason for including any method (primitive or composite) in the public interface for an object is a specific application, then that method should probably be removed from the public interface for the object.

(There are many other issues that could be discussed here. Most of them are related to software reusability, software reliability, and efficiency.)

Composite Objects

Our discussion of object cohesion in individual objects now shifts to composite objects. A **composite object** is an object that is conceptually composed of two, or more, other objects. (A composite object is said to be an *aggregation* of its component objects.) The objects that make up the composite object are referred to as **component objects**. In addition, the composition of a composite object is externally discernible, i.e.:

- the (externally discernible) state of a composite object is directly affected by the presence or absence of one, or more, component objects, and/or

- those outside of the composite object can directly query or change the states of the component objects via the methods in the public interface of the composite object.

Over and above an assessment of the cohesion of a composite object based on the methods in its public interface, we can judge the cohesion of a composite object based on its externally discernible component objects. A ranking of the cohesiveness of a composite object, based on its externally discernible component objects, and ordered roughly in terms of increasing goodness, is:

- the externally discernible component objects are not related to each other, and, taken as a collection, do not support (or seem to support) a single coherent object-oriented concept, i.e., there is no way to describe the collection other than to list the externally discernible component objects,

- two, or more, of the externally discernible component objects appear to have a logical, object-oriented relationship, but the collection of externally discernible component objects, taken as a whole, does not exhibit such a relationship,

- although the collection of externally discernible component objects, taken in isolation, does not represent a single stable object-oriented concept, the externally discernible component objects are bound together by how they are used in a particular application, or set of applications, e.g., they are all part of the information displayed on a single screen,

- a definite majority of the externally discernible component objects are necessary to support a single, coherent, object-oriented concept, but, when the composite object is considered in isolation, there is at least one externally discernible component object that does not directly support the single, coherent, object-oriented concept (there is an excellent chance that these extraneous externally discernible component objects were included for a specific application or set of applications),

- all of the externally discernible component objects are necessary to support a single coherent object-oriented concept, but even though a definite majority of the necessary externally discernible component objects are present, there are one, or more, externally discernible component objects that are missing, and

- all of the externally discernible component objects necessary to support a single coherent, application-independent, object-oriented concept are present, and there are no additional externally discernible component objects.

Objects encapsulate more than just methods and component objects. The public interface of an object may contain such things as exceptions, constants, and exportable definitions. In evaluating the cohesiveness of an object, we need to consider these items as well.

For example, suppose that we are dealing with a bounded list object, i.e., a list with a fixed upper limit to the number of items that it can contain. Suppose that we have defined an exception "underflow" that will be raised/activated/thrown when someone attempts to remove an element from an empty bounded list. However, if we have not also defined an exception "overflow" (to be raised/activated/thrown when someone attempts to add an item to a bounded list that is already full), then our bounded list object is not as cohesive as it could be. Said another way, we have not yet fully captured the abstraction of a bounded list.

To summarize, when we are attempting to assess the cohesion of an individual object in isolation, we focus on three areas:

- an assessment of the methods in the public interface,

  - Are all the methods appropriate for the given object?

  - Do we have at least a minimally sufficient set of primitive methods?

  - Do we have extra or application-specific methods?

- an assessment of the non-method items in the public interface, and

  - Are all the non-method items appropriate for the given object?

  - Do we have at least a minimally sufficient set of the non-method items?

  - Do we have extra or application-specific non-method items?

- for composite objects, an assessment of the component objects.

  - Are all the component objects appropriate for the given object?

  - Do we have at least a minimally sufficient set of component objects?

- Do we have extra or application-specific component objects?

Specialization Hierarchies

The second dimension of object cohesion deals with objects that are part of a specialization hierarchy. By specialization we mean such things as inheritance or delegation. In such hierarchies we are concerned with two things:

- does the object represent a coherent and proper specialization with respect to the rest of the specialization hierarchy, and

- how cohesive is the specialization interface (if present) for the object?

Notice that the first consideration very definitely requires both knowledge of, and experience in, the application domain. The second consideration, on the other hand, can be assessed in a more mechanical nature.

The establishment of stable and usable specialization hierarchies is usually a long process that requires a great deal of knowledge and experience in the particular application domain. For example, the establishment of genus and species classification schemes for plants and animals has been going on for over 100 years and is still being refined.

To complicate matters, more than one hierarchical organization may be appropriate for the same set of objects. Consider a hierarchy of automobiles, for example. Should the hierarchy be based on manufacturers (e.g., General Motors, Volvo, and BMW), the price of the vehicles, or on the types and numbers of features? Experience has shown that multiple specialization hierarchies for the same set of objects can be quite useful — even though it may greatly complicate the job of the software engineer.

Before we can place objects into a specialization hierarchy, we need to establish the framework for the hierarchy. This means that we must have some taxonomy (classification scheme) already in mind. Next, we need to (at least informally) establish the criteria for placing a given object at a particular point in our hierarchy. Before placing any objects into the hierarchy, we need to know that both the framework and our placement criteria are viable.

We often hear about software engineers making frequent changes to specialization hierarchies. There are two major reasons for this:

- Instead of basing the hierarchy on an external or high-level criterion, the software engineer has chosen to base the hierarchy primarily on code reuse. This is what Sakkinen ([Sakkinen, 1989]) calls "incidental inheritance," and others have called "subclassing for reuse." The more detail-oriented the classification criteria, typically the more susceptible to change that criteria become.

- The people setting up the specification hierarchy lacked knowledge of, and/or experience in, the particular application domain.

Of course, there are other reasons; for example, not enough resources (e.g., time and money) were allocated for setting up the hierarchy.

Given a particular specification hierarchy, we can assess the cohesiveness of an object with respect to that hierarchy. The less cohesive an object is with respect to a given specialization hierarchy, the more likely it will be that that object will have to be changed at some point in the future. Besides knowledge and experience in the application domain, things that help in this assessment include excellent abstraction skills and the advice of P.-J. Courtois ([Courtois, 1985]) mentioned earlier in this chapter.

Since we made an assessment of the cohesion of an object in isolation based primarily on its public interface, it would seem reasonable to make an assessment of the cohesion of an object in a specialization hierarchy based in part on that object's specialization interface. Specifically, we can focus on three areas:

- an assessment of the methods in the specialization interface,

    - Are all the methods appropriate for specializations of the given object?

    - Do we have at least a minimally sufficient set of primitive methods for specializations of the given object?

    - Do we have an extra or application-specific methods?

- an assessment of the non-method items in the specialization interface,

    - Are all the non-method items appropriate for specializations of the given object?

    - Do we have at least a minimally sufficient set of the non-method items for specializations of the given object?

    - Do we have an extra or application-specific non-method items?

- and an assessment of the form and content of the state information that the object makes available to its specializations.

    - Are the form and content of the state information appropriate for specializations of the given object?

    - Do we have at least a minimally sufficient set of state information for specializations of the given object?

    - Do we have an extra or application-specific state information?

Next, we shift our attention to object cohesion in systems of objects. A **system of objects** is defined as two or more interacting or interrelated, non-nested objects. (We exclude simple aggregations, i.e., composite objects, from our definition of systems of objects.) Systems of objects fall into two general categories (See chapter 9 of this book for a more detailed discussion of systems of objects.):

- **kits**, which are collections of objects (e.g., classes, metaclasses, non-class instances, unencapsulated composite operations, other kits, and systems of interacting objects), all of which support a large, object-oriented concept, and

- **systems of interacting objects**, which are collections of objects in which there must be a direct or indirect *physical* connection between any two arbitrary objects within the collection.

One can think of kits as "a class taken to the next higher level." Specifically, kits provide a public interface that contains the items necessary to support a large object-oriented concept, e.g., windows, and they have a hidden (or body) part that supports the public interface. A first approximation of a kit would be a library, i.e., users of a kit may pick and choose which components they need, and leave the rest behind. Kits must be object-oriented, e.g., a "math kit" is an oxymoron.

A system of interacting objects, on the other hand, is most often treated as a single, monolithic unit. Specifically, those outside of the system of interacting objects do not have any access to the internal components of the system of interacting objects. ([Hailpern and Ossher, 1990] describes one code-level mechanism by which this might be accomplished.) You could say, with the exception of libraries and kits, each object-oriented application is a system of interacting objects.

Over and above an assessment of the cohesion of each of the components of a kit, we can judge the cohesion of a kit based on its externally-visible (accessible) components. A ranking of the cohesiveness of a kit, based on its externally visible components, and ordered roughly in terms of increasing goodness, is:

- the externally visible components of the kit do not seem to have any logical relationship,

- the externally visible components of the kit do indeed have a logical relationship, but it is not object-oriented, e.g., the relationship among the components is functional, and

- the externally visible components of the kit are all related in that they directly support a large, coherent, object-oriented concept.

(By "large," we mean an object-oriented concept that cannot be fully characterized by only one class, or only one instance.)

Over and above an assessment of the cohesion of each of its components, we assess the object cohesion of a system of interacting objects from two different directions: internal and external. A ranking of the cohesiveness of a system of interacting objects, based on its *external* characteristics, and ordered roughly in terms of increasing goodness, is:

- the system of interacting objects does not represent any coherent concept, i.e., there is no easy way to describe it,

- the system of interacting objects does represent a single, coherent concept, but the concept is not object-oriented, e.g., it is a functional concept,

- the system of interacting objects represents a single, coherent, object-oriented concept, but one or more of its necessary interfaces are missing,

- the system of interacting objects represents a single, coherent, object-oriented concept, but it has interfaces over and above a complete set of public interfaces,

- the system of interacting objects represents a single, coherent, object-oriented concept, it has no public interfaces above a complete set of public interfaces, but one or more of the public interfaces is not cohesive, and

- the system of interacting objects represents a single, coherent, object-oriented concept, it has no public interfaces above a complete set of public interfaces, and all of the public interfaces are cohesive.

Of course, an important part of the external view of the cohesion of any object (or system of objects) is whether or not it properly exhibits its externally discernible characteristics. This will directly affect our assessment of the cohesion of a given system of interacting objects, i.e., we must consider it along with all but the first point mentioned above.

Internally, the assessment of the cohesion of a system of interacting objects deals with such issues as:

- there must be a direct or indirect, physical connection among all of the internal components, and

- all components necessary to preserve and exhibit the externally defined characteristics of the system of interacting objects must be present.

Unfortunately, there are very few metrics for object cohesion. One of the few is [Chidamber and Kemerer, 1991].

Conclusion

We have discussed and reviewed the foundations for coupling and cohesion, and examined each in an object-oriented context. While many of the original (non-object-oriented) concepts do carry over into object-oriented software engineering, some have to be enhanced, and new ones had to be generated.

It is unfortunate that there is much more written about object coupling than there is about object cohesion. This is most probably because cohesion does not lend itself to easily identifiable characteristics in the same manner as coupling. You might say that coupling is more of a physical phenomenon and cohesion is more of a logical phenomenon.

Although we have presented a more detailed view of object cohesion than has previously been discussed, much work remains to be done. For example, a nomenclature scheme needs to be developed for the varying types of object cohesion we have described above.

Bibliography

[Agha, 1986]. G. Agha, *ACTORS, A Model of Concurrent Computation in Distributed Systems*, MIT Press, Cambridge, Massachusetts, 1986.

[Agha and Hewitt, 1987]. G. Agha and C. Hewitt, "Actors: A Conceptual Foundation for Concurrent Object-Oriented Programming," in *Research Directions in Object-Oriented Programming*, Edited by B. Shriver and P. Wegner, MIT Press, Cambridge, Massachusetts, 1987, pp. 47 - 74.

[America, 1987]. P. America, "Inheritance and Subtyping In a Parallel Object-Oriented Language," *ECOOP '87: Proceedings of the European Conference on Object-Oriented Programming, Lecture Notes on Computer Science, Volume 276*, Springer Verlag, New York, New York, 1987, pp. 234 - 242.

[Ammirati and Gerhardt, 1990]. J. Ammirati and M. Gerhardt, "Using Object-Oriented Thinking to Teach Ada," *Proceedings of the Seventh Washington Ada Symposium,* June 25-28, 1990, pp. 277 - 300.

[ARM, 1983]. Reference Manual for the Ada Programming Language, *ANSI/MIL-STD 1815A (1983)*, United States Department of Defense, February 1983.

[Aron, 1968]. J.D. Aron, "The Superprogrammer Project," *Software Engineering: Report on a Conference Sponsored by the NATO Science Committee*, Garmisch, Germany, October 7-11, 1968, pp. 50 - 52.

[Bach, 1988]. W.W. Bach, "Is Ada Really an Object-Oriented Programming Language," *Proceedings of Ada Expo 1988*, Galaxy Productions, Frederick, Maryland, 1988, 7 pages.

[Baker, 1972]. F.T. Baker, "Chief Programming Team Management of Production Programs," *IBM Systems Journal*, Vol. 11, No. 1, January 1972, pp. 56 - 73.

[Baker, 1991]. H. Baker, "Object-Oriented Programming in Ada83 — Genericity Rehabilitated," *Ada Letters*, Vol. XI, No. 9, November/December 1991, pp. 116 - 127.

[Baker and Mills, 1973]. F.T. Baker and H.D. Mills, "Chief Programming Teams," *Datamation*, Vol. 19, No. 12, December 1973, pp. 58 - 61.

[Bauer and Wossner, 1982]. F.L. Bauer and H. Wossner, *Algorithmic Language and Program Development*, Springer-Verlag, New York, New York, 1982.

[Beane et al., 1984]. J. Beane, N. Giddings, and J. Silverman, "Quantifying Software Designs," *Proceedings of the Seventh International Conference on Software Engineering*, 1984, pp. 314 - 322.

[Berard, 1985]. E.V. Berard, *An Object-Oriented Design Handbook for Ada Software*, EVB Software Engineering, Inc., Frederick, Maryland, 1985.

[Berard, 1986]. E.V. Berard, *Object-Oriented Design (Course Notes)*, EVB Software Engineering, Inc., Frederick, Maryland, 1986.

[Bergin and Greenfield, 1988]. J. Bergin and S. Greenfield, "What Does Modula-2 Need to Fully Support Object-Oriented Programming?," *SIGPLAN Notices*, Vol. 23, No. 3, March 1988, pp. 73 - 82.

[Bergland, 1981]. G.D. Bergland, "A Guided Tour of Program Design Methodologies," *IEEE Computer*, Vol. 14, No. 10, October 1981, pp. 18 - 37.

[Berlin, 1990]. L. Berlin, "When Objects Collide: Experiences With Reusing Multiple Class Hierarchies," *OOPSLA/ECOOP '90 Conference Proceedings,* special issue of *SIGPLAN Notices*, Vol. 25, No. 10, October 1990, pp. 181 - 193.

[Blair et al., 1991]. G. Blair, J. Gallagher, D. Hutchison, and D. Sheperd, *Object-Oriented Languages, Systems and Applications*, Halsted Press, New York, New York, 1991.

[Booch, 1986]. G. Booch, "Object Oriented Development," *IEEE Transactions on Software Engineering,* Vol. SE-12, No. 2, February 1986, pp. 211 - 221.

[Booch, 1987]. G. Booch, *Software Components With Ada*, Benjamin/Cummings, Menlo Park, California, 1987.

[Booch, 1991]. G. Booch, *Object-Oriented Design With Applications*, Benjamin/Cummings, Menlo Park, California, 1991.

[Borgida, 1985]. A. Borgida, "Language Features for Flexible Handling of Exceptions in Information Systems," *ACM Transactions on Database Systems*, Vol. 10, No. 4, December 1985, pp. 565 - 603.

[Borgida, 1986]. A. Borgida, "Exceptions in Object-Oriented Languages," *SIGPLAN Notices*, Vol. 21, No. 10, October 1986, pp. 107 - 119.

[Borning, 1986]. A.H. Borning, "Class Versus Prototypes in Object-Oriented Languages," *Proceedings of the 1986 Fall Joint Computer Conference*, IEEE Catalog Number 86CH2345-7, IEEE Computer Society Press, Washington, D.C., 1986, pp. 36 - 40.

[Budd, 1991]. T. Budd, *An Introduction to Object-Oriented Programming*, Addison-Wesley, Reading, Massachusetts, 1991.

[Bulman, 1989]. D. Bulman, "Objects Don't Replace Design," *Computer Language*, Vol. 6, No. 8, August 1989, pp. 151 - 152.

[Cameron, 1989]. R.D. Cameron, "Efficient High-Level Iteration With Accumulators," *ACM Transactions on Programming Language Systems*, Vol. 11, No. 2, April 1989, pp. 194 - 211.

[Card and Glass, 1990]. D.N. Card and R.L. Glass, *Measuring Software Design Quality*, Prentice Hall, Englewood Cliffs, New Jersey, 1990.

[Card et al., 1985]. D.N. Card, G.T. Page, and F.E. McGarry, "Criteria for Software Modularization," *Proceedings of the IEEE Eighth International Conference on Software Engineering*, August 1985, pp. 372 - 377.

[Card et al., 1986]. D.N. Card, V.E. Church, and W.W. Agresti, "An Empirical Study of Software Design Practices," *IEEE Transactions on Software Engineering*, Vol. 12, No. 2, February 1986, pp. 264 - 271.

[Chambers and Ungar, 1989]. C. Chambers and D. Ungar, "Customization: Optimizing Compiler Technology for Self, a Dynamically-Typed Object-Oriented Language," *SIGPLAN Notices*, Vol. 24, No. 7, July 1989, pp. 146 - 160.

[Chambers et al., 1989]. C. Chambers, D. Ungar, and Elgin Lee, "An Efficient Implementation of Self, a Dynamically-Typed Object-Oriented Language Based on Prototypes," *OOPSLA '89 Conference Proceedings*, special issue of *SIGPLAN Notices*, Vol. 24, No. 10, October 1989, pp. 49 - 70.

[Chidamber and Kemerer, 1991]. S.R. Chidamber and C.F. Kemerer, "Towards a Metrics Suite for Object-Oriented Design," *OOPSLA '91 Conference Proceedings*, special issue of *SIGPLAN Notices*, Vol. 26, No. 11, November 1991, pp. 197 - 211.

[Coad and Yourdon, 1990]. P. Coad and E. Yourdon, *OOA — Object-Oriented Analysis*, 2nd Edition, Prentice Hall, Englewood Cliffs, New Jersey, 1990.

[Coad and Yourdon, 1991]. P. Coad and E. Yourdon, *Object-Oriented Design*, Prentice Hall, Englewood Cliffs, New Jersey, 1991.

[Coggins, 1990]. J.M. Coggins, "Designing C++ Class Libraries," *Proceedings of the C++ Conference, San Francisco, California*, April 1990, USENIX Association, Berkeley, California, 1990, pp. 25 - 35.

[Cohen, 1986]. N.H. Cohen, *Ada As a Second Language*, McGraw-Hill, New York, New York, 1986.

[Constantine, 1967]. L.L. Constantine, *Concepts in Program Design*, Information and Systems Press, Cambridge, Massachusetts, 1967.

[Constantine, 1968]. L.L. Constantine, "Control of Sequence and Parallelism In Modular Programs," *AFIPS Proceedings of the 1968 Spring Joint Computer Conference*, Vol. 32, AFIPS Press, Montvale, New Jersey, 1968, page 409.

[Constantine, 1991]. L.L. Constantine, "Larry Constantine on Structured Methods and Object Orientation," *UNIX Review*, Vol. 9, No. 2, February 1991, pp. 30 - 31.

[Conte et al., 1986]. S.D. Conte, H.E. Sunsmore, and V.Y. Shen, *Software Engineering Metrics and Models*, Benjamin/Cummings, Menlo Park, California, 1986.

[Cook et al., 1989]. W. Cook, W. Hill, and P. Canning, "Inheritance Is Not Subtyping," Report STL-89-17 (Revision 1), Hewlett-Packard Laboratories, Palo Alto, California, 1989, 11 pages. Also in the *Proceedings of the Seventeenth Symposium on Principles of Programming Languages*, January 1990, pp. 125 - 135.

[Courtois, 1985]. P.J. Courtois, "On Time and Space Decomposition of Complex Structures," *Communications of the ACM*, Vol. 28, No. 6, June 1985, pp. 590 - 603.

[Dijkstra, 1969]. E.W. Dijkstra, "Structured Programming," *Software Engineering Techniques*, NATO Scientific Affairs Division, Brussels 39, Belgium, 1969, pp. 84 - 88. Reprinted in [Yourdon, 1979].

[Dony, 1988]. C. Dony, "An Object-Oriented Exception Handling System for an Object-Oriented Language," *ECOOP '88: Proceedings of the European Conference on Object-Oriented Programming, Lecture Notes on Computer Science, Volume 322*, Springer Verlag, New York, New York, 1988, pp. 146 - 161.

[Dony, 1990]. C. Dony, "Exception Handling and Object-Oriented Programming: Towards a Synthesis," *OOPSLA/ECOOP '90 Conference Proceedings,* special issue of *SIGPLAN Notices*, Vol. 25, No. 10, October 1990, pp. 322 - 330.

[Eckart, 1987]. J.D. Eckart, "Iteration and Abstract Data Types," *SIGPLAN Notices*, Vol. 22, No. 4, April 1987, pp. 103 - 110.

[Ejiogu, 1991]. L.O. Ejiogu, *Software Engineering With Formal Metrics*, QED Technical Publishing Group, Boston, Massachusetts, 1991.

[Fairley, 1985]. R. Fairley, *Software Engineering Concepts*, McGraw-Hill Book Company, New York, New York, 1985.

[Gabriel, 1989]. R.P. Gabriel, "Using the Common LISP Object System," *Computer Language*, Vol. 6, No. 8, August 1989, pp. 73 - 80.

[Goldberg and Robson, 1983]. A. Goldberg and D. Robson, *Smalltalk-80: The Language and Its Implementation*, Addison-Wesley, Reading, Massachusetts, 1983.

[Gomaa, 1984]. H. Gomaa, "A Software Design Method for Real-Time Systems," *Communications of the ACM*, Vol. 27, No. 9, September 1984, pp. 938 - 949.

[Goodenough, 1975]. J. Goodenough, "Exception Handling: Issues and a Proposed Notation," *Communications of the ACM*, Vol. 18, No. 12, pp. 683 - 696.

[Hailpern and Ossher, 1990]. B. Hailpern and H. Ossher, "Extending Objects to Support Multiple Interfaces and Access Control," *IEEE Transactions on Software Engineering*, Vol. 16, No. 11, November 1990, pp. 1247 - 1257.

[Harland, 1984]. D.M. Harland, *Polymorphic Programming Languages — Design and Implementation*, Halstead Press, New York, New York, 1984.

[Hatley and Pirbhai, 1987]. D. J. Hatley and I. A. Pirbhai, *Strategies for Real-Time System Specification*, Dorset House Publishing Company, New York, New York, 1987.

[Helm et al., 1990]. R. Helm, I.M. Holland, and D. Gangopadhyay, "Contracts: Specifying Behavioral Compositions in Object-Oriented Systems," *OOPSLA/ECOOP '90 Conference Proceedings,* special issue of *SIGPLAN Notices*, Vol. 25, No. 10, October 1990, pp. 169 - 180.

[IEEE, 1983]. IEEE, *IEEE Standard Glossary of Software Engineering Terminology*, The Institute of Electrical and Electronic Engineers, New York, New York, 1983.

[Jackson, 1983]. M. Jackson, *System Development*, Prentice Hall, Englewood Cliffs, New Jersey, 1983.

[Johnson and Foote, 1988]. R.E. Johnson and B. Foote, "Designing Reusable Classes," *Journal of Object-Oriented Programming*, Vol. 1, No. 2, July/August 1988, pp. 22-35.

[Keene, 1989]. S.E. Keene, *Object-Oriented Programming in Common Lisp*, Addison-Wesley, Reading, Massachusetts, 1989.

[Kilian, 1990]. M. Kilian, "Trellis: Turning Designs Into Programs," *Communications of the ACM*, Vol. 33, No. 9, September 1990, pp. 65 - 67.

[Knuth, 1974]. D.E. Knuth, "Structured Programming with GOTO's," *ACM Computing Surveys*, Vol. 6, No. 4, December 1974, pp. 261 - 302.

[Koenig and Stroustrup, 1990]. A. Koenig and B. Stroustrup, "Exception Handling for C++," *Journal of Object-Oriented Programming*, Vol. 3, No. 2, July/August 1990, pp. 16 - 33.

[Korson and McGregor, 1990]. T. Korson and J.D. McGregor, "Understanding Object-Oriented: A Unifying Paradigm," *Communications of the ACM*, Vol. 33, No. 9, September 1990, pp. 40 - 60.

[LaLonde et al., 1986]. W.R. LaLonde, D.A. Thomas, and J.R. Pugh, "An Exemplar Based Smalltalk," *OOPSLA '86 Conference Proceedings,* special issue of *SIGPLAN Notices*, Vol. 21, No. 11, November 1986, pp. 322 - 330.

[Lamb, 1990]. D.A. Lamb, "Specification of Iterators," *IEEE Transactions on Software Engineering*, Vol. 16, No. 12, December 1990, pp. 1352 - 1360.

[Lawless and Miller, 1991]. J.A. Lawless and M.M. Miller, *Understanding CLOS: The Common Lisp Object System*, Digital Press, Bedford, Massachusetts, 1990.

[Liberherr and Holland, 1989]. K.J. Liberherr and I.M. Holland, "Assuring Good Style for Object-Oriented Programs," *IEEE Software*, Vol. 6, No. 5, September 1989, pp. 38 - 48.

[Liberherr and Riel, 1988a]. K.J. Liberherr and A.J. Riel, "Demeter: A Case Study of Software Growth Through Parameterized Classes," *Proceedings of the 10th International Conference on Software Engineering*, April 11-15, 1988, pp. 254 - 264.

[Liberherr and Riel, 1988b]. K.J. Liberherr and A.J. Riel, "Demeter: a CASE Study of Software Growth Through Parameterized Classes," *Journal of Object-Oriented Programming*, Vol. 1, No. 3, August/September 1988, pp. 8 - 22.

[Liberherr and Riel, 1989]. K.J. Liberherr and A.J. Riel, "Contributions to Teaching Object-Oriented Design and Programming," *OOPSLA '89 Conference Proceedings,* special issue of *SIGPLAN Notices*, Vol. 24, No. 10, October 1989, pp. 11 - 22.

[Liberherr et al., 1988]. K.J. Liberherr, I. Holland, and A.J. Riel, "Object-Oriented Programming: An Objective Sense of Style," *OOPSLA '88 Conference Proceedings,* special issue of *SIGPLAN Notices*, Vol. 23, No. 11, November 1988, pp. 323 - 334.

[Lieberman, 1986]. H. Lieberman, "Using Prototypical Objects to Implement Shared Behavior In Object-Oriented Systems," *OOPSLA '86 Conference Proceedings,* special issue of *SIGPLAN Notices*, Vol. 21, No. 11, November 1986, pp. 214 - 223.

[Lieberman et al., 1988]. H. Lieberman, L. A. Stein, and D. Ungar, "Of Types and Prototypes: The Treaty of Orlando," *OOPSLA '87 Addendum to the Proceedings,* special issue of *SIGPLAN Notices*, Vol. 23, No. 5, May 1988, pp. 43 - 44.

[Liskov and Zilles, 1975]. B. Liskov and S.N. Zilles, "Specification Techniques for Data Abstraction," *IEEE Transactions on Software Engineering*, Vol. SE-1, No. 1, March 1975, pp. 7 - 19.

[Liskov et al., 1977]. B.H. Liskov, A. Snyder, R. Atkinson, and C. Schaffert, "Abstraction Mechanisms in CLU," *Communications of the ACM*, Vol. 20, No. 8, August 1977, pp. 564 - 576.

[Liskov et al., 1981]. B.H. Liskov, R. Atkinson, T. Bloom, E. Moss, J. C. Schaffert, R. Scheifler, and A. Snyder, *CLU Reference Manual*, Springer-Verlag, New York, New York, 1981.

[Lohse and Zweben, 1984]. J.B. Lohse and S.H. Zweben, "Experimental Evaluation of Software Design Principles: An Investigation Into the Effect of Module Coupling on System Modifiability," *Journal of Systems and Software*, Vol. 4, No. 4, November 1984, pp. 301 - 308.

[Loy, 1990]. P.H. Loy, "Comparisons of O-O and Structured Development," *Software Engineering Notes*, Vol. 15, No. 1, January 1990, pp. 44 - 48.

[Madsen et al., 1990]. O.L. Madsen, B. Magnusson, and B. Møller-Pedersen, "Strong Typing of Object-Oriented Languages Revisited," *OOPSLA/ECOOP '90 Conference Proceedings,* special issue of *SIGPLAN Notices*, Vol. 25, No. 10, October 1990, pp. 140 - 150.

[Meyer, 1992]. B. Meyer, *Eiffel: The Language*, Prentice Hall, Englewood Cliffs, New Jersey, 1992.

[Micallef, 1988]. J. Micallef, "Encapsulation, Reusability and Extensibility in Object-Oriented Programming Languages," *Journal of Object-Oriented Programming*, Vol. 1, No. 1, April/May 1988, pp. 12 - 36.

[Miller, 1956]. G. A. Miller, "The Magical Number Seven, Plus or Minus Two: Some Limits on our Capacity for Processing Information," *The Psychological Review*, Vol. 63, No. 2, March 1956, pp. 81 - 97. Reprinted in [Yourdon, 1982], pp. 443 - 460.

[Milner, 1978]. R. Milner, "A Theory of Type Polymorphism in Programming," *Journal of Computer and System Sciences*, Vol. 17, 1978, pp. 348 - 375.

[Milner, 1984]. R. Milner, "A Proposal for Standard ML," *ACM Symposium on Lisp and Functional Programming*, August 1984, pp. 184 - 197.

[Moon, 1986]. D.A. Moon, "Object-Oriented Programming With Flavors," *OOPSLA Conference Proceedings*, (Special Issue of *SIGPLAN Notices*, Vol. 21, No. 11, November 1986), Association for Computing Machinery, New York, New York, 1986, pp. 1 - 8.

[Morgan, 1988]. T.M. Morgan, "Configuration Management and Version Control in the Rational Programming Environment," in *Ada In Industry: Proceedings of the Ada-Europe International Conference*, Munich 7-9 June, 1988, Cambridge University Press, Cambridge, United Kingdom, 1988, pp. 17 - 28.

[Moss and Kohler, 1987]. J.E.B. Moss and W.H. Kohler, "Concurrency Features for the Trellis/Owl Language," *Proceedings of the European Conference on Object-Oriented Programming 1987*, Paris, France, pp. 223 - 232.

[Myers, 1973a]. G.J. Myers, *Composite Design: The Design of Modular Programs*, Technical Report No. TR00.2406, IBM Corporation, Poughkeepsie, New York, January 29, 1973.

[Myers, 1973b]. G.J. Myers, "Characteristics of Composite Design," *Datamation*, Vol. 19, No. 9, September 1973, pp. 100 - 102.

[Myers, 1975]. G. J. Myers, *Reliable Software through Composite Design*, Van Nostrand Reinhold Company, New York, New York, 1975.

[Myers, 1976]. G.J. Myers, *Software Reliability: Principles and Practices*, John Wiley & Sons, New York, New York, 1976.

[Myers, 1978]. G.J. Myers, *Composite/Structured Design*, Van Nostrand Reinhold, New York, New York, 1978.

[Naur and Randell, 1969]. P. Naur and B. Randell, Editors, *Software Engineering: Report on a Conference Sponsored by the NATO Science Committee*, Garmisch, Germany, October 7-11, 1968.

[O'Brien et al., 1987]. P.D. O'Brien, D.C. Halbert, and M.F. Kilian, "The Trellis Programming Environment," *OOPSLA '87 Conference Proceedings,* special issue of *SIGPLAN Notices,* Vol. 22, No. 12, December 1987, pp. 91 - 102.

[Page-Jones, 1988]. M. Page-Jones, *The Practical Guide to Structured Systems Design,* Second Edition, Yourdon Press, Englewood Cliffs, New Jersey, 1988.

[Parnas, 1972]. D.L. Parnas, "On the Criteria To Be Used in Decomposing Systems Into Modules," *Communications of the ACM,* Vol. 5, No. 12, December 1972, pp. 1053-1058.

[Parnas, 1979]. D.L. Parnas, "Designing Software for Ease of Use and Extension," *IEEE Transactions on Software Engineering,* Vol. 5, No. 2, March 1979, pp. 128 - 157.

[Parnas et al., 1983]. D.L. Parnas, P.C. Clements, and D. M. Weiss, "Enhancing Reusability with Information Hiding," *ITT Proceedings of the Workshop on Reusability in Programming,* 1983, pp. 240 - 247.

[Porter, 1992]. H.H. Porter, III, "Separating the Subtype Hierarchy from the Inheritance Implementation," *Journal of Object-Oriented Programming,* Vol. 4, No. 9, February 1992, pp. 20 - 22, 24 - 29.

[Prieto-Diaz and Arango, 1991]. R. Prieto-Diaz and G. Arango, Editors, *Domain Analysis and Software Systems Modeling,* IEEE Computer Society Press, Los Alamitos, California, 1991.

[Rational, 1986]. Rational, Inc., *Large-System Development and Rational Subsystems,* Document Control Number 6004, Rational, Inc., Mountain View, California, November 1986.

[Ross, 1989]. D. Ross, "The Form of a Passive Iterator," *Ada Letters,* Vol. 9, No. 2, March/April 1989, pp. 102 - 105.

[Sage and Palmer, 1990]. A.P. Sage and J.D. Palmer, *Software Systems Engineering,* John Wiley & Sons, New York, New York, 1990.

[Sakkinen, 1989]. M. Sakkinen, "Disciplined Inheritance," *ECOOP '89: Proceedings of the European Conference on Object-Oriented Programming, British Computer Society Workshop Series,* Cambridge University Press, Cambridge, United Kingdom, 1989, pp. 39 - 56.

[Schaffert et al., 1986]. C. Schaffert, T. Cooper, B. Bullis, M. Killian, and C. Wilpolt, "An Introduction to Trellis/Owl," *OOPSLA '86 Conference Proceedings,* special issue of *SIGPLAN Notices,* Vol. 21, No. 11, November 1986, pp. 9 - 16.

[Shaw, 1981]. M. Shaw, Editor, *Alphard: Form and Content,* Springer-Verlag, New York, New York, 1981.

[Shaw et al., 1981]. M. Shaw, W.A. Wolf, and R. London, "Abstraction and Verification in Alphard: Iteration and Generators," *Alphard: Form and Content,* Springer-Verlag, New York, New York, 1981, pp. 73 - 116.

[Shlaer and Mellor, 1992]. S. Shlaer and S.J. Mellor, *Object Lifecycles: Modeling the World In States,* Yourdon Press: Prentice Hall, Englewood Cliffs, New Jersey, 1992.

[Simon, 1962]. H.A. Simon, "The Architecture of Complexity," *Proceedings of the American Philosophical Society,* Vol. 106, December 1962, pp. 467 - 482.

[Simon, 1981]. H.A. Simon, *The Sciences of the Artificial, Second Edition,* MIT Press, Cambridge, Massachusetts, 1981.

[Simon and Ando, 1961]. H.A. Simon and A. Ando, "Aggregation of Variables in Dynamic Systems," *Econometrica,* Vol. 29, April 1961, pp. 111 - 138.

[Snyder, 1986]. A. Snyder, "Encapsulation and Inheritance in Object-Oriented Programming Languages," *OOPSLA '86 Conference Proceedings,* special issue of *SIGPLAN Notices,* Vol. 21, No. 11, November 1986, pp. 38 - 45.

[Snyder, 1987a]. A. Snyder, "Inheritance and the Development of Encapsulated Software Components," *Proceedings of the Twentieth Hawaii International Conference on System Sciences,* Kona, Hawaii, January 1987, pp. 227 - 238.

[Snyder, 1987b]. A. Snyder, "Inheritance and the Development of Encapsulated Software Components," *Research Directions in Object-Oriented Programming*, The MIT Press, Cambridge, Massachusetts, 1987, pp. 165 - 188.

[Sommerville, 1989]. I. Sommerville, *Software Engineering, Third Edition,* Addison-Wesley Publishing Company, Reading, Massachusetts, 1989.

[Stein, 1987]. L.A. Stein, "Delegation Is Inheritance," *OOPSLA '87 Conference Proceedings,* special issue of *SIGPLAN Notices*, Vol. 22, No. 12, December 1987, pp. 138 - 146.

[Stevens, 1981]. W.P. Stevens, *Using Structured Design: How to Make Programs Simple, Changeable, Flexible, and Reusable*, John Wiley & Sons, New York, New York, 1981.

[Stevens et al., 1974]. W. P. Stevens, G. J. Myers and L. L. Constantine, "Structured Design," *IBM Systems Journal*, Vol. 13, No. 2, May 1974, pp. 115 - 139.

[Stroustrup, 1991]. B. Stroustrup, *The C++ Programming Language, Second Edition*, Addison-Wesley, Reading, Massachusetts, 1991.

[Taenzer et al., 1989]. D. Taenzer, M. Ganti, and S. Podar, "Problems in Object-Oriented Software Reuse," *ECOOP '89: Proceedings of the European Conference on Object-Oriented Programming, British Computer Society Workshop Series*, Cambridge University Press, Cambridge, United Kingdom, 1989, pp. 25 - 38.

[Taylor and Hecht, 1990]. D.K. Taylor and A. Hecht, "Using CASE for Object-Oriented Design with C++," *Computer Language*, Vol. 7, No. 11, November 1990, pp. 49 - 57.

[Troy and Zweben, 1981]. D.A. Troy and S.H. Zweben, "Measuring the Quality of Structured Designs," *Journal of Systems and Software*, Vol. 2, No. 2, June 1981, pp. 113 - 120.

[Ungar and Smith, 1987]. D. Ungar and R.B. Smith, "Self: The Power of Simplicity," *OOPSLA '87 Conference Proceedings,* special issue of *SIGPLAN Notices*, Vol. 22, No. 12, December 1987, pp. 227 - 242.

[Wand and Weber, 1990]. Y. Wand and R. Weber, "An Ontological Model of an Information System," *IEEE Transactions on Software Engineering*, Vol. 16, No. 11, November 1990, pp. 1282 - 1292.

[Ward and Mellor, 1985]. P. T. Ward and S. J. Mellor, *Structured Development for Real-Time Systems, Volumes 1, 2 and 3*, Yourdon Press, New York, New York, 1985.

[Wegmann, 1986]. A. Wegmann, "Object-Oriented Programming Using Modula-2," *Journal of Pascal, Ada & Modula-2*, Vol. 5, No. 3, May-June 1986, pp. 5 - 17.

[Wegner, 1990]. P. Wegner, "Concepts and Paradigms of Object-Oriented Programming," *OOPS Messenger*, Vol. 1, No. 1, August 1990, pp. 7 - 87.

[Wild, 1991]. F.H. Wild, III, "Managing Class Coupling: Apply the Principles of Structured Design to Object-Oriented Programming," *UNIX Review*, Vol. 9, No. 10, October 1991, pp. 44 - 47.

[Wirfs-Brock and Wilkerson, 1989]. A. Wirfs-Brock and B. Wilkerson, "Variables Limit Reusability," *Journal of Object-Oriented Programming*, Vol. 2, No. 1, May/June 1989, pp. 34 - 40.

[Wirfs-Brock et al., 1990]. R. Wirfs-Brock, B. Wilkerson, and L. Wiener, *Designing Object-Oriented Software*, Prentice Hall, Englewood Cliffs, New Jersey, 1990.

[Wirth, 1983]. N. Wirth, *Programming In Modula-2,* Second Edition, Springer-Verlag, New York, New York, 1983.

[Yourdon, 1975]. E. Yourdon, *Techniques of Program Structure and Design*, Prentice Hall, Englewood Cliffs, New Jersey, 1975.

[Yourdon, 1979]. E. N. Yourdon, Editor, *Classics in Software Engineering*, Yourdon Press, New York, New York, 1979.

[Yourdon, 1982]. E. Yourdon, Editor, *Writings of the Revolution*, Yourdon Press, New York, New York, 1982.

[Yourdon and Constantine, 1979]. E. Yourdon and L.L. Constantine, *Structured Design: Fundamentals of a Discipline of Computer Program and Systems Design,* Prentice Hall, Englewood Cliffs, New Jersey, 1979.

8   Object and Class Specifications

> In our description of nature the purpose is not to disclose the real essence of the phenomena but only to track down, so far as it is possible, relations between the manifold aspects of our experience.
>
> — *Niels Bohr, Atomic Theory and the Description of Nature (1934)*

Prologue

I have frequently mentioned the fact that object-oriented approaches enhance software reusability — often focusing on the reusability of individual objects. The most common analogy I used was that of "computer chips." "Just as an electronics engineer builds complex hardware from reusable integrated circuits," I said, "so too can software engineers assemble complex software applications from reusable objects."

Around 1985, a hardware engineer challenged that contention. He cited the fact that whenever he was considering the use of a specific chip, he could examine a "data sheet" for that chip. The "data sheet" contained virtually everything a hardware engineer needed to know to make a decision on the appropriateness of a given chip for a given application. "Where," he said, "was the software equivalent of the 'data sheet,' i.e., an application-independent specification, for my so-called reusable objects?"

At the time, I had to admit that there was no standard means of documenting individual objects. Since his comment was one that I was hearing with increasing frequency, I decided to propose a consistent means of documenting individual objects. What I came up with was the "object and class specification."

In truth, "object and class specifications" (OCS) are really just "object specifications." However, the usage of the terms "object" and "class" were being used inconsistently. Today, we know that classes are indeed objects, but, in the mid-1980s, some people were using the term "object" to mean strictly "an instance of a class." These folks often ran into trouble when confronted with metaclasses, i.e., classes whose instances themselves were classes.

To tell even more truth, OCSs are not (supposed to be) used primarily for documenting objects after the fact. They are meant to capture the original design of the object, i.e., OCSs are created before lower-level implementations (e.g., source code) of objects are created.

The first object and class specifications (OCSs) were simply a textual description of the given object, and a graphical representation (using a semantic network) of the object's externally discernible structure. As we and our clients began to use OCSs on real applications, we found that this form was insufficient. Hence, we began to add other sections. Each additional section, and each modification to an existing section was added in response to a real need expressed by more than one client. Although the current five-part structure of the OCS has not changed in the past few years, most organizations modify the basic OCS to suit their own needs.

As a side note, "OCS" is often pronounced "ox," and the plural ("OCSs") is sometimes (humorously) pronounced "oxen."

Individual Objects Versus Systems of Objects

OCSs are used to document individual objects, as opposed to systems of objects. By "individual objects," we mean classes, metaclasses, parameterized classes, and their instances. In truth, we seldom use OCSs to document "non-class instances," i.e., objects that cannot be used directly to create other instances. For example, in an object-oriented application, we would produce an OCS for a class representing a "list of names," but not for instances of that class. So while an application might contain literally thousands of objects, we usually only produce object and class specifications for those that represent patterns, e.g., classes and metaclasses.

[Sometimes, we find ourselves working with a language or a system that supports "prototypes" (sometimes referred to as "exemplars," e.g., [LaLonde et al., 1986]) instead of (or in addition to) classes. (See, e.g., [Borning, 1986] and [Liberman, 1986].) Languages such as Self ([Chambers and Ungar, 1989], [Chambers et al., 1989], and [Ungar and Smith, 1987]) and most actor languages ([Agha, 1986]) use prototypes in place of classes. In these situations, it would not be unusual, in fact it would be normal, to document non-class instances with OCSs.]

A **system of objects** is defined as two or more interacting or interrelated, non-nested objects, that fall into two general categories:

- **kits**, which are collections of objects (e.g., classes, metaclasses, non-class instances, unencapsulated composite operations, other kits, and systems of interacting objects), all of which support a large, object-oriented concept, e.g., windows, switches, and insurance policies.

- **systems of interacting objects**, which are collections of objects in which there must be a direct or indirect physical connection between any two arbitrary objects within the collection.

(See chapter 9 of this book for a more detailed discussion of systems of objects.)

Kits are documented with a "kit specification" (KS). Kit specifications, in turn, usually contain many OCSs. Systems of interacting objects are documented using a "system of interacting objects specifications" (SIOS), and these also often contain many OCSs.

Sometimes people confuse the documentation of an individual object with the documentation for an object-oriented life-cycle process. The results of an object-oriented requirements analysis (OORA) effort are documented using an "object-oriented requirements specification" (OORS), and these contain many OCSs. Object-oriented design (OOD) efforts are documented using an "object-oriented design specification" (OODS), and OODSs also contain many OCSs.

When Do We Create OCSs?

Regardless of the software engineering process, or where we are in the object-oriented software life-cycle, whenever we identify a new class, metaclass, or parameterized class, it is advisable to document it with an OCS. (If we are dealing with "prototypes," each new prototype should be documented with an OCS.) OCSs may be created, for example, during analysis, design, maintenance, and domain analysis. One should not be able to tell by examining an OCS, during which software engineering process it was created.

OCSs are reusable software. Specifically, they are created with the intention that they will be reused — preferably without changes. OCSs created during analysis on one project, for example, might be reused during design on another project. As an organization's reusability system acquires more OCSs, the need to create new OCSs, as opposed to reusing existing OCSs, diminishes.

What View of an Object Does an OCS Provide?

OCSs provide an external, high-level, programming-language-independent view of an object. Specifically, OCSs provide a user of an object with an accurate and complete description of the externally discernible characteristics of an object. OCSs do *not* contain information about the underlying implementation of an object, nor are they meant to suggest specific internal implementation mechanisms.

Further, OCSs may be produced for objects which will not necessarily be implemented as code software. For example, an OCS may be produced for a hardware object, a flesh and blood human being object, or a document object. In addition, an object described using an OCS may have multiple implementations, e.g., using several different programming languages.

Although it is often overpowering, software engineers should avoid the temptation to tailor the OCS for a specific implementation, e.g., a specific implementation language. An OCS should represent the best possible external design for a given object. Software engineers should keep in mind that even with a well-written OCS, there is still some discretion left to the coder of an object. They should also keep in mind that some OCSs will be implemented via hardware or "flesh and blood."

The Basic Structure of an OCS

Each object and class specification is divided into five parts, i.e.:

- a *Precise and Concise Description* that provides an "executive summary" for the object. Precise and Concise Descriptions may be graphical, textual, or otherwise.

- *Graphical Representations* of the object that model both the static and dynamic characteristics of the object. Most often, we use semantic networks for the static characteristics, and state transition diagrams for the dynamic characteristics.

- both suffered and required *Operations* for the object, including a very brief description of the algorithms for each operation.

- a description of the *State Information* associated with the object, described in a manner that decouples the states from the operations that may query or change these states. This information is very helpful designing the methods associated with each operation.

- descriptions of any exported *Constants and Exceptions* for the object. This section describes the non-operation items in the public interface for the object.

An OCS is typically five to six pages. Small OCSs can be three (and very rarely, two) pages in length, and very large OCSs may be eight to nine pages in length. (The reader is referred to the Appendix of this book for examples of OCSs.)

The Precise and Concise Description

The first part of each OCS is a precise and concise description of the object. This description may be textual, graphical, a mixture of both, or otherwise. For the most part, it may be considered to be an "executive overview" of the object itself. However, we should remember that the precise and concise description does contain information found nowhere else in the OCS.

Precise and concise descriptions are typically two-thirds of a page to a full page in length. They should seldom exceed a page and a half in length. Precise and concise descriptions that are shorter than a half a page are usually incomplete.

A precise and concise description must contain at least the following:

- a concise general description of the object. Among other things, this should connect the object with its "real world" (physical or logical) counterpart.

- a list of the suffered and required operations for the object (one may mention specific methods only for purposes of clarity). Details of the operations (e.g., descriptions of their methods) are more appropriately addressed in the Operations section of the OCS.

- a list of exceptions exported by the object. Descriptions of the conditions under which each exception will be raised (thrown, activated) will be covered in the Constants and Exceptions part of the OCS.

- a list of any constants exported by the object. A statement about the purpose and relative usefulness of each constant can be found in the Constants and Exceptions part of the OCS.

- a list of any variables, constants, and/or classes imported by the object, i.e., used to parameterize the object. If we are dealing with a metaclass or a parameterized object, this is the only place in the OCS where we usually find information on the parameters for these items.

- any explicit restrictions placed on the states which the object may assume. More details on this can be found in the State Information section of the OCS.

Each precise and concise description must be created with the idea that it be:

- accurate,

- easily verifiable,

- loosely coupled, if at all, with any other objects and OCSs (it is in the precise and concise description that the coupling of an OCS to other OCSs most often occurs),

- general enough make the OCS very reusable, while specific enough to be meaningful, and

- as complete as possible, while being concise and to the point.

The following should be taken into consideration when developing a precise and concise description:

- Where appropriate, you may use a requirements specification language. See, e.g., [Alford, 1985] and [Borgida et al., 1985].

- One may also choose to formalize the precise and concise description with mathematical techniques, e.g., Vienna Development Methodology (e.g., [Chedgey et al., 1987], [Jackson, 1985] and [Jones, 1986]), OBJ and its derivatives (e.g., [Gallimore et al., 1989], [Goguen, 1984], and [Grogono and Bennett, 1989]), Z (e.g., [Spivey, 1988] and [Spivey, 1989]), and C.A.R. Hoare's communicating sequential processes (e.g., [Hoare, 1985])

- The precise and concise description should be created with automation in mind, e.g., hypertext.

- The precise and concise description must go through explicit, although possibly informal, verification.

The precise and concise description is one of the places in the OCS where there is plenty of "wiggle room," i.e., room to introduce changes and enhancements. (Specifically, we are referring to the tailoring of the OCS format for a particular site.) For example, if an organization has a requirement for some very specific, external, object-oriented information — and this information is not covered by any other part of the OCS — the information is often incorporated into the precise and concise description.

Those charged with assuring the quality of an OCS will ask the following questions when they are examining the precise and concise description:

- Are all the operations mentioned? (Methods need not be discussed, unless appropriate.)

- Are all exceptions and constants mentioned?

- Is the state information mentioned?

- Are any relevant constraints on the class mentioned?

- Is duplication of information within the precise and concise description kept to a minimum?

- Has object coupling been minimized, e.g., has there been any unnecessary mention of specific other objects?

Graphical Representations

The cliché about a picture being worth a thousand words is largely true. For many people, graphics are one of the most effective and efficient means of transferring information. This is the primary reason for including graphical representations in the OCS. There are, of course, other reasons. For example, some information can be verified more systematically in graphical form than the same information in textual form.

Originally, aside from any graphics contained in the precise and concise description, the only graphics included in the OCS were semantic networks. (See, e.g., [Barr and Feigenbaum, 1981], [Schalkoff, 1990], and [Winston, 1984].) The effective use of semantic networks, however, required that we overcome two major problems, i.e.:

- no consistent or standard set of semantic relationships existed, and

- there was no convenient mechanism for systematically expressing constraints in semantic relationships.

We overcame these problems by defining both a standard set of semantic relationships and a constraint expression mechanism.

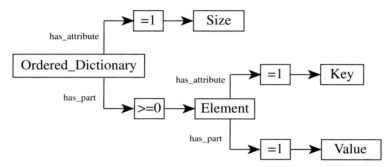

Figure 1:   **A semantic network for an ordered dictionary object shows that ordered dictionaries can be thought of as containing pairs of "keys" and "values."** Users of ordered dictionary objects can also query an ordered dictionary as to its size.

Because of the nature of some objects, their semantic networks are extremely simple, i.e., they are "just a box with a label." However, within the context of an OCS (i.e., the documentation of a single object in isolation), the semantic network for a given object may show one or more of the following types of semantic relationships:

- *aggregation*: This is the classic "has part" semantic relationship and describes the externally discernible structure of composite objects. A **composite object** is an object which is conceptually composed of two, or more, other objects. The objects which make up the composite object are referred to as **component objects**. (A composite object is said to be an aggregation of its component objects.) In addition, the composition of a composite object is externally discernible, i.e.:

  - the (externally discernible) state of the composite object is directly affected by the presence or absence of one, or more, component objects, and/or

  - those outside of the composite object can directly query or change the states of the component objects via the interface of the composite object.

- *metrics*: This semantic relationship describes the externally measurable characteristics of an object, e.g., size, weight, voltage, volume, speed, and colors. We labeled this semantic relationship as "has attribute."

- *allowable values*: Oftentimes, we place restrictions on the externally discernible states that an object can assume. If we feel that it will be of some use in understanding a given object (in isolation), we may include this information in the semantic network of the object. The label we use is "value can be."

- *property relationships*: Properties (e.g., [Zdonik, 1986]) document the concepts that come into existence when one object is placed into the context of another object. For example, a "name object" in isolation does not have a "location," and neither does a "list object." However, when we place a name in a list, we may properly ask, "what is the location of that name within the given list?" Location is the concept that came into existence when we placed one object (i.e., the name) into the context of another object (i.e., the list). This semantic relationship is labeled "can be a."

Although semantic networks can easily document generalization-specialization relationships (e.g., base class - derived class), we do not normally show such relationships within an OCS. This is primarily to reduce object coupling. Alan Snyder ([Snyder, 1986]) states the problem in the following manner:

> "A deeper issue raised by inheritance is whether or not the use of inheritance itself should be part of the external interface (of the class or the objects). In other words, should the clients of a class (necessarily) be able to tell whether or not a class is defined using inheritance?"

Lastly, we do not show semantic relationships that depict contextual (re)usage of objects within the context of an OCS — and, again, object coupling is the primary reason for this decision.

(Note: Outside of the context of an OCS, e.g., within the context of an application involving many objects, we freely and often show generalization-specialization relationships and contextual (re)usage of objects in our semantic networks.)

We noticed that all our standard semantic relationships expressed only static relationships, i.e., we had no means of graphically illustrating the dynamic properties of an object. This lead us to consider state transition diagrams.

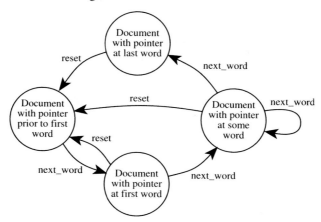

Figure 2:   **This state transition diagram shows some of the state transitions for a document object.** (The OCS for the document object would contain additional state transition diagrams so that all allowable state transitions can be shown.) This state transition diagram will be accompanied by a set of notes to explain questions a reader of the OCS might have.

State transition diagrams (e.g., [Hatley and Pirbhai, 1987], [Rumbaugh et al., 1991], and [Shlaer and Mellor, 1992]) were a natural means of showing the dynamic properties of an object. (Please note that discussions of concepts such as Mealy state machines and Moore state machines (e.g., [Hatley and Pirbhai, 1987]) occasionally have a place when describing the dynamic properties of some, but not all, objects. Further note that the concept of "finite state automata" (e.g., [Aho et al., 1986]) is seldom applicable to objects since few objects have definitive "start states" and "stop states.")

There were, however, three additional problems that we had to address:

- Some objects were capable of spontaneously changing their own state. Specifically, state changes in these objects could be caused by means other than invoking a state-changing method in the public interface of the object. These "objects with life" are sometimes called "actors" ([Agha, 1986]) or "active objects" ([Booch, 1991]).

  The problem arose when software engineers attempted to show both spontaneous and non-spontaneous state transitions on the same state transition diagram. Although this was often possible, most software engineers wanted to separate the two categories (i.e., spontaneous and non-spontaneous) of state transitions assigning each category to its own state transition diagram. We found this approach extremely useful and have encouraged it.

- Some state transition diagrams, although complete, were overly complex. For example, they contained more than "7 plus or minus 2" states ([Miller, 1956]), or it was difficult to cleanly illustrate all possible state transitions. This problem was solved by allowing software engineers to use a set of partial state transition diagrams to illustrate dynamic behavior. Specifically, a software engineer could choose to represent the dynamic behavior of an object either with a single, complete state transition diagram, or with a set of partial state transition diagrams.

- Some object behavior required two or more objects, or involved concurrency and/or other complex timing relationships. At one time we considered such tools as statecharts and their derivatives (e.g., [Coleman et al., 1992], [Harel, 1987], [Harel et al., 1987], and [Hayes and Coleman, 1991]). Petri nets and Petri net graphs (e.g., [Agerwala, 1979], [Bruno and Balsamo, 1986], [Bruno and Marchetto, 1985], [Ghezzi et al., 1989], [Ghezzi et al., 1991], [Peterson, 1977], [Peterson, 1981], and [Reisig, 1985]), however, offered a number of advantages over statecharts. Therefore, in an OCS, we recommend the use of Petri net graphs to show behavior requiring two or more objects, or behavior that involves complex timing relationships.

Each of these graphics (i.e., semantic networks, state transition diagrams, and Petri net graphs) are considered "engineering drawings" and, as such, are usually accompanied by a set of notes when they appear in an OCS.

In using these graphical techniques, it is important to realize that an OCS is used to document an individual object, not a system of objects. Further, this individual object sees all other objects as "black boxes," i.e., it has no knowledge of the underlying implementation of these other objects. Finally, software engineers must strive to minimize object coupling, and should not introduce unnecessary object coupling through inappropriate use of the graphical representations.

The quality assurance for the graphical representations must take the above into consideration. Quality assurance techniques specific to a particular graphical representation technique must also be considered.

Operations

The third section of the OCS documents the suffered and required operations (and their corresponding methods) for the object. An **operation** is an item that exists in the public interface for an object and is the name of an encapsulated functional capability for the object, i.e., an operation "advertises" a capability. (Many people refer to operations as "selectors," "method selectors," or "method interfaces." See, e.g., [Goldberg and Robson, 1983].) A **method** is the specific algorithm which actually accomplishes the requested operation, i.e., a method represents a capability which is advertised by an operation. We further stipulate that one operation may have many methods associated with it, possibly within the same encapsulating object.

(There is a tendency to refer to combinations of an operation and one of its associated methods as an "operation." Specifically, in many contexts, the terms "operation" and "subprogram" (e.g., function, procedure, and subroutine) are interchangeable. There is also a tendency to use the term "message" to mean both a request sent to an object, and as a synonym for a "method selector.")

Suffered operations are those operations which reside in the public interface for an object, and are actions that happen to the object. Specifically, suffered operations change or query the states of the objects in which they are encapsulated. **Required operations** for an object are operations suffered by objects *other than the encapsulating object,* and are *required by* the encapsulating object to ensure the desired and correct characteristics of the encapsulating object. Whereas we speak of suffered operations as being exported, in a very real sense, required operations must be imported.

A **primitive method** is any method that cannot be implemented simply, efficiently, and reliably without direct knowledge of the underlying implementation of the object in which it is encapsulated. A **composite method** is an method constructed from two or more primitive methods — sometimes from different objects. We stipulate that all methods encapsulated within an object should be primitive methods with respect to the encapsulating object.

We can identify three broad categories of primitive methods, i.e., selectors, constructors, and iterators. The terms "selector" and "constructor" to describe different categories of methods can be traced to the work of Barbara Liskov (e.g., [Liskov and Zilles, 1975]). The concept of an "iterator" had its formal origins in the programming language Alphard ([Shaw, 1981]), and has been discussed frequently in the literature, e.g., [Eckart, 1987], [Lamb, 1990], and [Shaw et al., 1981].

Selectors are encapsulated primitive methods that return state information about their encapsulating object, and cannot, by definition, alter the state of the object in which they are encapsulated. (Note that this is a general software engineering definition, and is not to be confused with the concept of a "method selector," e.g., as in Smalltalk.) Selectors are discussed in, e.g., [Bauer and Wossner, 1982], [Booch, 1986], [Booch, 1987], and [Booch, 1991].

Constructors are primitive methods that can (and often do) change the state of their encapsulating object to accomplish their function. (When necessary, constructors can also return state information about the object in which they are encapsulated.) We can think of constructors as methods that "construct a new, or altered, version of an object." Constructors are discussed in [Bauer and Wossner, 1982], [Booch, 1986], and [Booch, 1987]. Note that this is a more general, software engineering definition of the term "constructor," and not the more restrictive definition of the term as it is defined in, say, C++ ([Stroustrup, 1991]).

If we are dealing with a homogeneous composite object (See, e.g., chapter 7 of this book.), we can consider the inclusion of an iterator capability in its interface. An **iterator capability** (often simply referred to as an **iterator**) allows its users to systematically visit all the nodes in a homogeneous composite object and to perform some user-supplied operation at each node.

In designing a complete set of primitive methods for a given object, it is useful to identify some guidelines, e.g.:

- *Fundamental Rule*: The operations and methods for any software object must resemble the operations and methods for the corresponding "real world" object as closely as possible. Therefore, an appropriate set of operations and methods for a software object can be established, in large part, by examining the corresponding "real world" object.

  Consider, for example, a temperature sensor. In the "real world," the methods appropriate for a hardware sensor might be: enable the sensor, disable the sensor, and interrogate the sensor to determine the current temperature. The operations and methods for the software sensor should closely follow those for the hardware sensor.

- *Rule of Thumb*: If a particular object is conceptually very close to a primitive object (i.e., an object that is defined in the standard for the implementation language, and is globally known), then its operations and methods will be very similar to those of the primitive object upon which it is built.

  Consider, for example, a class representing "degrees Kelvin" (a temperature scale whose smallest value is zero). A software engineer may elect to build this class on top of a primitive class representing floating point numbers. Methods such as addition, subtraction, division, multiplication, and exponentiation which are appropriate for floating point numbers are probably also appropriate for objects of class Degrees_Kelvin. However, some methods, e.g., methods dealing with negative values, are probably not appropriate.

- *Rule of Thumb*: If a constructor method is required to place an object in a specific state, a corresponding selector method, that can query the object to determine if the object is in that state, is often also required. Conversely, if a selector method is required to determine if an object is in a specific state, a corresponding constructor method, that can cause the object to be in that state, is often also required. This is referred to as the "**selector-constructor pair rule**."

  Consider a counter object. A constructor method that increments the value of the counter is required. However, a selector method that determines the current value of the counter is also required. Notice that if a constructor method which decrements the value of the counter is also required, the same selector method may be used to detect that state as well.

The "selector-constructor pair" rule does not mean that selectors and constructors always come in pairs. The following situations are not all that uncommon:

- a single selector method which queries states established by several different constructors, e.g., value_of, increment, and decrement in the counter object,

- a selector method which queries a state which never changes, e.g., a sensor may be assigned permanently to a port address which can be queried, but never changed,

- a selector method which queries a state which changes; however the state cannot be changed via a software operation, e.g., a selector method which queries the current temperature value stored in a temperature sensor, and

- a constructor method which alters the state of an object, and whose state may not be queried, e.g., in an embedded system, there may be a port which may only be written to, and which maintains no status information.

When we are designing a complete set of primitive methods for composite objects, we take all of the above rules into account. In addition, we also use the following guidelines:

- Create constructors and selectors based on the "real world" view of the abstraction.

- If the object maintains state information which is not encapsulated within one of its component objects, add selectors and constructors appropriate for this information.

- Augment the above, where appropriate, by additional operations associated with the "mixins" of the object. We refer to the classes which encapsulate "minor" characteristics that are intended to be provided to other classes via multiple inheritance as "**mixins**." (See, e.g., [Stefik and Bobrow, 1985].)

- Consider issues of concurrency and memory management. Add additional operations, if necessary, to handle these items. (See, e.g., [Booch, 1987].)

- Examine the object for completeness. Add additional operations for reusability where appropriate.

When we are designing a complete set of primitive methods for a *heterogeneous* composite object, there is one additional consideration. For each component object there should be a selector method that returns the component object, and a constructor method that sets the component object. Note that either the selector or the constructor may not be appropriate, but at least one must be present.

When we are designing a complete set of primitive methods for *homogeneous* composite objects, we again use the above general guidelines. We have one other guideline for homogeneous composite objects. Specifically, if it is appropriate, we will add either an active (open) or passive (selective or constructive) iterator. (For a discussion of active versus passive iterators, see, for example, chapter 7 of [Booch, 1987].)

We should also take the following items into account when designing methods for composite objects in general:

- All methods must be primitive methods. (Among other things, allowing encapsulated non-primitive methods increases the chance for object coupling and allows for the possibility of large numbers of encapsulated methods.)

- An object should have, at most, about 24 operations in its interface. (This should be taken as an approximation, not as a "hard and fast" upper limit.) Most well-designed composite objects have fewer. Remember, you must include all inherited operations in this count, e.g., those supplied via mixins.

For *heterogeneous* composite objects, if you find that either you need more than 24 methods, or that some of the "necessary" methods are not primitive, you may have a candidate for a family of objects, you may have a candidate for a kit, you may have component objects at differing levels of abstraction, or you have a poorly-designed object.

If we are designing a *homogeneous* composite object, we have a slight variation on the above. Specifically, if you find that either you need more than 24 methods, or that some of the "necessary" methods are not primitive, you may have a candidate for a family of objects, you may have a candidate for a kit, or you have a poorly designed object.

The number 24 (i.e., our previously-mentioned maximum number of operations advisable in the interface of an object) is *not* a "magic number," i.e., it is *not* a nice-sounding number that has no basis in fact. This suggested upper limit to the number of operations in the public interface for a given object is derived from three different sources.

(Before we begin this discussion, keep in mind that this limit should be used as a "mile marker," not a "micrometer." We are *not* saying, for example, that all objects with 23 operations in their public interface are better than all objects with 25 operations in their interface. This number should be used as a guide, not an absolute standard. Objects with more than 24 operations in their public interface should be subjected to extra scrutiny, but they should not be rejected out of hand.)

The first source is the research done by George Miller ([Miller, 1956]) in the 1950s. Miller was able to quantify one of the limits of the human mind. He knew that, as human beings had to juggle more items simultaneously in their minds, the greater was the likelihood of mistakes. He found that up to 7 ± 2 items, the probability of a mistake was roughly linearly proportional to the number of items involved. For example, if you had to concentrate on 6 items, your probability of making a mistake was roughly twice what it would be if you only had to deal with 3 items. However, as the number of items was increased beyond 7 ± 2, the error rate climbed disproportionately. For example, if you had to deal with 12 items simultaneously, your chances of making a mistake would be significantly more than twice what they were had you been dealing with only 6 items.

Based on the above discussion, you might think that we should limit the number of items in the public interface of an object to a maximum of 9. However, as software engineers, we have found that we can exceed this limit, when necessary, by a significant amount without incurring an unacceptable reliability penalty. In the case of the number of operations in the public interface to an object, this upper limit appears to be between 20 to 24.

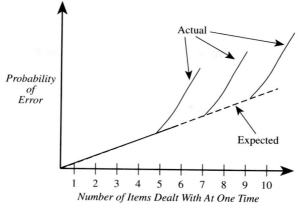

Probability
of
Error

Actual

Expected

1 2 3 4 5 6 7 8 9 10
Number of Items Dealt With At One Time

Figure 3:   **The psychological research done by George Miller in the 1950s revealed that there was a limit to the number of items a human mind could effectively deal with at one time, i.e., 7±2.** Increasing the number of items beyond this point dramatically increased the likelihood of errors.

The second source for the upper limit of 24 operations in the public interface comes from the work of Grady Booch. Booch developed a library of 500 reusable object-oriented components, first in Ada ([Booch, 1987]), and later in C++ ([Booch and Vilot, 1990]). These components represented primarily homogeneous composite objects. Booch observed that the formatted public interfaces for these objects (e.g., package specifications in Ada or header files in C++), with all the comments removed, should take up no more than two printed pages. Abiding by this rule, he found that he seldom exceeded an upper limit of 20 to 24 operations.

The third source of the upper limit comes from my own experience in developing object-oriented components and applications, and from my experiences in providing consulting to my clients who are (and were) developing object-oriented applications in a variety of programming languages.

One of the first things I and my clients noticed was the inverse relationship between the complexity of the public interface for an object and the probability that that object would be reused. Specifically, we found that, if given a choice of (re)using one of several different implementations of the same object, software engineers would consistently pick the object with the simplest interface. (All objects involved in the selection process were written by someone other than the person making the selection.) Even objects with as few as 15 operations in their public interface were often regarded as "overly complex." In short, keeping the number of operations in the public interface for an object to a useful minimal set significantly increased the chances for that object to be reused.

Objects that encompassed application-specific operations in their public interfaces, often exceeded the 20 to 24 upper limit. An application-specific operation is an operation that is necessary for a particular application, but is either not needed, or very likely to require modifications, when the object is reused in other applications. Application-specific operations frequently require unnecessary object coupling, and significantly reduce the cohesion of their encapsulating object. (See chapter 7 of this book.) If you find that you have more than 20 to 24 operations in the public interface to an object, it is very probable that you have included some application-specific operations.

Software engineers sometimes attempt to make one object serve too many purposes. In reality, they have identified one object where there really should be a family of objects. The "excess operations" should really be assigned to the appropriate family members. (See, e.g., [Booch, 1987], [Booch and Vilot, 1990], [Margono and Berard, 1987], and [Russell, 1987].)

When we are identifying methods for an object, we must be sure to include not only the methods that objects *suffer*, but also methods that objects *require*. Often, attention is focused only on the methods that an object suffers, and methods that it requires are completely ignored. A definition of an object is not complete if only the methods that it suffers are defined. The methods that it requires must be defined as well.

When we document methods in an OCS, we separate the suffered methods from the required methods, and the methods from the methods.

State Information

The **state** of an object encompasses both the characteristics of an object, and the current values for those characteristics. We often view the state (sometimes referred to as the "state information") for an object as that information which we can query and/or change via interactions with the object's interface. Specifically, state information is *externally discernible*. Sometimes, however, a system may be impacted by changes in the externally discernible state of an object that are neither detectable nor changeable via the public interface for that object. This occurs with "objects with life."

By definition, an "object with life" (an active object, or actor) is capable of spontaneously changing its own state. Another way of saying this is that, for an object with life, it is possible for the state of the object to be changed without invoking any of the operations in the public interface to the object. However, we are only interested in those spontaneous changes in state which we can detect either via invocation of selector methods in the interface to the object, or that cause the object to interact with other objects.

(Some people use the terms "state" and "value" to mean the same thing. Still others attach special — and different — meanings to each of these terms. We will tend to use them interchangeably.)

Since the concept of state is fundamental to the concept of object-orientation, it is not unusual to see it mentioned in an OCS. However, there are reasons for its specific inclusion. The most common reason is to aid in the understanding and development of methods for the operations in the public interface of the object. For example, suppose that we have identified a suffered method that tests for the equality of two objects. In reality this operation is testing for the equality of the *states* of the two objects.

Some objects define restrictions on the states which they may assume. It is important for the software engineer to identify accurately any explicit restrictions placed on the states which an object may assume. Examples of restrictions include:

- an explicit upper limit to the number of items which may be contained in a homogeneous composite object,

- explicit bounds on the range of values a simple object may take on, and

- an explicit maximum length of time that an object may remain in a specific state.

All state information associated with an object must be documented. This documentation must clearly identify that state information which can be changed spontaneously by the object itself. (Note that state information which is changed spontaneously may also, in some instances, be changed by constructor methods in the software interface to the object.) Each piece of state information should be categorized as one or both of the following:

- changeable via methods in the public interface, or

- changed spontaneously.

The documentation of the state information for an object must also mention all explicit restrictions placed on the states which that object may assume.

We note the following with respect to state information:

- Constants are objects whose state is constant. Examples of constant objects include: empty lists, null items, and hexadecimal bus addresses.

- The same piece of state information may be interpreted in different ways, e.g., there may be two different selectors, number_of_items and is_empty that both query the same piece of state information.

- Some pieces of state information are explicitly maintained by the object, e.g., current address, while others are derived when needed, e.g., current speed.

- Some pieces of state information may have to be constructed by a user of an object, i.e., the user may have to invoke a series of methods in a specified order to obtain the information.

- State information that is changed spontaneously may also be either changeable via a constructor operation in the software interface, or detectable via a selector operation in the software interface.

- Monolithic (i.e., non-composite) objects can have composite state. (For example, a temperature sensor might be enabled/disabled, and would also "know" the current temperature.)

- State information must have some value to its users.

- While the user of an object may query or alter the state of an object, the underlying mechanisms for doing so, i.e., the methods, are unknown to the user.

- State information may be altered or queried by means other than operations in the interface to an object, e.g., hardware may alter the temperature value stored in a temperature_sensor object.

Constants and Exceptions

The last section of each OCS deals with those items in the public interface for an object that are not methods. Although, depending on the implementation mechanisms, an object may have such things as variables and exportable type/class definitions in its interface, we generally restrict this section to the discussion of encapsulated constants and exceptions.

Constants are objects of constant state provided in the public interface of an object. They are intended to be made available to users of the object, and are not considered to be part of state information for the encapsulating object. In some cases, constants are not absolutely necessary, but are provided for the convenience of the user. In other cases, however, constants are a necessity.

As an example of the former, consider a bounded list object that contains a constant representing the maximum number of items that may be placed in the list in its public interface. A user of the list object might determine how many more items can be placed in the list by invoking a method that returns the current number of items in the list and subtracting that number from the constant.

All constants which are exported by the object must be documented. Documentation for a constant must include:

- the name of the constant,

- the value of the constant (in the interest of "information hiding, " the precise value is not absolutely necessary, but there must be an adequate general description of the value), and

- a brief explanation of how the constant is expected (or required) to be used.

Now, let us shift our attention to exceptions. An older technique for the communication of problems is "error codes." A typical scenario for using error codes is:

- one of the parameters returned by a subroutine, or the value returned by a function, is an error code,

- if the value of the error code is zero, there were no detected errors; if the value of the error code is non-zero an error has occurred, and

- sometimes specific errors are indicated by specific values of the error code.

While it was good for routines to have some mechanism for detecting and communicating error conditions, there were two major problems with error codes, i.e.:

1. No one was obligated or forced to check the error codes returned by subprograms.

2. If specific values were assigned to the error code to indicate specific errors, then every program which called the subprogram had to be aware of some, or all, of these specific values, and the meanings of these values. If the values changed (additions, deletions, or modifications), all routines which invoked the subprogram would have to be examined for the impact of the change. Unfortunately, there was often nothing in the interface of the subprogram, with the exception of comments, which could convey the changes.

A mechanism which overcomes much of the negative impact of these problems is exceptions.

> [An exception is] an event that causes suspension of normal program execution.

> — *[IEEE, 1983]*

> An exception is the occurrence of an abnormal condition during the execution of a software element.
>
> — *[Meyer, 1988]*

The term "**exception**" is used to indicate *both* "an abnormal condition" and "the mechanism for notifying the system that an abnormal condition has occurred." In the case of the latter, we refer to the activation of the mechanism as "raising an exception." Thus, when an abnormal condition (i.e., an exception) is encountered, a notification mechanism is activated (i.e., the appropriate exception is raised). Exceptions are usually named (there can be "anonymous exceptions"), and the name of the exception typically reflects the abnormal condition that was detected, e.g., Storage_Error, UNEXPECTED, Overflow, and DivisionByZeroSignal.

Executing a sequence of statements as a *direct* result of a specific exception being raised is referred to as "**handling the exception**." Once an exception is handled, it is no longer active (i.e., it is no longer raised). Most programming languages which support exceptions will also allow a programmer to re-raise an exception, or to raise a new exception, during the handling process. What happens after an exception is handled varies depending on the semantics of the programming language, and on how the source code was written.

The specific sequence of statements which handles the raised exception is referred to as an "**exception handler**." Depending on the programming language, and the design of the handler, an exception handler may handle only one specific exception, or it may be capable of handling a number of different exceptions.

There are two general categories of exceptions, i.e., programming-language-defined and user-defined. In the case of programming-language-defined exceptions, the programming language itself will continually test for error conditions, and raise the appropriate exception when an abnormal condition is detected. A programming language which supports exceptions will identify a set of abnormal (or error) conditions for which it will *raise* (activate) exceptions. Examples of typical abnormal conditions include:

- division by zero,
- an attempt to read past the end of a file,
- an attempt to communicate with a non-existent parallel process, and
- attempting to use or allocate more memory than is available.

Users are often allowed to define their own exceptions. Unlike programming-language-defined exceptions, however, user-defined exceptions normally must be tested for and raised by the programmer. Examples of exceptions that might be created for user-defined objects include:

- Elevator_On_Bottom_Floor
- Out_Of_Bounds
- Temperature_Out_Of_Range
- Device_Not_On_Line

- Sensor_Not_Enabled

Unlike error codes, exceptions cannot be ignored. Still, this does not address the second problem we mentioned, i.e., what about changes to the exceptions. Notice that exceptions are not "buried in the body of the code." Rather, they are encapsulated and visible in the public interface to the object. If we delete an exception, or add a new one, for example, the modifier of the class will publish a new interface that will show any additions or deletions. (In the case of programming-language-defined exceptions, these are known globally.) We speak of the exceptions in the public interface of the object as being "exported" by the object.

Exceptions are often considered necessary for critical applications. See, for example, the discussion in Chapter 9 of [Stroustrup, 1991]. [Borgida, 1986], [Dony, 1988], [Dony, 1990], [Goodenough, 1975], and [Koenig and Stroustrup, 1990] are other examples of the many hundreds of references that discuss exceptions and exception handling.

All exceptions which are exported by the object must be documented. Documentation for an exception must include the name of the exception, and the conditions under which the exception will be raised. It is *not* advisable to specify which methods might cause the exception to be raised, since these might change.

Verification of an OCS

Each OCS must be verified in some manner. This process requires that we explicitly, and at least informally, verify each section of the OCS. Up to this point, we have suggested ways in which each section of the OCS can be verified in isolation. However, a much greater payoff is achieved when each section of the OCS is verified against the other sections. It is very important that both testing and software quality assurance check for consistency among the sections of the OCS.

While each section of the OCS overlaps partially with the other sections, each section contains at least some information not contained in any of the other sections. Therefore, verification of the OCS will involve three major components:

- the verification of the information contained in the OCS against what is known about the corresponding "real world" object,

- a check for consistency of each section of the OCS against all the other sections of the same OCS, and

- the specific verification of that information which is unique to each specific section of the OCS.

Verification of the Precise and Concise Description Section

Earlier, we said that the precise and concise description must contain the following:

- a concise general description of the object

- a list of the operations for the object (one may mention specific methods only for purposes of clarity)

- a list of exceptions associated with the object

- a list of any constants associated with the object

- a list of any variables, constants, and other objects imported by the object

- any explicit restrictions placed on the states which the object may assume

The "general description" part of the "precise and concise description" must accurately connect the software object with the "real world" object that it represents. Graphic, as well as textual, means may be used to accomplish this, e.g., it may be appropriate to show a picture, or other graphical representation, of the "real world" object.

The "operations" section of the precise and concise description must list all of the suffered and required operations. Methods for an operation are mentioned only if necessary, i.e., for clarity. The list of operations should be checked against the graphical representations, operations, and state information sections of the OCS. This list must be complete. (Details of the operations and methods will be covered in the "operations" section of the OCS.)

Any exceptions that will be raised by the object must be mentioned. The conditions necessary to cause each exception to be raised will be described in detail in the "constants and exceptions" of the OCS. The exceptions should be checked against the "operations" and "constants and exceptions" sections of the OCS.

Any constants exported (advertised) by the object must be mentioned. The details for each constant (i.e., what they represent, and how they are intended to be used) are provided in the "constants and exceptions" section of the OCS. The constants should be checked against the information provided in the "constants and exceptions" section of the OCS.

If we are dealing with a metaclass or a parameterized class, the constants, variables, and other objects imported by the object must be addressed in the precise and concise description of the OCS. The following must be present:

- an unambiguous description of each constant, variable, and any other object which is imported by the object (this description must include any specific restrictions that will be placed on each item), and

- a brief, and accurate, description of how each imported constant, variable, and other objects will be used by the importing object.

Each imported object will be associated with at least one required (imported) operation. Therefore, each of these items should be cross-checked against the list of required operations.

A software engineer may place explicit restrictions on the states which an object may assume. These should be mentioned in the precise and concise description, and checked against the more detailed descriptions of the restrictions contained in the "state information" section of the OCS.

Verification of the Graphical Representations Section

Verification of graphical representations involves verification of both the static and dynamic representations. Each of these representations is checked against the information contained in the rest of the OCS. For the static graphical representation:

- Check the composition against that described in the precise and concise description.

- Insure that all component objects are associated with a selector method, a constructor method, or both. (Be aware of the special cases associated with objects with life.)

- Check the components and other characteristics of the object against the state information for that object.

For the dynamic graphical representations:

- Check the states and the state transitions against those described in the precise and concise description.

- Insure that all selectors and constructors are accounted for in the dynamic representations. For constructor methods involving two, or more, instances of the same object, ensure that a Petri net graph has been constructed and is accurate when compared with the operations and methods.

- Check the states of the object against the state information for that object.

- Identify constructor methods which will cause exceptions to be raised when applied to objects in a given state, and check these exceptions against the exceptions listed in the precise and concise description and the constants and exceptions section.

Verification of the Operations Section

For each operation, suffered or required:

- Verify that a method has been specified.

- Verify that each operation was mentioned in the precise and concise description.

For each required operation:

- Verify that the operation is associated with a specific imported object. This information should be in the precise and concise description. (Be aware of the special cases associated with objects with life. Specifically, an object with life may have a required operation that has no corresponding imported object.)

- Identify which suffered operations will use the required operations. (Note: Verification of this information may require a knowledge of the internal structure of the object.)

For each suffered operation:

- If the operation is a constructor, ensure that it is addressed by at least one edge in the state transition diagram(s).

- If the operation is a selector, identify the states in the state transition diagram(s) which the selector can detect, or can be used in combination with other selectors to detect.

- Identify all possible exceptions which may be raised by the invocation of the operation, and check these against those mentioned in the "constants and exceptions" section.

- Verify all suffered operations against the "state information" section.

Verification of the State Information Section

For each piece of state information:

- Ensure that the state information is at least mentioned in the precise and concise description.

- Verify that the state information is consistent with both the static and dynamic graphical representations.

- If the state is not one which is changed spontaneously, it must be either explicitly queried or explicitly changed by one or more suffered operations.

- If the state is one which is changed spontaneously, ensure that it is explicitly referenced in at least one state transition diagram or Petri net graph.

Verification of the Constants and Exceptions Section

For each constant in the public interface:

- Ensure that the constant was mentioned in the precise and concise description.

- Identify the suffered operations that may use the constant, and how the constant may be properly used by these operations.(Be aware of the special cases associated with objects with life. Specifically, an object with life may have an exported constant that is not used by any suffered operation.)

- Ensure that there is a description of both the constant and its intended use.

For each exception:

- Ensure that the exception was mentioned in the precise and concise description.

- Using the dynamic graphical representation, identify all combinations of states and constructor methods which will cause the exception to be raised.

- Identify the specific suffered operations (constructors and selectors) which may raise the exception.

- Ensure that the conditions under which the exception will be raised are precisely defined.

Additional OCS Issues

There are a number of important issues that the software engineer must keep in mind during the design of both individual OCSs and libraries of OCSs.

Each OCS represents (and documents) a single object. However, as with computer hardware, specific circumstances may require specific variations of the object. These variations (we will call them "forms," e.g., [Booch, 1987]) will preserve the basic, object-oriented abstraction while introducing more specialized concepts which will make some "family members" better suited to specific classes of applications.

There will be one complete OCS for each different family member (i.e., each different form). As much as possible, each OCS should be self-contained, and independent of OCSs for other members of the same family. (This is the classic trade-off between "ease of creation" and "ease of use." For example, some software engineers are tempted to create inheritance hierarchies of OCS, and include in an individual OCS only those characteristics that differentiate it from more general OCSs. Unfortunately, this makes understanding an individual OCS more difficult since many "OCSs" may have to be assembled in one place before an individual "OCS" can be understood. A tool that automatically generates a complete OCS from a hierarchy of information is a more recommended approach.)

Most (but not all) of the authors who have proposed "families of components" have also suggested taxonomies (classification schemes) for family members. Very often the elements of a given taxonomy may be combined (within a given set of rules) to define a multitude of forms. (See, e.g., [Margono and Berard, 1987].) However, at present, even the best-defined taxonomies fall far short of describing all possible useful families and family members.

In addition to the need for taxonomies to describe various forms of smaller objects (e.g., classes, metaclasses, and their instances), we will need taxonomies for "kits" and "systems of interacting objects" as well. It has already been demonstrated that at least some of the suggested taxonomies for individual objects will also be appropriate for collections of objects. In any event, we do not yet have a taxonomy, or collection of taxonomies, which covers all known useful variations of objects. (Note: It is highly likely that we will need at least some application-domain-specific taxonomies.)

The chosen taxonomy for objects should be reflected in the name of each specific OCS, e.g., "Bounded List," "Temperature Sensor," "Protected Button," and "Multi-Guarded Un-bounded Managed Graphics Window With Iterators."

"**Conceptual integrity**" means being true to a concept, or, more simply, being consistent. Realizing that an installation may be maintaining a library containing hundreds of OCSs, it is imperative that all OCSs be consistent in style and content. An organization should decide on the specific style and content for an OCS, and that organization's software quality assurance function must ensure that the standard is enforced.

Object-oriented approaches emphasize reusability. Portability is a major component of reusability. Care must be taken in the construction of an OCS to minimize (if not eliminate) all application-, environment-, and domain-specific information. However, a balance must be struck between making an OCS so specific that it is non-portable, and making an OCS so general that its usefulness is diminished.

All OCSs should be created with the intention that they will be reused *without* modifications. A well-designed OCS can be adapted to a specific application through its parameters (i.e., the imported objects, operations, constants, and variables), or through contextual usage. A software engineer should never have to modify an OCS, except under the following circumstances:

- a new form, which conforms to a previously-defined taxonomy, is needed for an object (and even here we are not modifying the original OCS, but, instead, a copy), or

- a highly application-specific variation on an object is needed (again we are modifying a copy of the original OCS).

Remember, anytime an OCS is physically modified, its reliability is greatly impaired, and a significant amount of new work is necessary to test, debug, quality assure, and catalog the newly-modified OCS.

One definition of software **reliability** is the probability that the software will not cause the failure of a system for a specified time under specified conditions. Any potentially unreliable situations (e.g., misuse of suffered operations, inappropriate imported classes) should be identified where appropriate in the OCS. Remember, software reliability must be engineered from the beginning.

Maintainability is a measure of the ease of maintenance for a piece of software. Ideally, a well-constructed and verified OCS will require no maintenance. However, each OCS should be constructed with the idea that it will be changed, and designed so that the impact of any change on any part of the OCS will have a negligible impact on any other parts of the OCS. (See the discussion of "cognitive dissonance" in [Weinberg, 1971].)

The concept of accuracy in an OCS has several dimensions, including:

- Care must be taken so that the OCS accurately reflects its corresponding "real world" object while taking into account any necessary software-related issues.

- The methods used in both the suffered and required operations must be both appropriate, and as accurate as necessary.

- The OCS must supply enough information so that the software engineer can make reasonable estimates as to both the resources needed and the associated costs for the overall system. Software engineers are often called upon to make informed trade-offs.

- The software engineer must have a good deal of confidence that the proposed solution can indeed be constructed within the imposed constraints and will indeed behave as described. The accuracy of the information contained in the OCS is thus essential.

Software safety has been defined as "the probability that conditions that can lead to a mishap (hazard) do not occur, whether or not the intended function is performed." ([Leveson, 1986]) In truth, software safety is very much a function of how an object is used. Specifically, unlike software reliability, software safety cannot be controlled appreciably by the software itself. In creating OCSs, the software engineer must consider situations in which an object might be used in an unsafe manner, and alert users (typically in the precise and concise description) as to the more probable, potentially unsafe usages of an object.

Software security is defined as the degree to which a piece of software protects itself, or is protected, from unauthorized, and sometimes malicious, actions. We live in a time of heightened awareness of the importance of system security. The security of a system is determined, in part, by the security of the components which make up the system. The software engineer should ask himself or herself about the security impact of a particular object, and, where appropriate, mention this impact in the precise and concise description.

We differentiate "garbage collection" (something the underlying implementation does) from "storage reclamation" (something a software engineer can effect). A software engineer is interested in memory management issues for a number of reasons:

- The software engineer may wish to assure consistency in the behavior of an object across a number of different implementations.

- Memory management has an impact on efficiency. For example, there may be a significant amount of overhead associated with dynamic allocation. This impact may be significant enough, in some instances, to be addressed at the OCS level.

- Some systems may preclude the use of software-controlled memory management. This may result in exclusion of use for some objects.

Memory management issues will impact an OCS in several areas:

- The name of the object may reflect memory management capability, or lack thereof.

- The precise and concise description will mention the topic if appropriate.

- Both the required and suffered operations, and their associated methods, will be impacted.

- Storage reclamation will require specific types of state information.

- There may be a need for some memory management specific exceptions.

In more traditionally designed systems, concurrency issues were typically handled at a very high level, and in a centralized location (e.g., in the "main routine"). In object-oriented systems, at least part of the responsibility for handling concurrency is placed in the objects themselves. For example, Booch ([Booch, 1987]) refers to at least three different forms of an object which deal specifically with concurrency issues.

Concurrency issues will impact an OCS in several areas:

- The name of the object may reflect an ability to deal with concurrency, or lack thereof.

- The precise and concise description will mention the topic if appropriate.

- Both the required and suffered operations, and their associated methods will be impacted.

- Concurrency will require the protection of specific types of state information.

- There may be a need for some concurrency-specific exceptions.

Efficiency is often a major consideration in the design of a system. Unfortunately, the implementations of many systems are often needlessly corrupted due to an overemphasis on efficiency. The most common dimensions for efficiency are time and space. Often, one must be traded off against the other.

Efficiency issues will impact an OCS in several areas:

- The name of the object may reflect an emphasis on a particular type of efficiency.

- The precise and concise description will mention the topic if appropriate.

- The outside view of an object, and hence its semantic network, may be impacted by efficiency considerations.

- Both the required and suffered operations, and their associated methods, will be impacted.

- Efficiency considerations may require specific types of state information.

- There may be a need for some efficiency-specific exceptions.

OCSs are (reusable) software, and, hence, must be configuration managed. Configuration management concerns itself with three main issues:

- naming of components,

- tracking of components, and

- tracking of information relating to the tracked components.

(See, e.g., [Ambriola and Bendix, 1989], [Babich, 1986], [Bryan et al., 1980], [Ghezzi et al., 1991], [Morgan, 1988], [Ternes, 1987], and [Thomas and Johnson, 1988].)

Each OCS will have its own change history, and will also have its own associated testing and software quality assurance information. This additional information should be maintained in a manner which makes it easy to associate it with its specific OCS. In addition, once an OCS is created, verified, and quality assured, it may be reused in many different applications. As an organization creates new applications it will be both reusing existing OCSs and creating new ones. This implies that an automated mechanism for storing, retrieving, and tracking OCSs will greatly enhance the object-oriented software engineering process. Issues that need to be considered in the selection or development of such a (configuration management/ reusability) system include:

- Since the OCS contains both graphical and textual information, the system must handle each equally well.

- The system should also be able to easily associate other items with an OCS, e.g., testing information, software quality assurance information, change histories, and application-specific information.

Many times, the information contained in an OCS alone is sufficient to produce a code software version of the object. However, there are times when an OCS will have to be augmented, i.e., with application-specific (i.e., non-reusable, or reusable on a very limited basis) information. This information is often "brought forward" from previously supplied requirements information, but may also come from other sources.

In some cases, two or more alternative object designs are based on a single OCS. (This is especially true in situations where the same OCS will be implemented in more than one programming language, or where the implementation language offers a variety of implementation options.) In turn, one or more source code implementations may be based on each design. All valid alternatives must fit within the constraints specified in both the OCS and in the application-specific information.

Observations on the OCS Creation Process

People have been creating OCSs since 1986, and there is an accumulated body of knowledge on what to expect. For example, the first time a software engineer attempts to create an OCS, the process sometimes takes as long as one or two days. This is primarily due to two reasons. First, there is the impact of the learning process, i.e., the software engineer is learning as well as doing. Second, the process of creating an OCS is often the first time a programmer has been forced to consider an object in isolation, i.e., apart from an actual application. (Of course, for some programmers, it is difficult to think in terms of concepts, rather than in terms of code.) After some practice, though, it is not unusual for a software engineer to develop three to four OCSs over the course of a single day.

The first time software engineers attempt to create an OCS, they will often develop the sections in a sequential manner, i.e., they will develop the precise and concise description first, then the graphical representations section, then the operations section, and so forth. During this process, "flat forehead syndrome" usually develops. For example, the software engineer develops the precise and concise description, and then proceeds to develop the graphical representations section. In the process of creating the graphical representations, the software engineers will often uncover a concept that should have been included in the precise and concise description, or a concept that they specified incorrectly in the precise and concise description. At this point, they hit themselves on the forehead, and return to the precise and concise description to introduce the change.

This process (of uncovering omissions and other errors, and performing the necessary updating of the appropriate sections of the OCS) is repeated as the software engineer progresses sequentially through the OCS. However, by the time the software engineer is finished with his or her first OCS, they are very familiar and comfortable with the object documented by the OCS.

Sometimes I am called upon to investigate problems with an on-going project. A common problem on many projects is the "code first, think later" phenomenon (a process favored by some programmers, and, unfortunately, encouraged by many managers). When I arrive at the project site, it is not uncommon for there to be no documentation whatsoever for any of the individual objects, and very little other documentation. I explain to the programmers and their management that:

- If the designs for individual objects are not well-thought-out, then frequent changes will be necessary and destructive "ripple effects" (i.e., the propagation of change requirements) will abound. Objects should be complete, highly cohesive, and loosely coupled with other objects.

- If there are no specifications, or incomplete specifications, for individual objects, then the black-box testing of these individual objects will be hampered.

- Many software engineers will often have to interface with an object created by another software engineer. Without a complete specification, or with only the (ever changing) source code to go on, this can be difficult.

- The longer an error exists in a system, the more psychological resistance there is to removing the error, and the more expensive it is to actually remove that error. Said another way, error prevention is less expensive, and less dangerous than error removal. Thinking through the design of individual objects is virtually always cheaper than the "code first, think later" approach.

With the (sometimes reluctant) backing of management, I require that no object will be coded until an OCS is first created for that object. In addition, as time and other resources permit, OCSs will be retroactively created for existing "source code objects." At this point, many of the programmers begin complaining loudly about "wasted time." However, after a few weeks of creating and reviewing OCSs, and catching errors early, the complaints usually die down.

Software quality assurance must keep a very close eye on the first OCSs that are produced by a software engineer. Common problems associated with OCS creation are tendencies to:

- *introduce object coupling*: It takes a while for software engineers to grasp the fact that an OCS documents an object in isolation, and that every effort should be made to reduce object coupling. Each OCS should be examined to ensure that any application-, environment-, and programming language-specific items are minimized in (if not totally eliminated from) each OCS.

- *obscure the connection with the "real world object"*: Sometimes a software engineer reduces the description of an object to "algorithms and data structures," i.e., it is difficult to tell from the information contained in the OCS which specific object is being documented. One commonly used trick used to avoid this problem is to require a "dictionary definition" for the object as part of the precise and concise description.

- *be incomplete*: Some programmers are anxious to get through with the documentation and start coding. This often results in sketchy, incomplete OCSs. Although page count is generally a poor indicator of quality, one or two-page, or one-column OCSs are often symptomatic of deeper problems. OCS should also contain complete, grammatically correct sentences.

- *slant the OCS toward a particular programming language*: It is common to hear an argument such as "but we are going to be using C++ anyway — why shouldn't we have a strong programming language flavor to our OCSs?" Arguments against a programming language slant are numerous, and include: avoidance of object coupling, multiple implementations of the same object, software reusability, and ever changing languages and language standards. Object-oriented approaches are supposed to be closer to the real world and farther away from underlying implementations. The more a software engineer can think in terms of engineering and less in terms of code, the better will be the objects designed by that engineer.

- *produce an OCS after, not before, the code for an object has been written*: Except for re-engineering situations, OCSs must be produced and reviewed before coding can begin. OCSs produced after coding has been completed usually have a strong programming language flavor.

- *focus only on "software objects"*: During the early parts of a software development effort, there is a strong tendency on the parts of some software engineers to make arbitrary and ad hoc decisions as to which objects will be implemented in code software. Sometimes OCSs are only created for these objects. While we are not advocating creation of OCSs for all objects, there are some tangible benefits to creating OCSs for "non-software objects," including a better understanding of the overall system, and the distinct possibility that a non-software object on one project may be implemented as a software object on another project.

Another observation commonly made about OCSs is that the sections can be produced in any order. Sometimes, as a learning exercise, more than one person is assigned the task of developing a single OCS, and each is assigned one or more sections of the OCS. When the sections are assembled, differences in understanding and points of view emerge. Generally however, for conceptual integrity reasons, it is not advisable to have more than one person working on the same OCS.

Some software engineers have commented on the redundancy present in the various sections of the OCS. I first inform these individuals that the structure and content of the OCS is market-driven, i.e., the OCS is the way it is (including the redundancy) because of requests from practitioners working on real projects. I also allude to the fact that OCSs are designed with tailoring in mind, and each site can decide what should stay and what should go. Lastly, I mention the fact that no one section of the OCS totally overlaps with any other section of the OCS, i.e., removal of any one section will result in the loss of some information.

Three other reasons commonly cited for the overlap in the sections of the OCS are:

- The very concept of verification implies that there must be some overlapping of information, i.e., one cannot verify an item against another item that shares nothing in common with the first item. Restating the same information in a different form, and then checking for consistency is a commonly used technique to determine if one really understands the given information.

- Different views of the same information can be more meaningful to some people than the original view. For example, many people find graphical representations easier to understand than textual descriptions. However, others have commented that some things that are relatively easy to express and understand in text form, are cumbersome to express graphically.

- Some forms of information are easier to handle in certain situations than are other forms with the "same" informational content. For example, people have commented that it is easier to generate some test cases using a state transition diagram than it would be if all they had was a list of suffered operations.

Summary

We have discussed the history, technical basis, content, and real life experiences associated with OCSs. Based on years of so-called real world experiences, we have found OCSs to be a useful tool in the understanding and development of object-oriented applications. This is over and above their usefulness in documenting reusable object-oriented components.

Bibliography

[Agerwala, 1979]. T. Agerwala, "Putting Petri Nets to Work," *IEEE Computer*, Vol. 12, No. 12, December 1979, pp. 85 - 94.

[Agha, 1986]. G. Agha, *ACTORS, A Model of Concurrent Computation in Distributed Systems*, MIT Press, Cambridge, Massachusetts, 1986.

[Aho et al., 1986]. A.V. Aho, R. Sethi, and J.D. Ullman, *Compilers: Principles, Techniques, and Tools*, Addison-Wesley Publishing Company, Reading, Massachusetts, 1986.

[Alford, 1985]. M. Alford, "SREM at the Age of Eight: The Distributed Computing Design System," *Computer,* Vol. 18, No. 4, April 1985, pp. 36 - 46.

[Ambriola and Bendix, 1989]. V. Ambriola and L. Bendix, "Object-Oriented Configuration Control," *Proceedings of the 2nd International Workshop on Software Configuration Management*, special issue of *Software Engineering Notes*, Vol. 17, No. 7, November 1989, pp. 133 - 136.

[Babich, 1986]. W.A. Babich, *Software Configuration Management*, Addison-Wesley Publishing Company, Reading, Massachusetts, 1986.

[Barr and Feigenbaum, 1981]. A. Barr and E.A. Feigenbaum, Editors, *The Handbook of Artificial Intelligence, Volume 1*, HeurisTech Press, Stanford, California, 1981.

[Bauer and Wossner, 1982]. F.L. Bauer and H. Wossner, *Algorithmic Language and Program Development*, Springer-Verlag, New York, New York, 1982.

[Booch, 1986]. G. Booch, "Object Oriented Development," *IEEE Transactions on Software Engineering,* Vol. SE-12, No. 2, February 1986, pp. 211 - 221.

[Booch, 1987]. G. Booch, *Software Components With Ada*, Benjamin/Cummings, Menlo Park, California, 1987.

[Booch, 1991]. G. Booch, *Object-Oriented Design With Applications*, Benjamin/Cummings, Menlo Park, California, 1991.

[Booch and Vilot, 1990]. G. Booch and M. Vilot, "The Design of the C++ Booch Components," *OOPSLA/ECOOP '90 Conference Proceedings,* special issue of *SIGPLAN Notices*, Vol. 25, No. 10, October 1990, pp. 1 - 11.

[Borgida, 1986]. A. Borgida, "Exceptions in Object-Oriented Languages," *SIGPLAN Notices*, Vol. 21, No. 10, October 1986, pp. 107 - 119.

[Borgida et al., 1985]. A. Borgida, S. Greenspan, and J. Mylopoulos, "Knowledge Requirements as the Basis for Requirements," *IEEE Computer,* Vol. 18, No. 4, April 1985, pp. 82 - 91.

[Borning, 1986]. A.H. Borning, "Class Versus Prototypes in Object-Oriented Languages," *Proceedings of the 1986 Fall Joint Computer Conference*, IEEE Catalog Number 86CH2345-7, IEEE Computer Society Press, Washington, D.C., 1986, pp 36 - 40.

[Bruno and Balsamo, 1986]. G. Bruno and A. Balsamo, "Petri Net-Based Object-Oriented Modeling of Distributed Applications," *OOPSLA '86 Conference Proceedings,* special issue of *SIGPLAN Notices*, Vol. 21, No. 11, November 1986, pp. 284 - 293.

[Bruno and Marchetto, 1985]. G. Bruno and G. Marchetto, "A Methodology Based on High-Level Petri Nets for the Specification and Design of Control Systems," *Proceedings of the Third International Workshop on Software Specification and Design*, August 1985, IEEE Catalog No. 85 CH2138-6, IEEE Computer Society Press, Washington, D.C., pp. 30 - 34.

[Bryan et al., 1980]. W. Bryan, C. Chadbourne and S. Siegel, Editors, *Tutorial: Software Configuration Management*, IEEE Computer Society Press (catalog number EHO-169-3), Silver Spring, Maryland, 1980.

[Chambers and Ungar, 1989]. C. Chambers and D. Ungar, "Customization: Optimizing Compiler Technology for Self, a Dynamically-Typed Object-Oriented Language," *SIGPLAN Notices*, Vol. 24, No. 7, July 1989, pp. 146 - 160.

[Chambers et al., 1989]. C. Chambers, D. Ungar, and E. Lee, "An Efficient Implementation of Self, a Dynamically-Typed Object-Oriented Language Based on Prototypes," *OOPSLA '89 Conference Proceedings,* special issue of *SIGPLAN Notices*, Vol. 24, No. 10, October 1989, pp. 49 - 70.

[Chedgey et al., 1987]. C. Chedgey, S. Kerney, and H.-J. Kugler, "Using VDM in an Object-Oriented Development Method for Ada Software," *VDM '87 VDM — A Formal Method At Work, Proceedings of the 1987 European Symposium*, Springer Verlag Lecture Notes On Computer Science, Number 252, pp. 63 - 76.

[Coad and Yourdon, 1990]. P. Coad and E. Yourdon, *OOA — Object-Oriented Analysis*, 2nd Edition, Prentice Hall, Englewood Cliffs, New Jersey, 1990.

[Coleman et al., 1992]. D. Coleman, F. Hayes, and S. Bear, "Introducing Objectcharts or How to Use Statecharts in Object-Oriented Design," *IEEE Transactions on Software Engineering*, Vol. 16, No. 1, January 1992, pp. 9 - 18.

[Dony, 1988]. C. Dony, "An Object-Oriented Exception Handling System for an Object-Oriented Language," *ECOOP '88: Proceedings of the European Conference on Object-Oriented Programming, Lecture Note on Computer Science, Volume 322*, Springer Verlag, New York, New York, 1988, pp. 146 - 161.

[Dony, 1990]. C. Dony, "Exception Handling and Object-Oriented Programming: Towards a Synthesis," *OOPSLA/ECOOP '90 Conference Proceedings,* special issue of *SIGPLAN Notices*, Vol. 25, No. 10, October 1990, pp. 322 - 330.

[Eckart, 1987]. J.D. Eckart, "Iteration and Abstract Data Types," *SIGPLAN Notices*, Vol. 22, No. 4, April 1987, pp. 103 - 110.

[Gallimore et al., 1989]. R. Gallimore, D. Coleman, and V. Stravridou, *Computer Journal*, "UMIST OBJ: A Language for Executable Program Specifications," *Computer Journal*, Vol. 32, No. 5, October 1989, pp. 413 - 421.

[Ghezzi et al., 1989]. C. Ghezzi, D. Mandrioli, S. Morasca, and M. Pezze, "A General Way to Put Time in Petri Nets," *Proceedings of the Fifth International Workshop On Software Specification and Design,* May 19-20, 1989, Pittsburgh, Pennsylvania, IEEE Computer Society Press, Washington, D.C., May 1989, pp. 60 - 67.

[Ghezzi et al., 1991]. C. Ghezzi, M. Jazayeri, and D. Mandrioli, *Fundamentals of Software Engineering*, Prentice Hall, Englewood Cliffs, New Jersey, 1991.

[Goguen, 1984]. J.A. Goguen, "Parameterized Programming," *IEEE Transactions on Software Engineering*, Vol. SE-10, No. 5, September 1984, pp. 528 - 543.

[Goldberg and Robson, 1983]. A. Goldberg and D. Robson, *Smalltalk-80: The Language and Its Implementation*, Addison-Wesley, Reading, Massachusetts, 1983.

[Goodenough, 1975]. J. Goodenough, "Exception Handling: Issues and a Proposed Notation," *Communications of the ACM*, Vol. 18, No. 12, pp. 683 - 696.

[Grogono and Bennett, 1989]. P. Grogono and A. Bennett, "Polymorphism and Type Checking in Object-Oriented Languages," *SIGPLAN Notices*, Vol. 24, No. 11, November 1989, pp. 109 - 115.

[Harel, 1987]. D. Harel, "Statecharts: A Visual Formalism for Complex Systems," *Science of Computer Programming*, Vol. 8, No. 3, June 1, 1987, pp. 231 - 274.

[Harel et al., 1987]. D. Harel, A. Pnueli, J.P. Schmidt, and R. Sherman, "On the Formal Semantics of Statecharts," *Proceedings of the Second IEEE Symposium on the Logic of Computer Science*, 1987, pp. 54 - 64.

[Hatley and Pirbhai, 1987]. D. J. Hatley and I. A. Pirbhai, *Strategies for Real-Time System Specification*, Dorset House Publishing Company, New York, New York, 1987.

[Hayes and Coleman, 1991]. F. Hayes and D. Coleman, "Coherent Models for Object-Oriented Analysis," *OOPSLA '91 Conference Proceedings,* special issue of *SIGPLAN Notices*, Vol. 26, No. 11, November 1991, pp. 171 - 183.

[Helm et al., 1990]. R. Helm, I.M. Holland, and D. Gangopadhyay, "Contracts: Specifying Behavioral Compositions in Object-Oriented Systems," *OOPSLA/ECOOP '90 Conference Proceedings,* special issue of *SIGPLAN Notices*, Vol. 25, No. 10, October 1990, pp. 169 - 180.

[Hoare, 1985]. C.A.R. Hoare, *Communicating Sequential Processes*, Prentice Hall, Englewood Cliffs, New Jersey, 1985.

[IEEE, 1983]. IEEE, *IEEE Standard Glossary of Software Engineering Terminology*, The Institute of Electrical and Electronic Engineers, New York, New York, 1983.

[Jackson, 1985]. M.I. Jackson, "Developing Ada Programs Using the Vienna Development Method (VDM)," *Software Practice and Experience*, Vol. 15, No. 3, March 1985, pp. 305 - 318.

[Jones, 1986]. C.B. Jones, *Systematic Software Development Using VDM,* Prentice Hall, Englewood Cliffs, New Jersey, 1986.

[Koenig and Stroustrup, 1990]. A. Koenig and B. Stroustrup, "Exception Handling for C++," *Journal of Object-Oriented Programming*, Vol. 3, No. 2, July/August 1990, pp. 16 - 33.

[LaLonde et al., 1986]. W.R. LaLonde, D.A. Thomas, and J.R. Pugh, "An Exemplar Based Smalltalk," *OOPSLA '86 Conference Proceedings,* special issue of *SIGPLAN Notices*, Vol. 21, No. 11, November 1986, pp. 322 - 330.

[Lamb, 1990]. D.A. Lamb, "Specification of Iterators," *IEEE Transactions on Software Engineering*, Vol. 16, No. 12, December 1990, pp. 1352 - 1360.

[Leveson, 1986]. N.G. Leveson, "Software Safety: What, Why, and How," *ACM Computing Surveys*, Vol. 18, No. 2, June 1986, pp. 125 - 164.

[Lieberman, 1986]. H. Lieberman, "Using Prototypical Objects to Implement Shared Behavior In Object-Oriented Systems," *OOPSLA '86 Conference Proceedings,* special issue of *SIGPLAN Notices*, Vol. 21, No. 11, November 1986, pp. 214 - 223.

[Liskov and Zilles, 1975]. B. Liskov and S.N. Zilles, "Specification Techniques for Data Abstraction," *IEEE Transactions on Software Engineering*, Vol. SE-1, No. 1, March 1975, pp. 7 - 19.

[Margono and Berard, 1987]. J. Margono and E.V. Berard, "A Modified Booch's Taxonomy for Ada Generic Data-Structure Components and Their Implementation," *Ada Components: Libraries and Tools - Proceedings of the Ada-Europe International Conference,* Stockholm, 26-28 May, 1987, Edited by S. Tafvelin, Cambridge University Press, Cambridge, United Kingdom, pp. 61 - 74.

[Meyer, 1988]. B. Meyer, *Object-Oriented Software Construction*, Prentice Hall, Englewood Cliffs, New Jersey, 1988.

[Miller, 1956]. G. Miller, "The Magical Number Seven, Plus or Minus Two: Some Limits On Our Capacity for Processing Information," *The Psychological Review*, Vol. 63, No. 2, March 1956, pp. 81-97.

[Morgan, 1988]. T.M. Morgan, "Configuration Management and Version Control in the Rational Programming Environment," in *Ada In Industry: Proceedings of the Ada-Europe International Conference,* Munich, 7-9 June, 1988, Cambridge University Press, Cambridge, United Kingdom, 1988, pp. 17 - 28.

[Peterson, 1977]. J.L. Peterson, "Petri Nets," *ACM Computing Surveys*, Vol. 9, No. 3, September 1977, pp. 223 - 252.

[Peterson, 1981]. J.L. Peterson, *Petri Net Theory and the Modeling of Systems*, Prentice Hall, Englewood Cliffs, New Jersey, 1981.

[Prieto-Diaz and Arango, 1991]. R. Prieto-Diaz and G. Arango, Editors, *Domain Analysis and Software Systems Modeling*, IEEE Computer Society Press, Los Alamitos, California, 1991.

[Rational, 1986]. Rational, Inc., *Large-System Development and Rational Subsystems*, Document Control Number 6004, Rational, Inc., Mountain View, California, November, 1986.

[Reisig, 1985]. W. Reisig, *Petri Nets: An Introduction*, Springer-Verlag, New York, New York, 1985.

[Rumbaugh et al., 1991]. J. Rumbaugh, M. Blaha, W. Premerlani, F. Eddy, and W. Lorensen, *Object-Oriented Modeling and Design*, Prentice Hall, Englewood Cliffs, New Jersey, 1991.

[Russell, 1987]. G. E. Russell, "Experiences Implementing a Reusable Data-Structure Component Taxonomy." *Proceedings of the Joint Ada Conference, Fifth National Conference on Ada Technology and Washington Ada Symposium,* March 16-19, 1987, U.S. Army Communications-Electronics Command, Fort Monmouth, New Jersey, pp. 8 - 18.

[Schalkoff, 1990]. R.J. Schalkoff, *Artificial Intelligence: An Engineering Approach*, McGraw-Hill Publishing Company, New York, New York, 1990.

[Shaw, 1981]. M. Shaw, Editor, *Alphard: Form and Content*, Springer-Verlag, New York, New York, 1981.

[Shaw et al., 1981]. M. Shaw, W.A. Wolf, and R. London, "Abstraction and Verification in Alphard: Iteration and Generators," *Alphard: Form and Content*, Springer-Verlag, New York, New York, 1981, pp. 73 - 116.

[Shlaer and Mellor, 1992]. S. Shlaer and S.J. Mellor, *Object Lifecycles: Modeling the World In States*, Yourdon Press: Prentice Hall, Englewood Cliffs, New Jersey, 1992.

[Snyder, 1986]. A. Snyder, "Encapsulation and Inheritance in Object-Oriented Programming Languages," *OOPSLA '86 Conference Proceedings,* special issue of *SIGPLAN Notices*, Vol. 21, No. 11, November 1986, pp. 38 - 45.

[Spivey, 1988]. J.M. Spivey, *Understanding Z: A Specification Language and Its Formal Semantics*, Cambridge University Press, Cambridge, United Kingdom, 1988.

[Spivey, 1989]. J.M. Spivey, *The Z Notation: A Reference Manual*, Prentice Hall, Englewood Cliffs, New Jersey, 1989.

[Stefik and Bobrow, 1985]. M. Stefik and D.G. Bobrow, "Object-Oriented Programming: Themes and Variations," *The AI Magazine*, Vol. 6, No. 4, Winter 1985, pp. 40 - 62.

[Stroustrup, 1991]. B. Stroustrup, *The C++ Programming Language,* Second Edition, Addison-Wesley, Reading, Massachusetts, 1991.

[Ternes, 1987]. D. H. Ternes, "Developmental Software Configuration and Integration in a Large Ada Project." *Using Ada: Proceedings of the 1987 ACM SIGAda International Conference on the Ada Programming Language,* Boston, Massachusetts, December 9-11, pp. 65 - 74.

[Thomas and Johnson, 1988]. D. Thomas and K. Johnson, "Orwell: A Configuration Management System for Team Programming," *SIGPLAN Notices*, Vol. 23, No. 11, November 1988, pp. 135 - 141.

[Ungar and Smith, 1987]. D. Ungar and R.B. Smith, "Self: The Power of Simplicity," *OOPSLA '87 Conference Proceedings,* special issue of *SIGPLAN Notices*, Vol. 22, No. 12, December 1987, pp. 227 - 242.

[Weinberg, 1971]. G. M. Weinberg, *The Psychology of Computer Programming*, Van Nostrand Reinhold Company, New York, New York, 1971.

[Winston, 1984]. P.H. Winston, *Artificial Intelligence,* Second Edition, Addison-Wesley, Reading, Massachusetts, 1984.

[Zdonik, 1986]. S.B. Zdonik, "Why Properties are Objects or Some Refinements of 'is-a'," *Proceedings of the 1986 Fall Joint Computer Conference*, IEEE Catalog Number 86CH2345-7, IEEE Computer Society Press, Washington, D.C., 1986, pp 41 - 47.

9   Large Object-Oriented Entities (Systems of Objects)

To put it quite bluntly: as long as there were no machines, programming was no problem at all; when we had a few weak computers, programming was a mild problem, and now we have gigantic computers, programming has become an equally gigantic problem.

> — *Edsger Dijkstra [Dijkstra, 1972].*

The programming and software engineering literature is almost uniform in agreeing that large programming systems tend to be more expensive to produce and to have longer schedules than do smaller programs.

> — *Capers Jones [Jones, 1986]*

As a result of structural complexity, it is notoriously difficult for someone unfamiliar with a large system to gain an understanding of it and notoriously easy to make a modification to a system that has unexpected and devastating consequences. These problems can be ameliorated by documentation that makes global structure visible and can thus impart an understanding of overall structure.

> — *Harold Ossher [Ossher, 1987]*

Prologue

A colleague of mine is fond of telling the following story:

The family that lives next door to you has a 10 year old boy. For the boy's birthday, the parents buy him a hammer, a hand saw, a box of nails, and some boards of varying sizes. The child later uses these items to build a simple 'tree fort' in a large tree in the family's back yard.

The boy seems to have a natural talent for woodworking, so on his fifteenth birthday, he receives a power saw, and several other 'professional' woodworking tools. During one of your visits with his parents, you suggest (only slightly in jest) that you would like him to build a deck in your back yard. You offer to buy the materials and to pay a fixed fee for his efforts. He accepts the offer.

Being more sophisticated than he was in his earlier years, he submits a few trial drawings that detail the general shape and total usable surface area for the deck. You select one and he begins work. Half way through his construction efforts, he acknowledges that the project was more involved than he had anticipated, but completes the work only two weeks later than he had originally planned.

Once the deck is completed, he invites you out to examine the finished product. You notice some small imperfections, e.g., the deck has a noticeable tilt, and some of the planks are further apart than they should be in some places. Still, while the deck will not win any design or construction awards, it is perfectly serviceable.

The boy's parents, however, are overly proud of the boy's magnum opus. They suggest that next year, their son will be designing skyscrapers that will rival the Sears Tower in downtown Chicago.

There is usually a chuckle at this point in the story. This is because the listeners know that it is highly unlikely that the boy will be designing any serious buildings. There are at least four years of university training in architecture, and a significant apprenticeship that must come first. Even then, there will probably be some competition to determine the best design for a given building.

The major points here are the stark and very real differences between a toy application (e.g., the deck) and a real application (e.g., a skyscraper), and between the skills of an untrained amateur and a seasoned and educated professional.

In the development of software, people seem particularly oblivious to these distinctions. If a person is familiar with the syntax and semantics of a given programming language, and has written some relatively small applications, this person is not necessarily qualified to design or otherwise develop large and/or critical software. Some managers do not realize that there is a great deal of difference between the skill set of a coder and the skill set of a systems designer. They appear to cling to the very outdated notion of the "one-size-fits-all" programmer, i.e., any software practitioner can perform any function on any project.

These problems are exacerbated in the development of large software applications. Techniques that seem inconsequential on small, non-critical projects can be deadly on large and/or critical projects. Concepts that might be considered "overkill" on a small project are absolutely essential for a large project.

The Impact of Size

Fred Brooks, Jr. was one of the first to document many of the problems associated with large software system development. In his book, *The Mythical Man-Month* ([Brooks, 1975]), he details the lessons he learned in the development of IBM's OS/360 in the mid-1960s, e.g.:

- "Adding manpower to a late software project makes it later."

- "I will contend that conceptual integrity is the most important consideration in systems design. It is better to have a system omit certain anomalous features and improvements, but to reflect one set of design ideas, than to have one that contains many good but independent and uncoordinated ideas."

By the early 1970s, the increasingly larger size of software applications was already a major concern (e.g., [Dijkstra, 1972]). The oft-cited article by DeRemer and Kron ([DeRemer and Kron, 1976]) showed that by the mid-1970s people were already looking for strategies and techniques that would be applicable to large systems development. This work has continued in earnest, e.g., [Goguen, 1986], [Jacobson, 1986], and [Purtilo et al., 1991].

Today, we have a better appreciation of why the engineering of large software systems is significantly more difficult than we might expect. (See, e.g., [Boehm, 1981] and [Glass, 1982].) Some of the more commonly cited reasons (see also chapter 4 of this book) include:

- as the size of the software product goes up, so does the error density,

- as the size of the software product goes up, new types of activities become necessary,

- as the size of the software product goes up, the number of necessary human interactions increases dramatically, and

- the overall complexity of software component interactions increases dramatically with system size.

These, and other, factors significantly contribute to the markedly lower programmer productivity rates observed in large systems development. (See, e.g., [Jones, 1978] and [Jones, 1986].)

Nowadays, we expect large software engineering efforts to be different from small software engineering efforts. Larger efforts not only require more personnel, but also additional types of personnel. Larger efforts require more formalized approaches than do smaller, ad hoc efforts. Finally, the architectures, and the components that make up these architectures will be different for large software products — when compared to small software products.

Much of the work on large software systems has focused on three areas:

- approaches for the design and/or development of large systems, e.g., [Gallo et al., 1989] and [Purtilo et al., 1991],

- mechanisms for describing the global architecture of large systems, e.g., [Ossher, 1984], [Ossher, 1987], and [Ossher, 1989], and

- ways to identify, specify, and design large software components, e.g., Chapter 17 of [Booch, 1987], [Buhr and Zarnke, 1988], [Hailpern and Ossher, 1990], [Helm et al., 1990], [Jacobson, 1986], [Parnas et al., 1984], and [Rational, 1986].

In this chapter, we will focus on the last point. We will first attempt to understand the nature of large object-oriented components, and then briefly address some design and specification issues for these entities.

Large Software Components

The size of the largest components in any system is usually directly proportional to the size of the overall system, i.e., the larger the overall system, the larger will be the size of its largest components. For example, while it would be impossibly difficult to think of General Motors strictly in terms of the myriad of parts that make up each of its automobiles and trucks, it is fairly easy to think of the company in terms of five car lines, i.e., Chevrolet, Buick, Oldsmobile, Pontiac, and Cadillac.

In the late 1940s and very early 1950s, programmers had to deal with individual lines of code. This meant that, if the system was comprised of 500 lines of code, the programmer had to deal with 500 individual items. Soon, however, the use of subprograms allowed lines of code to be bundled into more manageable units.

A **subprogram** is a programming-language-defined encapsulation mechanism that allows programmers to package one or more lines of code into a single unit. This single unit, in turn, can be addressed as a monolithic entity within a larger program. Subprograms usually have a single (hopefully well-defined) interface, and programmers need not concern themselves with the details of the underlying implementations of the subprograms they use. (We note, however, that not all programming languages provide a significant amount of information hiding for their subprogram, e.g., the implementation of a Cobol paragraph is much more visible than the implementation of a Fortran subroutine. Further, most programming languages, unfortunately, provide mechanisms for violating both the information hiding and encapsulation of subprograms.) Examples of subprograms include Fortran's subroutines and functions, Pascal's procedures, Cobol's paragraphs, and C's functions.

Subprograms allow programmers to reduce the overall complexity of software systems. For example, 100 subroutines each containing 100 lines of code are much easier to handle than 10,000 individual lines of code. Well-designed subprograms can reduce overall development time, and simplify the testing, integration, and configuration management processes.

Starting in the mid-1960s, programming languages began to emerge that allowed for larger groupings than mere subprograms, e.g., Simula's classes ([Dahl and Nygaard, 1966]), Smalltalk's classes ([Goldberg and Robson, 1983]), Self's prototypes ([Ungar and Smith, 1987]), Modula's modules ([Wirth, 1983]), and Ada's packages ([ARM, 1983]). These larger units can physically encapsulate one or more subprograms and other programming language items, e.g., constants, exceptions, and state information representation mechanisms. Although often exclusively associated with the object-oriented programming languages, these larger units also show up in "object-based" programming languages, e.g., Ada, as well. (See [Wegner, 1990].)

As with subprograms, these larger units are recognized syntactically and semantically as single entities by their respective programming language. Also like subprograms, the larger units present a public interface to the outside world, and hide their underlying implementations, often using varying degrees of information hiding. The larger program units, if properly handled, can reduce overall development time as well as integration time. Unfortunately they can also mildly complicate the configuration management process, and frequently require special testing strategies.

Unlike subprograms the semantics of their respective programming languages often allows these larger units to make some of their encapsulated characteristics selectively available to other program units. The semantics of some programming languages requires that software engineers specify each of the individual characteristics they wish to acquire from the larger units. Other programming languages, i.e., object-oriented programming languages, can automatically provide a pre-determined set of information via mechanisms such as inheritance (e.g., [Sakkinen, 1989]) or delegation (e.g., [Borning, 1986] and [Liberman, 1986]).

Even though these larger program units allow for more manageable software systems, they too have their limits. As progressively larger object-oriented systems were constructed, items such as classes proved insufficiently large. People sought out other, object-oriented mechanisms to aid them in conquering complexity. Some have proposed further programming language enhancements such as "patterns" in BETA ([Kristensen et al., 1987]). In this article, however, we will restrict ourselves to two distinct varieties of "systems of objects."

A **system of objects** is defined as two or more interacting or interrelated, non-nested objects. (We exclude simple aggregations, i.e., composite objects, from our definition of systems of objects.) Systems of objects fall into two general categories:

- **kits**, which are collections of objects (e.g., classes, metaclasses, non-class instances, unencapsulated composite operations, other kits, and systems of interacting objects) all of which support a single, large, coherent, object-oriented concept, e.g., windows, switches, and insurance policies. There may indeed be some physical connection among some of the members of a given kit. However, kits are "granular," i.e., while all the components of a kit are logically related, there are very few physical connections that bind them together.

- **systems of interacting objects**, which are collections of objects (e.g., classes, metaclasses, non-class instances, unencapsulated composite operations, kits, and other systems of interacting objects) all of which support a single, large, coherent, object-oriented concept, and in which there must be a direct or indirect physical connection between any two arbitrary objects within the collection. Further, systems of interacting objects have at least one internal, independently executing thread of control. Lastly, systems of interacting objects may exhibit multiple, completely-disjoint public interfaces.

Peter Coad ([Coad and Yourdon, 1990]) describes "subjects" in a manner that makes them somewhat resemble kits. Sally Shlaer and Steve Mellor ([Shlaer and Mellor, 1992]) talk about "domains," although not all domains are based on a single, coherent, object-oriented concept. Further, "domain" is more commonly associated with "domain analysis," e.g., [Prieto-Diaz and Arango, 1991]. Booch and others (e.g., [Booch, 1987], [Booch, 1991], [Morgan, 1988], and [Rational, 1986]) describe "subsystems." However, the stated definitions and use of "subsystems" encompass systems of interacting objects as well as kits. [Helm et al., 1990] refers to systems of interacting objects as "behavioral compositions." Rebecca Wirfs-Brock, and others, have defined the concept of "frameworks" (e.g., [Wirfs-Brock et al., 1990]). Frameworks, as they are defined, most closely resemble kits.

Kits

a set of tools, articles for special use, parts to be assembled etc.

— [Mish, 1988]

In the early 1980s, Rational, Inc. was developing the environment for their first machine. Although they were attempting to use an object-oriented approach, they found that, as their system grew larger and larger, classes, metaclasses, parameterized classes, and non-class instances were not enough. They needed something to handle very large object-oriented concepts. Specifically, Rational was interested in concepts that involved:

- more than one non-nested object,

- more than just individual classes, metaclasses, parameterized classes, and their instances, and

- components that were bound together much more in a *logical* manner than in a physical manner.

Rational referred to their concept as "subsystems" (e.g., [Rational, 1986]). Later, when Grady Booch joined Rational, he formalized the concept, e.g., chapter 17 of [Booch, 1987]. Booch has often referred to subsystems as the concept of a class taken to the next higher level of abstraction, e.g., subsystems are to classes as classes are to methods.

There are, however, many problems with the name "subsystems." First, most software engineers seldom associate the term exclusively with object-oriented concepts. Second, both Rational and Booch often used the term to refer to both library-like collections and large, physically cohesive system components. Therefore, we have defined the concept of a "kit" to more accurately capture the spirit of a collection of (generally) loosely coupled items that support some well-defined, large object-oriented concept.

Consider, for example, the concept of a dialog window. A single dialog window class in isolation does not fully define the concept of a dialog window. We must also include classes for radio buttons, scroll bars (both vertical and horizontal), push buttons, editable text, static text, pictures, check boxes, and pop-up menus, to more fully capture the idea of dialog windows. Further, notice that all dialog windows do not contain all of the above items. Still, we would like to have these objects at our disposal when we are called upon to fashion a new instance of the dialog window class. This collection could quite properly be called a "dialog window kit."

Now, consider what we might place in a "Gregorian date kit." In addition to a parameterized Gregorian date class, we might include several different month classes, day classes, and year classes. We could also include a number of unencapsulated composite operations (these are referred to as "free subprograms" in [Booch, 1991]). The unencapsulated composite operations might accomplish such things as converting a Gregorian date to a Julian date, incrementing the value of a particular date by a specified number of days, and decrementing the value of a particular date by a specified number of months.

Kits have three main parts:

- an **export** (or visible) part that contains classes, metaclasses, parameterized classes, non-class instances, systems of interacting objects, other kits, and unencapsulated composite operations that are to be made available to the clients of the kit,

- a **body** (or hidden) part that contains classes, metaclasses, parameterized classes, non-class instances, systems of interacting objects, other kits, and unencapsulated composite operations, that are necessary to support those items in the export (or visible) part, as well as the overall object-oriented concept, and

- an **import** (or requirements) part that describes the objects and unencapsulated composite operations that are necessary to support the kit, i.e., they are the parameters for the "instantiation" of the kit.

People sometimes confuse kits with smaller objects, e.g., classes. Kits, however, differ from classes in the following ways:

- Kits are not supported by most commonly used programming languages (although, e.g., the Rational Environment does automatically support the concept). Therefore, their structure and interfaces can often only be supported in a logical (as opposed to physical) manner. This also implies:

  - Kits cannot be compiled as a recognized programming language unit.

  - Kits cannot be referred to as a unit within a given programming language.

  - Kits cannot inherit characteristics as a unit, although their individual components may.

  - Kits cannot provide inheritable characteristics as a unit, although their individual components may.

- Kits are, by definition, much larger than classes. For example, in a given programming language, kits may be a factor of 20-50 times larger than a class in the same language, in terms of lines of source code.

- Kits cannot provide items which are not in the form of stand-alone compilation units. Specifically, one should be able to access easily the individual object code for any item advertised in the export (visible) part of the kit. Items such as unencapsulated exceptions are therefore usually not provided by kits.

- Kits may offer items in their interface which may not normally be offered by classes, e.g., classes, other kits, and systems of interacting objects.

A common misconception is that kits may contain only source code. Specifications for objects (e.g., Object and Class Specifications) and unencapsulated composite operations can (and should) also be included. Software engineers should also consider including testing information, software quality assurance information, graphical representations, and any other information that will enhance the understandability and completeness of the kit. Some software engineers define a **kit specification** as all the source code for kit components, any supporting documentation for these components, and any other documentation necessary to understand the structure and use for the kit.

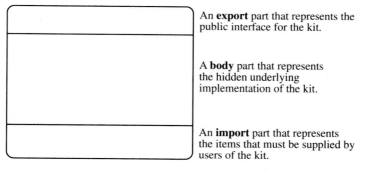

An **export** part that represents the public interface for the kit.

A **body** part that represents the hidden underlying implementation of the kit.

An **import** part that represents the items that must be supplied by users of the kit.

Figure 1:   **The original graphic for kits (i.e., Booch's graphic for a "subsystem") showed three parts for a kit.** One of the purposes that this graphic served was to differentiate kits from more traditional object-oriented program units, which are usually thought of as having two parts.

Kit Name

Dialog Window Kit

Gregorian Date Kit

Figure 2:   **Schematic graphics for kits show only the name of the kit within a rectangle with rounded corners.** Since the public (visible) interface for a given kit can be extremely complex, seldom is it advisable to show this interface graphically.

At this point, someone could quite reasonably suggest that it might be simpler just to encapsulate composite methods within the relevant object. This suggestion is further bolstered by the feeling of some people that any unencapsulated methods are undesirable in a "truly object-oriented system." Before we can explore this idea, we need to establish some definitions:

- A **primitive method** is any method that cannot be implemented simply, efficiently, and reliably without direct knowledge of the underlying implementation of the object in which it is encapsulated. A **composite method** is any method constructed from two or more primitive methods — sometimes from different objects.

- A **sufficient set of primitive methods** for an object is the minimum set of primitive operations to accomplish all necessary work with the object. (For any one object (or category of objects) there may be multiple sufficient sets.) Sufficient sets of primitive methods may be augmented with additional primitive methods so that the augmented set of primitive methods more fully captures the abstraction represented by the object. We call such augmented sets of methods for a given object **complete sets of primitive methods**.

- An **unencapsulated composite operation** ("free subprogram") is any method that is not physically encapsulated (syntactically and semantically) within a specific object. (For a different perspective, see the discussions of "generic functions" in [Keene, 1989] and [Lawless and Miller, 1991].)

When we design any object we are often concerned with both reliability (e.g., [Malaiya and Srimani, 1990], [Musa et al., 1990], and [Myers, 1976]) and reusability (e.g., [Biggerstaff and Perlis, 1989a], [Biggerstaff and Perlis, 1989b], [Prieto-Diaz and Arango, 1991], and [Tracz, 1988]). (Of course, we are also concerned with other items, e.g., modifiability, efficiency, and understandability.) The following considerations will impact the design of our individual objects:

- The number of primitive methods for any object is typically bounded, and complete sets of primitive methods for any given object seldom include more than about 24 methods, whereas the number of composite methods for any given object is typically unbounded. (See chapter 8 of this book.)

- As the number of encapsulated methods increases, the reliability, reusability, and sometimes even the efficiency, of an object decrease.

- Composite methods are often application-specific, whereas primitive methods are object-specific. This means that objects containing composite methods are more likely to change, and are more vulnerable to changes within the application itself.

- Changes can, and often do, have a negative impact on the reliability of any software. (See, e.g., [Weinberg, 1983].)

If we are building only small, non-critical applications, and we are not very concerned with reusability, reliability, modifiability, and understandability, then the nature of the methods encapsulated in any one object are not of great concern to us. However, this is seldom the case.

Our problem can be stated as follows:

- We want to be able to reuse objects unchanged from application to application, and, for that matter, even within the same application.

- At the same time, we want to keep individual objects practical and manageable. Objects that encapsulate many methods will be difficult to understand, have questionable reliability, and may (depending on development system capabilities) not be acceptably efficient. Therefore, we have an interest in keeping the number of methods for any one object to a minimum, while striving to make the same object reusable without changes. Said another way we want each object to have a well-chosen complete set of primitive methods.

- We also want to have a means of preserving and managing potentially reusable *composite* methods. However, given the previous points, it does not seem advisable to do this by encapsulating them in a particular object.

There have been a number of proposed solutions for this problem. One common suggestion is to have a "pure" general object (i.e., an object that contains only a complete set of primitive methods), and to add the composite methods in specializations of the object. This is an example of poor software engineering, e.g.:

- Specializations are not intended to be used simply as configuration management tools, i.e., we need a better reason for creating a specialization (e.g., a subclass, derived class, child class, or extension) than simply as a place to put a reusable composite method.

- If there is more than one reusable composite method, how do we place the methods in the specializations, e.g. all in one specialization, one per specialization, or several in each specialization?

What we need is a mechanism that allows us to use the "pure" general object alone, and will also allow us to select only those composite methods that we need, when we need them. Kits offer us this flexibility. Although, kits are not directly supported by commonly used object-oriented programming languages, they are supported by some software engineering environments, e.g., Rational ([Rational, 1986]).

There are four commonly used types of kit:

- kits containing a single (meta)object or parameterized object (sometimes also containing variations based on different complete sets of primitive operations), along with a collection of unencapsulated composite operations for that (meta)object or parameterized object,

- kits containing a collection of differing objects and other items necessary to support a large object-oriented concept that is based on a particular composite object,

- kits containing a collection of variations on an individual object, specifically, variations on form (other object-oriented items and unencapsulated composite operations may also be included), and

- kits containing a collection of very similar (meta)objects and/or parameterized objects.

Let us now discuss each of these options in turn.

As an example of the first type of kit, suppose that we have designed a parameterized ordered list class. The public interface for this parameterized class contains a complete set of primitive operations. We have also created an unencapsulated composite operation "exchange," that replaces a given old item in the list with a given new item. (This operation was written using the primitive operations of "delete" and "add" available in the public interface of the list class.) The combination of the parameterized ordered list class and this single unencapsulated composite operation is an extremely trivial example of an "ordered list kit." Of course, in practice, such kits often contain many unencapsulated composite operations.

The "Gregorian date kit" we discussed earlier is an example of the second type of kit. A "dialog window kit" that contained one or more parameterized dialog window classes, scroll bar classes, radio button classes, check box classes, push button classes, pop-up menu classes, static text classes, editable text classes, icon classes, and picture classes would also fall under this category. (In effect, it would be a "dialog window building kit.") Taking this further, the X Window System™, Motif™, and Open Look™ could be structured as a collection of kits, or kits of kits.

Kits that fall under the second category we described are the most common form of kits — both because of their utility and because of their ease of creation. A software engineer merely identifies a useful composite object, or family of closely-related composite objects, the most useful component objects, and a set of useful/reusable unencapsulated composite methods for these objects. These are then combined to form the kit.

In [Booch, 1987], Grady Booch defines **form** as "a time and space variation of the components for a specific abstraction." The particular book ([Booch, 1987]) describes basic abstractions (e.g., lists, stacks, queues, strings, graphs, sets, and bags) and time and space variations on these abstractions. By "time variations" Booch means primarily those versions of the abstractions that might be best suited to a sequential environment, and other versions that would be able to handle themselves in a parallel environment. By "space variations," Booch is referring primarily to an object's ability to retain a fixed maximum size, or to grow and shrink based on both demand and available computer resources.

One abstraction can have many different time and space variations (forms). Some researchers have identified up to 600 useful forms for each basic abstraction. The third type of kit suggested above could be constructed by gathering all the useful forms for a basic abstraction, along with a set of useful/reusable unencapsulated composite methods for the abstraction and specific forms. This type of kit, although easy to construct, is not commonly used.

The second most commonly used type of kit is the fourth (and last) type mentioned above. In 1986, one of my clients was constructing an embedded real-time application in an object-oriented manner. They notice that they had significant numbers of very similar abstractions. For example, their application dealt with many different switches, e.g., single-pole-single-throw, double-pole-double-throw, and many others. They began to create kits that very closely resembled "parts drawers," e.g., if you needed access to a number of different switches, lamps, or buttons, you merely selected the appropriate kit.

One might justifiably ask, "When do I know I need a kit?" Given that kits are very appropriate for such things as graphical user interfaces (GUI), virtually any object-oriented application that requires a GUI could make use of kits. However, we would like some more general guidelines. Here are a few situations that might lead you to kits:

- You have a very reusable composite object that you can parameterize based primarily on its component objects.

- You need to create some composite methods for a given object, and you want these methods available for more than just your immediate application.

- You recognize the need for variations on an object that do not (generally) involve variations on functionality, e.g., a version of the object for concurrent environments.

- You have a number of very closely related, but different, objects.

In [Booch, 1987], (although he is talking about what he calls "subsystems") Booch poses the following guidelines for kits:

- The larger the overall system, the greater the probability for the creation of kits.

- An optimally designed kit is one that requires the full-time resources of one or two developers, e.g., roughly 20,000 to 30,000 lines of documented source code.

- For complex systems, multiple levels of kit decomposition may be necessary.

- Kits should be designed with reuse in mind. However, remember the axiom that the larger a piece of software, the more difficult it is to reuse that piece of software.

Kit documentation should contain the following:

- Any necessary, and helpful, graphics for both the kit and its components.

- A list of objects and other items (e.g., unencapsulated composite methods) that are available in the export part of the kit. This list should be accompanied by any necessary documentation for the items in the interface of the kit.

- A description of the internal structure of the kit. (This should only be made available to the creators and maintainers of the kit.)

- A description of the requirements (e.g., necessary objects and unencapsulated methods) for the kit.

- A description of the purpose, and suggested use, of the kit.

Kit documentation is collectively referred to as a **kit specification** (KS). Kit specifications usually include all the source code for kit components, any supporting documentation for these components, and any other documentation necessary to understand the structure and use for the kit. It is not unusual to see kit documentation taking up several "three-ring binders."

Although kits are more common in larger systems, they show up even in small systems. Probably the most common example is the use of a graphical user interface (GUI). Even a program that only presents a simple message (e.g., "hello world") in a text window will make use of one or more window kits.

Systems of Interacting Objects

Consider a simple "Gregorian date" object, i.e., a date that is a simple aggregation of a month object, a day object, and a year object. The public interface to the Gregorian date object provides the operations: set the month, return the month, set the day, return the day, set the year, return the year, test for equality (between two Gregorian dates), and copy (the value of one Gregorian date object into another, designated Gregorian date object). Internally, the Gregorian date object resembles a box with three bins, i.e., one bin each for the aggregated month object, day object, and year object.

The Gregorian date object is not an "active object," i.e., it does not possess an internal, independently executing thread of control. (For discussions of, "active objects," "objects with life," and "actors," see such references as [Agha and Hewitt, 1987] and [Booch, 1991].) Specifically, the only time a Gregorian date object changes its state is when one of the state-changing methods in its interface (e.g., set the month) is activated/invoked.

Now consider a different object. Suppose that we are designing an "electronic message system" (EMS). One of the primary object-oriented components of the EMS is a "post office." Externally, the post office resembles an ordinary object, e.g., in its public interface we find three operations: is there any mail (for a given recipient), pick up mail (for a given recipient), and send mail (to one or more recipients). With respect to the post office object these are all primitive operations.

An examination of the underlying implementation of the post office object, however, reveals a fairly involved situation. Specifically, we find a number of objects involved, i.e.:

- a collection of mailboxes object,

- many individual mailboxes,

- many individual message objects, and

- a clerk object.

As it turns out, the clerk object is an active object, i.e., it can spontaneously change its own state. Following the clerk object for a time, we find that it is quite active, and interacts with a number of objects, e.g.:

- The clerk object monitors an event queue. When someone asks if there is any mail for a given recipient, this request is converted into an event object and placed in the event queue. Likewise, requests to pick up and send mail are also converted into event objects and placed in the event queue.

- The clerk object queries the event queue object to determine if any events are present. If an event is present, the clerk object removes the event object from the event queue and then extracts information from the event object via the operations in the public interface of the event object.

- The clerk object can ask what type of event the event object represents. For example, if the event object is a query to see if there is any mail for a particular recipient, the clerk can retrieve the name and address for the recipient in question from the event object. Using the address object, the clerk attempts to extract a mailbox object from the collection of mailboxes object. (If a corresponding mailbox is not found, an appropriate exception will be raised/thrown/activated.) The clerk object then determines if there is any mail in the extracted mailbox object. If mail is present, the clerk object iterates over the messages objects contained in the mailbox object, searching for a match with the supplied recipient name object. Depending on whether a match is found, the clerk object sets the value of a response object, and deposits the response object in an outgoing queue object.

Of course, the underlying implementation of the post office object could be considerably enhanced (or, made more complex, depending on your point of view). For example, additional clerk objects could be added, as well as additional event and response queue objects.

In any event, the post office object appears quite different from the simple Gregorian date object. Whereas the Gregorian date object is a simple aggregation, the post office object, as we have described it, is truly a system of interacting objects. A **system of interacting objects** is a collection of two or more objects that meet the following criteria:

- the collection represents a (large) object-oriented concept,

- the objects within the collection exhibit a high degree of logical cohesion, i.e., they all directly support the overall object-oriented concept represented by the collection,

- there is also a very high degree of physical cohesion among all the objects, i.e., there is a direct or indirect physical connection among all the objects within the collection (of course, in the interests of minimizing object coupling, these connections are kept as tenuous as possible),

- within the collection there is at least one independently executing thread of control, and there may be multiple threads of control (e.g., as with agents and agencies — see, for example, [Adams and Nabi, 1989] and [Fenton and Beck, 1989]), and

- the collection presents at least one, and possibly many, cohesive and object-oriented public interfaces.

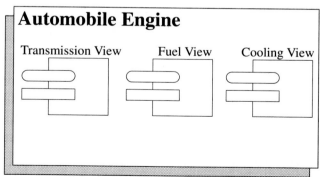

Figure 3:   **A graphic for a system of interacting objects shows the overall object (the Automobile Engine) and its three disjoint public interfaces (the Transmission View, the Fuel System View, and the Cooling System View).** The bounding rectangle represents the physical cohesion of the overall object, and the program unit graphics suggest the (small) object-like interfaces presented to the public.

Let us return to the post office object. The public interface we described originally could be considered to be the "lobby" or "general public" interface. We could add another, totally disjoint public interface that would represent the "loading dock" at the rear of the post office. Although users of the lobby interface, and users of the loading dock interface both interact with the post office object, they are presented with different views of the post office object.

Consider another example, i.e., an automobile engine. Automobile engine objects are made up of many different smaller objects, some of which themselves may also be systems of interacting objects. The automobile engine presents a number of disjoint public interfaces, e.g., an interface to the transmission, an interface to the fuel system, and an interface to the cooling system.

In creating a graphic to represent a system of interacting objects, a number of goals had to be met:

- The graphic had to clearly partition and represent multiple views of a system of interacting objects.

- Each view of the system of interacting objects had to be very object-like. Specifically, from the viewer's standpoint, the system of interacting objects had to appear as a single object with an object-like interface. Each view was represented as a collection of methods, exceptions, constants, and any other items appropriate for the public interface of an object.

- There had to be a way of encapsulating all the views to show that they were indeed just different views of the same system of interacting objects.

- The graphic had to be manageable. Specifically, the graphic had to be easy to create and able to represent potentially many different views.

- It should not be easy to confuse the graphic with other graphics — especially program unit graphics.

(We also had to come up with a schematic version of the system of interacting objects graphic that could be used when space was at a premium.)

Figure 4:   **A graphic representing a schematic (lacking in detail, to be defined/elaborated elsewhere) system of interacting objects shows only one interface icon**. Although it is possible to have a system of interacting objects with only one public interface, the lack of a label for the interface in the graphic above tells us that this is a schematic.

The appearance of, and requirement for, multiple disjoint interfaces for an object is very closely related to the size of an object. A simple list object needs only a single relatively simple interface. Organizations, automobile engines, post offices, and other large objects often require multiple interfaces to manage the complexity of their interactions and interrelationships with the outside world. Hailpern and Ossher ([Hailpern and Ossher, 1990]) have described a means of accomplishing both multiple object interfaces ("views") and controlling access to each of these interfaces. [Helm et al., 1990] describes a formal means ("contracts") of specifying the explicit behavior of systems of interacting objects ("behavioral compositions").

Systems of interacting objects are documented using a **system of interacting objects specification** (SIOS). Although the external specification of a system of interacting objects can be somewhat small (e.g., 5-20 typeset pages), the internal specification for a system of interacting objects (i.e., one that specifies the internal architecture of the system) can be quite complicated, and take up hundreds of pages. An SIOS should include the following:

- any necessary, and helpful, graphics for both the system of interacting objects and its components,

- a thorough description of the interface(s) for the system of interacting objects,

- a description of the internal structure of the system of interacting objects (this should only be made available to the creators and maintainers of the system of interacting objects), and

- a description of the purpose, and suggested use, of the system of interacting objects.

We make the observation that the internal documentation for a system of interacting objects very closely resembles the documentation produced as the result of an object-oriented design (OOD) effort.

Object-oriented applications that include systems of interacting objects are typically medium to large in size. (In truth, every stand-alone object-oriented application, with the general exception of kits and libraries, is a system of interacting objects.) Further, for very large object-oriented applications, it is quite normal for systems of interacting objects to themselves contain systems of interacting objects.

Sometimes the construction of a potentially reusable system of interacting objects is unintentional. Suppose we are chartered with the development of a system to control and otherwise schedule the elevators in a large building. We construct the application in an object-oriented manner, e.g., elevators, motors, buttons, lamps, and requests are all objects. We complete our project and view the elevator scheduler as a stand-alone object-oriented application.

Our customer is delighted with the product, and proposes that we create a "building system." This system will not only deal with the elevators, but will also handle heating, ventilating and air conditioning, and building security. Our stand-alone elevator scheduler and controller is now a system of interacting objects within a larger system, i.e., the building system. We will have to re-examine the interface(s) to the elevator scheduler and controller to determine how they may have to be modified to accomplish the new interrelationships.

Conclusion

Object-oriented development of large systems is different from the development of small object-oriented applications. One of the differences is the emergence of large object-oriented entities. We have discussed two such entities, kits and systems of interacting objects. Although both are logically very cohesive — each representing a single, coherent object-oriented concept — kits are not very physically cohesive in that they allow users to select and use individual components of the kit. Systems of interacting objects, on the other hand, are very physically cohesive — representing a single monolithic entity. In addition, systems of interacting objects may present multiple, completely disjoint interfaces to the outside world.

Object-oriented development of large systems has traditionally involved significant numbers of both kits and systems of interacting objects, but kits in particular are very applicable even for small systems. Unfortunately, no *commonly used* object-oriented programming languages or environments directly support either concept.

Our discussion of these large object-oriented entities was very high-level. There is obviously much more that could be said about the design, implementation, usage, and documentation for these entities.

Bibliography

[Adams and Nabi, 1989]. S.S. Adams and A.K. Nabi, "Neural Agents — A Frame of Mind," *OOPSLA '89 Conference Proceedings,* special issue of *SIGPLAN Notices*, Vol. 24, No. 10, October 1989, pp. 139 - 150.

[Agha and Hewitt, 1987]. G. Agha and C. Hewitt, "Actors: A Conceptual Foundation for Concurrent Object-Oriented Programming," in *Research Directions in Object-Oriented Programming*, Edited by B. Shriver and P. Wegner, MIT Press, Cambridge, Massachusetts, 1987, pp. 47 - 74.

[ARM, 1983]. Reference Manual for the Ada Programming Language, *ANSI/MIL-STD 1815A (1983)*, United States Department of Defense, February 1983.

[Biggerstaff and Perlis, 1989a]. T. Biggerstaff and A.J. Perlis, *Software Reusability, Volume 1: Concepts and Models*, Addison-Wesley, Reading, Massachusetts, 1989.

[Biggerstaff and Perlis, 1989b]. T. Biggerstaff and A.J. Perlis, *Software Reusability, Volume 2: Applications and Experience*, Addison-Wesley, Reading, Massachusetts, 1989.

[Boehm, 1981]. B. W. Boehm, *Software Engineering Economics*, Prentice Hall, Englewood Cliffs, New Jersey, 1981.

[Booch, 1987]. G. Booch, *Software Components With Ada*, Benjamin/Cummings, Menlo Park, California, 1987.

[Booch, 1991]. G. Booch, *Object-Oriented Design With Applications*, Benjamin/Cummings, Menlo Park, California, 1991.

[Borning, 1986]. A.H. Borning, "Class Versus Prototypes in Object-Oriented Languages," *Proceedings of the 1986 Fall Joint Computer Conference*, IEEE Catalog Number 86CH2345-7, IEEE Computer Society Press, Washington, D.C., 1986, pp 36 - 40.

[Brooks, 1975]. F. P. Brooks, Jr., *The Mythical Man-Month*, Addison-Wesley Publishing Company, Reading, Massachusetts, 1975.

[Buhr and Zarnke, 1988]. P.A. Buhr and C.R. Zarnke, "Nesting In an Object-Oriented Language Is Not for the Birds," *ECOOP '88: Proceedings of the European Conference on Object-Oriented*

Programming, Lecture Notes on Computer Science, Volume 322, Springer Verlag, New York, New York, 1988, pp. 128 - 145.

[Coad and Yourdon, 1990]. P. Coad and E. Yourdon, *OOA — Object-Oriented Analysis,* 2nd Edition, Prentice Hall, Englewood Cliffs, New Jersey, 1990.

[Dahl and Nygaard, 1966]. O.J. Dahl and K. Nygaard, "SIMULA — an ALGOL-Based Simulation Language," *Communications of the ACM,* Vol. 9, No. 9, September 1966, pp. 671 - 678.

[DeRemer and Kron, 1976]. F. DeRemer and H.H. Kron, "Programming-in-the-Large Versus Programming-in-the-Small," *IEEE Transactions on Software Engineering,* Vol. SE-2, No. 2, June 1976, pp. 80 - 86, reprinted in *IEEE Tutorial: Software Design Techniques,* Third Edition, edited by P. Freeman and A.I. Wasserman, IEEE Catalog Number EHO161-0, IEEE Computer Society Press, Silver Spring, Maryland, 1983, pp. 237 - 243.

[Dijkstra, 1972]. E.W. Dijkstra, "The Humble Programmer," *Communications of the ACM,* Vol. 15, No. 10, October 1972, pp. 859 - 866.

[Fenton and Beck, 1989]. J. Fenton and K. Beck, "Playground: An Object-Oriented Simulation System With Agent Rules for Children of All Ages," *OOPSLA '89 Conference Proceedings,* special issue of *SIGPLAN Notices,* Vol. 24, No. 10, October 1989, pp. 123 - 138.

[Gallo et al., 1989]. T. Gallo, G. Serrano, and F. Tisato, "ObNet: An Object-Oriented Approach for Supporting Large, Long-Lived, Highly Configurable Systems," *Proceedings of the Eleventh International Conference on Software Engineering,* Pittsburgh, Pennsylvania, May 15-18, 1989, pp. 138 - 144.

[Glass, 1982]. R. Glass, *Modern Programming Practices: A Report From Industry,* Prentice Hall, Englewood Cliffs, New Jersey, 1982.

[Goguen, 1986] J.A. Goguen, "Reusing and Interconnecting Software Components," *IEEE Computer,* Vol. 19, No. 2, February 1986, pp. 16 - 28.

[Goldberg and Robson, 1983]. A. Goldberg and D. Robson, *Smalltalk-80: The Language and Its Implementation,* Addison-Wesley, Reading, Massachusetts, 1983.

[Hailpern and Ossher, 1990]. B. Hailpern and H. Ossher, "Extending Objects to Support Multiple Interfaces and Access Control," *IEEE Transactions on Software Engineering,* Vol. 16, No. 11, November 1990, pp. 1247 - 1257.

[Helm et al., 1990]. R. Helm, I.M. Holland, and D. Gangopadhyay, "Contracts: Specifying Behavioral Compositions in Object-Oriented Systems," *OOPSLA/ECOOP '90 Conference Proceedings,* special issue of *SIGPLAN Notices,* Vol. 25, No. 10, October 1990, pp. 169 - 180.

[Jacobson, 1986]. I. Jacobson, "Language Support for Changeable Large Real Time Systems," *OOPSLA '86 Conference Proceedings,* special issue of *SIGPLAN Notices,* Vol. 21, No. 11, November 1986, pp. 377 - 384.

[Jones, 1978]. T.C. Jones, "Measuring Programming Quality and Productivity," *IBM Systems Journal,* Vol. 17, No. 1, 1978, pp. 39 - 63.

[Jones, 1986]. C. Jones, *Programming Productivity,* McGraw-Hill, New York, New York, 1986.

[Keene, 1989]. S.E. Keene, *Object-Oriented Programming in Common Lisp,* Addison-Wesley, Reading, Massachusetts, 1989.

[Kristensen et al., 1987]. B.B. Kristensen, O.L. Madsen, B. Moller-Pedersen, and K. Nygaard, "The BETA Programming Language," in *Research Directions in Object-Oriented Programming,* B. Shriver and P. Wegner, Editors, The MIT Press, Cambridge, Massachusetts, 1987, pp. 7 - 48.

[Lawless and Miller, 1991]. J.A. Lawless and M.M. Miller, *Understanding CLOS: The Common Lisp Object System*, Digital Press, Bedford, Massachusetts, 1990.

[Lieberman, 1986]. H. Lieberman, "Using Prototypical Objects to Implement Shared Behavior In Object-Oriented Systems," *OOPSLA '86 Conference Proceedings,* special issue of *SIGPLAN Notices*, Vol. 21, No. 11, November 1986, pp. 214 - 223.

[Malaiya and Srimani, 1990]. Y.K. Malaiya and P.K. Srimani, Editors, *Software Reliability Models: Theoretical Developments, Evaluation and Applications*, IEEE Computer Society Press, Los Alamitos, California, 1990.

[Mish, 1988]. F.C. Mish, Editor in Chief, *Webster's Ninth New Collegiate Dictionary*, Merriam-Webster Inc., Springfield, Massachusetts, 1988.

[Morgan, 1988]. T.M. Morgan, "Configuration Management and Version Control in the Rational Programming Environment," in *Ada In Industry: Proceedings of the Ada-Europe International Conference,* Munich, 7-9 June, 1988, Cambridge University Press, Cambridge, United Kingdom, 1988, pp. 17 - 28.

[Musa et al., 1990]. J.D. Musa, A. Iannino, and K. Okumoto, *Software Reliability: Professional Addition*, McGraw-Hill Publishing Company, New York, New York, 1990.

[Myers, 1976]. G. J. Myers, *Software Reliability Principles and Practices*, John Wiley & Sons, New York, New York, 1976.

[Ossher, 1984]. H. Ossher, "Grids: A New Program Structuring Mechanism Based on Layered Graphs," *Proceedings of the Eleventh Annual ACM Symposium on Principles of Programming Languages,* Salt Lake City, Utah, January 15-18, 1984, pp. 11 - 22.

[Ossher, 1987]. H.L. Ossher, "A Mechanism for Specifying the Structure of Large, Layered Systems," in *Research Directions in Object-Oriented Programming*, B. Shriver and P. Wegner, Editors, The MIT Press, Cambridge, Massachusetts, 1987, pp. 219 - 252.

[Ossher, 1989]. H. Ossher, "A Case Study in Structure Specification: A Grid Description of Scribe," *IEEE Transactions on Software Engineering*, Vol. 15, No. 11, November 1989, pp. 1397 - 1416.

[Parnas et al., 1984]. D.L. Parnas, P.C. Clements, and D.M. Weiss, "The Modular Structure of Complex Systems," *Proceedings of the Seventh International Conference on Software Engineering,* March 26-29, 1984, IEEE Computer Society Press, Washington, D.C., 1984, pp. 408 - 447.

[Prieto-Diaz and Arango, 1991]. R. Prieto-Diaz and G. Arango, Editors, *Domain Analysis and Software Systems Modeling*, IEEE Computer Society Press, Los Alamitos, California, 1991.

[Purtilo et al., 1991]. J. Purtilo, A. Larson, and J. Clark, "A Methodology for Prototyping-In-the-Large," *Proceedings of the Thirteenth International Conference on Software Engineering*, May 13-17, 1991, Austin, Texas, pp. 2 - 12.

[Rational, 1986]. Rational, Inc., *Large-System Development and Rational Subsystems*, Document Control Number 6004, Rational, Inc., Mountain View, California, November, 1986.

[Sakkinen, 1989]. M. Sakkinen, "Disciplined Inheritance," *ECOOP '89: Proceedings of the European Conference on Object-Oriented Programming, British Computer Society Workshop Series*, Cambridge University Press, Cambridge, United Kingdom, 1989, pp. 39 - 56.

[Shlaer and Mellor, 1992]. S. Shlaer and S.J. Mellor, *Object Lifecycles: Modeling the World In States*, Yourdon Press: Prentice Hall, Englewood Cliffs, New Jersey, 1992.

[Tracz, 1988]. W. Tracz, Editor, *Software Reuse: Emerging Technology*, IEEE Catalog Number EH0278-2, Computer Society Order Number 846, IEEE Computer Society Press, Washington, D.C., 1988.

[Ungar and Smith, 1987]. D. Ungar and R.B. Smith, "Self: The Power of Simplicity," *OOPSLA '87 Conference Proceedings,* special issue of *SIGPLAN Notices*, Vol. 22, No. 12, December 1987, pp. 227 - 242.

[Wegner, 1990]. P. Wegner, "Concepts and Paradigms of Object-Oriented Programming," *OOPS Messenger*, Vol. 1, No. 1, August 1990, pp. 7 - 87.

[Weinberg, 1983]. G. M. Weinberg, "Kill That Code," *Infosystems*, August 1983, page 49.

[Wirfs-Brock et al., 1990]. R. Wirfs-Brock, B. Wilkerson, and Lauren Wiener, *Designing Object-Oriented Software*, Prentice Hall, Englewood Cliffs, New Jersey, 1990.

[Wirth, 1983]. N. Wirth, *Programming In Modula-2,* Second Edition, Springer-Verlag, New York, New York, 1983.

10   Object-Oriented Domain Analysis

The whole secret of the study of nature lies in learning how to use one's eyes.

— *George Sand (Amandine Aurore Lucie Dupin, Baronne Dudevant) in Nouvelles Lettres d'un Voyageur [1869]*

Prologue

If you were to ask a good number of people why they were using, or were seriously thinking about using, an object-oriented approach to software engineering, you would get responses such as enhanced interoperability, software solutions which are easily modified and extended, simpler, more straightforward solutions, and better suitability for real-time systems. However, probably the most common answer would be: enhanced reusability.

Like object-orientation, software reusability is a very much misunderstood concept. Many people think that the pinnacle of software reuse is a "library of math functions." What most software professionals do not realize is that software reusability, like object-orientation, impacts everything, from management practices to software development standards, and much more.

Software Reusability

Software components (routines), to be widely acceptable to different machines and users, should be available in families arranged according to precision, robustness, generality and time-space performance. Existing sources of components — manufacturers, software houses, users' groups and algorithm collections — lack the breadth of interest or coherence of purpose to assemble more than one or two members of such families, yet software production in the large would be enormously helped by the availability of spectra of high quality routines, quite as mechanical design is abetted by the existence of families of structural shapes, screws, or resistors.

— *Doug McIlroy (in [Naur and Randell, 1969])*

Specialists in every part of software have a curious vision of the world: All parts of software but his are simple and easily parameterized; his is totally variable.

— *A. J. Perlis (in [Naur and Randell, 1969])*

In talking about the implementation of software components, the whole concept of how one designs software is ignored. Yet this is the key thing.

— *K. Kolence (in [Naur and Randell, 1969])*

A comparison with our hardware colleagues is relevant.

— *Peter Naur (in [Naur and Randell, 1969])*

Reusable code is taken seriously in Japan and should be here too. ... To me this is the most important branching point. In the long run, it will determine which companies will stay in business and which ones won't.

— *Capers Jones (ComputerWorld, November 24, 1986, page 19)*

> The results of a California study proved that software systems are highly redundant, with 75% of the application code, 50% of the systems programs and 70% of telecommunications programs sharing identical code or functions.
>
> — News item from ComputerWorld, November 24, 1986, page 19

One of my primary areas of interest is software reusability. I have conducted research on, taught courses about, and developed products using software reusability technology. Here are some of the things I found:

- Software practitioners often incorrectly limit their definition of "software" to source code and object code. In truth, software includes such things as:

    - code fragments,

    - modules, i.e.:

        - subprograms, e.g., procedures, functions, subroutines, paragraphs, and

        - larger collections, e.g., Smalltalk's classes ([Goldberg and Robson, 1983]), C++'s classes ([Stroustrup, 1991]) Modula's modules ([Wirth, 1983]), and Ada's packages ([Cohen, 1986]),

    - large object-oriented entities, e.g., kits ([Levy and Ripken, 1987], [Rational, 1986], and chapter 9 of this book),

    - scaffolding code and documentation (i.e., software items produced during the development of a software product that are not part of the delivered software product),

    - test data,

    - plans, policies, standards, and procedures, and

    - products of analysis, design, and software quality assurance efforts.

- Management and technical staff alike often avoid thinking about software reuse until too late, i.e., the "coding phase." They fail to realize that reusability impacts everything including management, contracting and legal issues, in-house development standards, and relationships with subcontractors. (See, e.g., [Berard, 1987].)

- The later in the software engineering of a software product that one delays reusability considerations the smaller the payoff one obtains from software reuse. Waiting until the coding phase of software development to consider software reuse yields a very small return for one's software reuse investment.

- Although many people pitch software reusability on the grounds that it will "save money," both management and technical staffers are seldom swayed by this argument — even when presented with hard data to back up the argument.

- Software reusability can have a very positive impact on software reliability, software efficiency, and "time to market."

- Training is essential. Simply purchasing libraries of reusable components (e.g., [Dlugosz, 1991], [Dusink and van Katwijk, 1987], [Russell, 1987] and [Margono and Berard, 1987]) and/or software reusability systems (e.g., [Burton et al., 1987]) does not guarantee their (proper) use.

- The concepts of software reusability and object-oriented technology are so intertwined that it is often difficult to talk about one without mentioning the other, e.g., see [Frankowski, 1986], [Johnson and Foote, 1988], [Meyer, 1987], [Schmucker, 1986], [St. Dennis et al., 1986], [Devanbu and Bachman, 1989], and the panel ("Experiences With Reusability") at the 1988 OOPSLA.

- The major obstacles to software reusability are *not* technical, they are primarily cultural. (See, e.g., [Carstensen, 1987] and [Tracz, 1987].)

Probably the most commonly cited reasons for considering software reuse today include:

- lower development and post-development costs,

- lower end product costs,

- higher software engineering productivity,

- risk reduction,

- reduced time-to-market,

- reduction in time to implement modifications and enhancements,

- higher reliability,

- greater application efficiency, and

- increased ability to rapidly prototype.

Domain Analysis: Definitions

If you study software reusability for a little while, you will probably encounter some discussion of "domain analysis." Here are three alternative definitions of domain analysis:

> An investigation of a specific application area that seeks to identify the operations, objects, and structures that commonly occur in software systems within this area.
>
> — *Dan McNicholl (in [Booch, 1987])*

> Systems analysis states what is done for a specific problem in a domain while domain analysis states what can be done in a range of problems in a domain. … A domain analysis is only useful if many similar systems are to be built so that the cost of the domain analysis can be amortized over the cost of all the systems.
>
> The key to reusable software is captured in domain analysis in that it stresses the reusability of analysis and design, not code.
>
> — *Jim Neighbors (in [Neighbors, 1980])*

> The process of identifying, collecting, organizing, and representing the relevant information in a domain based on the study of existing systems and their development histories, knowledge captured from domain experts, underlying theory, and emerging technology within the domain.
>
> — *[Kang et al., 1990]*

(Note Neighbors's emphasis on the importance of non-code software. (See, also [Arango, 1989] and [Prieto-Diaz and Arango, 1991].))

In essence, "domain" in domain analysis refers to "application domain," e.g., graphical user interfaces, embedded missile applications, and decision support systems. The reason you are conducting an "analysis" is that you hope to identify reusable items within the domain, i.e., items which may be reused to build new applications which also fall within the same domain.

Although most people understand that the word "domain" in "domain analysis" refers to "application domain," **domain** can be defined more precisely as:

- a collection of current and future (software) applications that share a set of common characteristics, or

- a well-defined set of characteristics which accurately, narrowly, and completely describe a family of problems for which computer application solutions are being, and will be, sought.

Grady Booch ([Booch, 1987]) offers the following definitions of horizontal and vertical domain analysis:

> A **horizontal domain analysis** studies a number of different systems across a variety of applications.

> A **vertical domain analysis** studies a number of systems intended for the same class of applications.

There are different types of domain analysis beyond simple vertical and horizontal approaches. In general, each type of domain analysis is distinguished by the types of reusable items which are being sought, e.g.:

- **Functional domain analysis** seeks to identify reusable items localized around functions, e.g., functions, subroutines, procedures, and programs.

- **Object-oriented domain analysis** seeks to identify reusable items localized around objects e.g., classes, instances, systems of interacting objects, and kits.

[Kang et al., 1990] defines "**domain engineering**" as: "An encompassing process which includes domain analysis and the subsequent construction of components, methods, and tools that address the problems of system/subsystem development through the application of domain analysis products."

Historical Background

Although the concept of domain analysis (like the concept of software reusability) has been around for decades, probably the first work of any significance in the area is documented in the doctoral thesis of Jim Neighbors ([Neighbors, 1980]). It was not, however, until 1985 that the term "domain analysis" began showing up with any regularity in the literature, e.g., [Adelson and Soloway, 1985]. (See also [Hess et al., 1990].)

By 1988-89, there were quite a few articles on domain analysis, e.g., [Iscoe, 1988], [Prieto-Diaz, 1988], and [Simos, 1988]. The way we think about domain analysis has also changed. For example, by 1987 there was a recognized need for a formal approach to domain analysis (e.g., [RMISE, 1987]), and by 1989, proposed "formal" approaches did begin to appear (e.g., [Arango, 1989]).

In 1989, we began to see articles on object-oriented domain analysis. The first of these articles is [Shlaer and Mellor, 1989].

In this article, I will present a very brief introduction to object-oriented domain analysis. However, please note that, as with object-oriented requirements analysis (OORA) and object-oriented design (OOD), there is more than one school of thought on the process.

Domain Analysis Is Not a Life-Cycle Activity

One of the first items one encounters in the study of domain analysis, is that it is *not* a life-cycle activity. Specifically, an overall domain analysis effort goes on *in parallel* with the software life-cycles for the products which an organization produces and maintains. As we will see shortly, there is a synergistic relationship between the overall domain analysis effort and individual software projects.

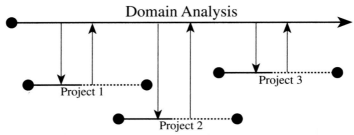

Figure 1:   **Domain analysis is independent of any particular project.** For domain analysis to be cost effective, the results must be accessible to many projects, and its interactions with any one project should serve to benefit other projects.

Christine Youngblut (in [Booch, 1987]) details some of the reasons for keeping domain analysis separate from any specific project:

- "When a component is developed in the context of some system, it is difficult to abstract from the concerns of that system to produce a truly flexible, unbiased component."

- "The additional requirements of a reusable component (increased quality assurance, testing, flexibility, etc.) mean that it is more expensive to produce than other components, and this may not have been allowed for in the project budgets and schedules."

- "It may be difficult to recognize that a particular part is highly reusable, and so many potentially useful components may be ignored."

Domain analysts regularly interact with the team members associated with a particular software product. The activities of the domain analyst (in these interactions) can involve:

- making project team members aware of new/updated reusable items,

- training project team members in software reusability concepts,

- instructing project team members in the use of the in-house software reusability system,

- assessing whether reusable items are being (re)used properly,

- assessing the level and quality of reuse for the project/product,

- soliciting potentially reusable items from the project/product,

- the gathering of software reusability metrics, and

- providing general reusability consulting.

Project team members for a given software product do not have to wait for the domain analysts to come to them. Examples of situations in which team members seek out interactions with domain analysis include:

- A potentially reusable object has been found, but the project does not have the resources to make it fully reusable, i.e., they will turn it over to the domain analysis group, who will consider making the object "fully reusable."

- A team member has identified an object which he or she feels should already be in the in-house reusability system, but is having trouble finding the object.

- A team member, or group of team members, has some specific reusability questions, and desires some reuse consulting.

- The quality of a given reusable object is suspect, and the team members bring this to the attention of the domain analysts.

- A particular project requires the use of (potentially generic) commercial off-the-shelf (COTS) reusable software that is not already in the in-house software reusability system. Team members can request that domain analysis procure the desired COTS software.

What Is a Domain Analyst?

One of the rarest species of software professional is the domain analyst. The reason for their rarity is that they must *simultaneously* possess all of the following characteristics:

- They must be familiar with the specific application domain, and with significant experience in that same domain. (This is a fairly easy requirement.)

- They must be familiar with the items (e.g., objects) which are to be considered for reuse, and with significant experience using these items. (If the domain analyst is familiar with the application domain but does not have a fundamental understanding of object-oriented concepts, he or she will not be able to easily recognize an object when he or she sees one.)

- They must have excellent abstraction skills. (Any analyst must be able to distinguish the general from the specific, and between concepts and implementations.)

- They must be versed in software reusability technology. (Software reusability technology is *not* trivial. For example, can the analyst examine an object in isolation and systematically determine if the object possesses a complete set of operations, constants, and exceptions?)

Steps in OODA

Oversimplifying, the steps in an OODA effort are:

- define the domain,

- collect a representative sample of domain artifacts,

- analyze the representative domain artifacts to identify reusable items,

- define reusability guidelines regarding the reusable items,

- demonstrate reuse using the reusable items and the guidelines, and

- make recommendations.

[Truth in advertising: True domain analysis is a never-ending process. Specifically, as long as an organization continues to develop and/or maintain software applications, the domain analysis effort will remain active. We will describe the steps here as if they were indeed sequential; however, in practice, each of these steps is more like an on-going activity.]

In the following discussions, "object" can be taken to mean one, or more, of the following: class, instance, metaclass, parameterized class, metaobject, kit, and system of interacting objects.

Defining the Domain

Defining an application domain requires two different (and often concurrent) activities:

- defining the types of items which populate the domain, and

- building one, or more, models of the domain.

There will typically be many items which populate a given domain. Assuming that we are conducting an object-oriented domain analysis effort, we can expect to be interested in:

- Items which are chiefly object-oriented in nature, e.g.:

  - specifications, source code, and object code for classes, metaclasses parameterized classes, and non-class instances,

  - specifications, source code, and object code for kits and systems of interacting objects,

  - unencapsulated composite operations,

  - test cases for object-oriented software,

  - commercial off-the-shelf (COTS) object-oriented software,

  - products of object-oriented analysis efforts, e.g., object-oriented requirements specifications and short maps, and

  - products of object-oriented design efforts, e.g., object-oriented design specifications.

- Items which are typically not object-oriented in nature, e.g.:

  - policies, procedures, plans, standards, and guidelines,

  - applications, and parts of applications, which were not created using an object-oriented approach,

- specifications for applications, and parts of applications, which were not created using an object-oriented approach,

- analysis and design logs,

- test cases for non-object-oriented software,

- commercial off-the-shelf (COTS) non-object-oriented software, and

- software engineering metrics, i.e., product metrics, process metrics, and people metrics.

For each category of items which populate the domain, we must define:

- the general defining characteristics for the category of item,

- the criteria which items within the category must meet to be considered as members of the domain,

- taxonomies (classification schemes),

- nomenclature, i.e., how to name each individual item, and

- hierarchies, sets, or other organizations.

The above information will help in the configuration management, identification, and quality assurance of the items of interest.

Domain analysis is much more than merely identifying potentially reusable items within a given application domain. Domain analysts must:

- demonstrate that they understand the context, overall structure, and organization of the domain, and

- understand how the components (including the reusable components) of a domain are interrelated.

This is usually accomplished by constructing many models of the domain. Hopefully, for object-oriented domain analysis, the models will be object-oriented in nature.

There are four major categories of models used in object-oriented software engineering:

- *textual models*: These are textual descriptions of both individual objects and systems of objects. They may be prose or mathematical in nature.

- *graphical models*: These graphically represent the characteristics of individual objects or systems of objects.

- *executable models*: These are models which execute on a computer and require special software.

- *others*: This general category includes all the models which do not fit into the above categories.

It is useful to define each domain as narrowly and as quantitatively as possible because:

- identification of candidate artifacts which fall (or will fall) within the domain will be easier,

- separation of domain-specific reusable items from non-domain-specific reusable items will be easier, and

- in general, analysis of the domain, and the resulting conclusions will be more meaningful.

(See also [McGraw and Harbison-Briggs, 1989].)

Collecting a Representative Sample of Applications in the Domain

This is a continually on-going effort and requires a careful analysis. The following must be considered:

- Are the applications in the sample truly representative of the applications in the domain, e.g., types, sizes, and languages?

- What is the likelihood that the applications in the sample contain a representative collection of reusable objects?

- Is there a high probability that future applications within the domain will have the same characteristics?

(When an organization first begins to use object-oriented technology, it is quite likely that any previously existing applications were *not* created in an object-oriented manner. Hence, the analysis of existing applications will require that the object-oriented domain analyst identify the *conceptual* (as opposed to *physical*) objects in each application.)

Analysis of the Sample

During the analysis of the representative sample of applications, the domain analyst must:

- identify candidate reusable objects,

- state why the objects are considered potentially reusable,

- identify variations on the objects which will also be reusable,

- determine the percentage of a typical application which might be constructed from the reusable objects,

- name, catalog, and otherwise apply configuration management to the reusable objects, and

- predict the relative usefulness of each object in terms of future applications.

(The most desirable form of reuse is reuse with *no* changes. Until they are properly trained, project software engineers will probably *not* be designing objects with reuse in mind. (Even after they are properly trained, project management may not allow them the resources (e.g., time) to correctly implement reusable objects.) Therefore, the domain analysts should not expect to find "complete" objects. More specifically, object-oriented domain analysts will often be expected to ensure that each object represents a complete abstraction. Further, the object-oriented domain analysts must make sure that each reusable object receives the proper amount of testing and quality assurance.)

Defining Reusability Guidelines

The domain analyst must provide software engineers with a set of meaningful guidelines for the reuse of the objects within the domain. For example the analyst should identify the criteria used to select an object for use in an application, and the trade-offs to be considered.

Demonstrations of Reuse Using the Reusable Objects

At least one representative example of an application constructed using the reusable objects must be developed. (In truth, an on-going series of sample applications will have to be constructed.) In addition to the application itself, a report describing the experiences of the developers, and the characteristics of reuse within the application must also be produced.

Making Recommendations

Based on the guidelines, and on the results of the demonstration, the domain analyst must provide recommendations for incorporating the reusable objects into current and future projects. The recommendations may also include recommendations for changes in life-cycle approaches, policies, standards, and tools.

Domain Analysis and Life-Cycle Activities

Software reusability is a key consideration during the object-oriented life-cycle. The analyst must both reuse existing objects, *and* create new ones in such a way that they can be easily reused. Some of the previously existing objects may very well have been created, not for any specific project, but as a normal product of domain analysis.

Object-oriented requirements analysis (OORA) and object-oriented design (OOD) are specific to a particular application within a domain. These processes, however, benefit from domain analysis in a number of ways:

- Since domain analysis has already identified a number of reusable objects within the domain, the analysts and the designers can use this information to help guide the analysis and design.

- If done well, domain analysis will contribute significantly to understanding how to design complete, robust objects.

- If done well, domain analysis will have identified those variations on an object that appear to be most useful within the domain, e.g., concurrent forms.

- Many of the same techniques used by the domain analyst can be used by the analysts and designers to help identify the objects within a specific application — as well as helping to understand the interactions of these objects.

As new applications are developed, new objects will be constantly uncovered. New relationships among new, and existing, objects will also be discovered. These new relationships will often suggest different and useful variations on the existing library of objects. In effect, the development and maintenance processes will be one of the most effective "feedback" mechanisms for domain analysis.

Other Uses for Domain Analysis

Although most people are drawn to domain analysis because of reusability, there are other benefits. For example, in the process of defining the domain, a fantastic amount of information about how an organization goes about its business is also uncovered. Many of my clients have remarked about how just going through the definition step was extremely worthwhile because they discovered so many things about the way they did business. Components and relationships that they never knew existed were uncovered by just attempting to define their application domain.

Another potential benefit of a well-done domain analysis effort is the optimization of business practices. Once an organization has constructed a few models of their domain, it is very common for them to note how they might optimize their day-to-day efforts. (As a side note: we have taught object-oriented domain analysis to people who have no connection to software engineering, e.g., a group of people who were attempting to optimize the manufacturing process for photographic paper.)

Conclusions

Over the past decade, domain analysis has gone from an idea to a defined practice. We now know more about the process and its relationship to other software engineering processes. In addition, the role of the domain analyst has become better understood. Finally, domain analysis in an object-oriented manner is different from the more traditional approaches to domain analysis in both the items considered for reuse and in the domain modeling approaches.

Bibliography

[Adelson and Soloway, 1985]. B. Adelson and E. Soloway, "The Role of Domain Experience in Software Design," *IEEE Transactions on Software Engineering*, Vol. SE-11, No. 11, November 1985, pp. 1351 - 1360.

[Arango, 1989]. G. Arango, "Domain Analysis: From Art to Engineering Discipline," *Proceedings of the Fifth International Workshop On Software Specification and Design,* May 19-20, 1989, Pittsburgh, Pennsylvania, IEEE Computer Society Press, Washington, D.C., May 1989, pp. 152 - 159.

[Berard, 1987]. E.V. Berard, "Software Reusability Cannot Be Considered in a Vacuum," *Digest of Papers COMPCON,* Spring 1987, IEEE Catalog Number 87CH2409-1, Computer Society Order Number 764, Computer Society Press of the IEEE, Washington, D.C., pp. 390 - 393.

[Booch, 1987]. G. Booch, *Software Components With Ada,* Benjamin/Cummings, Menlo Park, California, 1987.

[Brown and Quanrud, 1988]. G.R. Brown and R.B. Quanrud, "The Generic Architecture Approach to Reusable Software," *Proceedings of the Sixth National Conference on Ada Technology,* March 14-18, 1988, U.S. Army Communications-Electronics Command, Fort Monmouth, New Jersey, pp. 390 - 394.

[Burton et al., 1987]. B.A. Burton, R.W. Aragon, S.A. Bailey, K.D. Koehler, and L. A. Mayes, "The Reusable Software Library," *IEEE Software*, Vol. 4, No. 4, July 1987, pp. 25 - 33.

[Carstensen, 1987]. H.B. Carstensen, "A Real Example of Reusing Ada Software," *Proceedings of the Second National Conference on Software Reusability and Maintainability*, National Institute for Software Quality and Productivity, Washington, D.C., March 1987, pp. B-1 to B-19.

[Chan, 1987]. Y.K. Chan, "Lessons in Software Reusability in Large Complex Software Systems," *Proceedings of the Conference on Software Reusability and Portability,* National Institute for Software Quality and Productivity, Washington, D.C., September 16-17, 1987, pp. B-1 - B-7.

[Cohen, 1986]. N.H. Cohen, *Ada As a Second Language*, McGraw-Hill, New York, New York, 1986.

[Devanbu and Bachman, 1989]. P. Devanbu and R. Bachman, *OOPSLA Workshop on Domain Modeling in Software Engineering*, New Orleans, Louisiana, 1989.

[Dlugosz, 1991]. J.M. Dlugosz, "Libraries With Class," *Byte*, Vol. 16, No. 2, February 1991, pp. 164 - 166, 168.

[Dusink and van Katwijk, 1987]. E.M. Dusink and J. van Katwijk, "Reflections on Reusable Software and Software Components," *Ada Components: Libraries and Tools — Proceedings of the Ada-Europe International Conference,* Stockholm, 26-28 May, 1987, Edited by S. Tafvelin, Cambridge University Press, Cambridge, U.K., pp. 113 - 126.

[Fischer, 1987]. G. Fischer, "Cognitive View of Reuse and Redesign," *IEEE Software*, Vol. 4, No. 4, July 1987, pp. 60 - 72.

[Frankowski, 1986]. E. N. Frankowski. "Why Programs Built from Reusable Software Should be Single Paradigm," *Proceedings of the STARS Reusability Workshop*, March 24-27, 1986.

[Goldberg and Robson, 1983]. A. Goldberg and D. Robson, *Smalltalk-80: The Language and Its Implementation*, Addison-Wesley, Reading, Massachusetts, 1983.

[Hess et al., 1990]. J.A. Hess, W.E. Novak, P.C. Carroll, S.G. Cohen, R.R. Holibaugh, K.C. Kang, and A.S. Peterson, *A Domain Analysis Bibliography*, Special Report CMU/SEI-90-SR-3, Software Engineering Institute, Pittsburgh, Pennsylvania, 1990.

[Iscoe, 1988]. N. Iscoe, "Domain-Specific Reuse: An Object-Oriented and Knowledge-Based Approach," in *IEEE Tutorial: Software Reuse: Emerging Technology*, Edited by W. Tracz, IEEE Catalog No. EH0278-2, IEEE Computer Society Press, Washington, D.C., 1988, pp. 299 - 308.

[Johnson and Foote, 1988]. R. E. Johnson and B. Foote, "Designing Reusable Classes," *Journal of Object-Oriented Programming*, Vol. 1, No. 2, June/July 1988, pp. 22 - 35.

[Kaiser and Garlan, 1987]. G.E. Kaiser and D. Garlan, "Melding Software Systems from Reusable Building Blocks," *IEEE Software*, Vol. 4, No. 4, July 1987, pp. 17 - 24.

[Kang et al., 1990]. K.C. Kang, S.G. Cohen, J.A. Hess, W.E. Novak, and A.S. Peterson, *Feature-Oriented Domain Analysis (FODA) Feasibility Study*, Technical Report CMU/SEI-90-TR-21 (ESD-90-TR-222), Software Engineering Institute, Carnegie-Mellon University, Pittsburgh, Pennsylvania, November 1990.

[Levy and Ripken, 1987]. P. Levy and K. Ripken, "Experience in Constructing Ada Programs from Non-Trivial Reusable Modules," *Ada Components: Libraries and Tools — Proceedings of the Ada-Europe International Conference,* Stockholm, 26-28, May 1987, Edited by S. Tafvelin, Cambridge University Press, Cambridge, United Kingdom, pp. 100 - 112.

[Margono and Berard, 1987]. J. Margono and E.V. Berard, "A Modified Booch's Taxonomy for Ada Generic Data-Structure Components and Their Implementation," *Ada Components: Libraries and Tools - Proceedings of the Ada-Europe International Conference,* Stockholm, 26-28 May, 1987, Edited by S. Tafvelin, Cambridge University Press, Cambridge, United Kingdom, pp. 61 - 74.

[Matsumoto, 1984]. Y. Matsumoto. "Some Experiences in Promoting Reusable Software: Presentation in Higher Abstract Levels," *IEEE Transactions on Software Engineering*, Vol. SE-10, No. 5, September 1984, pp. 502 - 513.

[McGraw and Harbison-Briggs, 1989]. K.L. McGraw and K. Harbison-Briggs, *Knowledge Acquisition: Principles and Guidelines*, Prentice Hall, Englewood Cliffs, New Jersey, 1989.

[Meyer, 1987]. B. Meyer, "Reusability: The Case for Object-Oriented Design," *IEEE Software*, Vol. 4, No. 2, March 1987, pp. 50 - 64.

[Naur and Randell, 1969]. P. Naur and B. Randell, Editors, *Software Engineering: Report on a Conference Sponsored by the NATO Science Committee*, Garmisch, Germany, October 7-11, 1968.

[Neighbors, 1980]. J.M. Neighbors, "Software Construction Using Components," *Technical Report 160*, Department of Information and Computer Sciences, University of California, Irvine, 1980.

[Neighbors, 1984]. J.M. Neighbors, "The DRACO Approach to Constructing Software From Reusable Components," *IEEE Transactions on Software Engineering*, Vol. SE-10, No. 5, September 1984, pp. 564 - 574.

[Prieto-Diaz, 1988]. P. Prieto-Diaz, "Domain Analysis for Reusability," *Proceedings of COMPSAC '87*, 1987, pp. 23 - 29, reprinted in *IEEE Tutorial: Software Reuse: Emerging Technology*, Edited by W. Tracz, IEEE Catalog No. EH0278-2, IEEE Computer Society Press, Washington, D.C., 1988, pp. 347 - 353.

[Prieto-Diaz and Arango, 1991]. R. Prieto-Diaz and G. Arango, Editors, *Domain Analysis and Software Systems Modeling*, IEEE Computer Society Press, Los Alamitos, California, 1991.

[Rational, 1986]. Rational, Inc., *Large-System Development and Rational Subsystems*, Document Control Number 6004, Rational, Inc., Mountain View, California, November 1986.

[Reilly, 1987]. A. Reilly, "Roots of Reuse," *IEEE Software*, Vol. 4, No. 1, January 1987, page 4.

[RMISE, 1987]. Rocky Mountain Institute of Software Engineering, *Workshop on Software Reuse — Participant Proceedings*, October 1987, summary contained in [Tracz, 1988], pp. 41 - 53.

[Russell, 1987]. G.E. Russell, "Experiences Implementing a Reusable Data Structure Component Taxonomy," *Proceedings of the Joint Ada Conference, Fifth National Conference on Ada Technology and Washington Ada Symposium*, U.S. Army Communications-Electronics Command, Fort Monmouth, New Jersey, pp. 8 - 18.

[St. Dennis et al., 1986]. R. St. Dennis, P. Stachour, E. Frankowski, and E. Onuegbe, "Measurable Characteristics of Reusable Ada Software," *Ada Letters*, Vol. VI, No. 2, March-April 1986, pp. 41 - 50.

[Schmucker, 1986]. K.J. Schmucker, "Object Orientation," *MacWorld*, Vol. 3, No. 11, November 1986, pp. 119 - 123.

[Shlaer and Mellor, 1989]. S. Shlaer and S.J. Mellor, "An Object-Oriented Approach to Domain Analysis," *Software Engineering Notes*, Vol. 14, No. 5, July 1989, pp. 66 - 77.

[Simos, 1988]. M.A. Simos, "The Domain-Oriented Software Life-Cycle: Towards and Extended Process Model for Reusability," from [RMISE, 1987], reprinted in *IEEE Tutorial: Software Reuse: Emerging Technology*, Edited by W. Tracz, IEEE Catalog No. EH0278-2, IEEE Computer Society Press, Washington, D.C., 1988, pp. 354 - 364.

[Standish, 1984]. T. A. Standish. "An Essay on Software Reuse," *IEEE Transactions on Software Engineering*, Vol. SE-10, No. 5, September 1984, pp. 494-497.

[Stroustrup, 1991]. B. Stroustrup, *The C++ Programming Language,* Second Edition, Addison-Wesley, Reading, Massachusetts, 1991.

[Tracz, 1987]. W. Tracz, "Software Reuse: Motivators and Inhibitors," *Digest of Papers COMPCON*, Spring 1987, IEEE Catalog Number 87CH2409-1, Computer Society Order Number 764, Computer Society Press of the IEEE, Washington, D.C., 1987.

[Tracz, 1988]. W. Tracz, Editor *Software Reuse: Emerging Technology*, IEEE Catalog Number EH0278-2, Computer Society Order Number 846, IEEE Computer Society Press, Washington, D.C., 1988.

[Wirth, 1983]. N. Wirth, *Programming In Modula-2,* Second Edition, Springer-Verlag, New York, New York, 1983.

[Woodfield et al., 1987]. S.N. Woodfield, D.W. Embley, and D.T. Scott, "Can Programmers Reuse Software?," *IEEE Software*, Vol. 4, No. 4, July 1987, pp. 52 - 59.

11 Creation of and Conversion to Object-Oriented Requirements

A bad beginning makes a bad ending.

— Euripides, 485-406 B.C.

Man's drive for self-expression, which over the centuries has built his monuments, does not stay within set bounds; the creations which yesterday were the detested and the obscene become the classics of today.

— Matthew Tobriner, Judge, California Supreme Court, 1964

Prologue

Localization is the process of placing items in close physical proximity to each other, usually with the connotation of having some mechanism for precisely defining the boundaries of the "area" into which the items are being gathered. (For other definitions, see, e.g., [Ross et al., 1975] and [Booch, 1986].) Object-oriented approaches localize information around *objects* and functional decomposition approaches localize information around *functions*. Data-driven approaches localize information around *data and data structures*.

Traceability is the degree of ease with which a concept, idea, or other item may be followed from one point in a process to either a succeeding, or preceding, point in the same process. For example, one may wish to trace a requirement through the software engineering process to identify the delivered source code which specifically addresses that requirement. Traceability is greatly facilitated when the same localization scheme is used throughout the software engineering process.

Many software engineering projects begin with the establishment of requirements. Requirements embody the wants and needs of the client with regard to the software product. Care must be taken in the determination and creation of the requirements because they will be used as input to the "acceptance testing" process. (See, e.g., [Myers, 1976] and [Myers, 1979].) Specifically, the client will accept or reject the delivered software product based on how closely that product conforms to the stated requirements.

Based on experience, verifying that *object-oriented* code meets specific *functional* requirements is difficult. However, experience has also shown that verifying object-oriented code against object-oriented requirements is at least as easy as verifying functional code against functional requirements. This suggests that, if an object-oriented approach is going to be used for design and coding, the original requirements should be object-oriented, or should be converted to an object-oriented form.

(We should also note that, also based on experience, clients usually find object-oriented requirements easier to understand than functional requirements. My clients have also commented that their customers find object-oriented requirements to be more complete than functional requirements.)

The purpose of this chapter is to discuss the beginnings of an object-oriented requirements analysis effort. Specifically, its focus is on the initial gathering and formulation of object-oriented requirements, as opposed to the final packaging of the requirements. It is also the intent of this chapter to discuss the conversion of existing functional requirements into object-oriented requirements.

Establishing a Mindset

As a rule, most software people are quite comfortable with the concept of functional requirements. The concept of functions being performed by subroutines, procedures, paragraphs, and functions is very familiar to them. Further, they have conveyed this view of the world to many of their customers. This functional mindset is so well-entrenched (not only mentally, but also in existing standards, policies, and procedures) that many software personnel can conceive of no other mechanism for describing requirements.

Suppose, however, we were attempting to define the requirements for a piece of hardware, e.g., an automobile, a personal computer, or a stereo system. These items will still have to meet requirements, but notice how our view of requirements has shifted, e.g.:

- While functionality is still important, we now speak of the "functionality of a (tangible, hardware) component." Whereas in software there is a tendency to view the component and functionality as one and the same, this tendency is not as strong with hardware.

- We talk about how the components will interact to affect a solution, as opposed to "what functions will be invoked." More importantly, instead of describing an invocation hierarchy, we speak of components interacting with each other (often without the necessity of some "master routine" supervising these interactions).

- Our models make virtually no mention of "flow of data" and "flow of control." We may talk about "components controlling other components," or "components communicating with other components." We are not troubled by the fact that there may be many simultaneous, independently executing threads of control. (For example, we assume that the fuel gauge can function relatively independently of the engine temperature monitor.)

An object-oriented mindset is much closer to a hardware mindset than it is to the conventional software functional mindset. If you are having trouble imagining what a set of object-oriented requirements look like, ask yourself how a set of requirements for a computer or an automobile might be created. Remember, "functionality" is still important in object-oriented requirements, but it is now localized within objects and within descriptions of the interactions among objects.

What Do We Mean by "Requirements Analysis"?

Depending on who you talk to, you will get a variety of definitions for "software requirements analysis," e.g.:

- the first activity to occur in the software life-cycle,

- the establishment of *what* needs to be done (as opposed to a discussion of the details of *how* it is to be accomplished), and

- the analysis of requirements which have previously been established by the client.

While there have been attempts at standard definitions for "analysis" or "requirements analysis" (e.g., [IEEE, 1983]), it is difficult to define the process precisely. Still, if you were to examine studies of software development methodologies (e.g., [Agresti, 1986], [Bergland and Gordon, 1981], [Birrell and Ould, 1985], [Blank et al., 1983], [DoI, 1981], [Firth et al., 1988], [Freeman and Wasserman, 1982], [Freeman and Wasserman, 1983], and [Teledyne Brown Engineering, 1987]), certain trends would begin to emerge.

First, if we were to examine a dictionary, we might find the following definitions for "analysis":

- the separation of a thing into the parts or elements of which it is composed

- the examination of a thing to determine its parts or elements; also a statement showing the results of such an examination.

These definitions, however, do not completely describe what we mean by analysis in a software engineering context. Our comparative study of software development methodologies would show that we usually expect the following things from an analysis effort:

- an examination of a concept, system, or phenomenon with the intention of accurately understanding and describing that concept, system, or phenomenon,

- an assessment of the interaction of the concept, system, or phenomenon with its existing or proposed environment,

- the proposal of two to three alternative solutions for the client with an accurate and complete analysis of the alternatives, and

- an accurate and complete (primarily external) description of the solution to be delivered to the client.

Notice that the deliverables include not only "an 'analysis' of the client's problem," but also an accurate and complete (primarily external) description of the system to be delivered. In effect, we must demonstrate an adequate understanding of the original problem, *and* we must precisely and concisely describe the solution we will be delivering to the client. This solution must be within any client stipulated constraints.

Second, an examination of virtually all software requirements analysis methodologies shows that requirements analysis ends with the description of the "user interface." The user interface is a detailed description of the product as the user will see (interact with) it. Further, "user" can be taken to mean anything from a human user, to other software products, to computer hardware.

Third, while design activities tend to be programming language specific, analysis activities can ignore programming language to a large extent. In truth, requirements analysis for software applications is somewhat influenced by the choice of programming language. However, most approaches to requirements analysis strive to be highly independent of programming language considerations. Most of the suggested approaches to software design, on the other hand, must deal with programming language concepts (e.g., modules, packages, and software interfaces) directly.

Fourth, user visibility is very high during analysis, and very low during design. **User visibility** is a term used to describe the level of client involvement during the software life-cycle. User visibility is highest during the "analysis" and "use" phases. User visibility is lowest during the "design" and "coding" phases. During analysis, software engineers must accurately extract the client's requirements and state them in terms which can be easily verified by the client.

(Notice that some sources (e.g., [DeMarco, 1979]) advocate that everything mentioned during analysis should be easily understood by the (potentially non-technical) client. However, the analyst must have a high level of confidence that the proposed solution can indeed be constructed within any user-stipulated constraints, as well as on time and within budget. Therefore, it is likely that some of the technical information produced during the analysis effort will be more appropriate for software engineers than for (non-technical) clients.)

Fifth, the end of each phase (or partial phase) of the software life-cycle is a decision point. At each decision point, management must often make decisions on how to proceed, or whether to proceed. Without a system specified in sufficient detail, meaningful decisions are often difficult, if not impossible. The requirements analyst must propose a solution in sufficient detail to allow meaningful management decisions. The deliverables from an analysis effort should therefore include:

- a complete description of the "user interface," including such items as a detailed list of all system capabilities, timing constraints, report formats, system limitations, installation instructions, operating instructions, deliverable system documentation, necessary hardware and software, and reliability information,

- a discussion of delivery dates, estimates of system development costs, installation costs, operating costs, training costs, and transition plans,

- any necessary legal documents, and

- other information deemed useful by either the analyst or the client.

The Context for Object-Oriented Requirements Analysis

Some software engineering activities may have already been accomplished, or may be on-going, by the time one attempts to establish the object-oriented requirements for a given project. **Object-oriented domain analysis** (OODA) is an activity which identifies, documents, and configuration manages reusable object-oriented components within a given application domain. Rather than be associated with any one project, OODA is a continually on-going effort which interacts with many software engineering efforts.

During OORA, software engineers will both solicit reusable object-oriented components from the OODA effort, and contribute new candidate components to the OODA system. In reuse-conscious installations, there is a highly symbiotic relationship between the OODA effort and individual projects. (See, e.g., [Arango, 1989], [Booch, 1987], [Neighbors, 1980], and [Prieto-Diaz, 1988] for a general discussion of domain analysis, and, e.g., [Shlaer and Mellor, 1989] for one view of OODA.) This brings up another aspect of OORA, i.e., software reusability is key to a successful OORA effort. (Note that we do not wait until coding begins to consider software reusability.)

Reusability plays an important role during OORA, e.g.:

- The OORA analysts, using the in-house reusability system, search for past (or current) projects which may have something in common with the current effort. They have a number of reasons for this, e.g.:

  - One way to better understand how to solve a given problem is to examine how similar problems have been solved.

  - There may be parts of other analysis (or design) efforts which can be reused (in whole, or in part) on the current project.

  - The OORA analysts will have to quantify various options which they will be presenting to management and the client. Metrics from previous efforts can help raise the level of confidence in these quantifications. (Metrics are reusable too.)

- An analyst may desire a better understanding of a given object. If that object (in non-code and/or code form) already exists in the in-house reusability system, the analyst may extract that object for further study.

- The analyst may wish to prototype rapidly alternative scenarios. If some, or all, of the objects involved in these scenarios already exist in the in-house reusability system, they may be extracted and used in the prototype(s).

- Of course, the OORA analysts will be regularly searching the in-house reusability system for:

  - Object and Class Specifications (OCSs)

  - Kit Specifications (KS)

  - Systems of Interacting Objects Specifications (SIOS)

- An analyst may recognize that a variation on a previously existing reusable object is necessary. The analyst may then select the form of the previously existing object which is closest to the desired variation, and then modify a copy of this form to produce the desired variation.

An activity which usually immediately precedes many requirements analysis efforts is a **feasibility study**. Feasibility studies have two main goals:

- to determine the feasibility of attempting a specific project (or series of projects), and

- to accomplish the above with both a high level of confidence, and a minimum expenditure of resources.

Feasibility is typically much more than mere technical feasibility. Also important are financial, political, marketing, and time-related feasibility. (Feasibility studies are often conducted using the techniques of analysis, although the application of these techniques is usually much more informal (than during analysis).)

Beginning the Analysis Effort

Regardless of the life-cycle approach you have chosen (e.g., functional decomposition or object-oriented), there are two activities which must be accomplished before a meaningful analysis effort can begin, i.e., the sources of requirements information must be identified, and, once identified, the sources of requirements information must be characterized.

Very seldom are requirements for a given project contained in a single, self-contained document. The OORA analyst must identify all valid, worthwhile sources of requirements information. These sources can include, for example, pre-existing requirements documents, knowledgeable people, previously existing software (including prototypes), and descriptions of "real world" systems of objects.

[Notice that if a set of non-object-oriented requirements already exists, they can be used as input to the OORA process, i.e., they can be converted to object-oriented requirements. The "bad news" is that a conversion effort is necessary. The "good news" is that you have a "starting point" for the OORA effort, and there is already some understanding of the original problem.]

Characterizing the sources of requirements information involves two main activities: characterizing the source itself, and characterizing the information provided by the source. The following are important considerations when attempting to characterize a source of requirements information:

- the credibility of the source,

- the ease of access that the OORA analyst will have to the source,

- the level of authority associated with the source,

- the types of information which this source can provide,

- the responsiveness of the source, and

- the longevity of the source.

The following are important considerations when attempting to characterize the information provided by a source of requirements information:

- the form of the information provided, e.g., textual, graphical, verbal, machine-executable, and machine-readable,

- the completeness of the information provided,

- determining how current the information is,

- determining how volatile the information is,

- the relevance of the information,

- how can the information be verified,

- how understandable the information is,

- the importance and priority of the information, and

- the interrelationships among the pieces of information, e.g., how will a change in one piece of information impact other pieces of information?

Problems with Requirements

Even with careful identification of sources of information, and careful characterization of requirements information, there will still very likely be problems with the requirements information. Software engineers are very seldom (if ever) presented with a "clean" set of requirements. Software engineers will have to plan on addressing problems with any set of requirements.

Software engineers must make sure that they are addressing problems in the requirements — *not adding useless enhancements*. All too often, software engineers think that they, and not the client, know what the "real" requirements are. When attempting to fix "problems" in the requirements, software engineers should continually ask themselves, "is this a crucial and necessary fix, or is this an 'enhancement' for my own gratification?" All "fixes" and "enhancements" to the requirements must be cleared with the client.

Typical problems with requirements information include (See also [Gause and Weinberg, 1989].):

- *omissions*: Very often the initial set of user-supplied requirements (and information) is incomplete. This means that, during the course of analysis, the software engineer will have to either locate, or generate, new information. This new information is, of course, subject to the approval of the client. (Note that this location or generation of new information may be considered by some to be "design.")

- *contradictions*: Contradictions may be the result of incomplete information, imprecise specification methods, a misunderstanding, or lack of a consistency check on the requirements. If the user alone cannot resolve the contradictions, the software engineer may be required to propose a resolution to each problem.

- *ambiguities*: Ambiguities are often the result of incompletely defined requirements, lack of precision in the specification method, or a conscious decision to leave their resolution to the software engineers performing analysis. Resolution of ambiguities may require some "requirements design" decisions on the part of the software engineers.

- *duplications*: Duplications may be the outright replication of information in the same format, or the replication of the same information in several different places and formats. Sometimes duplications are not obvious, e.g., the use of several different terms to describe the same item. Software engineers must be careful when identifying and removing unnecessary duplications.

- *inaccuracies*: It is not uncommon for software engineers to uncover information which they suspect is incorrect. These inaccuracies must be brought to the client's attention, and resolved. Often, it is not until the client is confronted with a precisely described proposed solution that many of the inaccuracies in the original requirements come to light.

- *too much design*: One of the greatest temptations in software engineering is "to do the next guy's job," i.e., to both define a problem and to propose a (detailed) solution. One of the most difficult activities during analysis is the separation of "real requirements" from arbitrary (and unnecessary) design decisions made by those supplying the requirements.

  A **metarequirement** is a stipulation of a "design decision" which is both supplied *and* required by the client. For example, a client might require that data be encrypted using a specific algorithm, or that a specific location in memory be used to store a specific piece of information. Software engineers must carefully separate true metarequirements from unnecessary design decisions made by the client. Metarequirements should be kept to a minimum.

- *failure to identify priorities*: A software engineer must have some basis for making decisions. Without a clearly defined, well thought out, and comprehensive set of priorities, it will be difficult to select from a number of alternatives. Software engineers must realize that emphasis on one priority often inversely impacts several others, e.g., an overemphasis on efficiency very often impairs the reliability of the system.

- *irrelevant information*: Software engineers are often reluctant to throw away any information. Their clients often feel it is better to supply too much information rather than too little. Without some clear cut mechanisms to identify and remove irrelevant information, it will be difficult to develop accurate, cost-effective, and pragmatic solutions to a client's problems.

Creation of and Conversion to Object-Oriented Requirements

The chief differences between the original creation of object-oriented requirements, and the conversion of existing requirements to object-oriented form, is in the types of information available, and in the potential understanding of the problem. If someone has already established a set of non-object-oriented requirements (e.g., functional requirements), these non-object-oriented requirements are simply one of the sources of requirements information.

The understanding of the problem is a tricky issue. All too often, software engineers, their managers, and sometimes even their clients, think that the only way to understand a problem is strictly in functional terms. This can greatly hamper the generation of object-oriented requirements, e.g., while data flow diagrams are entirely appropriate in a functional decomposition approach, they are virtually useless in an object-oriented approach. Unfortunately, a functional decomposition approach to requirements analysis can sometimes make the establishment of object-oriented requirements more difficult than if the original set of (functional) requirements were completely discarded.

Given a reasonably complete, and reasonably accurate, set of functional requirements, and a skilled, object-oriented software engineer, a set of functional requirements can be converted to object-oriented requirements with a minimum of trouble. Further, if done well, object-oriented requirements tend to be more complete than functional requirements.

A Model

If we were to examine a number of different approaches to requirements analysis (e.g., [DeMarco, 1979] and the requirements analysis parts of [Marca and McGowan, 1988] and [Ward and Mellor, 1985]), we would see a common model consisting of three parts:

1. A series of graphical models (e.g., data flow diagrams, actigrams, and state transition diagrams). Some of these graphical models depict static relationships, while other show dynamic behavior. Many of these graphical techniques can be used at multiple levels of abstraction.

2. One or more repositories of information supporting the graphical models (e.g., the data dictionary in Structured Analysis).

3. A specified packaging of the analysis results, i.e., the deliverables. (e.g., the Structured Specification in Structured Analysis)

It is the intent of this article that we address the first two points. The last point, which potentially involves the creation of an object-oriented requirements specification (OORS), will be left for another time.

Object-Oriented Models

In constructing object-oriented models during object-oriented requirements analysis (OORA), we do not restrict ourselves to graphical models. In OORA, object-oriented models may be:

- *graphical*, e.g., semantic networks (e.g., [Barr and Feigenbaum, 1981] and [Winston, 1984]), state transition diagrams (e.g., [Shlaer and Mellor, 1988] and [Ward and Mellor, 1985]), Petri net graphs (e.g., [Peterson, 1981] and [Reisig, 1985]), object-message diagrams, and timing diagrams,

- *textual*, e.g., prose (e.g., [Abbott, 1983]), mathematical descriptions (e.g., [Jones, 1986]), and logical descriptions (e.g., [Conery, 1988]),

- *executable*, e.g., models created using object-oriented programming languages/environments (e.g., Smalltalk ([Goldberg, 1984]), Trellis ([O'Brien et al., 1987]), DSM ([Shah et al., 1989]), Actor ([Franz, 1990]), and Prograph ([Cox and Pietrzykowski, 1989])), and

- otherwise, e.g., CRC (Class-Responsibility-Collaboration) cards ([Beck and Cunningham, 1989]).

Some graphical modeling techniques are best for showing static relationships, e.g., semantic networks for depicting specialization and aggregation. Other graphical techniques can be used to demonstrate dynamic behavior, e.g., state transition diagrams and Petri net graphs. (For still other object-oriented graphical modeling techniques, see [Cunningham and Beck, 1986] and [Loomis et al., 1987].) Care must be taken to ensure that the selected graphical technique(s) either are object-oriented in nature, or encourage object-oriented thinking.

Textual models seem best for describing low-level items (e.g., internal methods). Russell J. Abbott ([Abbott, 1983]) and Grady Booch ([Booch, 1983]) have demonstrated how one can create simple textual models for small designs (or small parts of large designs). Few people have the training to effectively carry out the mathematical design of even small software systems.

Executable models, to be most effective, require high-level languages (or high-level interfaces), libraries of reusable, object-oriented components, and user-friendly environments. Even with these items, there are problems, e.g., some object-oriented modeling tools lack support for multiple inheritance, concurrency, and unencapsulated composite operations. Most importantly, we do not want the limitations of any programming language having an appreciable impact on our thinking during OORA. (Still, the future of object-oriented software engineering seems to lie in the direction of executable specifications.)

Supporting the Models: The "Object Dictionary"

Object-oriented models may be static or dynamic. They may show individual or group characteristics. They may be graphical, textual, executable, or otherwise. However, they all deal with objects. Objects are the physical and conceptual things we find in the world around us. An object may be hardware, software, a concept (e.g., velocity), or even "flesh and blood." Objects are complete entities, e.g., they are not "simply information," or "simply information and actions." (Software objects strive to capture as completely as possible the characteristics of the "real world" objects which they represent.) Finally, objects are "black boxes," i.e., their internal implementations are hidden from the outside, and all interactions with an object take place via a well-defined interface.

Objects encapsulate:

- knowledge of state,

- operations and their corresponding methods (operations "advertise" an object's capabilities to the external world, while methods are the actual internal implementations for the operations),

- in the case of composite objects, other objects (i.e., we may have both heterogeneous and homogeneous composite objects),

- [optionally] exceptions,

- [optionally] constants, and

- most importantly, concepts.

For small object-oriented systems, our objects may consist solely of classes, metaclasses, parameterized classes and/or instances. A **class** is an object which is used to create instances, i.e., a class is a template, description, pattern, or "blueprint" for a category or collection of very similar items. Among other things, a class describes the interface these items present to the outside world. (There are alternative definitions for "class.") An **instance** is a *specific* thing or characteristic. Instances are usually created using classes as templates. A **metaclass** is a class whose instances are themselves classes.

Systems engineering tells us that the size of the largest items in a system is directly proportional to the size of the overall system, i.e., as the size of the system goes up, so do the sizes of its largest components. While large and complex objects may often be represented using *only* classes, metaclasses, parameterized classes, and instances, these items are not sufficient for all large systems. Therefore, for large systems we should expect to find a significant need for kits and systems of interacting objects. (See chapter 9 of this book for a detailed discussion of both kits and systems of interacting objects.)

The major purpose of our "object dictionary" is to encapsulate the specifications for the objects (small and large) which populate our models. Therefore, we would expect to see the following items in our object-dictionary:

- specifications for small objects, i.e., classes, metaclasses, parameterized classes, and (occasionally) instances — here we are referring to object and class specifications (See chapter 8 of this book.),

- specifications for kits, and

- specifications for systems of interacting objects.

Please note that objects are more complex than mere data, and will require correspondingly more complex documentation.

(An interesting side note: Since objects, and their corresponding documentation are more complex than simple data and data descriptions, attempting to use a conventional "data dictionary" to store object-related information may prove less than satisfactory.)

Attacking an Analysis Problem

No two projects/products are the same. No two people think in exactly the same manner. Therefore, it should not be surprising that no two OORA efforts are the same. For example, some OORA analysts start by examining the available requirements information, and identifying as many different objects as possible. Other OORA analysts choose a more top-down approach, i.e., they identify the objects at the highest levels of abstraction, and then begin constructing object-oriented models of the problem (and sometimes potential solutions).

In truth, an object-oriented approach will be a mixture of composition and decomposition strategies. For small, easily-understood problems, a purely compositional approach may suffice. However, for larger, more complex problems, the initial approach will be more of an object-oriented decomposition process.

Short Maps

Regardless of whether they are using a compositional or a decompositional approach, OORA analysts will want to identify and track information relating to the objects in their system. A simple mechanism for doing this is a "short map." A **short map** resembles an index, i.e., it is simply a list of the candidate objects which were found in the requirements information, and associated with each candidate object, is a list of places where that object was found in the requirements information. The most useful short maps are those which reflect a survey of the entirety of the requirements information.

OCS Precursors

Once candidate objects have been identified, and a short map has been created, the OORA analyst may choose to reorganize the information in the original requirements. Using the short map, the OORA analyst selects each candidate object in turn, and gathers into one place everything that is know about that object. This collection of information for an object is referred to as an "**OCS precursor**."

(In truth, the information contained in an OCS precursor may describe a large object (i.e., a kit or system of interacting objects). In this case, the information will be used, in part, to produce a kit specification (KS) or a system of interacting objects specification (SIOS), rather than an OCS. However, the term is used by convention, and because the OORA analyst may not be able to tell (initially) about the size of the object.)

The analyst should look at the process of gathering information into an OCS precursor more as a "cut and paste" process, than as a "surgical extraction" process. Another commonly used analogy for OCS precursors is "a clippings file," i.e., as in clipped (cut out) newspaper articles.

The information in an OCS precursor is used for two purposes:

1. To create or select a specification for the general object, and

2. To aid in the construction of application-specific models of both the original problem and proposed solutions.

OCS precursors can contain up to four different types of information, i.e.:

1. information about the "pure object," i.e., information that is always true for the object, regardless of the applications in which it might be used,

2. application-specific information, i.e., information that relates to how the object will be used in, or will relate to, the application itself,

3. irrelevant information, and

4. incorrect information.

A good analyst will carefully identify, isolate, and remove irrelevant and/or incorrect information. Although irrelevant information may appear inconsequential, it increases the "clutter," and thus also increases the likelihood of error introduction.

The analyst should not fall into the trap of believing that an OCS precursor contains all the necessary/relevant information about the object it represents. Merely removing irrelevant and incorrect information from an OCS precursor, and then separating the application-specific information, will not necessarily result in a complete set of information about an object in isolation. (This is further hampered by the fact that, at present, the original information provided to (and/or acquired by) the analyst is most likely not in object-oriented form.)

Conclusion

Object-oriented approaches to analysis share much in common with more traditional methods of analysis. For example, OORA analysts can construct models of both the problem space and solution space. (For a discussion of the terms "problem space" and "solution space," see [Ledgard and Marcotty, 1986].) Further, the OORA analyst can support these models with an "object dictionary."

Regardless of the starting point, e.g., with or without a set of functional requirements, a set of object-oriented requirements can be produced. (This chapter, however, did not discuss the entire OORA process.)

Bibliography

[Abbott, 1983]. R.J. Abbott, "Program Design by Informal English Descriptions," *Communications of the ACM*, Vol. 26, No. 11, November 1983, pp. 882 - 894.

[Agresti, 1986]. W. W. Agresti, Editor, *Tutorial: New Paradigms for Software Development*, Institute of Electrical and Electronic Engineers (catalog number EH0245-1), Washington, DC, 1986.

[Arango, 1989]. G. Arango, "Domain Analysis: From Art to Engineering Discipline," *Proceedings of the Fifth International Workshop On Software Specification and Design,* May 19-20, 1989, Pittsburgh, Pennsylvania, IEEE Computer Society Press, Washington, D.C., May 1989, pp. 152 - 159.

[Barr and Feigenbaum, 1981]. A. Barr and E.A. Feigenbaum, Editors, *The Handbook of Artificial Intelligence,* Volume 1, HeurisTech Press, Stanford, California, 1981.

[Beck and Cunningham, 1989]. K. Beck and W. Cunningham, "A Laboratory for Teaching Object Oriented Thinking," *OOPSLA '89 Conference Proceedings,* special issue of *SIGPLAN Notices*, Vol. 24, No. 10, October 1989, pp. 1 - 6.

[Bergland and Gordon, 1981]. G. D. Bergland and R. D. Gordon, Editors, *Tutorial: Software Design Strategies*, Second Edition, IEEE Computer Society Press (catalog number EHO184-2), New York, New York, 1981.

[Birrell and Ould, 1985]. N. D. Birrell and M. A. Ould, *A Practical Handbook for Software Development*, Cambridge University Press, New York, New York, 1985.

[Blank et al., 1983]. J. Blank, M. M. H. Drummen, H. Gersteling, T. G. M. Janssen, M. J. Krijger, and W. D. Pelger, *Software Engineering: Methods and Techniques*, John Wiley & Sons, New York, New York, 1983.

[Booch, 1983]. G. Booch, *Software Engineering with Ada*, Benjamin/Cummings, Menlo Park, California, 1983.

[Booch, 1986]. G. Booch, *Software Engineering with Ada,* Second Edition, Benjamin/Cummings, Menlo Park, California, 1986.

[Booch, 1987]. G. Booch, *Software Components With Ada*, Benjamin/Cummings, Menlo Park, California, 1987.

[Booch, 1991]. G. Booch, *Object-Oriented Design With Applications*, Benjamin/Cummings, Menlo Park, California, 1991.

[Conery, 1988]. J.S. Conery, "Logical Objects," *in Proceedings of the 5th International Conference/ Symposium on Logic Programming,* Seattle, Washington, August 1988, MIT Press, Cambridge, Massachusetts, pp. 470 - 474.

[Cox and Pietrzykowski, 1989]. P.T. Cox and T. Pietrzykowski, "User-Oriented Software: A New Methodology for Software Development," *Computer Language*, Vol. 6, No. 9, September 1989, pp. 79 - 92.

[Cunningham and Beck, 1986]. W. Cunningham and K. Beck, "A Diagram for Object-Oriented Programs," *OOPSLA '86 Conference Proceedings,* special issue of *SIGPLAN Notices*, Vol. 21, No. 11, pp. 361 - 367.

[DeMarco, 1979]. T. DeMarco, *Structured Analysis and System Specification*, Yourdon Press, New York, New York, 1979.

[DoI, 1981]. Department of Industry, *Report on the Study of an Ada-based System Development Methodology,* Volume 1, Department of Industry, London, England, 1981.

[Firth et al., 1988]. R. Firth, L. R. Gold, R. Pethia, and B. Wood, *A Guide to the Assessment of Software Development Methods*, Technical Report CMU/SEI-88-TR-8, ESD-TR-88-009, Carnegie Mellon University, Software Engineering Institute, Pittsburgh, Pennsylvania, April 1988.

[Franz, 1990]. M. Franz, *Object-Oriented Programming: Featuring Actor*, Scott, Foresman and Company, Glenview, Illinois, 1990.

[Freeman and Wasserman, 1982]. P. Freeman and A. I. Wasserman, *Software Development Methodologies and Ada (Methodman)*, Department of Defense Ada Joint Program Office, Arlington, Virginia, 1982.

[Freeman and Wasserman, 1983]. P. Freeman and A. I. Wasserman, Editors, *Tutorial on Software Design Techniques*, Forth Edition, IEEE Computer Society Press (catalog number EHO205-5), Silver Spring, Maryland, 1983.

[Gause and Weinberg, 1989]. D.C. Gause and G.M. Weinberg, *Exploring Requirements: Quality Before Design*, Dorset House Publishing, New York, New York, 1989.

[Goldberg, 1984]. A. Goldberg, *Smalltalk-80: The Interactive Programming Environment*, Addison-Wesley, Reading, Massachusetts, 1984.

[Helm et al., 1990]. R. Helm, I.M. Holland, and D. Gangopadhyay, "Contracts: Specifying Behavioral Compositions in Object-Oriented Systems," *OOPSLA/ECOOP '90 Conference Proceedings,* special issue of *SIGPLAN Notices*, Vol. 25, No. 10, October 1990, pp. 169 - 180.

[IEEE, 1983]. IEEE, *Standard Glossary of Software Engineering Terminology* ANSI/IEEE Std 729-1983, Institute of Electrical and Electronics Engineers, New York, New York, 1983.

[Jones, 1986]. C.B. Jones, *Systematic Software Development Using VDM,* Prentice Hall, Englewood Cliffs, New Jersey, 1986.

[Ledgard and Marcotty, 1986]. H. Ledgard and M. Marcotty, *The Programming Language Landscape: Syntax, Semantics, Implementation,* Second Edition, Science Research Associates, Chicago, Illinois, 1986.

[Loomis et al., 1987]. M.E.S. Loomis, A.V. Shaw, and J.E. Raumbaugh, "An Object Modeling Technique for Conceptual Design," *Proceedings of ECOOP '87: European Conference on Object-Oriented Programming*, Springer Verlag, New York, New York, 1987, pp. 192 - 202.

[Marca and McGowan, 1988]. D.A. Marca and C.L. McGowan, *SADT — Structured Analysis and Design Technique*, McGraw-Hill Book Company, New York, New York, 1988.

[Morgan, 1988]. T.M. Morgan, "Configuration Management and Version Control in the Rational Programming Environment," in *Ada In Industry: Proceedings of the Ada-Europe International Conference,* Munich, 7-9 June, 1988, Cambridge University Press, Cambridge, United Kingdom, 1988, pp. 17 - 28.

[Myers, 1976]. G.J. Myers, *Software Reliability: Principles and Practices*, John Wiley & Sons, New York, New York, 1976.

[Myers, 1979]. G. J. Myers, *The Art of Software Testing*, John Wiley & Sons, New York, New York, 1979.

[Neighbors, 1980]. J.M. Neighbors, "Software Construction Using Components," *Technical Report 160*, Department of Information and Computer Sciences, University of California, Irvine, 1980.

[O'Brien et al., 1987]. P.D. O'Brien, D.C. Halbert, and M.F. Kilian, "The Trellis Programming Environment," *OOPSLA '87 Conference Proceedings,* special issue of *SIGPLAN Notices*, Vol. 22, No. 12, December 1987, pp. 91 - 102.

[Peterson, 1981]. J.L. Peterson, *Petri Net Theory and the Modeling of Systems*, Prentice Hall, Englewood Cliffs, New Jersey, 1981.

[Prieto-Diaz, 1988]. P. Prieto-Diaz, "Domain Analysis for Reusability," *Proceedings of COMPSAC '87*, 1987, pp. 23 - 29, reprinted in *IEEE Tutorial: Software Reuse: Emerging Technology*, Edited by W. Tracz, IEEE Catalog No. EH0278-2, IEEE Computer Society Press, Washington, D.C., 1988, pp. 347 - 353.

[Rational, 1986]. Rational, Inc., *Large-System Development and Rational Subsystems*, Document Control Number 6004, Rational, Inc., Mountain View, California, November, 1986.

[Reisig, 1985]. W. Reisig, *Petri Nets: An Introduction*, Springer-Verlag, New York, New York, 1985.

[Ross et al., 1975]. D. T. Ross, J. B. Goodenough, C.A. Irvine, "Software Engineering: Process, Principles, and Goals," *Computer*, Vol. 8, No. 5, May 1975, pp. 17 - 27.

[Shah et al., 1989]. A.V. Shah, J.E. Rumbaugh, J.H. Hamel, and R.A. Borsari, "DSM: An Object-Relationship Modeling Language," *OOPSLA '89 Conference Proceedings,* special issue of *SIGPLAN Notices*, Vol. 24, No. 10, October 1989, pp. 191 - 202.

[Shlaer and Mellor, 1988]. S. Shlaer and S.J. Mellor, *Object-Oriented Systems Analysis: Modeling the World In Data*, Yourdon Press: Prentice Hall, Englewood Cliffs, New Jersey, 1988.

[Shlaer and Mellor, 1989]. S. Shlaer and S.J. Mellor, "An Object-Oriented Approach to Domain Analysis," *Software Engineering Notes*, Vol. 14, No. 5, July 1989, pp. 66 - 77.

[Teledyne Brown Engineering, 1987]. *Software Methodology Catalog*, Technical Report MC87-COMM/ADP-0036, Teledyne Brown Engineering, Tinton Falls, New Jersey, October 1987.

[Ward and Mellor, 1985]. P.T. Ward and S.J. Mellor, *Structured Development for Real-Time Systems, Volumes 1-3*, Yourdon Press, New York, New York, 1985.

[Winston, 1984]. P.H. Winston, *Artificial Intelligence,* Second Edition, Addison-Wesley, Reading, Massachusetts, 1984.

12   Object-Oriented Requirements Analysis

Given for one instant an intelligence which could comprehend all the forces by which nature is animated and the respective positions of the beings which compose it, if moreover this intelligence were vast enough to submit these data to analysis, it would embrace in the same formula both the movements of the largest bodies in the universe and those of the lightest atom; to it nothing would be uncertain, and the future as the past would be present to its eyes.

— Pierre Simon de Laplace, Oeuvres, Volume VII, Théorie Analytique des Probabilités [1812-1820], introduction

Prologue

Before I begin a discussion of object-oriented requirements analysis (OORA), I must mention several very important points.

First, the development part of the object-oriented life-cycle is often best accomplished using a recursive/parallel approach, e.g., "analyze a little, design a little, implement a little, and test a little." (See chapter 5 of this book.) Therefore, even though I may talk about OORA as if it were performed at only one place during development, in reality, it may very likely be accomplished at many places.

Second, although it may be preceded by such things as feasibility studies, I will treat OORA as if it were the very first thing to be accomplished during the development of an object-oriented software product. For example, if you were to attempt an object-oriented approach using the classic waterfall life-cycle model (not recommended, but still possible), OORA would be followed by object-oriented design (OOD), which would, in turn, be followed by object-oriented programming (OOP), and so forth. During the recursive/parallel life-cycle, if OORA is used, it is the first process accomplished during each recursive application of "analyze a little, design a little, implement a little, test a little."

Third, the application of a formal OORA process is not always appropriate. If the project is small and/or non-critical, OOP may be all that is required. As we move to larger and/or more critical efforts, OOD becomes a necessary precursor to OOP. For still larger and more critical projects, we often turn to OORA, followed by OOD, followed by OOP. (Keep in mind that there is always at least an informal analysis effort that should take place at the beginning of any software development effort.)

Object-oriented requirements analysis (sometimes referred to as object-oriented analysis (OOA)) was virtually unheard of in the object-oriented programming community until the late 1980s. There are two main reasons why it is now being seriously considered:

- When object-oriented technology is applied to large and/or critical projects, the bottom-up approach, so common in OOP, often proves insufficient. Very few people, for example, can contemplate a project of, say, 100,000 lines of source code, and adequately identify most of the low-level components without some form of analysis. As object-oriented thinking moves into the mainstream, people are realizing that OOP techniques (e.g., identify classes, create objects, and send messages) *alone* may be very inadequate for large, critical efforts.

• Object-oriented technology is now being seriously considered by people who are accustomed to thinking in terms of life-cycle methodologies. These people include, for example, those developing large business applications, critical real-time applications, and large, complex software in general.

History

Although E.W. Dijkstra first described what he called "structured programming" in 1969 ([Dijkstra, 1969]), it was not until December of 1973 that many programmers became aware of the term. (The December 1973 issue of *Datamation* was devoted to the subject, e.g., [Baker and Mills, 1973], [Donaldson, 1973], [McCracken, 1973], and [Miller and Lindamood, 1973].) In 1974, the first widely-read article on "structured design" was published in the *IBM Systems Journal* ([Stevens et al., 1974]), and in late 1976, Tom McCabe began publicizing something called "structured testing," e.g., [McCabe, 1976].

By 1976, there was some early work going on in the area of "structured analysis," e.g., [SofTech, 1976]. (See also [Marca and McGowan, 1988], [Ross, 1977], and [Ross and Schoman, 1977].) In 1977, Gane and Sarson were describing their version of structured analysis ([Gane and Sarson, 1977]), which they later published in book form ([Gane and Sarson, 1979]). However, it was not until Tom DeMarco published his best selling book (DeMarco, 1979]) that structured analysis began to become generally accepted.

By 1983, it had become apparent that "standard structured analysis" was not adequate for real-time systems, e.g., it did very little in the area of such things as interrupts and scheduling of concurrent processes. A new, "real time flavor" of structured analysis began to emerge — often combined with an equally revised version of structured design. See, for example, [Gomaa, 1984], [Hatley and Pirbhai, 1988], and [Ward and Mellor, 1985]. This real time trend is also very apparent in modern OORA. (For those who are not as concerned with real time issues, OORA techniques can also be easily applied to non-real-time systems.)

(For general references on software requirements engineering, see [Dorfman and Thayer, 1990], and [Thayer and Dorfman, 1990]. Also, see chapter 11 of this book.)

The first significant object-oriented programming language was Simula ([Dahl and Nygaard, 1966]). Many of those in the object-oriented community who cast technology primarily in programming language terms (see chapter 1 of this book) contend that the concept of object-oriented analysis (or object-oriented requirements analysis) originated when the first object-oriented programming language emerged.

However, there are those in the object-oriented community who view object-oriented software engineering as primarily an *engineering* process with well-defined, coordinated tasks, and well-defined deliverables. For these people, concepts such as structured analysis predate the concept of object-oriented analysis — even though the earliest versions of structured analysis did not appear until a decade after Simula (and 4 years after the earliest versions of Smalltalk ([Goldberg and Kay, 1976])). The earliest versions of rigorous processes that were explicitly referred to as "OORA" and/or "OOA" did not show up until the last half of the 1980s, e.g., [Berard, 1988], [Coad, 1988], [McIntyre and Higgins, 1988], [Shlaer and Mellor, 1988], and [Smith and Tockey, 1988].

Grady Booch is the person chiefly responsible for introducing the concept of "object-oriented design" to the Ada community (e.g., [Booch, 1981] and [Booch, 1982]). By 1986, OOD (in some form or another) was being used on a significant percentage of Ada development efforts. However, there were some serious problems reported, e.g.:

- Traceability was difficult. (**Traceability** is a measure of the ease with which a concept, requirement, or idea may be traced from one point in the software life-cycle to another point.) For example, contractors were often (if not exclusively) furnished with *functional* requirements, and encouraged to develop *object-oriented* code. Tracing functional requirements to functional code was relatively easy since the localization (i.e., around functions) remained constant throughout the development effort. Changing localizations (i.e., from functional to object-oriented) in the middle of development made tracing requirements (and, hence, acceptance testing) very difficult.

- Testing and integration became a nightmare. A very common practice was to divide a large effort up into several (more manageable) *functional* pieces. Each of these functional pieces was given to a separate team which then designed and coded the piece in an "object-oriented" manner. Given that objects are *not* localized in a functional manner, this meant that the characteristics of a given object were often distributed unevenly among the functional pieces.

  What this meant was that each team had a very small probability of gaining a *complete* understanding of any particular object. For example, one team might see object X as having attributes A, B, and C, and another team would see object X as having attributes B, D, and F. These differences only became apparent when it came time to integrate the work of both teams, and the first team attempted to hand off their version of object X to the second team. Since integration often occurs fairly late in development, this made the required changes difficult and expensive.

- Needless to say, there was also a great deal of duplicated effort, since each separate team often (re-)developed objects which were already in use by other teams.

- Software engineers found that working with two, vastly different paradigms was difficult. For example, many of them had problems when attempting to "bridge the gap" between structured analysis and object-oriented design. (See, e.g., [Firesmith, 1991] and [Gray, 1988].)

By 1986, it had become obvious that some form of object-oriented requirements analysis was needed. Most efforts to develop an OORA methodology used either "classic" structured analysis, a real-time version of structured analysis, or a combination of either of these approaches with entity-relationship diagrams, as a starting point. (See, e.g., [Anderson et al., 1989], [Bailin, 1989], [Coad and Yourdon, 1990], [Khalsa, 1989], [Page-Jones and Weiss, 1989], [Shlaer and Mellor, 1988], [Smith and Tockey, 1988], [Stoecklin et al., 1988], [Toetenel et al., 1990], and [Ward, 1989].) To someone with a strong background in "conventional" object-oriented programming, these approaches seem strangely out of place.

Also in 1986, my clients, who were suffering from the problems I mentioned earlier, began to demand that I provide them with an object-oriented requirements methodology. By that time, I was also undertaking some large (e.g., approximately 300,000 lines of code) object-oriented development efforts of my own. Thus, I needed some practical approach to OORA for my own company.

My staff and I began to investigate the problem. From our consulting and training efforts with other organizations, and from our own experience, we knew the following:

- Attempting to base an OORA methodology on conventional requirements analysis techniques was a mistake. Whether you referred to these approaches as "functional decomposition" or "event-driven," they did not localize information around objects, and they ignored virtually all aspects of object-oriented technology.

- We would have to supply some form of graphical techniques to represent part of our analysis efforts. A purely textual approach was undesirable. Quite frankly, most of the time, people relate better to pictures than they do to words. When we began, we did not know which graphics we would use, but one of our most important criteria was that the graphics be object-oriented, or directly support object-oriented thinking.

- We had to have some mechanism for creating a specification for objects of interest. Structured analysis, for example, has a "data dictionary." We thought that we should have an "object dictionary," but we were not sure how to describe the "entries," i.e., the objects of interest.

- Merely specifying objects of interest was not enough. We had to have some mechanism(s) for showing how these objects were related, and how they would interact. It was a given that these techniques had to be graphical.

- Reusability was a key issue. We had evolved an OOD methodology which emphasized reusable objects, and we planned to extend this thinking into the OORA methodology.

- Whatever methods we came up with had to accurately reflect object-oriented thinking. Since we were already familiar with the standard object-oriented literature, we felt we had that area covered.

- The methodology had to be programming-language-independent to the highest degree possible. Developing a methodology which "reeked of Smalltalk," might not be all that applicable, for example, to projects which were going to be implemented in Eiffel ([Meyer, 1992]), C++ ([Stroustrup, 1991]), CLOS ([Lawless and Miller, 1991]), or Self ([Ungar and Smith, 1987]).

- The methodology had to be:
  - *Pragmatic*: Real people, working on real projects, under real constraints, had to be able to use the methodology.
  - *Quantifiable*: As much as possible, the methodology had to be precisely defined so that it was repeatable, and so that viable alternatives could be evaluated.

- *Widely applicable*: The approach should be one that can be used, with little, or no, modifications, on a complete spectrum of applications, e.g., from business, to scientific, to embedded real-time applications.

- *Tailorable*: Each organization (and, often, each project) may wish to emphasize different things. Some may want to delete items, others will want to add things, and still others may want to re-arrange the overall process.

Over the past six years, the OORA process, as I will describe it, has grown and matured. Techniques, graphics, and documentation have all been modified based on experience. The OORA process continues to mature.

OODA Will Impact OORA

All too often, people wait until it is time to produce source code before they think of software reusability. This ensures a minimal return on the reusability investment. Software engineers and their managers need to realize that:

- The earlier in the software life-cycle that reusability issues are addressed, the higher will be the payoff from an organization's reuse efforts.

- Much more than code software can be reused. Specifically, all items (e.g., analysis documentation) produced during a software engineering effort are candidates for reuse.

- Many existing policies, procedures, guidelines, standards, and practices are "reuse hostile," i.e., they actually inhibit software reusability.

Object-oriented approaches (e.g., OORA and OOD) force reusability issues to the earlier stages of the software life-cycle. This has an interesting effect, i.e., as software engineers learn about OORA and OOD, for example, they are also made to consider software reusability issues.

For organizations which continually develop (and maintain) significant amounts of software, an on-going object-oriented domain analysis (OODA) effort is strongly recommended. [Kang et al., 1990] defines **domain analysis** as "the process of identifying, collecting, organizing, and representing the relevant information in a domain based on the study of existing systems and their development histories, knowledge captured from domain experts, underlying theory, and emerging technology within the domain." (See also [Prieto-Diaz and Arango, 1991].) The primary motivation for domain analysis is software reusability.

Object-oriented domain analysis (OODA) seeks to identify reusable items localized around objects, e.g., classes, instances, systems of interacting objects, and kits. OORA analysts, and OOD designers will interact on a fairly frequent basis with the domain analysis effort.

Domain analysis is best accomplished independent of any particular software development effort. However, individual software engineering efforts will both make use of the products of the domain analysis effort, and contribute new products and information to the on-going domain analysis activities.

The OORA process is greatly facilitated if there is an on-going OODA effort within the organization. (See chapter 11 in this book for a detailed description of the role reusability plays during OORA.)

A Suggested OORA Methodology

There is more than one school of thought on how OORA might be accomplished, e.g., [Coad and Yourdon, 1990], [Freitas et al., 1990], [Hayes and Coleman, 1991], [Jochem et al., 1989], [Lee and Carver, 1991], [Ross, 1990], [Shlaer and Mellor, 1988], and the general references in [Wiener, 1991]. I share some ideas in common with other OORA methodologists, but both they and I would agree that what I am about to describe is significantly different from other OORA approaches.

In addition, although I will describe this process as if it were to be accomplished in one contiguous block of time, this is most often not the case. It is best accomplished in a recursive/parallel life-cycle.

I will list the steps to be accomplished as if they were in sequential order. However, in practice, some steps may be re-arranged (within limits), and many may be accomplished in parallel, e.g., it is possible to be working on step 1 and step 8 at the same time.

The general OORA process is:

1. Identify the sources of requirements information.

2. Characterize the sources of requirements information.

3. Identify candidate objects.

4. Build object-oriented models of both the problem, and the potential solution, as necessary.

5. Re-localize the information around the appropriate candidate objects.

6. Select, create, and verify candidate objects.

7. Assign the candidate objects to the appropriate section of the object-oriented requirements specification (OORS).

8. Develop and refine the precise and concise system description.

Now let's briefly look at each of these steps in slightly more detail.

There is nothing specifically object-oriented about the first two steps. Regardless of the approach to requirements analysis one chooses, they will have to be accomplished.

Very seldom are requirements for a given project contained in a single, self-contained document. The OORA analyst must identify all valid, worthwhile sources of requirements information. These sources can include, for example: pre-existing requirements documents, standards documentation, knowledgeable people, previously existing executable software, including prototypes, and descriptions of "real world" systems of objects.

When my clients actually attempt this step for real projects, they discover several things:

- There are actually many more sources of requirements than they thought existed. Simply listing the sources of requirements information, one per line, can consume many pages.

- Two, or more, different teams gathering these sources will often come up with very different lists. Specifically, while there will indeed be overlap between/among the lists, there will be significant differences. (It is very common to hear statements such as "I didn't know that that document existed." or "I didn't realize that that person had anything to do with the requirements for this project.")

- Although, most software engineers think that "information gathering" is an intuitive and ad hoc process, most are surprised to find that there are systematic methods for knowledge acquisition, e.g., [McGraw and Harbison-Briggs, 1989].

- The actual identification of sources of requirements information was a more time-consuming process than most people expected. For example, for one medium-sized project, a team of three people spent at least two weeks just identifying (not qualifying, and not describing — just identifying) sources of requirements information.

- The identification of sources of requirements information is an on-going process. During the development of any serious software, changes are continually introduced — even up to the point of delivery of the product. Changes are often accompanied by new sources of requirements information.

- It is sometimes difficult to uniquely identify a particular source of requirements information. Each source of requirements information must be identified in an unambiguous manner (ideally, so that someone who was not part of the identification process can find the specific source).

(If there is already a pre-existing set of "functional" requirements, there are systematic techniques for converting these requirements into object-oriented requirements. Keep in mind that one does *not* have to do functional requirements analysis first. You can start off with object-oriented requirements analysis.)

Characterizing the sources of requirements information is actually a two-part process. You must characterize the source of the information, and you must also characterize the information provided by the source. The source may be characterized in terms of availability, authority, credibility, responsiveness, longevity, ease of access, and types of information provided. The information provided by the source may be characterized in terms of form (e.g., textual, graphical, machine-readable, and verbal), completeness, how current the information is, which aspects of the product it addresses, and understandability, among others.

Identification of candidate objects requires that we define what "objects" are. The objects dealt with most frequently are: classes, metaclasses, parameterized classes, non-class instances, kits, and systems of interacting objects. Metaclasses are classes whose instances themselves are classes.

Each object will have to be documented in some form. Classes, metaclasses, parameterized classes, and, in rare cases, non-class instances, are usually documented with an object and class specification (OCS, pronounced "ox"). (See chapter 8 of this book.)

OCSs are used to document individual objects. However, the OORA analyst will often come across systems of objects. A **system of objects** is defined as two or more interacting or interrelated, non-nested objects. (We exclude simple aggregations, i.e., composite objects, from our definition of systems of objects.) Systems of objects fall into two general categories:

- **kits**, which are collections of objects all of which support a large, object-oriented concept, and

- **systems of interacting objects**, which are collections of objects in which there must be a direct or indirect physical connection between any two arbitrary objects within the collection.

(See chapter 9 of this book.)

In the process of identifying candidate object-oriented items, the OORA analyst should keep a record of where a particular piece of information was found. The collection of these records for all the object-oriented items is referred to as a "**short map**." The form of a short map is very similar to an index, i.e., the name of each object-oriented item is listed (typically in alphabetical order), followed by pointers indicating where information on the item can be found.

Simultaneously, with the identification of objects, software engineers can be creating models of both aspects of the problem, and sketches of potential solutions. There are four major categories of models used in object-oriented software engineering: textual models, graphical models, executable models, and other models. (See chapter 11 of this book for a more detailed discussion of these types of models.)

Each model should have an accompanying set of "engineering notes," and should also be supported by the "object dictionary."

A natural human tendency is to (re)localize "everything we know about an item" in one place. During the processes of identifying candidate objects and constructing models, we will be making decisions about which objects will be necessary for both a better understanding of the problem, and an implementation of a solution. Software engineers will want to localize in one place information regarding particular objects. (This localization is usually accomplished with the help of the short map.) These collections of information are referred to as "object and class specification precursors" or "**OCS precursors**."

OCS precursors typically contain: information about the object in isolation (the "pure object"), information about how the object is used in this particular application, irrelevant information, and, unfortunately, incorrect information.

This information is often incomplete and ambiguous, and software engineers must be careful to verify all available information on a particular object. To ensure a high degree of reusability, we must take care to separate the characteristics of the object "in isolation" from how the object is used in the application at hand.

At this point in the OORA process, after examining OCS precursors, the OORA analyst should have enough information to:

- Select a previously-defined OCS, kit specification, or system of interacting objects specification to use for the object which has been documented using the OCS precursor. (The OORA analyst may also wish to examine other information, e.g., any pre-existing code software that may be associated with an OCS or kit specification.)

- Use the information available from the particular OCS precursor to define a new object, or system of objects, and document that object, or system of objects, with an OCS, a kit specification, or system of interacting objects specification.

One OCS, for example, may inspire several different designs, and each design may be implemented in several different ways (e.g., in multiple programming languages). The "object dictionary" may be a full-blown reusability system, e.g., McDonnell Douglas's AMPEE, Rockwell's ROSES, and others. The reusability system may store other items along with the OCS, e.g., the design(s) and the source code.

In addition to information about the objects in isolation, OCS precursors contain application-specific information. This application information must not be discarded. The OORA analyst must use this application-specific information, where appropriate, in the application-specific section of the object-oriented requirements specification (OORS).

The object-oriented requirements specification (OORS) is the primary deliverable from the OORA process. If you are using a recursive/parallel approach, the OORS will be a "living document," i.e., we will be updating its contents even after we have begun to do some design. Of course, if you insist on "doing all of your object-oriented analysis at once," e.g., you are using a classic waterfall life-cycle approach, the OORS will be completed by the end of the "analysis phase."

The OORS is divided into two parts: an object-general section, and an application-specific section. Oversimplifying, reusable objects are placed into the object-general section, and application-specific objects, along with an object-oriented system specification, are placed in the application-specific section.

At sometime during the OORA process, the OORA analysts must create an accurate description of the system which will be delivered to the client. This description will most likely be a combination of textual and graphical information. This description must unambiguously describe the system which will be delivered to the client. It must therefore include the following:

- a complete description of the "user interface," including such items as a detailed list of all system capabilities, timing constraints, report formats, system limitations, installation instructions, operating instructions, deliverable system documentation, and reliability information,

- a discussion of delivery dates, estimates of system development costs, installation costs, operating costs, training costs, and transition plans,

- models of the system representing the system from the user's viewpoint (These models can be textual, graphical, executable, or otherwise.),

- any necessary legal documents, and

- other information deemed useful by either the analyst or the client.

V&V and SQA

Verification, validation, and software quality assurance are always important. Verification answers the question: "are we solving the problem correctly?" Validation answers the question: "are we solving the correct problem?" Software quality assurance ensures that we are addressing some aspect of the software life-cycle in an appropriate and approved manner. These processes will be done continually throughout the OORA process.

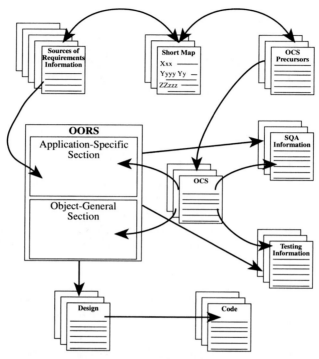

Figure 1:   **An OORA map showing a high-level view of the OORA process includes many of the typical OORA documents**. The object-oriented requirements specification (OORS) itself is the main deliverable from the OORA process.

Conclusion

As with structured analysis, object-oriented analysis has several different interpretations. Those in the object-oriented community that advocate formality and rigor in the software engineering process have advanced several different interpretations as to how to conduct an OOA/OORA effort.

What we have presented in this chapter is a high-level view of one systematic approach to OORA. This approach evolved based on the demands of my clients, and has been used on real projects with a good deal of success. The approach blends pragmatic software engineering concerns (e.g., identification and characterization of sources of information) with more explicitly object-oriented issues (e.g., the identification and specification of classes, meta-classes, and parameterized classes).

Bibliography

[Anderson et al., 1989]. J.A. Anderson, J. McDonald, L. Holland, and E. Scranage, "Automated Object-Oriented Requirements Analysis and Design," *Proceedings of the Sixth Washington Ada Symposium*, June 26-29, 1989, pp. 265 - 272.

[Bailin, 1989]. S. C. Bailin, "An Object-Oriented Requirements Specification Method," *Communications of the ACM*, Vol. 32, No. 5, May 1989, pp. 608 - 623.

[Baker and Mills, 1973]. F.T. Baker and H.D. Mills, "Chief Programming Teams," *Datamation*, Vol. 19, No. 12, December 1973, pp. 58 - 61.

[Beck and Cunningham, 1989]. K. Beck and W. Cunningham, "A Laboratory for Teaching Object Oriented Thinking," *OOPSLA '89 Conference Proceedings,* special issue of *SIGPLAN Notices*, Vol. 24, No. 10, October 1989, pp. 1 - 6.

[Berard, 1988]. E.V. Berard, *Object Oriented Requirements Analysis: Course Notes*, EVB Software Engineering, Frederick, Maryland, 1988.

[Berard, 1990]. E.V. Berard, "Object-Oriented Requirements Analysis," *Hotline On Object-Oriented Technology*, Vol. 1, No. 8, June 1990, pp. 9 - 11.

[Booch, 1981]. G. Booch, "Describing Software Design in Ada," *SIGPLAN Notices*, Vol. 16, No. 9, September 1981, pp. 42 - 47.

[Booch, 1982]. G. Booch, "Object Oriented Design," *Ada Letters*, Vol. I, No. 3, March-April 1982, pp. 64 - 76.

[Booch, 1986]. G. Booch, "Object Oriented Development," *IEEE Transactions on Software Engineering*, Vol. SE-12, No. 2, February 1986, pp. 211 - 221.

[Coad, 1988]. P. Coad, "Object-Oriented Requirements Analysis (OORA): A Practitioner's Crib Sheet," *Proceedings of Ada Expo 1988*, Galaxy Productions, Frederick, Maryland, 1988, 9 pages.

[Coad and Yourdon, 1990]. P. Coad and E. Yourdon, *OOA — Object-Oriented Analysis*, 2nd Edition, Prentice Hall, Englewood Cliffs, New Jersey, 1990.

[Cox and Pietrzykowski, 1989]. P.T. Cox and T. Pietrzykowski, "User-Oriented Software: A New Methodology for Software Development," *Computer Language*, Vol. 6, No. 9, September 1989, pp. 79 - 92.

[Dahl and Nygaard, 1966]. O.J. Dahl and K. Nygaard, "SIMULA — an ALGOL-Based Simulation Language," *Communications of the ACM*, Vol. 9, No. 9, September 1966, pp. 671 - 678.

[DeMarco, 1979]. T. DeMarco, *Structured Analysis and System Specification*, Yourdon Press, New York, New York, 1979.

[Dijkstra, 1969]. E. Dijkstra, "Structured Programming," Presented at the 1969 NATO Science Committee Conference, Reprinted in E. N. Yourdon, Editor, *Classics in Software Engineering*, Yourdon Press, New York, New York, 1979, pp. 113 - 125.

[Donaldson, 1973]. J.R. Donaldson, "Structured Programming," *Datamation*, Vol. 19, No. 12, December 1973, pp. 52 - 54.

[Dorfman and Thayer, 1990]. M. Dorfman and R.H. Thayer, Editors, *Standards, Guidelines, and Examples on System and Software Requirements Engineering*, IEEE Computer Society Press, Los Alamitos, California, 1990.

[Firesmith, 1991]. D. Firesmith, "Structured Analysis and Object-Oriented Development Are Not Compatible," *Ada Letters*, Vol. XI, No. 9, November/December 1991, pp. 56 - 66.

[Franz, 1990]. M. Franz, *Object-Oriented Programming: Featuring Actor*, Scott, Foresman and Company, Glenview, Illinois, 1990.

[Freeman and Wasserman, 1980]. P. Freeman and A. I. Wasserman, Editors, *Tutorial on Software Design Techniques*, Third Edition, Catalog No. EHO161-0, Institute of Electrical and Electronic Engineers, New York, New York, 1980.

[Freeman and Wasserman, 1983]. P. Freeman and A. I. Wasserman, Editors, *Tutorial on Software Design Techniques,* Forth Edition, Catalog No. EHO205-5, IEEE Computer Society Press, Silver Spring, Maryland, 1983.

[Freeman, 1979].P. Freeman, "A Perspective on Requirements Analysis and Specification," *IBM Design '79 Symposium*, 1979. Reprinted in [Freeman and Wasserman, 1980], pp. 86 - 96.

[Freitas et al., 1990]. M Freitas, A Moreira, and P. Guerreiro, "Object-Oriented Requirements Analysis in an Ada Project," *Ada Letters*, Vol. 10, No. 6, July-August 1990, pp. 97 - 109.

[Gane and Sarson, 1977]. C. Gane and T. Sarson, *Structured Systems Analysis: Tools and Techniques*, Improved System Technologies, New York, New York, 1977.

[Gane and Sarson, 1979].C. Gane and T. Sarson, S*tructured Systems Analysis: Tools and Techniques*, Prentice Hall, Englewood Cliffs, New Jersey, 1979.

[Goldberg and Kay, 1976]. A. Goldberg and A. Kay, Editors, *Smalltalk-72 Instructional Manual*, Technical Report SSL-76-6, Xerox PARC, Palo Alto, California, March 1976.

[Goldberg and Robson, 1983]. A. Goldberg and D. Robson, *Smalltalk-80: The Language and Its Implementation*, Addison-Wesley, Reading, Massachusetts, 1983.

[Gomaa, 1984]. H. Gomaa, "A Software Design Method for Real-Time Systems," *Communications of the ACM*, Vol. 27, No. 9, September 1984, pp. 938 - 949.

[Gray, 1988]. L. Gray, "Transitioning from Structured Analysis to Object-Oriented Design," *Proceedings of the Fifth Washington Ada Symposium*, June 27 - 30, 1988, Association for Computing Machinery, New York, New York, 1988, pp. 151 - 162.

[Hatley and Pirbhai, 1988]. D.J. Hatley and I.A. Pirbhai, *Strategies for Real-Time System Specification*, Dorset House Publishing, New York, New York, 1988.

[Hayes and Coleman, 1991]. F. Hayes and D. Coleman, "Coherent Models for Object-Oriented Analysis," *OOPSLA '91 Conference Proceedings,* special issue of *SIGPLAN Notices*, Vol. 26, No. 11, November 1991, pp. 171 - 183.

[Jochem et al., 1989]. R. Jochem, M. Rabe, W. Süssenguth, and P. Bals, "An Object-Oriented Analysis and Design Methodology for Computer Integrated Manufacturing Systems," *Technology of Object-Oriented Languages and Systems 1989 (TOOLS '89)*, Paris, France, November 13 - 15, 1989, pp. 75 - 84.

[Kang et al., 1990]. K.C. Kang, S.G. Cohen, J.A. Hess, W.E. Novak, and A.S. Peterson, *Feature-Oriented Domain Analysis (FODA) Feasibility Study*, Technical Report CMU/SEI-90-TR-21 (ESD-90-TR-222), Software Engineering Institute, Carnegie-Mellon University, Pittsburgh, Pennsylvania, November 1990.

[Khalsa, 1989]. G.K. Khalsa, "Using Object Modeling to Transform Structured Analysis Into Object-Oriented Design," *Proceedings of the Sixth Washington Ada Symposium*, June 26-29, 1989, pp. 201 - 212.

[Kilian, 1990]. M. Kilian, "Trellis: Turning Designs Into Programs," *Communications of the ACM*, Vol. 33, No. 9, September 1990, pp. 65 - 67.

[Lawless and Miller, 1991]. J.A. Lawless and M.M. Miller, *Understanding CLOS: The Common Lisp Object System*, Digital Press, Bedford, Massachusetts, 1990.

[Lee and Carver, 1991]. S. Lee and D.L. Carver, "Object-Oriented Analysis and Specification: A Knowledge Base Approach," *Journal of Object-Oriented Programming*, Vol. 3, No. 5, January/February 1991, pp. 35 - 43.

[Marca and McGowan, 1988]. D.A. Marca and C.L. McGowan, *SADT — Structured Analysis and Design Technique*, McGraw-Hill Book Company, New York, New York, 1988.

[McCabe, 1976]. T. McCabe, "A Complexity Measure," *IEEE Transactions on Software Engineering*, December 1976, pp. 308 - 320.

[McCracken, 1973]. D. McCracken, "Revolution in Programming: An Overview," *Datamation*, Vol. 19, No. 12, December 1973, pp. 50 - 52.

[McGraw and Harbison-Briggs, 1989]. K.L. McGraw and K. Harbison-Briggs, Knowledge Acquisition: Principles and Guidelines, Prentice Hall, Englewood Cliffs, New Jersey, 1989.

[McIntyre and Higgins, 1988]. S.C. McIntyre and L.F. Higgins, "Object-Oriented Systems Analysis and Design: Methodology and Application," *Journal of Management Information Systems*, Vol. 5, No. 1, Summer 1988, pp. 25 - 35.

[Meyer, 1992]. B. Meyer, *Eiffel: The Language*, Prentice Hall, Englewood Cliffs, New Jersey, 1992.

[Miller and Lindamood, 1973]. E.F. Miller and G.E. Lindamood, "Structured Programming: Top-Down Approach," *Datamation*, Vol. 19, No. 12, December 1973, pp. 55 - 57.

[Page-Jones and Weiss, 1989]. M. Page-Jones and S. Weiss, "Synthesis: An Object-Oriented Analysis and Design Method," *Hotline on Object-Oriented Technology*, Vol. 1, No. 2, December 1989, pp. 12 - 14.

[Prieto-Diaz and Arango, 1991]. R. Prieto-Diaz and G. Arango, Editors, *Domain Analysis and Software Systems Modeling*, IEEE Computer Society Press, Los Alamitos, California, 1991.

[Reid, 1990]. T.F. Reid, "Object-Oriented Requirements Analysis: A Tool Vision," *Proceedings of the Seventh Washington Ada Symposium,* June 25-28, 1990, pp. 227 - 230.

[Ross, 1990]. D.L. Ross, "Issues in Object-Oriented Requirements Analysis," *Proceedings of the Seventh Washington Ada Symposium,* June 25-28, 1990, pp. 77 - 99.

[Ross, 1977]. D.T. Ross, "Structured Analysis (SA): A Language for Communicating Ideas," *IEEE Transactions on Software Engineering*, Vol. SE-3, No. 1, January 1977, pp. 16 - 34. Reprinted in [Freeman and Wasserman, 1983], pp. 96 - 114.

[Ross and Schoman, 1977]. D.T. Ross and K.E. Schoman, "Structured Analysis for Requirements Definition," *IEEE Transactions on Software Engineering*, Vol. SE-3, No. 1, January 1977, pp. 6 - 15. Reprinted in [Freeman and Wasserman, 1983], pp. 86 - 95.

[Shlaer and Mellor, 1988]. S. Shlaer and S.J. Mellor, *Object-Oriented Systems Analysis: Modeling the World In Data*, Yourdon Press: Prentice Hall, Englewood Cliffs, New Jersey, 1988.

[Smith and Tockey, 1988]. M. K. Smith and S.R. Tockey, "An Integrated Approach to Software Requirements Definition Using Objects," *Proceedings of Ada Expo 1988*, Galaxy Productions, Frederick, Maryland, 1988, 21 pages.

[SofTech, 1976]. *An Introduction to SADT: Structured Analysis and Design Technique*, SofTech, Inc., Waltham, Massachusetts, 1976.

[Stevens et al., 1974]. W. P. Stevens, G. J. Myers, and L. L. Constantine, "Structured Design," *IBM Systems Journal*, Vol. 13, No. 2, May 1974, pp. 115 - 139. Reprinted in P. Freeman and A. I. Wasserman, Editors, *Tutorial on Software Design Techniques*, Fourth Edition, IEEE Computer Society Press (catalog number EHO205-5), Silver Spring, Maryland, 1983, pp. 328 - 352.

[Stoecklin et al., 1988]. S.E. Stoecklin, E.J. Adams, and S. Smith, "Object-Oriented Analysis," *Proceedings of the Fifth Washington Ada Symposium,* June 27 - 30, 1988, Association for Computing Machinery, New York, New York, 1988, pp. 133 - 138.

[Stroustrup, 1991]. B. Stroustrup, *The C++ Programming Language,* Second Edition, Addison-Wesley, Reading, Massachusetts, 1991.

[Thayer and Dorfman, 1990]. R.H. Thayer and M. Dorfman, Editors, *System and Software Requirements Engineering*, IEEE Computer Society Press, Los Alamitos, California, 1990.

[Toetenel et al., 1990]. H. Toetenel, J. van Katwijk, and N. Plat, "Structured Analysis — Formal Design, Using Stream and Object-Oriented Formal Specification," *Proceedings of the ACM SIGSOFT International Workshop on Formal Methods in Software Development*, special issue of *Software Engineering Notes*, Vol. 15, No. 4, September 1990, pp. 118 - 127.

[Ungar and Smith, 1987]. D. Ungar and R.B. Smith, "Self: The Power of Simplicity," *OOPSLA '87 Conference Proceedings,* special issue of *SIGPLAN Notices*, Vol. 22, No. 12, December 1987, pp. 227 - 242.

[Walters, 1991]. N.L. Walters, "An Ada Object-Based Analysis and Design Approach," *Ada Letters*, Vol. XI, No. 5, July/August 1991, pp. 62 - 78.

[Ward, 1989]. P.T. Ward, "How to Integrate Object Orientation with Structured Analysis and Design," *IEEE Software*, Vol. 6, No. 2, March 1989, pp. 74 - 82.

[Ward and Mellor, 1985]. P.T. Ward and S.J. Mellor, *Structured Development for Real-Time Systems, Volumes 1, 2 and 3*, Yourdon Press, New York, New York, 1985.

[Wiener, 1991]. R.S. Wiener, Editor, *Focus On Analysis and Design*, SIGS Publications, Inc., New York, New York, 1991.

13   Object-Oriented Design

The Park [Central Park, New York City] throughout is a single work of art, and as such subject to the primary law of every work of art, namely, that it shall be framed upon a single, noble motive, to which the design of all its parts, in some more or less subtle way, shall be confluent and helpful.

— Frederick Lay Olmstead and Calvert Vaux in a report submitted with their plan (awarded first prize) for Central Park in New York City.

Prologue

Like structured programming, the term "object-oriented design" (OOD) means different things to different people. For example, OOD has been used to imply such things as:

- the design of individual objects, and/or the design of the individual methods contained in those objects (e.g., [Taylor and Hecht, 1990]),

- the design of an inheritance (specialization) hierarchy of objects,

- the design of a library of reusable objects (e.g., [Coggins, 1990]), and

- the process of specifying and coding an entire object-oriented application.

At one time, the lines were more clearly drawn, i.e., those with a software engineering background used the term "object-oriented *design*" almost exclusively, and almost never talked about "object-oriented *programming*" (OOP). Users of the so-called object-oriented programming languages (e.g., Smalltalk ([Goldberg and Robson, 1983])), used the term "object-oriented programming" almost exclusively. However, with the increased popularity in things object-oriented, even these people are using the term "object-oriented design" with increasing frequency.

Examples of non-formal approaches to OOD that are very close to coding are described in [Jalote, 1989], [Mullin, 1989], [Scharenberg and Dunsmore, 1991], and [Taylor and Hecht]. [Bailey, 1989] and [Clark, 1987] describe informal techniques for designing individual objects, while [Coggins, 1990] discusses approaches to the design of a library of classes.

Dave Bulman ([Bulman, 1989]) and others have observed that the mere identification and creation of objects, however, is not a substitute for "design." It is important to realize that, by "design," Bulman means the establishment of a system architecture. This includes not only the identification of system components (objects), but also the definitions of their interactions and interrelationships as well.

For Bulman and others with an engineering viewpoint, concepts such as structured design significantly predate the emergence of a formalized, repeatable process for *object-oriented* design. We note, however, that the earliest versions of structured design did not appear until eight years after Simula (and 2 years after the earliest versions of Smalltalk ([Goldberg and Kay, 1976])). The earliest versions of a rigorous process that was explicitly referred to as "OOD" did not show up until 1980, e.g., [Booch, 1981] and [Booch, 1982].

Almost everyone that advocates an engineering approach views object-oriented *design* as only one part of the software development life-cycle. It may be preceded by such activities as analysis and feasibility studies and followed by the production of source code. Those accomplishing object-oriented design will be expected to interact with testing, quality assurance, and management personnel. Only if the software problem is small, and of relatively low risk, will object-oriented design be the *first* life-cycle activity, and even then it will be followed by object-oriented programming.

OOD and the Software Life-Cycle

As we will define it, OOD is the phase of the software life-cycle in which the internal architecture of the system (e.g., the object definitions, their interrelationships, and their interactions) is both created and documented in an object-oriented manner. OOD usually occurs after object-oriented requirements analysis (OORA) and before coding (object-oriented programming) takes place. OORA defines both the client's needs and a proposed solution to the client's problem in an object-oriented manner *as it will appear to the client.* You can think of OORA as specifying the externally discernible (i.e., visible to users of the system) characteristics of the system, and of OOD as specifying the internal (i.e., hidden from users of the system) structure of the system.

OOD can be used in a more conventional (e.g., waterfall) life-cycle — although this is not the best approach. It is more appropriately handled within the context of a recursive/parallel life-cycle approach, i.e., "analyze a little, design a little, implement a little, and test a little." This means that OOD is usually not accomplished as a separate, *contiguous* life-cycle phase, i.e., we will be effecting OOD at many different points in the development part of the life-cycle. This has many interesting consequences. For example, in the recursive/parallel life-cycle the distinctions between analysis, design and programming become somewhat blurred, but the characteristic flavors are preserved.

The "good news" is that OOD and OORA are *more* consistent in their thinking than are, say, structured analysis and structured design. The "bad news" is that this higher level of consistency makes it harder to differentiate between the two. (See the discussion in chapter 5 of this book.)

History

While the significant history of object-oriented technology in general dates from at least 1966, the history of object-oriented design is much more recent. The object-oriented programming (OOP) community did not pay much attention to system design issues until very recently. (See, for example, [Beck and Cunningham, 1989], [Rosson and Gold, 1989], and [Wirfs-Brock and Wilkerson, 1989].) As it turns out, a significant amount of the early work in the definition of an explicit, formal OOD process occurred in the Ada ([ARM, 1983]) community.

(Please note that object-oriented programming languages, and their fundamental concepts, decidedly predate the introduction of Ada. Also note that Ada is *not* an object-oriented programming language, but rather an "object-based" programming language. (See [Wegner, 1990].) A good number of those who developed software engineering processes that were explicitly referred to as OOD — even though they were doing it in the context of the Ada community — did indeed cite the influences of object-oriented programming languages such as Smalltalk.)

In January of 1980, Grady Booch attended an Association for Computing Machinery (ACM) symposium on Ada in Boston, Massachusetts. There was a very clear message delivered at the conference: "the main thrust of any Ada training must be software engineering, i.e., language syntax and semantics are there to support specific, and important, software engineering concepts."

Booch then set out to find some mechanism for introducing software engineering into the Ada training efforts. He identified the work of Russell J. Abbott at California State University as being relevant (e.g., [Abbott, 1983]). Abbott had described a simple approach to design using nouns and verbs. Booch slightly formalized Abbott's approach, and referred to it as "object-oriented design" (see, e.g., [Booch, 1981] and [Booch, 1982]). By the time his first book ([Booch, 1983a]) was released Booch had a number of working examples.

(Many people did not understand Booch's intentions. They thought, for example, that OOD *always* required that one write a paragraph, and then underline nouns and verbs. Booch viewed the paragraph as a "crutch," i.e., one technique out of many which could help identify and define objects.)

By 1982, I had begun to develop some Ada training courses. These courses included simple object-oriented design exercises. Later, in 1984, I wrote a 300-page book on object-oriented design, i.e. *An Object-Oriented Design Handbook for Ada Software,* ([Berard, 1985]). By late 1985, both Booch and myself had begun to actively incorporate more classic object-oriented thinking (e.g., Smalltalk concepts) into our courses, consulting, and articles. (See also [Richardson et al., 1992].)

In February of 1986, Booch wrote an article ([Booch, 1986]) describing his revised (more correctly: evolving) thinking on object-oriented approaches. Realizing that object-oriented thinking is not limited to design and coding, Booch began to refer to his approach as "object-oriented *development*."

By 1986, other ideas of how to approach object-oriented design began to emerge. Ed Seidewitz and Mike Stark at NASA Goddard introduced what they referred to as "general object-oriented development" (GOOD). (See, e.g., [Seidewitz and Stark, 1986] and [Stark and Seidewitz, 1987].) CiSi (in France) began talking about their "hierarchical object-oriented design" (HOOD) method ([Heitz, 1988], [Heitz and Labreuille, 1988], and [Vielcanet, 1989]). Some folks at the Software Engineering Institute (SEI) in Pittsburgh, Pennsylvania have presented their views ([Lee et al., 1987]). Ken Shumate, then at Hughes, introduced what he called "layered virtual machine/object-oriented design" (LVM/OOD) — see, e.g., [Nielsen and Shumate, 1987] and [Shumate, 1988].

More recently, we have seen both enhancements of existing approaches (e.g., [Booch, 1990] and [Booch, 1991]), interesting combinations of views (e.g., [McQuown, 1989]), and an expanded effort to define OOD in the non-Ada arena, e.g., [Weiner, 1991], [Wirfs-Brock, 1990], and [Wirfs-Brock and Johnson, 1990]. We are also beginning to see more attempts at measuring the overall quality of an object-oriented design, e.g., [Chidamber and Kemerer, 1991].

There are other views on OOD that have evolved from fairly unusual perspectives. [Jochem et al., 1989] describes an approach that was influenced by computer integrated manufacturing (CIM). James Rumbaugh ([Blaha et al., 1988] and [Rumbaugh et al., 1991]) advocates an approach that is more closely based on data modeling than on object-oriented thinking. Peter Coad ([Coad and Yourdon, 1991]) describes a "multicomponent, multilayered" approach that is fairly unique.

Mixed Paradigms

There are methodologists who suggest mixing object-oriented approaches with other approaches, and giving each approach equal weighting. [Bewtra et al., 1990] suggests combining object-oriented technology with functional programming ([Backus, 1978] and [Backus, 1982]). [Pendley, 1989] describes a combination of object-oriented thinking and information engineering ([Finkelstein, 1989], [Martin, 1989], [Martin, 1990a], and [Martin, 1990b]). Stream and formal object-oriented specification techniques are advocated in [Toetenel et al., 1990].

Modifying Other Approaches to Encompass the Object-Oriented Paradigm

When moving from an older way of doing things to a newer way, it is seldom advisable to "throw out" everything connected with the old way. One oft-used strategy is to enlarge the older way so that it can encompass some or all of the aspects of the newer. [Henderson-Sellers, 1991], [Henderson-Sellers and Constantine, 1991], [Li, 1991], and [Ward, 1989] all suggest mechanisms for keeping much of traditional structured/functional-decomposition thinking while addressing object-oriented concerns. [Birchenough and Cameron, 1989], [Hull et al., 1989], and [Reed and Bynum, 1989] all describe OOD within the context of Jackson System Development (JSD) ([Jackson, 1983]).

Different Paradigms in the Same Life-Cycle

Experience has shown that simply attempting to integrate object-oriented thinking into the more traditional methodologies (e.g., structured) is a mistake. The major problem is that of localization, i.e., the placing of related items in close physical proximity to each other. Functional approaches, for example, tend to localize information around functions, whereas object-oriented approaches tend to localize information around objects. A functional decomposition "front end" to an object-oriented process, in effect, breaks up objects and scatters their parts. Later, these parts must be retrieved and relocalized around objects.

There have been quite a number of attempts to reconcile the output of a non-object-oriented process with the input requirements of an OOD process, e.g., [Alabiso, 1988], [Brown and Dobbs, 1989], [Gray, 1987], [Gray, 1988], [Khalsa, 1989], and [Lukman, 1991]. None of these scenarios are as clean and easy as using an object-oriented approach from the very beginning of the software life-cycle.

Transitioning from OORA

Assuming that one has a large enough (or critical enough) project, a formal OORA process immediately precedes OOD. OORA will have identified some objects which are necessary for setting the context for the application, but will not be considered during the design process. We generally refer to these objects as "**analysis objects**." There are two other types of objects which will be identified in OORA:

- Objects that are part of the "user interface," where a "user" can be a human, another piece of software, or a piece of hardware. (Remember, that most traditional analysis methodologies stop at the "user interface.") Examples of these objects include windows and read-only ports. These objects are collectively referred to as "**interface objects**."

- Objects that exist inside the proposed system, but become visible to the outside through the user interface. Examples of these objects include such things as messages in an electronic messaging system, and purchase orders (in a more traditional business application). One can accurately think of these objects as the inputs and outputs for the system. Since these objects commute into and out of the system, they are collectively referred to as "**commuting objects**."

As a direct result of the OOD process, the designer must deliver an internal architecture for the system that causes the system to exhibit the externally discernible characteristics that were established during the OORA process. The OOD designer must directly incorporate both the interface objects and the commuting objects into his or her design. However, although the OOD designer generally cannot introduce new interface and commuting objects, he or she will be specifying new objects that exist entirely inside of the system, i.e., these objects are not visible to those outside of the system (i.e., users). We refer to objects created during the design process, and not visible to those outside of the system, collectively as "**design objects**."

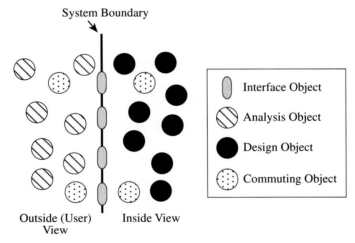

Figure 1:   **The boundary between the software engineering activities of "analysis" and "design" has traditionally also been the boundary between the external or user's view of a system, and the underlying implementation (i.e., internal architecture) for that system.** This boundary has been most commonly referred to as the "user's interface."

OODA Will Impact OOD

Object-oriented approaches such as OOD force reusability issues to the earlier stages of the software life-cycle. This has an interesting effect, i.e., as software engineers learn about OOD they are also made to consider software reusability issues.

For organizations which continually develop (and maintain) significant amounts of software, an on-going object-oriented domain analysis (OODA) effort is strongly recommended. (See chapters 10 and 12 of this book for definitions of domain analysis.) **Object-oriented domain analysis** (OODA) seeks to identify reusable items localized around objects e.g., classes, instances, systems of interacting objects, and kits. OOD designers will interact on a fairly frequent basis with the domain analysis effort.

Domain analysis is best accomplished independent of any particular software development effort. However, individual software engineering efforts will both make use of the products of the domain analysis effort, and contribute new products and information to the on-going domain analysis activities.

Reusability plays an important role during OOD, e.g.:

- The OOD designers, using the in-house reusability system, search for past (or current) projects which may have something in common with the current effort. They have a number of reasons for this, e.g.:

  - One way to better understand how to solve a given problem is to examine how similar problems have been solved.

  - There may be parts of other design (or analysis) efforts which can be reused (in whole, or in part) on the current project.

  - The OOD designers will have to quantify various options which they will be presenting to management and to each other. Metrics from previous efforts can help raise the level of confidence in these quantifications. (Metrics are reusable too.)

- A designer may desire a better understanding of a given object. If that object (in non-code and/or code form) already exists in the in-house reusability system, the designer may extract that object for further study.

- The designer may wish to prototype rapidly alternative scenarios. If some, or all, of the objects involved in these scenarios already exist in the in-house reusability system, they may be extracted and used in the prototype(s).

- Of course, the designers will be regularly searching the in-house reusability system for object and class specifications (OCSs), kit specifications (KS), and systems of interacting objects specifications (SIOS).

- For each object specification (OCS, KS, or SIOS), there may be one or more reusable designs. The OOD designers will use the in-house reusability system to identify previously existing designs for objects.

- A designer may recognize that a variation on a previously existing reusable object is necessary. The designer may then select the form of the previously existing object which is closest to the desired variation, and then modify a copy of this form to produce the desired variation.

A Mechanism for Accomplishing OOD

The method I am about to describe here is a method I currently advocate. It is the result of 10 years of continual evolution, and has actually been used to develop large, object-oriented applications. However, not everyone agrees that it is the best approach.

Although, I will present the following steps as if they were sequential, some of them may be re-ordered, and some may even be accomplished in parallel. The overall seven-step process looks like this:

- Identifying candidate objects
  - Developing an object-oriented model of the solution
  - Identifying objects of interest from the model
  - Associating attributes with the objects of interest
- Identifying operations suffered by, and required of, candidate objects
  - Identifying operations of interest
  - Associating attributes with the operations of interest
  - Handling composite operations
    - Decomposition into primitive operations
    - Decoupling of objects
- Selecting, creating, and verifying objects for design
  - Binding objects and operations
  - Examining objects for completeness
- Deciding on programming language implementations for objects
  - Objects identified during analysis
  - Objects identified during design
- Creating object-oriented graphical models
- Establishing the interface for each object-oriented item
- Implementing each object-oriented item
  - Refinement of the interface objects
  - Refinement of the other objects
  - Recursive application of the object-oriented development process

The first part of the OOD process requires that the software engineer accomplish two different goals: identify the objects of interest, and specify how these objects will interact and interrelate to effect a solution for the problem. One might say that the software engineer must construct an object-oriented model (strategy) of the proposed solution. There are four major categories of models used in object-oriented software engineering: textual models, graphical models, executable models, and other models. (See also, chapter 12 of this book.)

It is strongly suggested that the software engineers construct more than one model of a potential solution. While all the models of the same strategy should be at generally the same level of abstraction, each should show something (e.g., different objects or different interactions) that the others do not. (See, for example, Figures 2 and 3.)

The strategy for the proposed solution must explicitly solve the problem at hand. Further, it must solve the problem within any stated or implied constraints. In addition, the strategy must be object-oriented, i.e., the objects in the model must be readily apparent, as well as their interactions and interrelationships. The strategy should also attempt to maintain a uniform level of abstraction — showing at most three levels, and those only when absolutely necessary.

> "The concordance utility prompts the user for a command. Based on the command, the concordance utility will allow a user to create a concordance for a user-specified document, store a concordance within the collection of concordances, retrieve a specified concordance from the collection of concordances, display a given concordance or otherwise modify the concordance or collection of concordances. Where necessary, users will be prompted for the names of documents, and/ or names of concordances. If an invalid document name, invalid concordance name, or invalid command is entered, an error message will be displayed."

Figure 2:   **A textual model of a strategy for solving a given problem identifies not only the objects involved, but their interactions and interrelationships as well.** "Concordance," "document," and even "user" are all candidate objects.

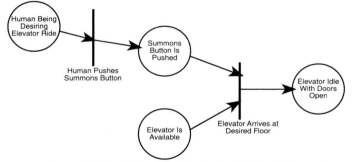

Figure 3:   **A graphical model, or a series of graphical models, can be used to illustrate a partial or full strategy for meeting the client's needs.** Some of the object states in this Petri net graph are rather simple, e.g., "summons button is pushed," while others are far more involved, e.g., "elevator is available."

Candidate Object	From which model(s)?	Do We Need It?	Type of Object	Name
build command	STD UI	Yes	Non-class instance	Build_Command
collection of concordances	Text	Yes	Metaclass	Concordance_Store Concordance_Dictionary
command	Text STD	Yes	Class	Command
compare command	STD UI	Yes	Non-class instance	Compare_Command
concordance	Text STD OMD UI	Yes	Metaclass	Concordance

Figure 4:   **This is a table showing objects identified from several models (STD = "state transition diagram," UI = "user interface," OMD = "object message diagram").** "Do We Need It?" refers to whether we need the candidate object to effect a solution to the original problem, and "Name" is used for tracking (configuration management) purposes.

Once the strategy is agreed upon, the objects of interest can be identified. (Here, we extend the concept of object to include large object-oriented entities (kits and systems of interacting objects) as well.) The designer will accomplish this by re-examining the models and producing a report of the objects that he or she found.

The designer should also gather information about each object of interest and localize it with the appropriate object. This information may be referred to as "annotations" or "attributes" for each candidate object. This information may come from several different sources, e.g., the original requirements, the models themselves, the mind of the software engineer, and technical references.

Candidate Object	Attributes
Command	• Command is a monolithic class. • Instances of class Command may take on the following values: build, store, retrieve, display, compare, quit, status, delete, update and remove.
Concordance_Store	• Concordance_Store is a homogeneous composite metaclass. • Concordance_Stores are homogeneous composite objects capable of storing many concordances. • Concordance_Store is parameterized by its component class: concordance. • Concordance_Stores may be empty.
Reference	• Reference is a heterogeneous composite parameterized class. • Its component classes are Line_Number and Page_Number. • Reference is parameterized by Line_Number and Page_Number.

Figure 5: **This table of objects attributes or object annotations reveals information that the designer feels is important regarding the objects listed.** This information is not meant to be exhaustively complete. Rather, these are "engineering notes" that the designer makes for himself, herself, or others.

The next major step requires the designer to identify suffered and required operations for each object. A "suffered" operation is something which happens to a given object, e.g., adding an element to a list, directing an elevator to go up, and querying a temperature sensor as to its current value. A "required" operation is an operation for an object other than the encapsulating object, and is necessary to ensure the correct and desired characteristics of the encapsulating object. For example, if we wish a list object to be ordered, it will require that the items contained in the list furnish a "<" (less than) operation.

(It is primarily (but not exclusively) through operations that objects are coupled. Unnecessary object coupling reduces both the reusability and reliability of our objects. The identification and separation of required operations is a means of reducing object coupling.)

Operations can be identified directly from the object-oriented model we constructed in the first step (e.g., the verbs and verb phrases in the paragraph), or they may come indirectly from the suggested interactions in the model. In either case, the designer should associate attributes with each operation (suffered and required). As with attributes of objects, the attributes for operations can come from several different sources, and should be viewed as engineering notes.

Candidate Operation	From which models?	Do We Need It?	Object	Name
acknowledge	STD	No		
build	STD OMD UI	Yes	composite	Build
compare	STD OMD UI	Yes	Concordance	Equality_Test
create	Text	Yes	composite	Build
delete	STD OMD UI	Yes	Concordance_Dictionary	Delete

Figure 6:   **This is a table showing operations identified from several models (STD = "state transition diagram," UI = "user interface," OMD = "object message diagram").** "Object" refers to the object in which the operation will be encapsulated. If this column contains the word "composite," that means that the operation is a composite of other, more primitive operations, and must be further decomposed.

During OOD, as during OORA, the software engineer will very likely encounter composite methods. A **primitive method** is an method that cannot be implemented simply, efficiently, and reliably without direct knowledge of the underlying implementation of the object in which it is encapsulated. A **composite method** is any method constructed from two or more primitive methods — sometimes from different objects. The designer must take care to decompose each composite method. In the process of decomposing each composite method, additional primitive methods, and/or object coupling, may be uncovered.

At this point in the OOD process, the designer can begin specifying *complete* objects. By combining objects and their respective suffered methods, a more complete picture of each object begins to emerge. Several things may happen, i.e.:

- The software engineer may recognize an object which is already available in the object library maintained by his or her organization. If this is the case, the library object will be extracted.

- The software engineer may recognize that the desired object is a variation on an object currently in the object library. The currently existing object will then be used as the basis for the creation of a new object.

- The software engineer may not find any existing object in the object library which closely (or exactly) meets the criteria for the needed object. In this case, a new object specification will be created.

In any of the above cases, we must verify that we have chosen, or created, a correct and appropriate object. If we create new objects, or modify existing objects, these objects will have to be tested and quality assured, and then placed in the library (as well as being used for this specific project).

Object	Suffered Operations	Required Operations	Instances
Command	set_from_string		Build_Command Compare_Command Retrieve_Command Remove_Command Store_Command Quit_Command Update_Command Display_Command Delete_Command Status_Command
Concordance	equality_test clear get_entry_dictionary set_entry_dictionary	equality_test (Name) equality_test (Entry_Dictionary)	none
Concordance_ Dictionary	get get_concordance get_name size_of next add remove exists?	less_than (Name)	none

Figure 7: **Having identified the objects and operations of interest, we now reconcile them.** Notice that operations that are required by one object will have to be supplied by one or more other objects.

We are usually not selecting or creating *code* software just yet. It is more likely that we are selecting or creating *non-code* software, i.e., specifications for objects, e.g., object and class specifications (OCSs). However, our in-house software reusability system may contain both code and non-code versions for many objects. We may even be swayed in our decision as to which object to select based on whether there is a code software implementation of a particular object specification.

Before any object can be considered usable, it must be examined for completeness. We do not want to have to modify any object (other than supplying parameters) when we reuse it. For example, our immediate application may only require that we add items to a list, but never delete them. If we place an add operation in the interface to the list, but no delete operation, the object is incomplete. It is very important that every object we create (either entirely new, or as a variation on an existing object) be examined for completeness.

Completeness entails more than just operations. For example, we may wish to add exportable constants and exceptions to our object definition.

The next major step in the OOD process is deciding on programming language implementations for our objects. This step involves both the objects identified during design, and those identified during analysis. Some programming languages, e.g., Smalltalk, C++ ([Stroustrup, 1991]), and Trellis ([Kilian, 1990]), have very specific mechanisms for implementing objects. Other languages, e.g., Ada, provide a variety of options. (Please note: I am *not* saying "Ada is better than...") The designer may wish to implement classes, instances, metaclasses, unencapsulated non-primitive operations, metaoperations, and parallel program units, depending on the capabilities furnished by the implementation language of choice. (See Figure 8.)

The designer may then wish to show programming language relationships among the objects of interest. By "programming language relationships" I mean, for example, access to capabilities (dependencies), nesting, message sending, and aggregation. These relationships may also be shown graphically, e.g., using the graphics suggested by Booch (e.g., [Booch, 1991]). Figure 9 shows the use of such "program unit graphics."

Concordance_Dictionary

1. Concordance_Dictionary will be implemented using a dictionary template from our library. Name will be the key and Concordance the information associated with the key.

2. Iteration is provided by an active iterator that comes with the dictionary in the library. It includes the operations reset, next, get_key (get_name), get_info (get_concordance), the end_of_list test, the no_current_entry exception and the no_more_entries (no_more_concordances) exception.

3. The delete operation is implemented as remove in the dictionary.

Figure 8:   **A description of how a software engineer plans to implement the Concordance_Dictionary class in a C++ implementation shows the parameters selected for instantiating the template. The designer has selected an active (open) iterator capability.** (See [Booch, 1987] and [Booch and Vilot, 1990].)

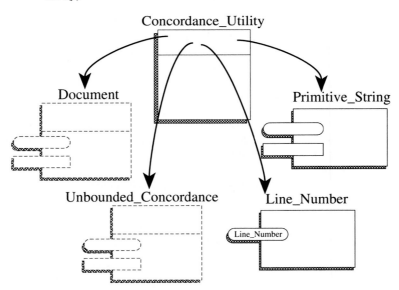

Figure 9:   **Program unit graphics are used to represent the architecture of the system.** The lines and the arrowheads indicate dependencies, e.g., the Concordance_Utility makes use of (needs, depends on) the Document template class.

We may choose to use the implementation language to precisely define the interfaces among the objects in the system. The early establishment of object interfaces allows for a greater degree of parallelism in the implementation of the object-oriented application.

Lastly, we have two main choices available to us:

- switch to OOP and implement the internal structures of our objects, or

- if the system is large enough, we may wish to re-apply the object-oriented development process (i.e., "analyze a little, design a little,...") to the products of our design effort.

The designer may then choose to use the implementation language to precisely define the interfaces among the objects in the system. The early establishment of object interfaces allows for a greater degree of parallelism in the implementation of the object-oriented application.

Summary

There are quite a few ideas on how to accomplish object-oriented design. While some restrict the definition of OOD to little more than coding decisions, others view OOD as an engineering process with well-defined steps and deliverables. In this chapter we have mentioned several engineering approaches, and shown one in detail. (A complete example of this particular OOD approach can be found in [Richardson et al., 1992].)

Bibliography

[Abbott, 1983]. R.J. Abbott, "Program Design by Informal English Descriptions," *Communications of the ACM*, Vol. 26, No. 11, November 1983, pp. 882 - 894.

[Alabiso, 1988]. B. Alabiso, "Transformation of Data Flow Analysis Models to Object-Oriented Design," *OOPSLA '88 Conference Proceedings,* special issue of *SIGPLAN Notices*, Vol. 23, No. 11, November 1988, pp. 335 - 353.

[ARM, 1983]. *Reference Manual for the Ada Programming Language, ANSI/MIL-STD 1815A (1983)*, United States Department of Defense, February 1983.

[Backus, 1978]. J. Backus, "Can Programming be Liberated From the von Neumann Style?: A Functional Style and Its Algebra of Programs," *Communications of the ACM*, Vol. 21, No. 8, August 1978, pp. 613 - 641.

[Backus, 1982]. J. Backus, "Function Level Computing," *IEEE Spectrum*, Vol. 19, No. 8, August 1982, pp. 22 - 27.

[Bailey, 1989]. S.C. Bailey, "Designing With Objects," *Computer Language*, Vol. 6, No. 1, January 1989, pp. 34 - 43.

[Beck and Cunningham, 1989]. K. Beck and W. Cunningham, "A Laboratory for Teaching Object Oriented Thinking," *OOPSLA '89 Conference Proceedings,* special issue of *SIGPLAN Notices*, Vol. 24, No. 10, October 1989, pp. 1 - 6.

[Berard, 1985]. E.V. Berard, *An Object-Oriented Design Handbook for Ada Software,* EVB Software Engineering, Inc., Frederick, Maryland, 1985.

[Bewtra et al., 1990]. M. Bewtra, S.C. Balin, and J.M. Moore, "An Ada Design and Implementation Toolset Based on Object-Oriented and Functional Programming Paradigms," *Proceedings of the Seventh Washington Ada Symposium,* June 25-28, 1990, pp. 213 - 226.

[Birchenough and Cameron, 1989]. A. Birchenough and J.R. Cameron, "JSD and Object-Oriented Design," *JSP & JSD: The Jackson Approach to Software Development*, IEEE Computer Society Press, Washington, D.C., 1989.

[Blaha et al., 1988]. M.R. Blaha, W.J. Premerlani, and J.E. Rumbaugh, "Relational Database Design Using an Object-Oriented Approach," *Communications of the ACM*, Vol. 31, No. 4, April 1988, pp. 414 - 427.

[Booch, 1981]. G. Booch, "Describing Software Design in Ada," *SIGPLAN Notices*, Vol. 16, No. 9, September 1981, pp. 42 - 47.

[Booch, 1982]. G. Booch, "Object Oriented Design," *Ada Letters*, Vol. I, No. 3, March-April 1982, pp. 64 - 76.

[Booch, 1983a]. G. Booch, *Software Engineering with Ada*, Benjamin/Cummings, Menlo Park, California, 1983.

[Booch, 1983b]. G. Booch, "Object Oriented Design," *IEEE Tutorial on Software Design Techniques*, Fourth Edition, P. Freeman and A.I. Wasserman, Editors, IEEE Computer Society Press, IEEE Catalog No. EHO205-5, IEEE-CS Order No. 514, pp. 420 - 436.

[Booch, 1986]. G. Booch, "Object Oriented Development," *IEEE Transactions on Software Engineering*, Vol. SE-12, No. 2, February 1986, pp. 211 - 221.

[Booch, 1990]. G. Booch, "On the Concepts of Object-Oriented Design," in *Modern Software Engineering: Foundations and Current Perspectives*, P.A. Ng and R.T. Yeh, Editors, Van Nostrand Reinhold, New York, New York, 1990, pp. 165 - 204.

[Booch, 1991]. G. Booch, *Object-Oriented Design With Applications*, Benjamin/Cummings, Menlo Park, California, 1991.

[Boyd, 1987]. S. Boyd, "Object-Oriented Design and PAMELA: A Comparison of Two Design Methods for Ada," *Ada Letters*, Vol. 7, No. 4, July-August 1987, pp. 68 - 78.

[Brown and Dobbs, 1989]. R.J. Brown and V. Dobbs, "A Method for Translating Functional Requirements for Object-Oriented Design," *Proceedings of the Seventh Annual National Conference on Ada Technology*, March 1989, pp. 589 - 599.

[Bulman, 1989]. D.M. Bulman, "An Object-Based Development Model," *Computer Language*, Vol. 6, No. 8, August 1989, pp. 49 - 59.

[Byrne and Wiatrowski, 1986]. W.E. Byrne and E. Wiatrowski, "Object-Oriented Design With Graphical Abstraction," *Proceedings of the Third National Conference on Methodologies and Tools for Real-Time Systems*, National Institute for Software Quality and Productivity, Washington, D.C., September 1986, pp. C-1 to C-19.

[Chidamber and Kemerer, 1991]. S.R. Chidamber and C.F. Kemerer, "Towards a Metrics Suite for Object-Oriented Design," *OOPSLA '91 Conference Proceedings,* special issue of *SIGPLAN Notices*, Vol. 26, No. 11, November 1991, pp. 197 - 211.

[Clark, 1987]. R.G. Clark, "Designing Concurrent Objects," *Ada Letters*, Volume VII, No. 6, Fall 1987, pp. 107 - 109.

[Coad and Yourdon, 1991]. P. Coad and E. Yourdon, *Object-Oriented Design,* Prentice Hall, Englewood Cliffs, New Jersey, 1991.

[Coggins, 1990]. J.M. Coggins, "Designing C++ Class Libraries," *Proceedings of the C++ Conference,* San Francisco, California, April 1990, USENIX Association, Berkeley, California, 1990, pp. 25 - 35.

[Colbert, 1989]. E. Colbert, "The Object-Oriented Software Development Method: A Practical Approach to Object-Oriented Development," *Proceedings of TRI-Ada '89 — Ada Technology In Context: Application, Development, and Deployment,* October 23-26, 1989, Association for Computing Machinery, New York, New York, pp. 400 - 415.

[Cox and Pietrzykowski, 1989]. P.T. Cox and T. Pietrzykowski, "User-Oriented Software: A New Methodology for Software Development," *Computer Language*, Vol. 6, No. 9, September 1989, pp. 79 - 92.

[Davis and Irving, 1989]. N.W. Davis and M. Irving, "Practical Experiences of Ada and Object-Oriented Design In Real-Time Distributed Systems," *Ada: the Design Choice — Proceedings of the Ada-Europe Conference,* Madrid, 13-15 June, 1989, Cambridge University Press, Cambridge, United Kingdom, 1989, pp. 59 - 79.

[Finkelstein, 1989]. C. Finkelstein, *An Introduction to Information Engineering: From Strategic Planning to Information Systems*, Addison-Wesley, Reading, Massachusetts, 1989.

[Franz, 1990]. M. Franz, *Object-Oriented Programming: Featuring Actor*, Scott, Foresman and Company, Glenview, Illinois, 1990.

[Goldberg and Robson, 1983]. A. Goldberg and D. Robson, *Smalltalk-80: The Language and Its Implementation*, Addison-Wesley, Reading, Massachusetts, 1983.

[Gray, 1987]. L. Gray, "Procedures for Transitioning from Structured Methods to Object-Oriented Design," *Proceedings of the Conference on Methodologies and Tools for Real-Time Systems IV*, National Institute for Software Quality and Productivity, Washington, D.C., September 14-15, 1987, pp. R-1 to R-21.

[Gray, 1988]. L. Gray, "Transitioning from Structured Analysis to Object-Oriented Design," *Proceedings of the Fifth Washington Ada Symposium,* June 27 - 30, 1988, Association for Computing Machinery, New York, New York, 1988, pp. 151 - 162.

[Heitz, 1988]. M. Heitz, "HOOD: A Hierarchical Object-Oriented Design Method," *Proceedings of the Third German Ada Users Congress,* January 1988, Gesellschaft für Software Engineering, Munich, West Germany, pp. 12-1 - 12-9.

[Heitz and Labreuille, 1988]. M. Heitz and B. Labreuille, "Design and Development of Distributed Software Using Hierarchical Object Oriented Design and Ada," in *Ada In Industry: Proceedings of the Ada-Europe International Conference,* Munich, 7-9 June, 1988, Cambridge University Press, Cambridge, United Kingdom, 1988, pp. 143 - 156.

[Henderson-Sellers, 1991]. B. Henderson-Sellers, "Hybrid Object-Oriented/Functional Decomposition Methodologies for the Software Engineering Lifecycle," *Hotline on Object-Oriented Technology*, Vol. 2, No. 7, May 1991, pp. 1, 2 - 8.

[Henderson-Sellers and Constantine, 1991]. B. Henderson-Sellers and L.L. Constantine, "Object-Oriented Development and Functional Decomposition, *Journal of Object-Oriented Programming*, Vol. 3, No. 5, January/February 1991, pp. 11 - 17.

[Hull et al., 1989]. M. Hull, A. Zarea-Aliabadi, and D. Gutherie, "Object-Oriented Design, Jackson System Development (JSD) Specifications and Concurrency," *Software Engineering Journal*, Vol. 4, No. 2, March 1989, pp. 79 - 86.

[Jackson, 1983]. M. A. Jackson, *System Development*, Prentice Hall, Englewood Cliffs, New Jersey, 1983.

[Jalote, 1989]. P. Jalote, "Functional Refinement and Nested Objects for Object-Oriented Design," *IEEE Transactions on Software Engineering*, Vol. 15, No. 3, March 1989, pp. 264 - 270.

[Jamsa, 1984]. K.A. Jamsa, "Object Oriented Design vs. Structured Design — A Student's Perspective," *Software Engineering Notes*, Vol. 9, No. 1, January 1984, pp. 43 - 49.

[Jochem et al., 1989]. R. Jochem, M. Rabe, W. Süssenguth, and P. Bals, "An Object-Oriented Analysis and Design Methodology for Computer Integrated Manufacturing Systems," *Technology of Object-Oriented Languages and Systems 1989 (TOOLS '89)*, Paris, France, November 13 - 15, 1989, pp. 75 - 84.

[Kang et al., 1990]. K.C. Kang, S.G. Cohen, J.A. Hess, W.E. Novak, and A.S. Peterson, *Feature-Oriented Domain Analysis (FODA) Feasibility Study*, Technical Report CMU/SEI-90-TR-21 (ESD-90-TR-222), Software Engineering Institute, Carnegie-Mellon University, Pittsburgh, Pennsylvania, November 1990.

[Khalsa, 1989]. G.K. Khalsa, "Using Object Modeling to Transform Structured Analysis Into Object-Oriented Design," *Proceedings of the Sixth Washington Ada Symposium*, June 26-29, 1989, pp. 201 - 212.

[Kilian, 1990]. M. Kilian, "Trellis: Turning Designs Into Programs," *Communications of the ACM*, Vol. 33, No. 9, September 1990, pp. 65 - 67.

[Ladden, 1988]. R.M. Ladden, "A Survey of Issues To Be Considered In the Development of an Object-Oriented Development Methodology for Ada," *Software Engineering Notes*, Vol. 13, No. 3, July 1988, pp. 24 - 31.

[Lee et al., 1987]. K.J. Lee, M.S. Rissman, R.D. D'Ippolito, C. Plinta, and R. Van Scoy, *An OOD Paradigm for Flight Simulators*, Technical Report CMU/SEI-87-TR-43 (ESD-TR-87-206), Software Engineering Institute, Pittsburgh, Pennsylvania, 1987.

[Li, 1991]. X. Li, "Integration of Structured and Object-Oriented Programming," in *Focus On Analysis and Design*, SIGS Publications, Inc., New York, New York, 1991, pp. 54 - 60.

[Lukman, 1991]. J.T. Lukman, "Transforming the 2167A Requirements Definition Model Into an Ada-Object-Oriented Design," *Proceedings of the Ninth Annual National Conference on Ada Technology*, March 4-7, 1991, pp. 200 - 205.

[Martin, 1989]. J. Martin, *Information Engineering, Book 1: Introduction*, Prentice Hall, Englewood Cliffs, New Jersey, 1989.

[Martin, 1990a]. J. Martin, *Information Engineering, Book 2: Planning and Analysis*, Prentice Hall, Englewood Cliffs, New Jersey, 1990.

[Martin, 1990b]. J. Martin, *Information Engineering, Book 3: Design and Construction*, Prentice Hall, Englewood Cliffs, New Jersey, 1990.

[Masiero and Germano, 1988]. P. Masiero and F.S.R. Germano, "JSD As An Object-Oriented Design Method," *Software Engineering Notes*, Vol. 13, No. 3, July 1988, pp. 22 - 23.

[McQuown, 1989]. K. McQuown, "Object-Oriented Design in a Real-Time Multiprocessor Environment," *Proceedings of TRI-Ada '89 — Ada Technology In Context: Application, Development, and Deployment*, October 23-26, 1989, Association for Computing Machinery, New York, New York, pp. 570 - 588.

[Mullin, 1989]. M. Mullin, *Object-Oriented Program Design: With Examples in C++*, Addison-Wesley Publishing Company, Reading, Massachusetts, 1989.

[Nielsen and Shumate, 1987]. K.W. Nielsen and K. Shumate, "Designing Large Real-Time Systems With Ada," *Communications of the ACM*, Vol. 30, No. 8, August 1987, pp. 695 - 715.

[Pendley, 1989]. J. Pendley, "Using Information Engineering and Ada Object-Oriented Design Methods in Concert — A Case Study," *Proceedings of the Sixth Washington Ada Symposium*, June 26-29, 1989, pp. 11 - 19.

[Prieto-Diaz and Arango, 1991]. R. Prieto-Diaz and G. Arango, Editors, *Domain Analysis and Software Systems Modeling*, IEEE Computer Society Press, Los Alamitos, California, 1991.

[Rajlich and Silva, 1988]. V. Rajlich and J. Silva, "Two Object-Oriented Decomposition Techniques," *Proceedings of the Fifth Washington Ada Symposium*, June 27-30, 1988, Association for Computing Machinery, New York, New York, 1988, pp. 171 - 176.

[Reed and Bynum, 1989]. G.P. Reed and Donald E. Bynum, "Analyzing Systems for Object-Oriented Design," *Proceedings of the Sixth Washington Ada Symposium*, June 26-29, 1989, pp. 195 - 200.

[Richardson et al., 1992]. J.E. Richardson, R.C. Schultz, and E.V. Berard, *A Complete Object-Oriented Design Example*, Berard Software Engineering, Gaithersburg, Maryland, 1992.

[Rosson and Gold, 1989]. M.B. Rosson and E. Gold, "Problem-Solution Mapping In Object-Oriented Design," *OOPSLA '89 Conference Proceedings,* special issue of *SIGPLAN Notices*, Vol. 24, No. 10, October 1989, pp. 7 - 10.

[Rumbaugh et al., 1991]. J. Rumbaugh, M. Blaha, W. Premerlani, F. Eddy, and W. Lorensen, *Object-Oriented Modeling and Design*, Prentice Hall, Englewood Cliffs, New Jersey, 1991.

[Safford, 1987]. H.D. Safford, "Ada Object-Oriented Design Saves Costs," *Government Computer News*, Vol. 6, No. 19, September 25, 1987, page 108.

[Scharenberg and Dunsmore, 1991]. M.E. Scharenberg and H.E. Dunsmore, "Evolution of Classes and Objects During Object-Oriented Design and Programming," *Journal of Object-Oriented Programming*, Vol. 3, No. 5, January/February 1991, pp. 18 - 28.

[Seidewitz and Stark, 1986]. E. Seidewitz and M. Stark, *General Object-Oriented Software Development*, Document No. SEL-86-002, NASA Goddard Space Flight Center, Greenbelt, Maryland, 1986.

[Shumate, 1988]. K. Shumate, "Layered Virtual Machine/Object-Oriented Design," *Proceedings of the Fifth Washington Ada Symposium,* June 27 - 30, 1988, Association for Computing Machinery, New York, New York, 1988, pp. 177 - 190.

[Stark and Seidewitz, 1987]. M. Stark and E.V. Seidewitz, "Towards a General Object-Oriented Ada Life-Cycle," *Proceedings of the Joint Ada Conference, Fifth National Conference on Ada Technology and Washington Ada Symposium*, U.S. Army Communications-Electronics Command, Fort Monmouth, New Jersey, pp. 213 - 222.

[Stroustrup, 1991]. B. Stroustrup, *The C++ Programming Language,* Second Edition, Addison-Wesley, Reading, Massachusetts, 1991.

[Taylor and Hecht, 1990]. D.K. Taylor and A. Hecht, "Using CASE for Object-Oriented Design with C++," *Computer Language*, Vol. 7, No. 11, November 1990, pp. 49 - 57.

[Toetenel et al., 1990]. H. Toetenel, J. van Katwijk, and N. Plat, "Structured Analysis — Formal Design, Using Stream and Object-Oriented Formal Specification," *Proceedings of the ACM SIGSOFT International Workshop on Formal Methods in Software Development*, special issue of *Software Engineering Notes*, Vol. 15, No. 4, September 1990, pp. 118 - 127.

[Vidale and Hayden, 1987]. R.F. Hayden and C.R. Hayden, "A Student Project to Extend Object-Oriented Design," *Proceedings of the Ada Software Engineering Education and Training Symposium*, June 9-11, 1987, pp. 89 - 98.

[Vielcanet, 1989]. P. Vielcanet, "HOOD Design Method and Control/Command Techniques of the Development of Realtime Software," *Proceedings of the Sixth Washington Ada Symposium*, June 26-29, 1989, pp. 213 - 219.

[Ward, 1989]. P.T. Ward, "How to Integrate Object Orientation with Structured Analysis and Design," *IEEE Software*, Vol. 6, No. 2, March 1989, pp. 74 - 82.

[Wasserman et al., 1989]. A.I. Wasserman, P. Pircher, and R.J. Muller, "An Object-Oriented Design Method for Code Generation," *Software Engineering Notes*, Vol. 14, No. 1, January 1989, pp. 32 - 55.

[Wasserman et al., 1990]. A.I. Wasserman, P. Pircher, and R.J. Muller, "An Object-Oriented Design Notation for Software Design Representation," *IEEE Computer*, Vol. 23, No. 3, March 1990, pp. 50 - 63.

[Wegner, 1990]. P. Wegner, "Concepts and Paradigms of Object-Oriented Programming," *OOPS Messenger*, Vol. 1, No. 1, August 1990, pp. 7 - 87.

[Wiener, 1991]. R.S. Wiener, Editor, *Focus On Analysis and Design*, SIGS Publications, Inc., New York, New York, 1991.

[Wirfs-Brock and Wilkerson, 1989]. R. Wirfs-Brock and B. Wilkerson, "Object-Oriented Design: A Responsibility-Driven Approach," *OOPSLA '89 Conference Proceedings,* special issue of *SIGPLAN Notices*, Vol. 24, No. 10, October 1989, pp. 71 - 76.

[Wirfs-Brock and Johnson, 1990]. R.J. Wirfs-Brock and R.E. Johnson, "Surveying Current Research in Object-Oriented Design," *Communications of the ACM*, Vol. 33, No. 9, September 1990, pp. 105 - 124.

[Wirfs-Brock et al., 1990]. R. Wirfs-Brock, B. Wilkerson, and L. Wiener, *Designing Object-Oriented Software*, Prentice Hall, Englewood Cliffs, New Jersey, 1990.

14   Evaluating An Object-Oriented Programming Language

Give us the tools, and we will finish the job.

— *Winston Churchill (February 9, 1941)*

We dissect nature along lines laid down by our native language ... Language is not simply a reporting device for experience but a defining framework for it.

— *Benjamin Whorf (1897 - 1941) in* "Thinking in Primitive Communities"

Prologue

Object-oriented software engineering (OOSE) is an extremely hot topic. There is a rapidly increasing number of books, articles, seminars, conferences, and products which focus on the technology. Only a few years ago, the discussion was largely limited to programming language features. Today, software engineers are investigating and using such things as "object-oriented requirements analysis" (OORA), "object-oriented design" (OOD), "object-oriented database systems" (OODBS), "object-oriented computer hardware" (OOCH), and "object-oriented computer aided software engineering" (OO CASE).

The character of object-oriented applications has also changed. Originally, most object-oriented applications were small and non-critical. Object-oriented software engineering was chiefly experimental, i.e., *not* production-oriented. In the beginning, slow programming language interpreters, highly non-portable languages and environments, lack of concurrency-related features, and fairly limited access to low-level machine characteristics were all tolerable.

As we moved to the early 1980s, the methodologies, tools, environments, and programming languages became progressively better. Object-oriented technology was successfully employed on a number of large and/or critical projects. However, the use of object-oriented technology was still fairly uncommon.

Today, object-oriented software engineering is entering the mainstream. Object-oriented technology must continue to demonstrate its suitability for applications which are both large and critical. Software engineers who are using object-oriented concepts must consider such issues as efficiency, low-level hardware characteristics, portability, and concurrency. They must do this in a way that preserves the desirable features, *and the essence*, of the object-oriented paradigm.

In each object-oriented application, one of the tools that will have to be considered is, of course, the implementation language. At one time, the choice was simple — there was only one language (i.e., Smalltalk) which claimed to be "object-oriented." Now there are scores of languages, and a plethora of variants, all of which claim some degree of object-orientation.

The issue is further complicated by those who advocate the (occasional) use of traditionally "non-object-oriented" programming languages in object-oriented applications.

Historical Background

In the very early 1970s, things were simple. There was only one programming language which called itself "object-oriented," i.e., Smalltalk ([Goldberg and Robson, 1983]). Further, all that anyone seemed interested in was "object-oriented programming" (OOP). No one even suggested such things as formalized, repeatable, and transferable processes for "object-oriented design" (OOD) or "object-oriented requirements analysis" (OORA).

During the 1980s, there was an explosive growth in object-oriented programming languages (OOPLs). Initially, most of these languages attempted to define themselves in terms of the Smalltalk paradigm. As our understanding of object-oriented concepts matured, however, the deviations from Smalltalk concepts among so-called object-oriented programming languages became more pronounced.

(The 1980s also saw the birth and evolution of formalized OOD, OORA, and object-oriented domain analysis (OODA), and the introduction of object-oriented database systems (OODBS). As our understanding and usage of OOPLs increased, so did our understanding of object-oriented software engineering (OOSE) in general.)

By the late 1980s, there was not only an increased interest in OOPLs, but also an increased interest in:

- attempts to evaluate, classify, or justify a given programming language as being "object-oriented," e.g., [Bach, 1988], [Buzzard and Mudge, 1985], [Cook, 1986], [Touati, 1987], and [Wolf, 1989],

- adding, or suggesting, "object-oriented extensions" to existing programming languages, e.g., [Bergin and Greenfield, 1988], [Cox, 1986], [Di Maio et al., 1989], [Donaldson, 1989], [Forestier et al., 1989], [Moon, 1986], [Simonian and Crone, 1988a], [Simonian and Crone, 1988b], [Waurzyniak, 1989], and [Wegner, 1983], and

- developing applications using an object-oriented approach, but using traditionally "non-object-oriented," programming languages, e.g., [Edelson, 1987], [Jacky and Kalet, 1987], and [Zaniolo, 1984].

All of this has stimulated efforts to define the criteria for calling a language an object-oriented programming language. For example, Peter Wegner, in [Wegner, 1986], offered:

> We define 'object-oriented' so that it includes prototypical object-oriented languages like Smalltalk and Loops, but excludes languages like Ada, Modula, and Clu which have data abstractions but are not generally considered object-oriented. Support of data abstraction is a necessary but not sufficient condition for a language to be object-oriented. Object-oriented languages must additionally support both the management of collections of data abstractions by requiring data abstractions to have a type, and the composition of abstract data types through an inheritance mechanism:
>
> object-oriented = data abstraction + abstract data types + type inheritance.

There have been a number of good overview articles describing the characteristics found in many different object-oriented programming languages, e.g. [Stefik and Bobrow, 1985], [Wegner, 1987a], [Wegner, 1987b], [Wegner, 1989], and [Wegner, 1990]. The reader should be aware that not all authors agree on "the basics," *and* that the technology is constantly evolving.

However, there are a good many problems which arise when people attempt to classify a particular programming language as either object-oriented or non-object-oriented.

Problems with Evaluations

Some "litmus tests" for object-oriented programming languages are based on how close a programming language is in concept and implementation to Smalltalk. There are obvious problems with this approach, e.g., since a language that is not Smalltalk must differ from Smalltalk in some (usually significant) ways, what are acceptable deviations? Further, as we begin to understand more about the object-oriented paradigm, some people have begun to point out "deficiencies" in Smalltalk, for example, the lack of type checking (see, e.g., [Johnson, 1986]). Is a programming language which "corrects" these deficiencies more object-oriented than even Smalltalk itself?

A major source of problems in any comparison scheme is the confusion between *concepts* and *implementations*. For example, in Smalltalk, objects communicate (i.e., work gets done) via "message passing." Messages are sent from one object to another. CLOS ([Keene, 1989]) does not have message passing in the Smalltalk sense, but instead uses a generalization that is more Lisp-like, i.e., generic functions. Is this an acceptable "deviation"? The important question here is: when *physical* differences arise, how great must these differences be before "reasonable people" can agree that the differences are not only physical differences, but also *conceptual* differences.

The greatest problem is determining just what "object-oriented characteristics" a programming language must possess to be considered a "true" OOPL. There are more than a few contenders for object-oriented programming language characteristics. There are also different views on how many of these characteristics a programming language must have before it is given the label "object-oriented." Adding to the confusion, are the differing interpretations of these characteristics.

Evaluation Criteria

We will now briefly discuss some of the more commonly mentioned object-oriented programming language characteristics. For most characteristics, we will also mention some object-oriented programming languages that appear to lack that characteristic.

Encapsulation is a packaging mechanism that is often confused with information hiding. In languages such as Smalltalk, the encapsulation is physical, i.e., it is accomplished via the syntax and semantics of the language. For example, Smalltalk offers a "class" construct which allows a programmer to physically encapsulate the methods, operations, and other features which logically constitute a class. The Common Lisp Object System (CLOS), on the other hand, does not provide much *physical* encapsulation, and instead emphasizes *logical* encapsulation. (See, e.g., [Gabriel, 1989], [Keene, 1989], and [Lawless and Miller, 1991].)

Information hiding is the suppression of details. Most commonly, the concept of information hiding is coupled with the concept of abstraction to reveal details at a given level of abstraction, and to hide, or cover up, details at lower levels of abstraction. In Smalltalk, objects are black boxes, i.e., their internal implementations are hidden from those outside of the object. (To be technically accurate, they are hidden from objects which are outside of the object's subclass-superclass chain. See, e.g., [Snyder, 1986].)

C++ ([Stroustrup, 1991]), on the other hand, allows "violations" of strict information hiding via *friend functions*. These functions allow objects to have access to the internals of other objects. Flavors ([Moon, 1986]) and Loops ([Bobrow, 1983]) allow instances to directly access the internals of other objects.

Data abstraction is a form of abstraction where we avoid focusing on details of the underlying algorithms (i.e., they are an abstraction), *and* we are not concerned with the type of data that those algorithms manipulate. Data abstraction allows objects to be treated as black boxes, e.g., "name objects" may be added to "directory objects" without regard to the underlying implementation of the name objects. (See, e.g., [Liskov, 1988].) Data abstraction is implemented directly in languages such as Simula ([Dahl and Nygaard, 1966]), Smalltalk, Ada, Modula ([Wirth, 1983]), and Clu ([Liskov et al., 1977]), but is not directly available in common programming languages, e.g., C, Pascal, Fortran, and Cobol.

Data abstraction is also necessary for the implementation of some metaclasses and parameterized classes. A metaclass is a class whose instances are themselves classes. Some object-oriented programming languages (e.g., Trellis ([Schaffert et al., 1986])) do not allow for straightforward implementation of user-defined metaclasses or parameterized classes.

Inheritance is a mechanism whereby an object acquires characteristics from one or more other objects, and, by induction, from all of antecedent generalizations of these other objects. Inheritance is implemented in a dynamic manner in languages such as Smalltalk and C++, but may also be accomplished via other mechanisms, e.g., via preprocessors ([Donaldson, 1989]) or using existing features of a language ([Perez, 1988]). The chief question seems to be: "must a given programming language implement inheritance in exactly the same manner as Smalltalk to be considered object-oriented?"

In some "classless" object-oriented languages (e.g., Self ([Ungar and Smith, 1987])), mechanisms which differ (slightly) from inheritance (e.g., delegation) are used. There have been attempts to reconcile these differing mechanisms, e.g., the "Treaty of Orlando" ([Lieberman et al., 1988]). There are also extensions of the Smalltalk type of inheritance. For example, Smalltalk has only single inheritance (i.e., each subclass has exactly one immediate superclass), and Eiffel ([Meyer, 1992]) supports multiple inheritance (i.e., each subclass may have *more than one* immediate superclass).

Some have observed that Smalltalk-like inheritance can mitigate some of the benefits of information hiding, e.g., [Snyder, 1986]. Further, Smalltalk-like inheritance can have undesirable side-effects when changes are made to the subclass-superclass hierarchy. Finally, Markku Sakkinen, for example, has postulated that inheritance is one of the "less important properties of objects." (See [Sakkinen, 1989].)

A **class** is an object which is used to create *instances*, where an instance is a *specific* thing or characteristic. More precisely, a class is a template, description, pattern, or "blueprint" for a category of very similar items. Among other things, a class describes the interface these items will present to the outside world. Classes first appeared in Simula, and are called "classes" in languages such as Smalltalk, C++, and Eiffel ([Meyer, 1992]).

(We should also note that some people restrict the definition of "object" to mean an instance of a class. One place where this line of reasoning breaks down is if you allow for classes whose instances themselves can be classes, i.e., metaclasses.)

Some object-oriented programming languages specifically avoid classes. For example, David Ungar's Self uses no classes, and creates new objects from existing (prototypical) objects. Beta ([Kristensen et al., 1987]) "replaces classes, procedures, functions, and types by a single abstraction mechanism called the *pattern*." Actor languages (e.g., [Agha, 1986]) lack both classes *and* an inheritance mechanism.

Whereas a *class* defines the structure and characteristics of its instances, a ***type*** defines those operations in which an object may participate, and under what circumstances the object may *legally* participate in those operations. Simula, which many consider to be the first object-oriented programming language had types. Smalltalk, on the other hand, has, in effect, no types, but there are typed extensions to Smalltalk, e.g., [Johnson, 1986]. C++ also supports some typing, i.e., more than C, and much less than Ada ([DoD, 1983]).

Binding is the association of one thing with another. (Alternatively, a binding is an assignment of a value to a property of something.) It can mean, for example, the association of variable names with variable values. In the object-oriented world, binding is commonly used to mean the association of method names with particular methods.

Binding may be either static (or early), i.e., accomplished at compile time, or dynamic (or late), i.e., accomplished at run-time. Of course, "lateness" is a matter of degree. For example, while "compile time" and "run time" usually define the bounds of when binding occurs, there are several places in between (e.g., "link time") where binding can also occur. The question to ask here is: "must a programming language support dynamic (late) binding to be considered 'object-oriented,' and, if so, how late must this binding occur?"

(There are other dimensions to binding. For example, in LISP and similar languages, one can speak of "shallow binding" and "deep binding." In deep binding, values are stored in some form of linked structure, whereas in shallow binding, values are stored in some easily accessible memory location.)

Message passing is a means of communication among objects within an application. In Smalltalk, messages have a prescribed format, and are handled in a specified manner. However, Wegner ([Wegner, 1987], page 512) observes: "... the term 'message passing' has several different meanings. The first object-oriented language, Simula, had coroutines, an asynchronous (quasi-parallel) form of message-passing in which the sender saves its state and must be explicitly reawakened by a resume call rather than by an automatic reply from the receiver. Smalltalk and Loops equate message-passing with remote procedure calls, a synchronous form of message-passing in which the sender must wait for a reply form the receiver before continuing. Modules in distributed systems may communicate by rendez-vous, which combines remote procedure call with synchronization between the calling and called processes by asynchronous message-passing, or both."

Wegner continues, "Objects certainly need to communicate, but any form of message-passing appears to be compatible with object-oriented programming."

Polymorphism is a measure of the degree of difference in how each item in a specified collection of items must be treated at a given level of abstraction. Polymorphism is increased when any unnecessary differences, at any level of abstraction, within a collection of items are eliminated. (See [Gabriel, 1989], [Harland, 1984], [Milner, 1978] and [Milner, 1984].) Most often we hear discussions of polymorphism in terms of "overloading of operation names or designators," i.e., which particular method (algorithm) will be used for a given operation, given a specific operand (or operands). (Polymorphism is, of course, a much broader concept.) Using the operation/operand theme, we can provide examples of several different types of polymorphism, i.e.:

- *general polymorphism* — where the same method is used regardless of the type (or form) of the operands,

- *ad hoc polymorphism* — where a different method is selected based on the type (or form) of the operands, and

- *parameterized polymorphism* — where the user of the polymorphic abstraction must supply some information, in the form of parameters, to the abstraction.

In truth, even such languages as Fortran are somewhat polymorphic, e.g., the same addition operator ("+") is used for both integers and reals, although the method for each is different. However, it is the polymorphic extensions, and the ability to have user-defined polymorphic relationships which are attractive in many object-oriented languages. (Few, if any, object-oriented languages are as polymorphic as the ML language ([Milner, 1984]).)

David M. Harland (in [Harland, 1984], page 32), commenting on what many refer to as "type polymorphism," observes that "polymorphism in variables and routines [means] that we [can] hold, take, and return differently typed variables at different times." James O. Coplien (in [Coplien, 1992], page 108) relates polymorphism to inheritance by observing that, in a C++ inheritance hierarchy, all instances of classes that are within the same inheritance hierarchy can be treated as though they were all instances of the class at the root of the inheritance hierarchy.

Persistence is a measure of the volatility of the state of an object. In object-oriented circles, persistence is most often discussed in the context of distributed applications (e.g., [Low, 1988]), or, more commonly, in the context of object stores or databases (e.g., [Merrow and Laursen, 1987]). Although some people feel that persistence should be integrated into the programming language itself (e.g., [Atkinson et al., 1983]), this is *not* a very strong contender for a necessary characteristic of object-oriented programming languages.

One very important requirement for any object-oriented application is that it closely model the "real world," and the real world is usually highly concurrent (as opposed to strictly sequential). C++ is decidedly strictly sequential — although concurrent applications can be written in C++ with the use of appropriate libraries. There are, however, a number of concurrent object-oriented programming languages, e.g., Vulcan ([Kahn et al., 1987]), ABCL/1 ([Yonezawa et al., 1986]), and POOL-T ([America, 1987]). Unfortunately, none of these "concurrent object-oriented programming languages" appears headed for the mainstream.

Reflection is a process whereby a system knows about itself as a computational, or structural, entity, and has the capability to act on this knowledge. (See, e.g., [Ferber, 1989].) Reflection has been suggested as one method for dealing with concurrency in object-oriented systems. Very few, if any, people would include reflection as a minimum characteristic for an object-oriented programming language.

Minimum Criteria for Objects

What are the **minimum criteria** an item must meet to be considered an object? Depending on who you are talking to, an object can be a class, a metaclass, a parameterized class, a non-class instance, or some other item. The classic concept of an object is that it is a *complete* entity, having (at least the possibility of) the ability to maintain state, presenting a specified interface to the outside world, and hiding its internal implementation. Commonly used examples of objects include bank accounts, temperature sensors, stacks, and voltage.

Functional object-oriented programming languages, e.g., FOOPS ([Goguen and Meseguer, 1987]), allow "functions" to be objects. "Traits" ([Curry and Ayers, 1984]), "mixins" ([Smith et al., 1987] and [Stefik and Bobrow, 1985]), and "partial types" ([Halbert and O'Brien, 1987]) allow for the implementation of *partial* concepts as objects. (Partial types are more commonly referred to as "abstract classes." See, e.g., [Stroustrup, 1991].)

Peter Wegner ([Wegner, 1987b]) suggests the following "dimensions" of object-oriented language design: objects, classes (object types), inheritance, data abstraction, strong typing, concurrency, and persistence. He claims that these characteristics "span the design space of object-based languages." He also observes ([Wegner, 1987a]) "object-based languages must possess the first," i.e. objects, and that certain combinations of the above attributes may be incompatible. (See [Wegner, 1990] for a fairly complete description of Wegner's ideas.)

Other Problems In Evaluating the Object-Orientedness of a Programming Language

Even if a general agreement on object-oriented characteristics can be reached, there are other problems with the evaluation of a programming language for object-oriented software engineering. Very often, *all* the characteristics are given *equal* weight — although many, if not most, people have their own *intuitive* ranking of the importance of each characteristic. A variation on this problem is the "all or nothing" syndrome, i.e., if a programming language is missing, or has a poor implementation of, even one characteristic, the programming language is not considered object-oriented.

Bigotry is often a major problem with programming language evaluation. Software engineers are, after all, human beings, and are thus subject to human frailties. I have read quite a number of evaluations and comparisons of programming languages, and I would have a hard time trying to identify even one which was totally free of bias. Unfortunately, I have read too many that do little to hide their strong (non-technical) prejudice against a particular language.

Sloppiness is another major problem with evaluations. Many times I have gotten the distinct impression that the authors of the evaluation have not used, or even looked at, the programming languages they are evaluating. Sometimes they seem to have scanned a list of reserved words, and, not finding words such as "object" or "class," they assume the language does not support object-oriented programming.

Another problem is the confusion about the original goals for the programming language itself. Specifically, very few programming languages were created *solely* with the idea of implementing a pure object-oriented programming language. For example, the Ada programming language was implemented for large, real-time, embedded applications where reliability is critical. Some of the thinking behind Ada conflicts with some of the traditional object-oriented implementation philosophy.

Evaluation Methodology

Sometimes the evaluation criteria for an object-oriented programming language seems biased in one direction, e.g., "how many of Smalltalk's features does this language possess?" As part of the evaluation of any candidate language for object-oriented software engineering, I propose that three main questions be asked, specifically:

1. What features does the candidate programming language have that many "object-oriented" programming languages seem to lack?

2. What features does the candidate programming language have in common with most "object-oriented" programming languages?

3. What features do most "object-oriented" programming languages have that the candidate programming language seems to lack?

Using the Ada programming language as an example, let us provide some sample answers to these questions. (Please note that we are not saying that Ada is better than X, or that Ada is not as good as Y. We are merely using the language as an example. Further, we stipulate from the outset that Ada is not an object-oriented programming language, but rather an object-based programming language.):

*   Under the category of features that Ada *possesses*, and that many object-oriented programming languages seem to *lack* we have, for example:

    *   **the capability of creating parameterized classes**. Assuming that one can fashion a class in Ada using a package which exports a type, for example, a parameterized class can be created by making that package generic. (With generic classes in Eiffel, and the arrival of templates in C++, this argument is not as strong as it once was.)

    *   **exceptions** (see, e.g., [Dony, 1988]). Ada provides both language-defined exceptions, and the capability for user defined exceptions. (I should point out that Ada's exception mechanism differs from that found in some object-oriented programming languages, e.g., Mesa ([Mitchell et al., 1979]).) Exception-like mechanisms have been added to Smalltalk implementations, and soon, C++ implementations will also feature exceptions.

    *   **concurrency**. Ada provides concurrency via its tasking mechanism. While it is true that there are a growing number of concurrent object-oriented programming languages, the most popular object-oriented programming languages still lack concurrency, or a mature, well-understood means for handling concurrency. Of course, one could argue whether support for concurrency should be supported directly by the programming language, or via, for example, support libraries.

- **types (strong typing)**. Many people have complained about Ada's strong typing. This makes the trend toward more strongly typed object-oriented programming languages that much more ironic.

- **the ability to address low-level, machine-dependent items**. Ada provides access to low-level aspects of the environment via such things as representation clauses. Few of the most popular object-oriented programming languages directly allow access to low-level, machine-dependent items. For example, while C++ does seem to provide some access to the hardware, Smalltalk and Eiffel generally avoid the issue.

- **a high degree of portability**. Many programmers confuse "compilability" with "portability." Just because there are many implementations of a compiler for a given language, does not mean that they will all compile the same code, or that the compiled code will exhibit the same semantics. (In truth, the main reason for the possibility of producing highly portable Ada source code has more to do with the infrastructure of Ada technology (e.g., validation) than with the language itself.)

- Under the category of features that Ada *shares in common* with most object-oriented programming languages we have, for example:

  - **encapsulation**: Ada's package construct allows for the encapsulation of operations, methods, exceptions, constants, and other items which can be associated with an object (e.g., a class, an instance, or a metaclass).

  - **information hiding**: Ada's private types provide an excellent mechanism for hiding information.

  - **data abstraction**: Ada's generics afford a software engineer the capability to make both subprograms and packages generic. Used well, they make the implementation of data abstraction fairly easy.

  - **some types of polymorphism**: Ada's ability to overload operators, and names, as well as Ada's ability to parameterize generic packages, provide some level of software engineer controlled polymorphism.

- Under the category of features that Ada *lacks* in comparison with most object-oriented programming languages we have, for example:

  - **Smalltalk-like inheritance mechanism**: No claim can be made that Ada, in isolation, closely mirrors Smalltalk-like inheritance. There are ways of *simulating* this mechanism within the language (e.g., [Perez, 1988]), and ways to implement a static "layers of abstraction" approach to inheritance. (We should also note that there is a distinct difference between genericity (provided by Ada's generics) and inheritance. See, e.g., [Meyer, 1986].)

  - **some forms of polymorphism**: The Ada language is not as polymorphic as Lisp and its object-oriented derivatives (e.g., Flavors), and nowhere near as polymorphic as ML ([Milner, 1984]). Being a very strongly typed language, some forms of polymorphism (e.g., arrays with components of different types) are precluded by definition. (Yes, there are ways around this using, for example, variant records or access types and unchecked_conversion, but these are not *direct* methods.)

- **dynamic binding**: Ada's emphasis on reliability shifts part of the burden to the programming language itself. In languages which feature dynamic binding (e.g., Objective-C™ ([Cox, 1986])), the onus is more on the software engineer, and less on the language, in terms of reliability. Therefore, dynamic binding is an attribute which directly conflicts with the original intentions of the Ada language.

- **some types of parameters**: Not all Ada objects are first-class objects. For example, objects implemented using types exported from (generic) packages, and objects implemented using task types can participate in a quite a number of expressions, and can be passed as parameters. However objects implemented using objects exported from packages, and objects implemented using tasks (and *not* task types) cannot behave as first class objects. Further, Ada's current non-support (or extremely limited support) for such items as "package types," "subprogram types," "procedure parameters," and "exceptions as parameters," precludes some types of desirable polymorphic behavior.

[Note: A number of extensions to the Ada language (e.g., DRAGOON ([Di Maio et al., 1989]), Classic Ada™ ([Donaldson, 1989]), Ada++ ([Forestier et al., 1989]), and InnovAda ([Simonian and Crone, 1988a])) do address each of these points. However, they are not part of the current language definition ([DoD, 1983]).]

Other Considerations

Of course, there are other considerations in the choice of an implementation language e.g., availability on the desired platforms, interfacing to other applications, customer requirements, and staff training.

If one is developing a small and/or non-critical application, then all that may be required is object-oriented programming (coding). However, for large and/or critical applications, it is likely that one, or more, of the following may be necessary: object-oriented design (OOD), object-oriented requirements analysis (OORA), and object-oriented domain analysis (OODA). In addition, object-oriented thinking will permeate post-development life-cycle activities, management practices, development standards, organizational policies and procedures, and software quality assurance, among others.

This is an important point. As we move away from the myopic view of considering what goes on during coding, and move toward a more comprehensive (e.g., total life-cycle) perspective on software engineering, our evaluation criteria for an object-oriented programming language changes. Potential flaws, which were virtually unnoticed during the development of small, non-critical applications, become glaring deficiencies in large and/or critical software applications.

It is crucial that a given programming language closely mirror the thought processes which were introduced during requirements analysis and carried over to design. For example, if we find it natural to talk about metaclasses or parameterized classes during analysis and design, it is more than a little helpful if our implementation language allows us to implement these items directly. The same is true for concepts such as concurrency and inheritance.

Summary

Deciding whether a given programming is "object-oriented" is not as simple as some people would have it. When there were only a few OOPLs, and few object-oriented applications, decisions were easy. However, that is no longer the case.

We can be sure of several things. First, new concepts and new interpretations of older concepts regarding object-oriented programming languages will continue to emerge. Second, new "object-oriented" programming languages and "object-oriented extensions" of older (non-object-oriented) programming languages will also continue to emerge. Third, there will continue to be a good deal of confusion, e.g., the all too typical confusion of concepts with implementations.

What is important is that there must be a direct correlation between "object-orientedness" and software engineering utility.

Bibliography

[Agha, 1986]. G. Agha, "An Overview of Actor Languages," *SIGPLAN Notices*, Vol. 18, No. 6, June 1983, pp. 58 - 67.

[America, 1987]. P. America, "POOL-T: A Parallel Object-Oriented Language," in *Object-Oriented Concurrent Programming*, A. Yonezawa and M. Tokoro, Editors, MIT Press, Cambridge, Massachusetts, 1987, pp. 199 - 220.

[Atkinson et al., 1983]. M.P. Atkinson, P.J. Bailey, W.P. Cockshott, K.J. Chisholm, and R. Morrison, "An Approach to Persistent Programming," *Computer Journal*, Vol. 26, No. 4, 1983, pp. 360 - 365.

[Bach, 1988]. W.W. Bach, "Is Ada Really an Object-Oriented Programming Language," *Proceedings of Ada Expo 1988*, Galaxy Productions, Frederick, Maryland, 1988, 7 pages.

[Bailin, 1988]. S.C. Bailin, "An Object-Oriented Specification Method for Ada," *Proceedings of the Fifth Washington Ada Symposium,* June 27 - 30, 1988, Association for Computing Machinery, New York, New York, 1988, pp. 139 - 150.

[Bergin and Greenfield, 1988]. J. Bergin and S. Greenfield, "What Does Modula-2 Need to Fully Support Object-Oriented Programming?," *SIGPLAN Notices*, Vol. 23, No. 3, March 1988, pp. 73 - 82.

[Bobrow, 1983]. D.G. Bobrow, *The LOOPS Manual*, Rank Xerox, Inc., Palo Alto, California, 1983.

[Buzzard and Mudge, 1985]. G.D. Buzzard and T.N. Mudge, "Object-Based Computing and the Ada Programming Language," *IEEE Computer,* Vol. 18, No. 3, March 1985, pp. 12 - 19.

[Cook, 1986]. S. Cook, "Languages and Object-Oriented Programming," *Software Engineering Journal*, Vol. 1, No. 2, 1986, pp. 73 - 80.

[Coplien, 1992]. J.O. Coplien, *Advanced C++: Programming Styles and Idioms*, Addison-Wesley, Reading, Massachusetts, 1992.

[Cox, 1986]. B.J. Cox, *Object Oriented Programming: An Evolutionary Approach*, Addison-Wesley, Reading, Massachusetts, 1986.

[Curry and Ayers, 1984]. G.A. Curry and R.M. Ayers, "Experience with Traits in the Xerox Star Workstation," *IEEE Transactions on Software Engineering*, Vol. SE-10, No. 5, September 1984, pp. 519 - 527.

[Dahl and Nygaard, 1966]. O.J. Dahl and K. Nygaard, "SIMULA — an ALGOL-Based Simulation Language," *Communications of the ACM*, Vol. 9, No. 9, September 1966, pp. 671 - 678.

[Di Maio et al., 1989]. A. Di Maio, C. Cardigno, R. Bayan, C. Destombes, and C. Atkinson, "DRAGOON: An Ada-Based Object-Oriented Language," *Ada: the Design Choice — Proceedings of the Ada-Europe Conference,* Madrid, 13-15 June, 1989, Cambridge University Press, Cambridge, United Kingdom, 1989, pp. 39 - 48.

[DoD, 1983]. U.S. Department of Defense, *Reference Manual for the Ada Programming Language, (ANSI/MIL-STD-1815A-1983),* Government Printing Office, Washington, D.C., 1983.

[Donaldson, 1989]. C.M. Donaldson, "Dynamic Binding and Inheritance in an Object-Oriented Ada Design," *Ada: the Design Choice — Proceedings of the Ada-Europe Conference,* Madrid, 13-15 June, 1989, Cambridge University Press, Cambridge, United Kingdom, 1989, pp. 16 - 25.

[Dony, 1988]. C. Dony, "An Object-Oriented Exception Handling System for an Object-Oriented Language," *ECOOP '88: Proceedings of the European Conference on Object-Oriented Programming, Lecture Notes on Computer Science,* Volume 322, Springer Verlag, New York, New York, 1988, pp. 146 - 161.

[Edelson, 1987]. D.R. Edelson, "How Objective Mechanisms Facilitate the Development of Large Software Systems in Three Programming Languages," *SIGPLAN Notices,* Vol. 22, No. 9, September 1987, pp. 54 - 63.

[Ferber, 1989]. J. Ferber, "Computational Reflection In Class Based Object-Oriented Languages," *OOPSLA '89 Conference Proceedings,* special issue of *SIGPLAN Notices,* Vol. 24, No. 10, October 1989, pp. 317 - 326.

[Forestier et al., 1989]. J.P. Forestier, C. Fornarino, and P. Franchi-Zannettacci, "Ada++: A Class and Inheritance Extension for Ada," *Ada: the Design Choice — Proceedings of the Ada-Europe Conference,* Madrid 13-15 June 1989, Cambridge University Press, Cambridge, United Kingdom, 1989, pp. 3 - 15.

[Gabriel, 1989]. R.P. Gabriel, "Using the Common LISP Object System," *Computer Language,* Vol. 6, No. 8, August 1989, pp. 73 - 80.

[Goguen and Meseguer, 1987]. J.A. Goguen and J. Meseguer, "Unifying Functional, Object-Oriented and Relational Programming With Logical Semantics," in *Research Directions in Object-Oriented Programming,* B. Shriver and P. Wegner, Editors, The MIT Press, Cambridge, Massachusetts, 1987, pp. 417 - 477.

[Goldberg and Robson, 1983]. A. Goldberg and D. Robson, *Smalltalk-80: The Language and Its Implementation,* Addison-Wesley, Reading, Massachusetts, 1983.

[Halbert and O'Brien, 1987]. D.C. Halbert and P.D. O'Brien, "Using Types and Inheritance in Object-Oriented Programming," *IEEE Software,* Vol. 4, No. 5, September 1987, pp. 71 - 79.

[Harland, 1984]. D.M. Harland, *Polymorphic Programming Languages — Design and Implementation,* Halstead Press, New York, New York, 1984.

[Jacky and Kalet, 1987]. J.P. Jacky and I.J. Kalet, "An Object-Oriented Programming Mechanism for Standard Pascal," *Communications of the ACM,* Vol. 30, No. 9, September 1987, pp. 772 - 776.

[Johnson, 1986]. R.E. Johnson, "Type-Checking Smalltalk," *OOPSLA '86 Conference Proceedings,* special issue of *SIGPLAN Notices,* Vol. 21, No. 11, November 1986, pp. 315-321.

[Kahn et al., 1987]. K. Kahn, E. Tribble, M. Miller, and D. Bobrow, "Vulcan: Logical Concurrent Objects," in *Research Directions in Object-Oriented Programming,* B. Shriver and P. Wegner, Editors, The MIT Press, Cambridge, Massachusetts, 1987, pp. 75 - 112.

[Keene, 1989]. S.E. Keene, *Object-Oriented Programming in Common Lisp,* Addison-Wesley, Reading, Massachusetts, 1989.

[Kristensen et al., 1987]. B.B. Kristensen, O.L. Madsen, B. Moller-Pedersen and K. Nygaard, "The BETA Programming Language," in *Research Directions in Object-Oriented Programming*, B. Shriver and P. Wegner, Editors, The MIT Press, Cambridge, Massachusetts, 1987, pp. 7 - 48.

[Lawless and Miller, 1991]. J.A. Lawless and M.M. Miller, *Understanding CLOS: The Common Lisp Object System*, Digital Press, Bedford, Massachusetts, 1990.

[Lieberman et al., 1988]. H. Lieberman, L. A. Stein, and D. Ungar, "Of Types and Prototypes: The Treaty of Orlando," *OOPSLA '87 Addendum to the Proceedings,* special issue of *SIGPLAN Notices*, Vol. 23, No. 5, May 1988, pp. 43 - 44.

[Liskov et al., 1977]. B.H. Liskov, A. Snyder, R. Atkinson, and C. Schaffert, "Abstraction Mechanisms in CLU," *Communications of the ACM*, Vol. 20, No. 8, August 1977, pp. 564 - 576.

[Liskov, 1988]. B. Liskov, "Data Abstraction and Hierarchy," *OOPSLA '87 Addendum to the Proceedings,* special issue of *SIGPLAN Notices*, Vol. 23, No. 5, May 1988, pp. 17 - 34.

[Low, 1988]. C. Low, "A Shared Persistent Object Store," *ECOOP '88: Proceedings of the European Conference on Object-Oriented Programming, Lecture Notes on Computer Science,* Volume 322, Springer Verlag, New York, New York, 1988, pp. 390 - 410.

[Merrow and Laursen, 1987]. T. Merrow and J. Laursen, "A Pragmatic System for Shared Persistent Objects," *OOPSLA '87 Conference Proceedings,* special issue of *SIGPLAN Notices*, Vol. 22, No. 12, December 1987, pp. 103 - 110.

[Meyer, 1986]. B. Meyer, "Genericity Versus Inheritance," *OOPSLA Conference Proceedings*, special issue of *SIGPLAN Notices*, Vol. 21, No. 11, November 1986, Association for Computing Machinery, New York, New York, 1986, pp. 391 - 405.

[Meyer, 1992]. B. Meyer, *Eiffel: The Language*, Prentice Hall, Englewood Cliffs, New Jersey, 1992.

[Milner, 1978]. R. Milner, "A Theory of Type Polymorphism in Programming," *Journal of Computer and System Sciences*, Vol. 17, 1978, pp. 348 - 375.

[Milner, 1984]. R. Milner, "A Proposal for Standard ML," *ACM Symposium on Lisp and Functional Programming*, August 1984, pp. 184 - 197.

[Mitchell et al., 1979]. J. Mitchell, W. Maybury, and R. Sweet, *Mesa Language Manual*, Technical Report, Xerox PARC, Palo Alto, California, 1979.

[Moon, 1986]. D.A. Moon, "Object-Oriented Programming With Flavors," *OOPSLA Conference Proceedings,* special issue of *SIGPLAN Notices*, Vol. 21, No. 11, November 1986, Association for Computing Machinery, New York, New York, 1986, pp. 1 - 8.

[Perez, 1988]. E.P. Perez, "Simulating Inheritance With Ada," *Ada Letters*, Vol. 8, No. 5, September-October 1988, pp. 37 - 46.

[Sakkinen, 1989]. M. Sakkinen, "Disciplined Inheritance," *ECOOP '89: Proceedings of the European Conference on Object-Oriented Programming, British Computer Society Workshop Series*, Cambridge University Press, Cambridge, United Kingdom, 1989, pp. 39 - 56.

[Schaffert et al., 1986]. C. Schaffert, T. Cooper, B. Bullis, M. Killian, and C. Wilpolt, "An Introduction to Trellis/Owl," *OOPSLA '86 Conference Proceedings,* special issue of *SIGPLAN Notices*, Vol. 21, No. 11, November 1986, pp. 9 - 16.

[Simonian and Crone, 1988a]. R. Simonian and M. Crone, "INNOVADA: An Object-Oriented Ada Environment," *Proceedings of the U.S. Army Information Systems Engineering Command Advanced Technology Office — Technology Strategies '88 Conference,* February 9-12, 1988, The American Defense Preparedness Association, Washington, D.C., pp. 63 - 74.

[Simonian and Crone, 1988b]. R. Simonian and M. Crone, "InnovAda: True Object-Oriented Programming In Ada," *Journal of Object-Oriented Programming*, Vol. 1, No. 4, November/December 1988, pp. 14 - 21.

[Smith et al., 1987]. R.G. Smith, P.S. Barth, and R.L. Young, "A Substrate for Object-Oriented Interface Design," in *Research Directions in Object-Oriented Programming*, B. Shriver and P. Wegner, Editors, The MIT Press, Cambridge, Massachusetts, 1987, pp. 253 - 315.

[Snyder, 1986]. A. Snyder, "Encapsulation and Inheritance in Object-Oriented Programming Languages," *OOPSLA '86 Conference Proceedings*, special issue of *SIGPLAN Notices*, Vol. 21, No. 11, November 1986, pp. 38 - 45.

[Stefik and Bobrow, 1985]. M. Stefik and D.G. Bobrow, "Object-Oriented Programming: Themes and Variations," *The AI Magazine*, 1985, pp. 40 - 62.

[Stein, 1987]. L.A. Stein, "Delegation Is Inheritance," *OOPSLA '87 Conference Proceedings*, special issue of *SIGPLAN Notices*, Vol. 22, No. 12, December 1987, pp. 138 - 146.

[Stroustrup, 1991]. B. Stroustrup, *The C++ Programming Language*, Second Edition, Addison-Wesley, Reading, Massachusetts, 1991.

[Touati, 1987]. H. Touati, "Is Ada an Object-Oriented Programming Language?," *SIGPLAN Notices*, Vol. 22, No. 5, May 1987, pp. 23 - 26.

[Ungar and Smith, 1987]. D. Ungar and R.B. Smith, "Self: The Power of Simplicity," *OOPSLA '87 Conference Proceedings*, special issue of *SIGPLAN Notices*, Vol. 22, No. 12, December 1987, pp. 227 - 242.

[Waurzyniak, 1989]. P. Waurzyniak, "Borland Pulls Object Orientation Into Its Fold," *ComputerWorld*, Vol. 23, No. 18, May 1, 1989, page 37.

[Wegner, 1983]. P. Wegner, "On the Unification of Data and Program Abstraction in Ada," *Proceedings of the 10th Annual ACM Symposium on Principles of Programming Languages*, 1983, pp. 256 - 264.

[Wegner, 1986]. P. Wegner, "Classification in Object-Oriented Systems," *SIGPLAN Notices*, Vol. 21, No. 10, October 1986, pp. 173 - 182.

[Wegner, 1987a]. P. Wegner, "The Object-Oriented Classification Paradigm," in *Research Directions in Object-Oriented Programming*, B. Shriver and P. Wegner, Editors, The MIT Press, Cambridge, Massachusetts, 1987, pp. 479 - 560.

[Wegner, 1987b]. P. Wegner, "Dimensions of Object-Based Language Design," *OOPSLA '87 Conference Proceedings*, special issue of *SIGPLAN Notices*, Vol. 22, No. 12, December 1987, pp. 168 - 182.

[Wegner, 1989]. P. Wegner, "Learning the Language," *Byte*, Vol. 14, No. 3, March 1989, pp. 245 - 253.

[Wegner, 1990]. P. Wegner, "Concepts and Paradigms of Object-Oriented Programming," *OOPS Messenger*, Vol. 1, No. 1, August 1990, pp. 7 - 87.

[Wirth, 1983]. N. Wirth, *Programming In Modula-2*, Second Edition, Springer-Verlag, New York, New York, 1983.

[Wolf, 1989]. W. Wolf, "A Practical Comparison of Two Object-Oriented Languages," *IEEE Software*, Vol. 6, No. 5, September 1989, pp. 61 - 68.

[Yonezawa et al., 1986]. A. Yonezawa, J.-P. Briot, and E. Shibayama, "Object-Oriented Concurrent Programming in ABCL/1," *OOPSLA '86 Conference Proceedings*, special issue of *SIGPLAN Notices*, Vol. 21, No. 11, November 1986, pp. 258 - 268.

[Zaniolo, 1984]. C. Zaniolo, "Object-Oriented Programming in Prolog," *1984 International Symposium on Logic Programming*, Atlantic City, New Jersey, February 1984, IEEE Computer Society Press, Washington, D.C., pp. 265 - 270.

15 Issues in the Testing of Object-Oriented Software

Testing shows the presence, not the absence, of bugs.

— E.W. Dijkstra, [Randell and Buxton, 1970], page 21

Absence of evidence is not evidence of absence.

— Source Unknown

Prologue

In my presentations on object-oriented technology, I often inform my clients that object-oriented technology will impact everything in a software engineering organization, from contracting practices, to documentation standards, and, of course, to the choice of programming languages. One frequently asked question is, "Is the testing of object-oriented software different, and, if so, how is it different?" When I attempt to answer this question, I regularly uncover other problems.

Confusion with Other Technologies

It is not a good idea to assume, just because an organization is involved in software production or maintenance, that its staff has an adequate background in software testing technology. Very often, for example, testing is confused with debugging or software quality assurance.

- **Testing** is the process of examining something with the intention of finding errors. While testing may reveal a symptom of an error, it may not uncover the exact cause of the error.

- **Debugging** is the process of locating the exact cause of an error, and removing that cause.

- **Software quality assurance** assures the effectiveness of a software quality program within a software engineering organization.

(For a good working definition of "software error," see [Myers, 1976] and [Myers, 1979]. For an excellent general discussion of "quality," see [Crosby, 1979].)

General references on software testing technology include: [Basili and Selby, 1987], [Beizer, 1983], [Beizer, 1990], [DeMillo, et al., 1987], [Howden, 1987], [Laski, 1989], [Miller and Howden, 1981], [Myers, 1979], [Musa and Ackerman, 1989], [Parrington and Roper, 1989], and [Quirk, 1985]. There are currently only a very few references which specifically address the testing of object-oriented software, e.g., [Balfour, 1988], [Fiedler, 1989], [Grogono and Bennett, 1989], [Honda and Yonezawa, 1989], and [Perry and Kaiser, 1990].

General references on software debugging include: [Agrawal and Spafford, 1989], [Bates, 1989], [Brown and Sampson, 1973], [Dunn, 1984], [Gould and Drongowski, 1972], [Gould, 1975], [Hseush and Kaiser, 1988], [Lazzerini and Lopriore, 1989], [Podgurski and Clarke,

1989], and [Tassel, 1978]. Articles which specifically cover the debugging of object-oriented software (e.g., [Honda and Yonezawa, 1989]) are even rarer than those covering object-oriented testing.

General references on software quality assurance include: [Chow, 1985], [Dunn, 1990], [Dunn and Ullman, 1982], [Mizuno, 1983], and [Schulmeyer and McManus, 1987]. While there is a growing body of knowledge regarding the quality assurance of object-oriented software, I could find no specific references on the topic.

I have also included a few references which deal (at least in part) with the management of software testing (i.e., [Gunther, 1978] and [Humphrey, 1989]), and the management of software quality assurance (i.e., [Dunn, 1990]).

Some Basic Concepts and Definitions

We will need some basic working definitions, i.e.:

> **Software**: We will define software as "everything which is not hardware or 'flesh and blood' in a computer system." Therefore, in addition to source code and object code, we will include plans, policies, procedures, the results of analysis and design efforts, test cases, general documentation, and software tools in our definition of software. Given that all software should be tested, this implies that such items as designs and test cases should be submitted to some form of testing.

> **White-Box Testing**: White-box testing is the testing of the underlying implementation of a piece of software (e.g., source code) without regard to the specification (external description) for that piece of software. The goal of white-box testing of source code is to identify such items as (unintentional) infinite loops, paths through the code which should be allowed, but which cannot be executed (e.g., [Frankel and Weyuker, 1987]), and dead (unreachable) code.

Probably the most commonly used example of a white-box testing technique is "basis path testing." (See, e.g., [Beizer, 1990], [Chusho, 1987], [McCabe, 1976], [McCabe, 1982], and [McCabe, 1987]. For an opposing view see [Evangelist, 1984].) McCabe's approach requires that we determine the number of linearly independent paths through a piece of software (what he refers to as the cyclomatic complexity), and use that number coupled with a graph of the control flow through the same piece of software to come up with a set of test cases which will cause executable statements to be executed at least once.

McCabe's approach is an attempt to systematically address an even older concept in white-box testing, i.e., coverage. **Coverage** is simply a measure of the number and type of statements executed, as well as how these statements are executed. Glen Myers, in [Myers, 1979], describes several types of coverage. "Statement coverage," the weakest acceptable form of coverage, requires that enough test cases be written so that we can be assured that all executable statements will be executed at least once. "Condition coverage" requires that all statements be executed at least once, and that all binary decisions have a true and a false outcome at least once.

Here, we uncover two of problems with simple coverage concepts. Suppose, we are working with a programming language which supports exceptions. The raising (activating) of an exception will cause a change in control flow without the usual visible "test and branch" instructions. Each statement in a piece of software could potentially cause one or more exceptions to be raised, depending on conditions, e.g., improper input or division by zero.

Testing for all possible exceptions in all possible places where an exception could be raised is usually considered impractical. Therefore, we state that a minimum acceptable level of coverage must assure us that all possible exceptions are raised at least once. Restating our definition of "condition coverage," we say that enough test cases must be written so that we can reasonably be assured that all statements are executed at least once, all binary decisions take on a true and a false outcome at least once, and all exceptions are raised at least once.

The second problem has to do with interrupts. An **interrupt** is a low-level event, typically generated by the computer hardware, which requires that an executing piece of software respond in some manner. For example, an application may initiate a transfer of a large amount of information, and request that the hardware notify the application when the transfer is complete. While virtually unknown in some application domains, interrupts are common in low-level (i.e., very close to the hardware) applications. Like exceptions, interrupts cause changes in control flow without the usual visible "test and branch" instructions. Interrupts may occur at many different points in the execution of a piece of software. Therefore, it is, for all intents and purposes, impractical to exhaustively test all possible occurrences of all possible interrupts for a given piece of software. We will state that, in a situation where the software must explicitly deal with interrupts, a minimum acceptable level of coverage will require that all possible interrupts are forced to occur at least once.

Further revising our definition of "condition coverage," we say that enough test cases must be written so that we can be reasonably assured that all statements are executed at least once, all binary decisions take on a true and a false outcome at least once, all exceptions are raised at least once, and all possible interrupts are forced to occur at least once.

(In [Myers, 1979], Myers goes on to describe progressively more comprehensive forms of coverage, i.e., "condition coverage," "decision/condition coverage," and "multiple condition coverage.")

If we attempt to combine McCabe's approach with what we know about coverage, we arrive at some interesting observations. One can make a strong intuitive argument that, if done correctly, McCabe's approach will give us a very high degree of coverage, i.e., at least statement coverage, and quite possibly, as high as multiple condition coverage. However, we will be required to augment these test cases with additional test cases for exceptions and interrupts, where appropriate.

> **Black-Box Testing**: Black-box testing is the testing of a piece of software without regard to its underlying implementation. Specifically, it dictates that test cases for a piece of software are to be generated based solely on an examination of the specification (external description) for that piece of software. The goal of black-box testing is to demonstrate that the software being tested does not adhere to its external specification. (Note that if there is no "external specification" it will be difficult to conduct black-box testing.)

There are quite a number of black-box testing techniques. "Boundary value analysis," one of the most fruitful forms of black-box testing, requires that test cases be generated which are on, and immediately around, the boundaries of the input and output for a given piece of software. (See, e.g., [Myers, 1979].) "Equivalence class partitioning" is a formalization of the way many people already test software. An **equivalence class** is a collection of items which can all be regarded as identical at a given level of abstraction, e.g., a set of data items which will all evoke the same general behavior from a given software module. (See, e.g., [Knuth,

1973].) As described in [Myers, 1979], equivalence class partitioning can be a quite systematic approach to black-box testing.

In situations where there are many different combinations of inputs possible, [Myers, 1979] suggests a black-box technique called "cause-effect graphing." This technique helps software engineers identify those specific combinations of inputs which will be the most error prone. The intuition of a software engineer is an important part of any testing effort. This intuitive approach to testing can be slightly formalized under the black-box testing technique known as "error guessing."

> **Gray-Box Testing**: Gray-box testing is testing based on an examination of both the specification for a piece of software, and the underlying implementation (e.g., source code) for that piece of software. A typical goal of gray-box testing is to identify singularities in a piece of software, i.e., situations in which the behavior of a piece of software become unbounded.

Any good testing effort is a carefully planned combination of black-box, white-box, and gray-box testing techniques. Low-level testing — generally thought of as testing small amounts of software (e.g., a single function) — usually involves a significant amount of white-box testing. Higher-level testing (testing larger amounts of software, e.g., system and acceptance testing) is almost exclusively black-box in nature.

> **Static Testing**: Static testing is any testing of a piece of software which can be done without actually executing that piece of software. (Some people restrict the definition of static testing to any testing of a piece of software which does not involve the use of a computer.)

In addition to desk checking, structured walkthroughs and inspections are common, and extremely beneficial, examples of static testing. (See e.g., [Ackerman et al., 1989], [Fagan, 1976], [Fagan, 1986], [Freedman and Weinberg, 1982], and [Yourdon, 1978].)

> **Dynamic Testing**: Dynamic testing is any testing of a piece of software which involves the actual execution of that piece of software.

Since the introduction of concurrency also introduces non-determinacy, the dynamic testing of concurrent software is a difficult process. However there is a growing body of knowledge regarding the testing of concurrent software applications, e.g., [Carver, 1989], [Carver and Tai, 1989], [Tai, 1985a], [Tai, 1985b], [Tai, 1986], [Tai, 1987], and [Tai and Din, 1985]. (Of course, there is a corresponding interest in the debugging of concurrent software applications, e.g., [Honda and Yonezawa, 1989], [Hseush and Kaiser, 1988], and [Tai et al., 1989].)

> **Formal Testing**: The application of formal, or semi-formal, mathematical techniques to demonstrate the correctness of a piece of software.

In the early 1960s, E.W. Dijkstra recognized that a computer program could be viewed as a series of mathematical relationships. He reasoned that mathematical proofs of correctness for software should be possible. His first attempts were very frustrating and led to his early observations on seemingly chaotic way in which software was developed (e.g., [Dijkstra, 1965]), and later to what he called "structured programming" ([Dijkstra, 1969]).

Others, most notably C.A.R. Hoare, were also interested in what has become known as formal proofs of program correctness. (See, e.g., [Hoare, 1969], [Hoare, 1971], and [Hoare, 1972].) Many of these approaches involved the use of assertions (a statement about a particular state of affairs which is assumed to be true), e.g. [Anderson, 1979], [Berg et al., 1982], [Roe and Rowland, 1987], and [Shankar, 1982].

After a while, people began to realize that they did not have to wait until module testing to begin using formal techniques. Beginning in the 1970s, some people began creating the so-called "formal methods" for software development, e.g. Vienna Development Method (VDM) ([Jones, 1986]) and Z ([Abrial, 1980], [Hayes, 1987], [Sommerville, 1989], [Spivey, 1988], and [Spivey, 1989]). The intersection of formal specification techniques, functional programming, and object-oriented approaches, interestingly enough, has yielded OBJ and its descendants. (See, e.g. [Gallimore et al., 1989], [Goguen, 1984], and [Grogono and Bennett, 1989].)

Formal proofs of software correctness are difficult enough without having to do them by hand. That is why there is a significant effort to automate the process, e.g., [Gallimore et al., 1989]. C.A.R. Hoare has refined and expanded his earlier work into Communicating Sequential Processes (CSP), e.g., [Hoare, 1985]. Realizing the value of both formal proofs of correctness and automation, Bertrand Meyer included assertions in his object-oriented programming language Eiffel (e.g., [Meyer, 1992]).

(Please note that there are many more forms of testing (and many testing issues) than can possibly be covered in this small article. Please be sure to check some of the previously mentioned general references.)

Encapsulation and Information Hiding

When making the transition to a new technology, we should expect that some of what we currently know will still be important and useful. We can also expect that there will be those things which will have little or no relevance, and still others will have to be modified. This is indeed the case when we investigate the testing of object-oriented software.

Two concepts which will have a major impact on our testing strategies are information hiding and encapsulation. Since some people confuse these two concepts, let me provide some simple definitions. **Information hiding** requires that we suppress (or hide) some information regarding an item. (See, e.g., [Parnas, 1972] and [Ross et al., 1975].) The general idea is that we show only that information which is necessary to accomplish our immediate goals. If we were to show more information we increase the chances of errors, either at the present time, or when the software is later modified. There are degrees of information hiding, e.g., C++'s public, private and protected members ([Ellis and Stroustrup, 1990]), and Ada's private and limited private types ([Booch, 1986]).

Encapsulation, on the other hand, describes the packaging (or binding together) of a collection of items. Common low-level examples of encapsulation include records and arrays. Procedures, functions, and subroutines are other ways of encapsulating information. Object-oriented approaches require still higher levels of encapsulation, e.g., classes. (Yes, I know that not all object-oriented approaches are class-based (e.g., [Ungar and Smith, 1987]), but let me perpetuate the illusion of simplicity for the moment.) Among other things, classes can encapsulate methods, other objects, and exceptions. Depending on the programming language, and the decisions of the software engineer, items which are encapsulated in a class will have varying degrees of visibility (information hiding).

The Impact of Encapsulation on Testing

Let's look at the impact of encapsulation first. We will state that object-oriented approaches use different encapsulation strategies than do the more conventional approaches, and that this has a twofold impact on software testing:

1.   The basic testable unit will no longer be the subprogram, and

2.   We will have to modify our strategies for integration testing.

Let's examine each of these separately.

Most technical and managerial software personnel are very familiar with functional decomposition methodologies. Outside of complete programs, the typical program unit produced by such an approach is some form of subprogram, e.g., functions, procedures, subroutines, and paragraphs. Many software standards and procedures are based on subprogram "units." Specifically, the subprogram is considered to be the basic "building block" from which applications are fashioned. In a classic waterfall approach to software development, subprogram units are usually well defined by the end of the design phase, and some may have been introduced as early as the analysis phase.

There have long been rules for well-designed subprograms (e.g., [Myers, 1978] and [Yourdon and Constantine, 1979]). Even before there was any code written, a good subprogram unit had a well-defined interface, and performed a single specific function (i.e., it was functionally cohesive). Designs could be black-box tested in a static manner, and the specifications for each subprogram unit could then be used as the basis for black-box testing the module once the code was written.

Once an individual subprogram unit was thoroughly tested, it was seldom, if ever, tested as a unit again. If a subprogram unit was reused (either in the same application or in another application), however, its appropriateness had to be re-determined in each context. For example, was the function being performed the right one for the given context, and did the interface for the module mesh smoothly with the surrounding code.

Now, let's consider an object-oriented environment. Here, we are dealing with larger program units, e.g., a class. Further, the concept of a subprogram is not quite the same as it is in more traditional systems. Specifically, we tend to separate the specification (interface) for the subprogram from its implementation (body). We refer to the specification as a "method interface" (i.e., an advertised capability in the external interface the class presents to the outside world), and to the implementation as a "method" (i.e., the internal (hidden) algorithm by which the operation is carried out). We often further complicate matters by allowing one method interface to be supported by multiple methods.

For the moment, let's keep things simple. We will view a method interface plus one of its methods as the equivalent of a single subprogram in a more traditional environment. A class can therefore be though of as encapsulating many subprograms. In addition, the same subprogram may find itself encapsulated in a number of different classes — frequently in descendants (specializations) of the class in which it first appeared. We also stipulate that classes may also encapsulate exceptions, other objects, and various forms of state information.

In object-oriented systems, we will most often think of subprograms as being bound (encapsulated) within a larger entity, e.g., a class. Further, these subprograms will work in conjunction with the other items encapsulated within the same object. This means that, in an object-oriented environment, attempting to test a subprogram in isolation is virtually meaningless. *In effect, the smallest testable unit is no longer the subprogram, but classes and instances of classes.* This impact will be felt even at relatively high levels of abstraction when, for example, we submit the results of analysis or design to the testing process.

(Yes, I realize that some of these observations change when we talk about object-oriented development of large applications, but allow me to keep things simple for this article.)

Elaine J. Weyuker has propose 11 axioms for checking the completeness of a testing effort (e.g., [Weyuker, 1986], [Weyuker, 1988], and [Zweben and Gourlay, 1989]). Dewayne E. Perry and Gail E. Kaiser ([Perry and Kaiser, 1990]) cite Weyuker's work and discuss its implications with regard to testing object-oriented software. Let's look at some examples.

Weyuker's fifth axiom is about *antiextensionality*. It says that if I have two different algorithms that compute the same function (i.e., they are "semantically close"), an adequate test set for one algorithm is not necessarily an adequate test set for the other algorithm. This says that if we replace an inherited method with a locally defined method that performs "the same function," the test set for the inherited method is not guaranteed to be adequate for the locally defined method.

Weyuker's sixth axiom is referred to as the "*general multiple change*" axiom. This axiom says that if two programs are of the same shape, a test set that is adequate for one will not necessarily be adequate for the other. (Two programs are of the "same shape" if one can be transformed into the other through a simple replacement of one or more relational operators with other relational operators, one or more constants with other constants, and one or more arithmetic operators with other arithmetic operators.) This axiom tells us that when the same items are inherited along different ancestor paths (i.e., via changes in the precedence ordering in a multiple inheritance scheme) then different test sets will be needed.

Weyuker's seventh axiom is called the *antidecomposition* axiom. The antidecomposition axiom says that something tested in one context will have to be retested if the context changes. For example, suppose that I thoroughly test a method within the context of a given class. Next, suppose I create a specialization (e.g., a subclass or a derived class) based on this class, and that the specialization inherits the tested method from the generalization (e.g., a superclass or base class). Even though I have tested the method within the context of the generalization, I cannot begin to guarantee the appropriateness of the same method within the context of the specialization, unless I re-test the method within the context of the specialization.

Weyuker's eighth axiom is the *anticomposition* axiom. The anticomposition axiom stipulates that adequately testing each unit in isolation is usually insufficient to adequately test the entire (integrated) program. Suppose that we change the underlying implementation for a given object, but keep the interface constant. We might suspect that we could get away with simply retesting the modified object in isolation. This is not the case. In addition, we will have to retest all dependent units (e.g., specializations and units that directly reference the modified object) as well.

Integration Testing

Now, let's move to the second point, i.e., integration testing. In non-object-oriented approaches, once a unit (usually a subprogram) is tested in isolation, it is then integrated into the larger whole. If I do this on a non-incremental basis, this means that I test each unit in isolation, simultaneously integrate all units, and then attempt to test the resulting whole. (This is why non-incremental testing is sometimes called "big bang" testing.) With the exception of very small, non-critical systems, non-incremental testing is not advisable.

Incremental testing, on the other hand, dictates that I test each unit in isolation, and then integrate each unit, one at a time, into the system, testing the overall system as I go. There are quite a number of different approaches to incremental testing, e.g., top-down, bottom-up, sandwich, and modified sandwich. (See, e.g., [Myers, 1976] and [Myers, 1979].) Incremental testing is almost always preferable to non-incremental testing.

Let's consider what happens in an object-oriented approach. If we were using a functional decomposition approach, our smallest testable unit would be a subprogram, and, during integration testing (depending on our integration strategy) we would be integrating one, or a few, subprogram(s) at a time. In our object-oriented system, our smallest testable unit will be a class (or comparable object-oriented unit). Given that the methods associated with each method interface often take advantage of the underlying implementation of the class, it is difficult to claim that each method-interface/method combination can be tested in isolation.

Integrating "subprograms" into a class, one at a time, testing the whole as we go, may not be an option. For example, there are usually direct or indirect interactions among the components which make up the class. One method may require that the object be in a specific state — a state which can only be set by another encapsulated method, or combination of encapsulated methods. Reversing the order of integration may not help since each method may be used to test the other.

There are other implications for integration testing in an object-oriented application. For example, in non-object-oriented systems, invocation hierarchies (module A calls module B, which eventually returns control to module A, et cetera) are the norm. Object-oriented systems are not required to abide by a strict invocation hierarchy, e.g., object A may interact directly with object B without necessarily having to go through an intermediary (controlling) object. This has led some people to say things such as "object-oriented systems have no tops," i.e., there may not be a master controlling module at the apex of some invocation hierarchy.

If we are working with a system that "has no top," then it will be difficult to define such things as "top-down integration testing," "bottom-up integration testing," or "sandwich integration testing." All of these testing strategies assume that there must be a definite "top" and a definite "bottom" for the system. This means that new integration testing strategies will have to be developed.

The Impact of Information Hiding on Testing

Advocates of object-oriented technology are fond of citing the black-box nature of objects. Specifically, a user of an object is denied access to the underlying implementation. This creates problems during testing. For example, consider a simple list object. In its interface there are a number of methods, e.g., add, delete, and length. Suppose we add an item to the list using the "add" method. How can we be assured that the specific item was actually added? (If the list is ordered, e.g., how can we be assured that the item was added in the correct position?) Since we cannot directly inspect the underlying implementation, we must seek some other strategy.

(Unless, the final product will actually incorporate an interactive debugger, it is generally not advisable to use a debugger for testing. One of the most fundamental axioms of testing is that we must test the actual product, not a variation on the product.)

A general approach is to first establish an acceptable level of confidence in the state-reporting methods in the object's interface, i.e., those methods that do not change or alter the state of the object, but rather return information on some aspect of the object's state. For example, if we could trust the "length" method in our list object, we could use it to test the "add" and "delete" methods by looking for corresponding increases and decreases in the length after the invocation of these methods. Of course, if we had an acceptable level of confidence in the list's "delete" method, and that method returned or required the actual item to be deleted, we could use that method to help check the "add" method.

At the very least, test designers will have to plan class testing strategies carefully.

Other Issues

If one is working with a language which supports parameterized classes, there will be the issue of how one tests parameterized classes. Using the list example again, if one is able to create a parameterized list class, that class will allow users to define specific list classes, e.g., a list of names class or a list of numbers class. The testing effort will try to demonstrate that at least some of the instances of the list metaclass do not have their intended characteristics.

In testing a generalization-specialization hierarchy, testers will want to demonstrate that the desired combination of characteristics may not be present in a given specialization due to mistakes in the inheritance structure as defined by the software engineers. In languages which support multiple inheritance, testers will seek out improper conflict resolution. In the so-called "classless" object-oriented languages (e.g., Self), testers will attempt to highlight problems with delegation schemes.

Summary

Much of what we know about testing technology does indeed apply to object-oriented systems. However, object-orientation brings with it, its own specialized set of concerns. Fortunately, there is a significant amount of research being conducted, and there is already an existing experience base.

Bibliography

[Abrial, 1980]. J.R. Abrial, *The Specification Language Z: Basic Library*, Programming Research Group, Oxford University, United Kingdom, 1980.

[Ackerman et al., 1989]. A. F. Ackerman, L. Buchwald, and F. Lewski, "Software Inspections: An Effective Verification Process," *IEEE Software*, Vol. 6, No. 3, May 1989, pp. 31 - 36.

[Agrawal and Spafford, 1989]. H. Agarwal and E. Spafford, "Bibliography on Debugging and Backtracking," *Software Engineering Notes*, Vol. 14, No. 2, April 1989, pp. 49 - 56.

[Anderson, 1979]. R.B. Anderson, *Proving Programs Correct*, John Wiley and Sons, New York, New York, 1979.

[Balfour, 1988]. B. Balfour, "On 'Unit Testing' and other Uses of the Term 'Unit'," *MCC '88 Military Computing Conference,* Military Computing Institute, 1988, pp. 127 - 130.

[Basili and Selby, 1987]. V.R. Basili and R.W. Selby, "Comparing the Effectiveness of Software Testing Strategies," *IEEE Transactions on Software Engineering*, Vol. 13, No. 12, December 1987, pp. 1278 - 1296.

[Bates, 1989]. P. Bates, "Debugging Heterogeneous Distributed Systems Using Event-Based Models of Behavior," *SIGPLAN Notices*, Vol. 24, No. 1, January 1989, pp. 11 - 22.

[Beizer, 1983]. B. Beizer, *Software Testing Techniques*, Van Nostrand Reinhold, New York, New York, 1983.

[Beizer, 1990]. B. Beizer, *Software Testing Techniques,* Second Edition, Van Nostrand Reinhold, New York, New York, 1990.

[Berg et al., 1982]. H.K. Berg, W.E. Boebert, W.R. Franta, and T.G. Moher, *Formal Methods of Program Verification and Specification*, Prentice Hall, Englewood Cliffs, New Jersey, 1982.

[Booch, 1986]. G. Booch, *Software Engineering with Ada,* Second Edition, Benjamin/Cummings, Menlo Park, California, 1986.

[Brown and Sampson, 1973]. A.R. Brown and W.A. Sampson, *Program Debugging*, Macdonald, London, United Kingdom, 1973.

[Carver, 1989]. R. Carver, *Testing, Debugging, and Analysis of Concurrent Software*, Ph.D. Thesis, North Carolina State University at Raleigh, Raleigh, North Carolina, (UMI Order No. GAX89-18077), 1989.

[Carver and Tai, 1989]. R. Carver and K.C. Tai, "Deterministic Execution Testing of Concurrent Ada Programs," *Proceedings of TRI-Ada '89 — Ada Technology In Context: Application, Development, and Deployment,* October 23-26, 1989, Association for Computing Machinery, New York, New York, pp. 528 - 544.

[Chow, 1985]. T.S. Chow, Editor, *IEEE Tutorial: Software Quality Assurance: A Practical Approach*, IEEE Computer Society Press, Silver Spring, Maryland, 1985.

[Chusho, 1987]. T. Chusho, "Test Data Selection and Quality Estimation Based on the Concept of Essential Branches for Path Testing," *IEEE Transactions on Software Engineering*, Vol. SE-13, No. 5, May 1987, pp. 509 - 517.

[Crosby, 1979]. P. B. Crosby, *Quality is Free*, The New American Library, Inc., New York, New York, 1979. (Originally published by McGraw-Hill, Inc., New York, New York.)

[DeMillo et. al., 1987]. R. DeMillo, W. McCracken, R. Martin, J. Passafiume, *Software Test and Evaluation,* Benjamin/Cummings, Menlo Park, California, 1987.

[Dijkstra, 1965]. E.W. Dijkstra, "Programming Considered as a Human Activity," *Proceedings of the 1965 IFIP Congress*, North Holland Publishing Company, Amsterdam, The Netherlands, 1965, pp. 213 - 217.

[Dijkstra, 1969]. E. Dijkstra, "Structured Programming," in *Software Engineering Concepts and Techniques, Proceedings of the NATO Conferences*, Edited by J.N. Buxton, P. Naur, and B. Randell, Petrocelli/Charter, New York, New York, 1976, pp. 222 - 226.

[Dunn, 1984]. R. Dunn, *Software Defect Removal*, McGraw-Hill, New York, New York, 1984.

[Dunn, 1990]. R. H. Dunn, *Software Quality: Concepts and Plans*, Prentice Hall, Englewood Cliffs, New Jersey, 1990.

[Dunn and Ullman, 1982]. R. Dunn and R. Ullman, *Quality Assurance for Computer Software*, McGraw-Hill, New York, New York, 1982.

[Ellis and Stroustrup, 1990]. M.A. Ellis and B. Stroustrup, *The Annotated C++ Reference Manual*, Addison-Wesley, Reading, Massachusetts, 1990.

[Evangelist, 1984]. M. Evangelist, "An Analysis of Control Flow Complexity," *Proceedings of the Eighth International Computer Software and Applications Conference*, Chicago, Illinois, November 7-9, 1984, pp. 235 - 237, 239.

[Fagan, 1976]. M.E. Fagan, "Design and Code Inspections To Reduce Errors in Program Development," *IBM Systems Journal*, Vol. 15, No. 3, 1976, pp. 219 - 248.

[Fagan, 1986]. M.E. Fagan, "Advances in Software Inspections," *IEEE Transactions on Software Engineering*, Vol. 12, No. 7, July 1986, pp. 744 - 751.

[Fiedler, 1989]. S.P. Fiedler, "Object-Oriented Unit Testing," *Hewlett-Packard Journal*, Vol. 36, No. 4, April 1989, pp. 69 - 74.

[Frankel and Weyuker, 1987]. P.G. Frankel and E.J. Weyuker, "Data Flow Testing in the Presence of Unexecutable Paths," *Proceedings of the Workshop on Software Testing*, Banff, Canada, July 1987, pp. 4 - 13.

[Freedman and Weinberg, 1982]. D.P. Freedman and G.M. Weinberg, *Handbook of Walkthroughs, Inspections, And Technical Reviews*, Third Edition, little, Brown and Company, Boston, Massachusetts, 1982.

[Gallimore et al., 1989]. R. Gallimore, D. Coleman, and V. Stravridou, *Computer Journal*, "UMIST OBJ: A Language for Executable Program Specifications," *Computer Journal*, Vol. 32, No. 5, October 1989, pp. 413 - 421.

[Goguen, 1984]. J.A. Goguen, "Parameterized Programming," *IEEE Transactions on Software Engineering*, Vol. SE-10, No. 5, September 1984, pp. 528 - 543.

[Goguen and Meseguer, 1987]. J.A. Goguen and J. Meseguer, "Unifying Functional, Object-Oriented and Relational Programming With Logical Semantics," in *Research Directions in Object-Oriented Programming*, Edited by B. Shriver and P. Wegner, The MIT Press, Cambridge, Massachusetts, 1987, pp. 417 - 477.

[Grogono and Bennett, 1989]. P. Grogono and A. Bennett, "Polymorphism and Type Checking in Object-Oriented Languages," *SIGPLAN Notices*, Vol. 24, No. 11, November 1989, pp. 109 - 115.

[Gould, 1975]. J.D. Gould, "Some Psychological Evidence on How People Debug Computer Programs," *International Journal of Man-Machine Studies*, Vol. 7, No. 2, 1975, pp. 151 - 182.

[Gould and Drongowski, 1972]. J.D. Gould and P. Drongowski, *A Controlled Psychological Study of Computer Program Debugging*, Technical Report RC-4083, IBM Research Division, Yorktown Heights, New York, 1972.

[Gunther, 1978]. R.C. Gunther, *Management Methodology For Software Product Engineering*, John Wiley and Sons, New York, New York, 1978.

[Hayes, 1987]. I. Hayes, Editor, *Specification Case Studies*, Prentice Hall, London, United Kingdom, 1987.

[Hoare, 1969]. C.A.R. Hoare, "An Axiomatic Basis for Computer Programming," *Communications of the ACM*, Vol. 12, No. 10, October 1969, pp. 576 - 580, 583.

[Hoare, 1971]. C.A.R. Hoare, "Proof of a Program: FIND," *Communications of the ACM*, Vol. 14, No. 1, January 1971, pp. 39 - 45.

[Hoare, 1972]. C.A.R. Hoare, "Proof of Correctness of Data Representation," *Acta Informatica*, Vol. 1, 1972, pp. 271 - 181.

[Hoare, 1985]. C.A.R. Hoare, *Communicating Sequential Processes*, Prentice Hall, Englewood Cliffs, New Jersey, 1985.

[Honda and Yonezawa, 1989]. Y. Honda and A. Yonezawa, "Debugging Concurrent Systems Based on Object Groups," in *ECOOP '88: Proceedings of the European Conference on Object-Oriented Programming, Lecture Notes on Computer Science,* Volume 322, S. Gjessing and K. Nygaard, Editors, Springer Verlag, New York, New York, 1988, pp. 267 - 282.

[Howden, 1987]. W. Howden, *Software Engineering and Technology: Functional Program Testing*, McGraw-Hill, New York, New York, 1987.

[Hseush and Kaiser, 1988]. W. Hseush and G.E. Kaiser, "Data Path Debugging: Data-Oriented Debugging for a Concurrent Programming Language," *Proceedings of the ACM SIGPLAN/ SIGOPS Workshop on Parallel and Distributed Debugging,* Madison, Wisconsin, May 1988, pp. 236 - 246.

[Humphrey, 1989]. W.S. Humphrey, *Managing the Software Process*, Addison-Wesley Publishing Company, Reading, Massachusetts, 1989.

[Jones, 1986]. C.B. Jones, *Systematic Software Development Using VDM,* Prentice Hall, Englewood Cliffs, New Jersey, 1986.

[Knuth, 1973]. D.E. Knuth, *The Art of Computer Programming, Volume 1: Fundamental Algorithms,* Second Edition, Addison-Wesley Publishing Company, Reading, Massachusetts, 1973.

[Laski, 1989]. J. Laski, "Testing in the Program Development Cycle," *Software Engineering Journal*, Vol. 4, No. 2, March 1989, pp. 95 - 106.

[Lazzerini and Lopriore, 1989]. B. Lazzerini and L. Lapriore, "Abstraction Mechanisms for Event Control in Program Debugging," *IEEE Transactions on Software Engineering*, Vol. 15, No. 7, July 1989, pp. 890 - 901.

[Lin and LeBlanc, 1989]. C. Lin and R. LeBlanc, "Event Based Debugging of Object/Action Programs," *SIGPLAN Notices*, Vol. 24, No. 1, January 1989, pp. 23 - 34.

[McCabe, 1976]. T. McCabe, "A Complexity Measure" *IEEE Transactions on Software Engineering*, December 1976, pp. 308 - 320.

[McCabe, 1982]. T.J. McCabe, Editor, *IEEE Tutorial: Structured Testing*, IEEE Computer Society Press, Silver Spring, Maryland, 1982.

[McCabe, 1987]. T. McCabe, "Automating the Testing Process Through Complexity Metrics," *Conference Proceedings Software Testing and Validation*, September 23-24, 1987, National Institute for Software Quality and Productivity, Inc., 1987, pp. G-l - G-30.

[Meyer, 1992]. B. Meyer, *Eiffel: The Language*, Prentice Hall, Englewood Cliffs, New Jersey, 1992.

[Miller and Howden, 1981]. E. Miller, and W.E. Howden, *Tutorial: Software Testing and Validation Techniques*, IEEE Computer Society Press, Washington, D.C., IEEE Catalog No. EHO180-0, 1981.

[Mizuno, 1983]. Y. Mizuno, "Software Quality Improvement," *IEEE Computer*, Vol. 16, No. 3, March 1983, pp. 66 - 72.

[Musa and Ackerman, 1989]. J. Musa and A. F. Ackerman, "Quantifying Software Validation: When to Stop Testing?," *IEEE Software,* Vol. 6, No. 3, May 1989, pp. 19 - 27.

[Myers, 1976]. G.J. Myers, *Software Reliability Principles and Practices*, John Wiley & Sons, New York, New York, 1976.

[Myers, 1978]. G. J. Myers, *Composite/Structured Design*, Van Nostrand Reinhold Company, New York, New York, 1978.

[Myers, 1979]. G.J. Myers, *The Art of Software Testing*, John Wiley and Sons, New York, New York, 1979.

[Ostrand et al., 1987]. T.J. Ostrand, R. Sigal, and E. Weyuker, "Design for a Tool to Manage Specification Based Testing," *Workshop on Software Testing,* Banff, Canada, July 1987, pp. 41 - 50.

[Parnas, 1972]. D.L. Parnas, "On the Criteria To Be Used in Decomposing Systems Into Modules," *Communications of the ACM*, Vol. 5, No. 12, December 1972, pp. 1053-1058.

[Parrington and Roper, 1989]. N. Parrington and M. Roper, *Understanding Software Testing*, Halstead Press, New York, New York, 1989.

[Perry and Kaiser, 1990]. D.E. Perry and G. E. Kaiser, "Adequate Testing and Object-Oriented Programming," *Journal of Object-Oriented Programming*, Vol. 2, No. 5, January/February 1990, pp. 13 - 19.

[Podgurski and Clarke, 1989]. A. Podgurski and L. Clarke, "The Implications of Program Dependencies for Software Testing, Debugging, and Maintenance," *Software Engineering Notes*, Vol. 14, No. 8, December 1989, pp. 168 - 178.

[Quirk, 1985]. W.J. Quirk, Editor, *Verification and Validation of Real-Time Software*, Springer-Verlag, New York, New York, 1985.

[Randell and Buxton, 1970]. B. Randell and J.N. Buxton, Editors, *Software Engineering Techniques*, NATO Scientific Affairs Division, Brussels 39, Belgium, 1970.

[Roe and Rowland, 1987]. R.P. Roe and J.H. Rowland, "Some Theory Concerning Certification of Mathematical Subroutines by Black Box Testing," *IEEE Transactions on Software Engineering*, Vol. SE-13, No. 7, July 1987, pp. 761 - 766.

[Ross et al., 1975]. D.T. Ross, J.B. Goodenough, and C.A. Irvine, "Software Engineering: Process, Principles, and Goals," *IEEE Computer,* Vol. 8, No. 5, May 1975, pp. 17 - 27.

[Schulmeyer and McManus, 1987]. G.G. Schulmeyer and J.I. McManus, Editors, *Handbook of Software Quality Assurance*, Van Nostrand Reinhold, New York, New York, 1987.

[Shankar, 1982]. K. S. Shankar, "A Functional Approach to Module Verification," *IEEE Transactions on Software Engineering*, Vol. SE-8, No. 2, March 1982, pp. 147 - 160.

[Sommerville, 1989]. I. Sommerville, *Software Engineering,* Third Edition, Addison-Wesley Publishing Company, Reading, Massachusetts, 1989.

[Spivey, 1988]. J.M. Spivey, *Understanding Z: A Specification Language and Its Formal Semantics*, Cambridge University Press, Cambridge, United Kingdom, 1988.

[Spivey, 1989]. J.M. Spivey, *The Z Notation: A Reference Manual*, Prentice Hall, Englewood Cliffs, New Jersey, 1989.

[Tai, 1985a]. K.C. Tai, "Reproducible Testing of Concurrent Ada Programs," *Proceedings of SOFTFAIR II*, IEEE Computer Society Press, Silver Spring, Maryland, December, 1985, pp. 114 - 120.

[Tai, 1985b]. K.C. Tai, "On Testing Concurrent Programs," *Proceedings of COMPSAC '85*, IEEE Computer Society Press, Silver Spring, Maryland, October, 1985, pp. 310 - 317.

[Tai, 1986]. K.C. Tai, "Reproducible Testing of Ada Tasking Programs," *Proceedings of the IEEE Second International Conference on Ada Applications and Environments*, IEEE Computer Society Press, Silver Spring, Maryland, 1986, pp. 69 - 79.

[Tai, 1987]. K.C. Tai, "A Methodology for Testing Concurrent Ada Programs," *Proceedings of The Joint Ada Conference Fifth National Conference on Ada Technology and Washington Ada Symposium*, March 1987, pp. 459 - 464.

[Tai and Din, 1985]. K.C. Tai and C. Y. Din, "Validation of Concurrency in Software Specification and Design," *Third International Workshop on Software Specification and Design*, IEEE Computer Society Press, Silver Spring, Maryland, 1985, pp. 223 - 227.

[Tai et al., 1989]. K.C. Tai, R.H. Carver, and E.E. Obaid, "Deterministic Execution Debugging of Concurrent Ada Programs," *Proceedings of Compsac '89*, IEEE Computer Society Press, Silver Spring, Maryland, October 1989, pp. 102 - 109.

[Tassel, 1978]. D.V. Tassel, *Program Style, Design, Efficiency, Debugging, and Testing,* Second Edition, Prentice Hall, Englewood Cliffs, New Jersey, 1978.

[Ungar and Smith, 1987]. D. Ungar and R.B. Smith, "Self: The Power of Simplicity," *OOPSLA '87 Conference Proceedings,* special issue of *SIGPLAN Notices*, Vol. 22, No. 12, December 1987, pp. 227 - 242.

[Weyuker, 1986]. E.J. Weyuker, "Axiomatizing Software Test Data Accuracy," *IEEE Transactions on Software Engineering,* Vol. SE-12, No. 12, December 1986, pp. 1128 - 1138.

[Weyuker, 1988]. E.J. Weyuker, "The Evaluation of Program-Based Software Test Data Accuracy Criteria," *Communications of the ACM*, Vol. 31, No. 6, June 1988, pp. 668 - 675.

[Yourdon, 1978]. E. Yourdon, *Structured Walkthroughs, Second Edition*, Yourdon Press, New York, New York, 1978.

[Yourdon and Constantine, 1979]. E. Yourdon and L. L. Constantine, *Structured Design: Fundamentals of a Discipline of Computer Program and System Design*, Prentice Hall, Englewood Cliffs, New Jersey, 1979.

[Zweben and Gourlay, 1989]. S.H. Zweben and J. Gourlay, "On the Adequacy of Weyuker's Test Data Adequacy Axioms," *IEEE Transactions on Software Engineering*, Vol. 15, No. 4, April 1989, pp. 496 - 500.

16   Specifying Test Cases for Object-Oriented Software

> A problem may be characterized as a fact or group of facts for which we have no acceptable explanation, which seems unusual, or which fails to fit in with our expectations or preconceptions. It should be obvious that some prior beliefs are required if anything is to appear problematic. If there are no expectations, there can be no surprises.
>
> — *I.M. Copi, [Copi, 1968]*

Prologue

Very often articles, books, and courses on software testing go to great lengths to show how test cases for software can be systematically designed. It is also not uncommon to find "checklists" designed to assist the reviewer in verifying and/or validating software. (See, e.g., [Hetzel, 1988], [Hollocker, 1990], [Myers, 1979], [Schulmeyer, 1990], and [Yourdon, 1989].) However, it is very unusual to find a complete, generic specification for an individual test case — much less a specification for a test case for object-oriented software. Some examples do exist, e.g., ANSI/IEEE Std-829-1983 (contained in [IEEE, 1989]), the "IEEE Standard for Software Test Documentation."

People sometimes confuse such things as "test plans" and "test cases." A **"test plan"** or "testing plan" describes an overall systematic approach to the testing of software. Within a software engineering organization, the testing group maintains a generic test plan that is used to guide management decisions, and justify such things as staffing, tool acquisition and training. These generic plans are instantiated ("fleshed out") for individual projects and products. Examples of test plans can be found in [Andriole, 1986], [Evans, 1984], and [Gunther, 1978].

"Test cases" (sometimes referred to as "test designs"), on the other hand, document individual tests. Bill Hetzel ([Hetzel, 1988]) observes that "a document that defines overall testing objectives and the testing approach is called a test plan. A document or statement that defines what we have selected to be tested and describes the expected results is called a test design." In this article, we will focus not on the design or creation of individual test cases for object-oriented software, but rather on the documentation (specification) of these test cases.

Why Study Specifications for Test Cases for Object-Oriented Software?

One might question the usefulness of studying a generic specification for a test case. Of course, it is very important to know how to systematically design test cases for object-oriented software. Still, a great deal can be obtained by studying a suggested format for test case specification. For example, a generic test case specification can be used:

- as a checklist for items to be included in a specific test case,

- to gain a better understanding of the testing of object-oriented software,

- in the automation of the testing effort (Standardized approaches are easier to automate than are ad hoc approaches.),

- to facilitate the systematic review of test cases (Standardized approaches, once understood, are often easier to review than non-standard, and constantly varying approaches.), and

- to simplify regression testing. Boris Beizer ([Beizer, 1990]) defines **regression testing** as "any repetition of tests [after a change has been introduced] intended to show that the software's behavior is unchanged except insofar as required by the change to the software…" Having a standard approach to test case specification helps to simplify the testing effort and encourages automation, both of which aid regression testing.

The Characteristics of a Well-Specified Test Case

Testing is a comparison process. The designer of a test case must specify, in advance, the *expected* results, *expected* characteristics, and/or *expected* behavior of the item being tested. When the test is physically executed (run), the *actual* results, *actual* characteristics, and/or *actual* behavior, are recorded and compared with what was expected. Assuming that the test case has gone through explicit verification before it was executed, a **symptom of an error** is present whenever an *actual* item does not agree with its *expected* counterpart.

In general, a well-specified test case can be executed by a relatively non-technical person, or even by completely automated means. The major technical effort involved should be in the design of the test case, not in its specification or execution. A well-specified test case:

- is complete, i.e., any necessary information is supplied,

- is unambiguous, i.e., there is no doubt as to the information which must be supplied, or as to what the expected outcome must be,

- if necessary, clearly specifies the ordering of events,

- clearly shows the relationships (correlations) among its components,

- is specified to the point where it can be easily automated, or, at least, executed by a person with minimum knowledge of what is being tested (A well-specified test case is defined to the point where, if it is given to two or more people, without any additional information, it will be executed in the same general manner, and will yield the same results.), and

- has a unique identification.

Specifying Test Cases for Object-Oriented Software

Test cases for software developed using more traditional approaches, e.g., functional decomposition, have usually been expressed in terms of "input-processing-output." For example, in defining a test case for a piece of software, a software engineer would identify the specific input(s) for the software and the expected output(s). The "state" of the software (prior to, during, and after execution) was seldom, if ever, considered.

To begin to understand what is involved in testing objects, consider the following examples:

- Suppose we are to test a "bank account" object. Specifically, we are interested in the "deposit" operation in the bank account's interface. This operation may require two input parameters, i.e., the specific identification for the bank account, and the amount to be deposited. Let us further stipulate that the deposit operation has no output parameters. We note the following:

  - One might say that the (hopefully correctly) altered state of the bank account served as an "output" for the deposit operation.

  - One technique for checking the proper behavior of the deposit operation would be to know the balance of the bank account immediately prior to, and immediately after, when the deposit was made. This might very likely involve the sending of several additional messages (invoking of several additional operations).

  - It may be possible (or intended) that the deposit operation will raise exceptions for certain combinations of the current balance plus the deposit amount, or if the amount to be deposited is negative. If this is intended, a test case would have to provide for dealing with the exceptions, or even checking to see that the proper exception was raised.

- Consider the testing of a "list" object. Specifically, we are interested in testing the "length" operation, i.e., the operation which returns the number of items currently stored in the list. This operation may have only one parameter, e.g., the number of items currently contained in the list (i.e., an output parameter). We note the following:

  - One might say that the current state of the list served as an "input" for the length operation.

  - One technique for checking the proper behavior of the length operation would be to know the number of items contained in the list immediately prior to, and immediately after, when the length was requested. This might very likely involve the sending of several additional messages (invoking of several additional operations).

- Lastly, consider a "button" object, e.g., a button one might press to summon an elevator, or to turn on a lamp. This object may be an "active object" (see, e.g., [Booch, 1991]), meaning that it is capable of "spontaneously" changing its own state, i.e., from "not pressed" to "pressed." We note the following:

  - Testing this object may require the presence of several "external" objects, e.g., a finger (to press the button), a lamp, or an elevator.

  - For the test case to be effective, these external objects will probably have to have known initial states, known final states, and we may even be interested in some of their intermediate states.

For a given object, we will usually specify a series (list) of test cases. Each individual test case will contain:

- an identification that uniquely identifies the object being tested,

- a unique test case identification,

- a statement of the purpose for the test case, and

- a list of test case steps. Each test case step will contain:

    - a list of specified states for the object being tested,

    - a list of the messages/operations that are to be used in the execution of the test case step (if applicable),

    - a list of exceptions to be raised by the object being tested (if applicable),

    - a list of interrupts to be generated by the object being tested (if applicable),

    - a list of external conditions (if applicable), and

    - a list of additional comments (if necessary).

Let's now look at each of these items in turn.

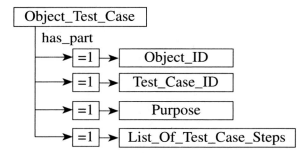

Figure 1:   **A semantic network showing the four main components of a test case specification for an object.** The bulk of the test case information is contained in the "list of test case steps" component.

Unique Object Identification

Each test case is associated with one object (or system of objects). Therefore, there must be some unambiguous mechanism for associating a specific test case with a specific object. In object-oriented systems, it is common for each object to have a unique name. For example, if we were interested in testing a bank account object, we might stipulate that we were testing "Eds_Bank_Account."

(In the spirit of reuse, we stipulate that one test case may be (re)used with (potentially) many different objects. However, each individual execution of the test case must be unambiguously associated with one specific object.)

Unique Test Case Identification

Each test case must have a unique identification. Keep the following in mind:

- For any given object, there are often many test cases.

- During the course of the development of even a medium-sized application, thousands of test cases may be generated.

- Not all test cases will be associated with a single object, i.e., they may be associated with a system of objects.

- If possible, test case identifications should provide some indication of the objects, or systems of objects, with which they are associated.

- Consider automation in the creation of a test case identification, e.g., the sorting of identifications.

- Some people consider the "unique object identification" to be part of the "unique test case identification."

Using the bank account example again, we might identify a specific test case as "first_deposit_test," "deposit_1," or even "first_deposit_equivalence_class."

The Purpose of the Test Case

In the process of evaluating the worth, appropriateness, and overall validity for any test case, it will be necessary to understand why the test case was constructed. Further, given a set of test cases for an object (or system of objects), a tester may desire some easy mechanism for determining if a sufficient set of test cases has been generated to achieve adequate testing, or if any duplication of effort has occurred.

Given a bank account object, and a particular type of black-box testing e.g., equivalence class partitioning, we might state the following purpose for one of our test cases:

> Given a known starting balance, a valid equivalence class of deposit amounts is all deposit amounts such that the starting balance plus the deposit amount is less than, or equal to, U.S. $100,000. This purpose of this test case is, given a bank account object with a known starting balance, to select a member of this valid equivalence class of deposit amounts, and to deposit this amount into the bank account.

A List of Test Case Steps

Each test case contains a collection of one or more test case steps. Further, depending on the type of object, or system of objects, we are testing, some of the test case steps may be able to proceed in parallel. Each test case step consists of:

- a list of states for the object (or system of objects) being tested,

- a list of messages/operations (if applicable),

- a list of exceptions raised by the object being tested (if applicable),

- a list of interrupts generated by the object being tested (if applicable),

- a list of external conditions (if applicable), and

- a list of comments (annotations), if applicable.

Let us look at each of these items in turn.

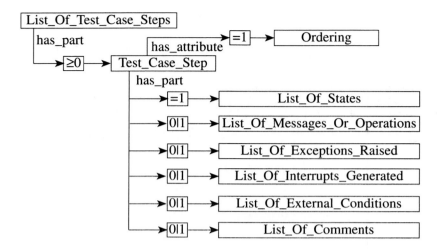

Figure 2: **A semantic network showing a breakdown of the six major components in a "test case step," within a "list of test case steps."** While five out of six of the components are listed as optional, at least one of these five components, other than the "list of comments," must be present.

A List of Specified States

The evaluation of a message (execution of an operation), for example, may be different depending on the initial and intermediate states of an object. In addition, during the execution of a particular test case, an object may proceed through a whole series of (important) states. In some cases, we may be more interested in the final state of the object than we are in the specific sequence of operations/messages, and/or sequence of external conditions, which were executed/evaluated/encountered in the process of getting the object to that state.

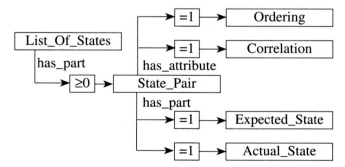

Figure 3: **A semantic network showing that the "list of states" is actually a list of "state pairs," i.e., for each expected state there is a corresponding actual state.** Notice that each state pair is usually correlated with some other part of the test case step, e.g., an operation/message.

For example, let us again consider testing the deposit operation for a bank account object. We may first wish to "open" a bank account, or at least make sure that it is already open. Next, we may wish to determine the current balance, and/or ensure that the current balance has a specific value. We then may "make the deposit." Lastly, we will want to know the final balance. The sequence of states in which we were interested was:

- is the bank account "open,"

- what is the "current balance" of the bank account, and

- what was the "current balance" of the bank account *after the deposit was made.*

Keep the following in mind when identifying a list of specified states for a given test case step:

- The states must be specified in an unambiguous manner. If equivalence classes of states are used, they should also be unambiguous.

- If there is a specific sequence or ordering of these states, the sequence or ordering should be unambiguous and readily apparent.

- If the states are supposed to be correlated with a specific operation/message, sequence of operations/messages, specific exception being raised, specific interrupt being generated, specific external condition, or sequence of external conditions, these correlations must be unambiguous and readily apparent.

In the design of any test case, a software engineer must specify the "expected results" in advance of running the test case. When the test case is executed, the "actual results" are compared with the "expected results." If they do not match, then the test case has detected a symptom of an error. Therefore, for each state in the list of specified states, the author of the test case must unambiguously specify the expected state. When the test case step is executed, the corresponding actual states will be recorded and compared with the expected states. Symptoms of errors are present when an actual state does not match its corresponding expected state.

Returning to our bank account example, the test case designer will stipulate that the *expected* sequence of states for the bank account object are: open, open with a known balance, and open with a new balance equal to the previous balance plus the deposit. When the test case is executed, the *actual* states will be recorded and associated with their corresponding expected states.

In the case of the bank account, we would expect that each of these could be determined by the sending of an appropriate message (invocation of an appropriate operation). (This, of course, assumes that we have already established an acceptable level of confidence in these messages/operations.) Therefore, each state will very likely be correlated with the sending of a specific message (invocation of a specific operation). However, we keep in mind that, for some objects, a specific state may be more directly correlated with a specific interrupt being generated, or a specific combination of external (to the object) conditions.

A List of Messages/Operations

Most, but not all, test case steps will involve the invocation of operations (sending of messages). For each operation/message involved in a test case step, the tester must supply:

- the name of the operation/message,

- the input parameters (if any) for the operation/message, and

- the output parameters (if any) for the operation/message.

We further note that some parameters may be both input and output.

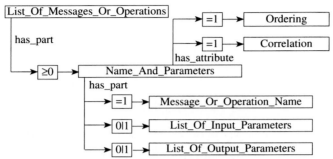

Figure 4:   **A semantic network showing that each message/operation is specified in terms of a name and optional lists of input parameters, output parameters, or both.** As with other components of a test case step, messages/operations are almost always correlated with other specific test case step components.

When the tester is creating the list of messages/operations for an individual test case step, he or she should keep the following in mind:

- Messages/operations must be specified in an unambiguous manner. If overloading is possible, it must be clear as to which specific method is intended.

- If there is a specific intended sequence (ordering) of the messages/operations, the sequence must be indicated in an unambiguous manner, and must be readily apparent.

- If a message/operation, or sequence of messages/operations, is supposed to be correlated with a specific state, specific sequence of states, a specific exception being raised, a specific interrupt being generated, a specific external condition, or specific sequence of external conditions, these correlations must be unambiguous and readily apparent.

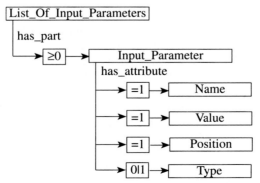

Figure 5:   **Input parameters are specified in terms of a formal parameter name, a value, a position, and, optionally, a type.** Not all object-oriented implementations support typing.

For each input parameter for a given message/operation, the test case must specify:

- the name of the parameter (by this, we mean the formal parameter name),

- the specific value for the parameter,

- the position of the input parameter, and

- the type of the input parameter (if applicable).

For each output parameter for a given message/operation, the test case must specify:

- the name of the parameter (by this, we mean the formal parameter name),

- the specific values (expected and actual) for the parameter,

- the position of the output parameter, and

- the type of the output parameter (if applicable).

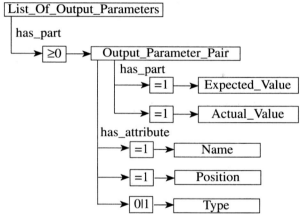

Figure 6: **If we are dealing with output parameters for a message/operation, we will specify the *expected* value for the output parameter.** When the test case is executed, the *actual* value for the corresponding output parameter will be recorded for comparison.

For each output parameter for each message/operation in the list of messages/operations, the author of the test case step must unambiguously specify the *expected* value of the output parameter. When the test case step is executed, the corresponding *actual* values for the output parameters will be recorded and compared with the expected values. Symptoms of errors are present when the *actual* value of an output parameter does not match the corresponding *expected* value for that output parameter.

Revisiting our bank account example, we might propose the following sequence of operations/messages in our testing of the "deposit" operation/message: "open," "is_open," "balance," "deposit," and "balance." (Of course, this assumes that we have previously established an acceptable level of confidence in the "open," "is_open," and "balance" operations/messages.) We would then detail the input and output parameters, e.g.:

- Operation: "Open"

- Input Parameter
  - Name: This_Bank_Account
  - Specific Value: "unopened" (the rest of the state information will be ignored)
  - Position: First, and only parameter
  - Type: Bank_Account
- Output Parameter
  - Name: This_Bank_Account
  - Expected Value: "opened" (the rest of the state information will be ignored)
  - Actual Value:
  - Position: First, and only parameter
  - Type: Bank_Account

We also note that this operation should be correlated with the state "bank account is open" in the list of specified states. This may be accomplished by having the state ("bank account is open") point to the operation ("open"), having the operation point to the state, having both the operation and state point to each other, or assigning the same "correlation value" to both the state and the operation. For example, "all items having a correlation value of 'X' are correlated with each other and there is no implied ordering or precedence."

A List of Exceptions Raised

It is not uncommon, nor unexpected, for some test cases to cause exceptions to be raised. Indeed, the primary purpose of a given test case may be to raise a specific encapsulated (within the object being tested) exception. In these instances, the test case designer will have to specify unambiguously a list of the exceptions that are expected to be raised. When the test case is run, then the actual exceptions raised (if they are raised) will be compared to the expected exceptions. When the actual exceptions do not correspond to the expected exceptions, then this indicates a symptom of an error. As with other items, exceptions have to be ordered, and correlated with other parts of the same test case.

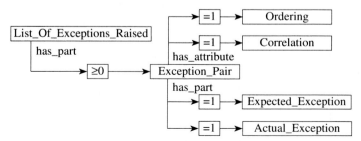

Figure 7:   **Some test cases are designed with the intention of raising specific exceptions.** For these test cases, the test case designer will specify the expected exception, and the executor of the test case will record the actual exception (if any) raised.

Suppose, for example, that if someone attempted to "open" an already "opened" bank account, the exception "opened" is supposed to be raised. In attempting to test this condition, a tester would have to ensure that a particular bank account object was already in the "open" state, and then request (most probably via a message/operation) that that account be opened. When the test case was executed, the actual exception raised (if any) would be recorded and compared with the expected exception — in our example, the exception "opened." Notice further that the expected exception will have to be correlated with both a specific state for the object, and a specific operation/message.

For any given test step, there may be more than one exception that will be raised, e.g., if there are multiple operations/messages, more than one of these operations/messages may raise an exception.

A List of Interrupts Generated

Objects that are very close to the hardware will occasionally have to generate interrupts. It will occasionally be necessary that the primary purpose for a given test case may be to cause an object to generate a specific interrupt. In these instances, the test case designer will have to specify unambiguously a list of the interrupts that he or she *expects* the object being tested to generate. When the test case is run, then the *actual* interrupts generated (if they are generated) will be compared to the expected interrupts. When the actual interrupts do not correspond to the expected interrupts, then this indicates a symptom of an error. As with other items, interrupts have to be ordered, and correlated with other parts of the same test case.

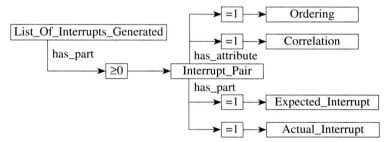

Figure 8:   **Some test cases, particularly for objects very close to low-level hardware, will require the generation of interrupts.** These interrupts will most likely be correlated with both specific states and specific messages/operations.

A List of External Conditions

An object (or system of objects) may be affected by, or may affect, conditions outside of the object. (For example, the change in state of a "button" object may require that a physical (hardware) button be pressed. Testing of a clock object may require the passage of time.) In general, the conduct and/or the results of a test case step may be different depending on the conditions which exist outside of the object being tested. There may be a whole series of external conditions whose ordering is important to the conduct and/or results of the test case step. Therefore, the specification of a test case step for an object must include all appropriate external conditions.

When a tester is creating a list of external conditions for a specific test case step, he or she should consider the following:

- External conditions must be specified in an unambiguous manner. If equivalence classes are used, they must also be unambiguous.

- If there is a specific intended sequence (ordering) of the external conditions, the sequence must be indicated in an unambiguous manner, and must be readily apparent.

- If an external condition or sequence of external conditions, is supposed to be correlated with a specific state, sequence of states, a specific message/operation, specific sequence of messages/operations, a specific exception, or a specific interrupt, these correlations must be unambiguous and readily apparent.

An "external condition" can take several forms, i.e.:

- an external (to the object being tested) object in a specific state,

- an externally (to the object being tested) raised exception with which the object being tested must deal,

- an externally (to the object being tested) generated interrupt to which the object being tested must respond, or

- the occurrence of an external (to the object being tested) event.

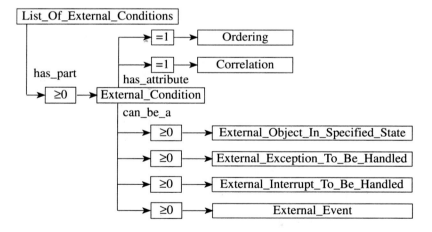

Figure 9:   **External conditions can be external objects in specified states, external exceptions and interrupts, and events.** In many cases "events" can be expressed in terms of objects, exceptions, and interrupts, but may be more straightforwardly described in other terms.

Although several items may make up the external conditions for an object being tested, it is the states of the external (to the object being tested) objects that allow us to test for errors. The designer of a test case involving external objects must unambiguously describe the expected states of these objects. When the test is executed, the actual states of these external objects will be captured and compared to the expected states. When the actual states are not identical to the expected states, this indicates a symptom of an error.

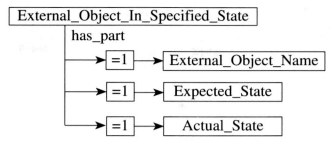

Figure 10: **External objects present another method for detecting symptoms of errors.** If the actual state of an external object is not what was specified for its expected state, we have uncovered a symptom of an error.

In truth, the detection of an external event will require a change in state for at least one object. Further, external exceptions and interrupts may be (at least part of) the mechanism by which an external event is detected. However:

- Some items are more easily stated in terms of events, e.g., the passage of a prescribed period of time.

- The designer of the test case may not know (or care) how a particular event is detected.

A List of Additional Comments

The tester may wish to annotate each test case step in some manner. Further, the tester may wish to attach a specific comment (engineering note) to a specific part of the test case step. Therefore, a list of comments will be an important part of any test case step.

In creating the list of comments for a specific test case step, the tester should keep the following in mind:

- The comments must convey meaningful information which is not readily apparent from an examination of the test case step.

- If the comment relates to a specific part of the test case step, it should be unambiguously associated with that part.

- The comments should be both precise and concise.

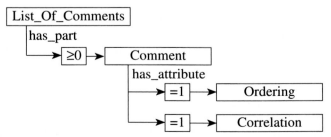

Figure 11: **Done correctly, comments are a necessary and helpful part of any test case, and test case step.** Of course, since some test cases may be quite intricate, comments must be correlated with the item being commented upon.

Conclusions

In testing objects, we are concerned with more than just "input parameters" and "output parameters." We must be concerned with the state of the object being tested, and quite possibly the states of other objects in the same system. In addition, we recognize that the testing of even a single operation in the interface to an object may involve a number of distinct steps.

Any effective testing effort is well planned. Test cases must be carefully designed, specified, reviewed, and executed. Without some systematic means of specifying a test case, it is difficult to evaluate the quality of individual test cases, much less the quality and effectiveness of an overall testing effort. In addition, well-specified test cases aid not only in the quality assurance of the testing effort, but also encourage such things as test automation, systematic regression testing, and test case reuse.

Overall, testing of objects is more involved than the testing of simple functions. This should not surprise us since objects themselves are more involved than are simple functions. We should note, however, that items such as exceptions and interrupts are hardly unique to object-oriented software.

Bibliography

[Andriole, 1986]. S.J. Andriole, Editor, *Software Validation, Verification, Testing, and Documentation*, Petrocelli Books, Princeton, New Jersey, 1986.

[Beizer, 1990]. B. Beizer, *Software Testing Techniques,* Second Edition, Van Nostrand Reinhold, New York, New York, 1990.

[Booch, 1991]. G. Booch, *Object-Oriented Design With Applications*, Benjamin/Cummings, Menlo Park, California, 1991.

[Copi, 1968]. I.M. Copi, *Introduction to Logic*, Macmillian Company, New York, New York, 1968.

[Evans, 1984]. M.W. Evans, *Productive Software Test Management*, John Wiley & Sons, New York, New York, 1984.

[Fiedler, 1989]. S.P. Fiedler, "Object-Oriented Unit Testing," *Hewlett-Packard Journal*, Vol. 36, No. 4, April 1989, pp. 69 - 74.

[Gunther, 1978]. R.C. Gunther, *Management Methodology For Software Product Engineering*, John Wiley & Sons, New York, New York, 1978.

[Hetzel, 1988]. B. Hetzel, *The Complete Guide to Software Testing,* Second Edition, QED Information Sciences, Inc., Wellesley, Massachusetts, 1988.

[Hollocker, 1990]. C.P. Hollocker, *Software Reviews And Audits Handbook*, John Wiley & Sons, New York, New York, 1990.

[IEEE, 1989]. Institute for Electrical and Electronics Engineers, *Software Engineering Standards,* Third Edition, IEEE, Inc., New York, New York, 1989.

[Myers, 1979]. G.J. Myers, *The Art of Software Testing*, John Wiley & Sons, New York, New York, 1979.

[Schulmeyer and McManus, 1987]. G.G. Schulmeyer and J.I. McManus, Editors, *Handbook of Software Quality Assurance*, Van Nostrand Reinhold, New York, New York, 1987.

[Yourdon, 1989]. E. Yourdon, *Structured Walkthroughs,* Fourth Edition, Prentice Hall, Englewood Cliffs, New Jersey, 1989.

17   Readings In Object-Oriented Technology

> There are more things in heaven and earth, Horatio, than are dreamt of in your philosophy.
>
> — *William Shakespeare,* Hamlet

> Now my suspicion is that the universe is not only queerer than we suppose, but queerer than we *can* suppose. … I suspect that there are more things in heaven and earth than are dreamed of, in any philosophy. That is the reason why I have no philosophy myself, and must be my excuse for dreaming.
>
> — *John Burdon Sanderson Haldane,* Possible Worlds *[1927]*

If you are interested in reading about any rapidly evolving technology, it is best to keep the following in mind:

- Read more than one source. Look for sources which have different, and possibly conflicting, views of the material. It is often difficult to determine fundamental facts when only one viewpoint is present.

- Very often, authors confuse concepts with implementations. Ask yourself if the author is discussing a concept, or a particular implementation of the concept.

- Always be on the lookout for new sources. In the software technology arena in particular, significant changes can take place in less than a month.

- Take care to distinguish between differing viewpoints and conflicting viewpoints.

There are many topic areas in object-oriented software technology, and literally thousands of books, articles, tutorials, and proceedings devoted, in whole, or in part, to object-oriented software concepts.

What we present here is fairly generic object-oriented technology material. The references that have been selected are generally well known, and represent a fair cross section of object-oriented technology. While any individual reference may or may not be an authoritative reference, readers who peruse more than a few references will begin to get an adequate appreciation of object-oriented technology.

Object-Oriented Programming

Object-oriented programming books most often tend to focus on programming language aspects of object-oriented technology. However, many fundamental concepts can be found in the books mentioned below:

[Cox, 1986]. B.J. Cox, *Object Oriented Programming: An Evolutionary Approach*, Addison-Wesley, Reading, Massachusetts, 1986.

[Goldberg and Robson, 1983]. A. Goldberg and D. Robson, *Smalltalk-80: The Language and Its Implementation*, Addison-Wesley, Reading, Massachusetts, 1983.

[Meyer, 1988]. B. Meyer, *Object-Oriented Software Construction*, Prentice Hall, Englewood Cliffs, New Jersey, 1988.

[Keene, 1989]. S.E. Keene, *Object-Oriented Programming in Common Lisp*, Addison-Wesley, Reading, Massachusetts, 1989.

[Stroustrup, 1991]. B. Stroustrup, *The C++ Programming Language,* Second Edition, Addison-Wesley, Reading, Massachusetts, 1991.

(If I could buy only one of these books, I would choose [Meyer, 1988]. [Stroustrup, 1991] would be my second choice.)

Object-Oriented Requirements Analysis

There are a number of publicly available courses on object-oriented requirements analysis. Since the technology is still new, these courses present many differing viewpoints and approaches. The following references will give the reader a quick survey of the more common ideas.:

[Anderson et al., 1989]. J.A. Anderson, J. McDonald, L. Holland, and E. Scranage, "Automated Object-Oriented Requirements Analysis and Design," *Proceedings of the Sixth Washington Ada Symposium*, June 26-29, 1989, pp. 265 - 272.

[Berard, 1990]. E.V. Berard, "Object-Oriented Requirements Analysis," *Hotline On Object-Oriented Technology*, Vol. 1, No. 8, June 1990, pp. 9 - 11.

[Coad and Yourdon, 1990]. P. Coad and E. Yourdon, *OOA — Object-Oriented Analysis*, Second Edition, Prentice Hall, Englewood Cliffs, New Jersey, 1990.

[de Champeaux and Faure, 1992]. D. de Champeaux and P. Faure, "A Comparative Study of Object-Oriented Analysis Methods," *Journal of Object-Oriented Programming*, Vol. 5, No. 1, March/April 1992, pp. 21 - 33.

[Shlaer and Mellor, 1988]. S. Shlaer and S.J. Mellor, *Object-Oriented Systems Analysis: Modeling the World In Data*, Yourdon Press: Prentice Hall, Englewood Cliffs, New Jersey, 1988.

[Stoecklin et al., 1988]. S.E. Stoecklin, E.J. Adams, and S. Smith, "Object-Oriented Analysis," *Proceedings of the Fifth Washington Ada Symposium,* June 27 - 30, 1988, Association for Computing Machinery, New York, New York, 1988, pp. 133 - 138.

(Outside of [Berard, 1990], I would recommend [de Champeaux and Faure, 1992]. [Coad and Yourdon, 1990] and [Shlaer and Mellor, 1988] are certainly very popular, but less object-oriented than they could be.)

Object-Oriented Design/Development

Most of the work which has been done in the area of object-oriented life-cycle issues, outside of object-oriented programming, has been accomplished within the Ada community. However, more non-Ada object-oriented software engineering sources are beginning to emerge. Some representative sources on OOD are:

[Abbott, 1983]. R.J. Abbott, "Program Design by Informal English Descriptions," *Communications of the ACM*, Vol. 26, No. 11, November 1983, pp. 882 - 894.

[Birchenough and Cameron, 1989]. A. Birchenough and J.R. Cameron, "JSD and Object-Oriented Design," *JSP & JSD: The Jackson Approach to Software Development*, IEEE Computer Society Press, Washington, D.C., 1989.

[Booch, 1986]. G. Booch, "Object Oriented Development," *IEEE Transactions on Software Engineering,* Vol. SE-12, No. 2, February 1986, pp. 211 - 221.

[Booch, 1990]. G. Booch, "On the Concepts of Object-Oriented Design," in *Modern Software Engineering: Foundations and Current Perspectives*, P.A. Ng and R.T. Yeh, Editors, Van Nostrand Reinhold, New York, New York, 1990, pp. 165 - 204.

[Booch, 1991]. G. Booch, *Object-Oriented Design With Applications*, Benjamin/Cummings, Redwood City, California, 1991.

[Heitz, 1988]. M. Heitz, "HOOD: A Hierarchical Object-Oriented Design Method," *Proceedings of the Third German Ada Users Congress*, January 1988, Gesellschaft für Software Engineering, Munich, Germany, pp. 12-1 - 12-9.

[Hruschka, 1990]. P. "Towards An Object-Oriented Method for System Architecture Design," *Proceedings of the 1990 IEEE International Conference on Computer Systems and Software Engineering — EuroComp '90*, Tel-Aviv, Israel, May 8 - 10, 1990, pp. 12 - 17.

[McQuown, 1989]. K. McQuown, "Object-Oriented Design in a Real-Time Multiprocessor Environment," *Proceedings of TRI-Ada '89 — Ada Technology In Context: Application, Development, and Deployment,* October 23-26, 1989, Association for Computing Machinery, New York, New York, pp. 570 - 588.

[Rumbaugh et al., 1991]. J. Rumbaugh, M. Blaha, W. Premerlani, F. Eddy, and W. Lorensen, *Object-Oriented Modeling and Design*, Prentice Hall, Englewood Cliffs, New Jersey, 1991.

[Stark and Seidewitz, 1987]. M. Stark and E.V. Seidewitz, "Towards a General Object-Oriented Ada Life-Cycle," *Proceedings of the Joint Ada Conference, Fifth National Conference on Ada Technology and Washington Ada Symposium*, U.S. Army Communications-Electronics Command, Fort Monmouth, New Jersey, pp. 213 - 222.

[Wasserman et al., 1990]. A.I. Wasserman, P. Pircher, and R.J. Muller, "An Object-Oriented Design Notation for Software Design Representation," *IEEE Computer*, Vol. 23, No. 3, March 1990, pp. 50 - 63.

[Wiener, 1991]. R.S. Wiener, Editor, *Focus On Analysis and Design*, SIGS Publications, Inc., New York, New York, 1991.

[Wirfs-Brock et al., 1990]. R. Wirfs-Brock, B. Wilkerson, and L. Wiener, *Designing Object-Oriented Software*, Prentice Hall, Englewood Cliffs, New Jersey, 1990.

In addition to the above references, the September 1990 issue of the *Communications of the ACM* (Vol. 33, No. 9) contains quite a few articles on object-oriented design approaches.

([Booch, 1991] is the clear favorite here, although [Rumbaugh et al., 1991] and [Wirfs-Brock et al., 1990] definitely have followings.)

Object-Oriented Databases

Object-oriented databases are *not* the same thing as relational databases. In effect, object-oriented database technology today is at the same point relational database technology was in the early 1980s. (I know more than a few vendors who would disagree with this point.) Some representative information on the subject can be found in:

[Ahmed et al., 1991]. S. Ahmed, A. Wong, D. Sriam, and R. Logcher, *A Comparison of Object-Oriented Database Management Systems for Engineering Applications*, Research Report No. R91-12, Order Number IESL90-03, 91-03, Massachusetts Institute of Technology, Department of Civil Engineering, Cambridge, Massachusetts, May 1991.

[Atkinson et al., 1989]. M. Atkinson, F. Bancilhon, D. DeWitt, K. Dittrich, D. Maier, and S. Zdonik, "The Object-Oriented Database System Manifesto," (Invited Paper), *Proceedings of the First International Conference on Deductive and Object-Oriented Databases*, Kyoto, Japan, December 4-6, 1989, pp. 40 - 57.

[Bertino and Martino, 1991]. E. Bertino and L. Martino, "Object-Oriented Database Management Systems: Concepts and Issues," *IEEE Computer*, Vol. 24, No. 4, April 1991, pp. 33 - 47.

[Brown, 1991]. A. Brown, *Object-Oriented Databases: Applications in Software Engineering*, McGraw-Hill, New York, New York, 1991.

[Bochenski, 1988]. B.A. Bochenski, "On Object-Oriented Programming, Databases," *Software*, Vol. 8, No. 11, September 1988, page 42.

[Cardenas and McLeod, 1990]. A.F. Cardenas and D. McLeod, Editors, *Research Foundations in Object-Oriented and Semantic Database Systems*, Prentice Hall, Englewood Cliffs, New Jersey, 1990.

[Cattell, 1991]. R.G.G. Cattell, *Object Data Management: Object-Oriented and Extended Relational Database Systems*, Addison-Wesley Publishing Company, Reading, Massachusetts, 1991.

[Dearle et al., 1991]. A. Dearle, G.M. Shaw, and S.B. Zdonik, *Implementing Persistent Object Bases, Principles and Practices: The Fourth International Workshop on Persistent Object Systems*, Morgan Kaufman Publishers, Inc., San Mateo, California, 1991.

[Dittrich, 1989]. K. Dittrich, Editor, *Advances in Object-Oriented Database Systems*, Springer-Verlag, New York, New York, 1989.

[Dittrich et al., 1991]. K.R. Dittrich, U. Dayal, and A.P. Buchmann, Editors, *On Object-Oriented Database Systems*, Springer-Verlag, New York, New York, 1991.

[Gupta and Horowitz, 1991]. R. Gupta and E. Horowitz, Editors, *Object-Oriented Databases With Applications to CASE, Networks, and VLSI CAD*, Prentice Hall, Englewood Cliffs, New Jersey, 1991.

[Hughes, 1991]. J.G. Hughes, *Object-Oriented Databases*, Prentice Hall, Englewood Cliffs, New Jersey, 1991.

[Kim, 1990]. W. Kim, *Introduction to Object-Oriented Databases*, The MIT Press, Cambridge, Massachusetts, 1990.

[Kim et al., 1990]. W. Kim, J.-M. Nicolas, and S. Nishio, Editors, *Deductive and Object-Oriented Database: Proceedings of the First International Conference on Deductive and Object-Oriented Databases (DOOD 89)*, Kyoto Research Park, Kyoto, Japan, 4-6 December, 1989, North-Holland (Elsevier), New York, New York, 1990.

[Nahoruaii and Petry, 1991]. E. Nahouraii and F. Petry, Editors, *IEEE Tutorial on Object-Oriented Databases*, IEEE Catalog Number EH0332-7, IEEE Computer Society Press, Los Alamitos, California, 1991.

[Zdonik and Maier, 1990]. S.B. Zdonik and D. Maier, Editors, *Readings in Object-Oriented Database Systems*, Morgan Kaufmann Publishers, Inc., San Mateo, California, 1990.

In addition to the above references, the November 1991 issue of the *Communications of the ACM* (Vol. 34, No. 11) contains quite a few articles on object-oriented databases.

(There is much, much interest in OODBSs. The first reference you should read is [Atkinson et al., 1989]. Many tend to favor [Cattell, 1991]. Good second choices are [Dearle et al., 1991], [Nahoruaii and Petry, 1991], and [Zdonik and Maier, 1990].)

Object-Oriented Computer Hardware

Even computer hardware can be constructed in an object-oriented manner. Here are three references:

[Myers, 1982]. G.J. Myers, *Advances in Computer Architecture,* Second Edition, John Wiley & Sons, New York, New York, 1982.

[Organick, 1983]. E. Organick, *A Programmer's View of the Intel 432 System*, McGraw-Hill, New York, New York, 1983.

[Pountain, 1988]. D. Pountain, "Rekursiv: An Object-Oriented CPU," *Byte*, Vol. 13, No. 11, November 1988, pp. 341 - 349.

([Pountain, 1988] would be my first choice.)

Metrics for Object-Oriented Software Engineering

As organizations begin shifting to object-oriented approaches, they find that some of the ways in which they used to measure things are less appropriate. People have already begun asking about *object-oriented* metrics. Although most work in this area is relatively new, there are a growing number of references, including:

[Chidamber and Kemerer, 1991]. S.R. Chidamber and C.F. Kemerer, "Towards a Metrics Suite for Object-Oriented Design," *OOPSLA '91 Conference Proceedings,* special issue of *SIGPLAN Notices*, Vol. 26, No. 11, November 1991, pp. 197 - 211.

[Duhl and Damon, 1988]. J. Duhl and C. Damon, "A Performance Comparison of Object and Relational Databases Using the Sun Benchmark," *OOPSLA '88 Conference Proceedings,* special issue of *SIGPLAN Notices*, Vol. 23, No. 11, November 1988, pp. 153 - 163.

[Hufnagel and Brown, 1989]. S.P. Hufnagel and J.C. Brown, "Performance Properties of Vertically Partitioned Object-Oriented Systems," *IEEE Transactions on Software Engineering*, Vol. 15, No. 8, August 1989, pp. 935 - 946.

[Liberherr and Holland, 1989]. K.J. Liberherr and I.M. Holland, "Assuring Good Style for Object-Oriented Programs," *IEEE Software*, Vol. 6, No. 5, September 1989, pp. 38 - 48.

[Liberherr and Riel, 1988]. K.J. Liberherr and A.J. Riel, "Demeter: a CASE Study of Software Growth Through Parameterized Classes," *Journal of Object-Oriented Programming*, Vol. 1, No. 3, August/September 1988, pp. 8 - 22.

([Chidamber and Kemerer, 1991] is the first choice, followed by [Liberherr and Holland, 1989].)

General Object-Oriented Technology References

There are a number of general references on object-oriented technology, including:

[ACM, 1986a]. Association for Computing Machinery, special issue of *SIGPLAN Notices on the Object-Oriented Programming Workshop*, Vol. 21, No. 10, October 1986.

[ACM, 1986b]. Association for Computing Machinery, *OOPSLA '86 Conference Proceedings,* special issue of *SIGPLAN Notices*, Vol. 21, No. 11, November 1986.

[ACM, 1987]. Association for Computing Machinery, *OOPSLA '87 Conference Proceedings,* special issue of *SIGPLAN Notices*, Vol. 22, No. 12, December 1987.

[ACM, 1988a]. Association for Computing Machinery, *OOPSLA '87 Addendum to the Proceedings,* special issue of *SIGPLAN Notices*, Vol. 23, No. 5, May 1988.

[ACM, 1988b]. Association for Computing Machinery, *OOPSLA '88 Conference Proceedings,* special issue of *SIGPLAN Notices*, Vol. 23, No. 11, November 1988.

[ACM, 1989]. Association for Computing Machinery, *OOPSLA '89 Conference Proceedings,* special issue of *SIGPLAN Notices*, Vol. 24, No. 10, October 1989.

[ACM, 1990]. Association for Computing Machinery, *OOPSLA/ECOOP '90 Conference Proceedings,* special issue of *SIGPLAN Notices*, Vol. 25, No. 10, October 1990.

[ACM, 1991]. Association for Computing Machinery, *OOPSLA/ECOOP '91 Conference Proceedings,* special issue of *SIGPLAN Notices,* Vol. 26, No. 11, November 1991.

[Aranow, 1992]. E. Aranow, "Object Technology Means Object-Oriented Thinking," *Software,* Vol. 12, No. 3, March 1992, pp. 41 - 44, 46 - 48.

[Bézivin and Meyer, 1991]. J. Bézivin and B. Meyer, Editors, *Technology of Object-Oriented Languages and Systems: Tools 4,* Prentice Hall, Englewood Cliffs, New Jersey, 1991.

[Bézivin et al., 1987]. J. Bézivin, J.-M. Hullot, P. Cointe, and H. Lieberman, *ECOOP '87: Proceedings of the European Conference on Object-Oriented Programming, Lecture Notes on Computer Science,* Volume 276, Springer Verlag, New York, New York, 1987.

[Blair et al., 1991]. G. Blair, J. Gallagher, D. Hutchison, and D. Sheperd, *Object-Oriented Languages, Systems and Applications,* Halsted Press, New York, New York, 1991.

[Budd, 1991]. T. Budd, *An Introduction to Object-Oriented Programming,* Addison-Wesley, Reading, Massachusetts, 1991.

[Cook, 1989]. S. Cook, *ECOOP '89: Proceedings of the European Conference on Object-Oriented Programming, British Computer Society Workshop Series,* Cambridge University Press, Cambridge, United Kingdom, 1989.

[Gjessing and Nygaard, 1988]. S. Gjessing and K. Nygaard, *ECOOP '88: Proceedings of the European Conference on Object-Oriented Programming, Lecture Notes on Computer Science,* Volume 322, Springer Verlag, New York, New York, 1988.

[Khoshafian and Abnous, 1990]. S. Khoshafian and R. Abnous, *Object Orientation: Concepts, Languages, Databases, User Interfaces,* John Wiley & Sons, Inc., New York, New York, 1990.

[Kim and Lochovsky, 1989]. W. Kim and F. Lochovsky, *Object-Oriented Concepts, Databases, and Applications,* ACM Press/Addison Wesley, Reading, Massachusetts, 1989.

[Korson, et al., 1991]. T. Korson, V. Vaishnavi, and B. Meyer, Editors, *Technology of Object-Oriented Languages and Systems: Tools 5,* Prentice Hall, Englewood Cliffs, New Jersey, 1991.

[Millikin, 1989]. M.D. Millikin, "Object Orientation: What It Can Do For You," *ComputerWorld,* Vol. 23, No. 11. March 13, 1989, pp. 103 - 113.

[Peterson, 1987a]. G.E. Peterson, *Tutorial: Object-Oriented Computing, Volume 1: Concepts,* IEEE Catalog Number EH0257-6, IEEE Computer Society Press, Washington, D.C., 1987.

[Peterson, 1987b]. G.E. Peterson, *Tutorial: Object-Oriented Computing, Volume 2: Implementations,* IEEE Catalog Number EH0257-6, IEEE Computer Society Press, Washington, D.C., 1987.

[Salmons and Babitsky, 1992]. J. Salmons and T. Babitsky, *1992 International OOP Directory,* SIGS Publications, Inc., New York, New York, 1992.

[Shriver and Wegner, 1987]. B. Shriver and P. Wegner, Editors, *Research Directions in Object-Oriented Programming,* The MIT Press, Cambridge, Massachusetts, 1987.

[Taylor, 1990]. D.K. Taylor, *Object-Oriented Technology: A Manager's Guide,* Addison-Wesley, Reading, Massachusetts, 1990.

(A good first choice would be [Blair et al., 1991]. [Taylor, 1990] is a clear favorite among managers. Those who consider themselves to be very technical should plan on eventually getting the OOPSLA series, the ECOOP series, and the TOOLS series. Those looking for a source book of object-oriented technology products and services should definitely acquire [Salmons and Babitsky, 1992].)

Appendix: Object and Class Specifications

Object and Class Specification

Class: Bounded List

1.0 Precise and Concise Description

1. A *linear list* (or simply, list) is defined to be "a set of $n >= 0$ nodes X[1],... X[n] whose structural properties essentially involve only the linear (one-dimensional) relative positions of the nodes:..., if $n > 0$, X[1] is the first node; when $1 < k < n$, the k th node X[k] is preceded by X[k - 1] and followed by X[k + 1]; and X[n] is the last node." (See [Knuth, 1973].) The number of elements (n) is called the *length* of the list. If $n = 0$, then the list is said to be *empty*.

2. A **bounded** list is a list which has a *fixed limit* on the maximum number of elements that can be stored in it. A user will have to specify the maximum length of a bounded list when a list object is declared.

3. The following is a list of operations that can be applied to a bounded list: clear a list, insert an element into a list, remove an element from a list, find out the current length of a list, copy a list to another list, check whether one list is equal to another list, determine if a given element is contained in a bounded list, return the value of the element at a specified location, check whether a list is empty, check whether a list is full, append one list to the end of another list, and break a list into two parts.

4. The user is not concerned with the type of elements that can be put in the list. The class of the elements to be placed in the list must be supplied by users of this class. The following required operations for the list must be applicable to the class of the elements to be placed in the list. The required operations are: assignment (of the value of one element to another), and test for equality (of the value of one element with another).

5. Users of the bounded list class must also supply a class which will be used to "count" the number of elements in a given bounded list, and which will also be used to identify locations within the list. The required operations for this class are assignment (of one value of an instance of this class to another), test for equality (of the value of an instance of this class with another), set to "zero" (set the value of an instance of this class to indicate no elements in a given bounded list), increment ("by one"), and decrement ("by one").

6. This class will export the exceptions Underflow, Overflow, and Element_Not_Found.

7. This class will export the constant "empty list."

[Knuth, 1973]. D.E. Knuth, *The Art of Computer Programming, Volume 1: Fundamental Algorithms*, Second Edition, Addison-Wesley, Reading, Massachusetts, 1973.

2.0   Graphical Representations

2.1   Static Representations

2.1.1   Semantic Networks

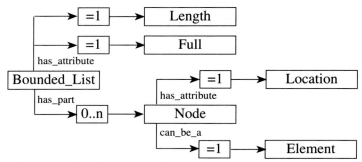

2.1.2   Notes on the Semantic Networks

1. The attribute "(is the bounded list) empty" can be determined directly from the "length (of the bounded list)" attribute. Hence, we do not show this attribute separately.

2. The constraint "0.. n" for the has_part relationship between Bounded_List and Node refers to the fact that bounded lists may have no more than "n" nodes.

2.2   Dynamic Representations

2.2.1   State Transition Diagrams

2.2.1.1 State Transition Diagrams for Non-Spontaneous State Changes

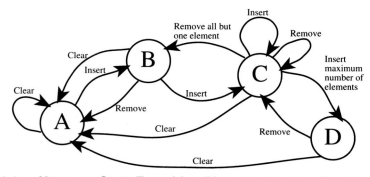

2.2.1.1.1   Notes on State Transition Diagrams for Non-Spontaneous State Changes

1. **Node A** represents an empty bounded list. **Node B** represents a bounded list with one element. **Node C** represents a bounded list containing more than 1 element, but not full. **Node D** represents a full bounded list.

2. The state transition "insert maximum number of elements" represents any combination of operations which will result in a bounded list containing the maximum number of elements.

3.   The state transition "remove all but one element" represents any combination of operations which will result in a bounded list containing only one element.

4.   The selector operation **Length_Of** may be used to determine if a bounded list is empty, contains one element, or contains some elements.

5.   The selector operation **Is_Full** may be used to determine if a bounded list contains its maximum allotted number of elements.

6.   The selector operation **Is_Empty** may be used to determine if a bounded list contains no elements.

7.   The following operations all require two or more bounded lists, and thus cannot be accurately shown on a single STD:

   a.   "=" : This selector operation is the test for equality of two bounded lists. This operation compares the states of two different bounded lists.

   b.   **Copy**: This constructor operation copies one entire bounded list to another bounded list. Since the Copy operation produces an exact copy of an existing bounded list, the resulting copy may be in any one of the states shown in the STD.

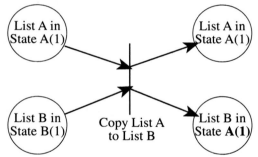

   c.   **Append**: This constructor operation appends one bounded list to another bounded list. The Append operation will result in a bounded list which may be in any one of the states shown in the STD.

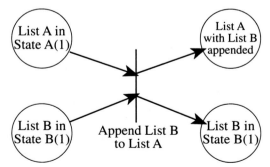

   d.   **Break_Up**: This constructor operation splits a given list at a specified location and puts the results in two sublists. The original bounded list will become an empty list. Depending on both the state of the original bounded list and the location specified for breaking the list, each of the two sublists may be in any of the states shown in the STD.

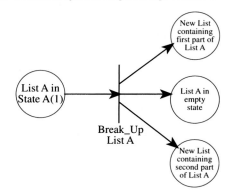

3.0   Operations

3.1   Required Operations

Operation	Method
Assignment	of the value of an element to be placed in the list to another element of the same class
Test for equality	of one of the elements to be placed in the list with another element of the same class
Assignment	of the value of an instance of the class used to "count" the number of elements in a given bounded list to another instance of the same class
Test for equality	of the value of an instance of the class used to "count" the number of elements in a given bounded list against another instance of the same class
Set to "zero"	an instance of the class used to "count" the number of elements in a given bounded list
Increment "by one"	the value of an object of the class used to "count" the number of elements in a given bounded list
Decrement "by one"	the value of an object of the class used to "count" the number of elements in a given bounded list

3.2   Suffered Operations

Operation	Method
Clear	the contents of a given bounded list, i.e., removes all elements from the specified bounded list

Insert	a given element into a given bounded list
Remove	a given element from a specified bounded list
Length_Of	a specified bounded list
Copy	the contents of a given bounded list into another specified bounded list producing a bounded list identical in contents to the original bounded list
"="	tests for the equality of two specified bounded lists. Two bounded lists are equal if the current lengths of both lists are the same, and if the values of the corresponding elements in both lists are the same
Exists	tests for the existence of a given element in a specified bounded list
Element	Returns the value of the element at the specified location within the bounded list
Is_Empty	determines if a given bounded list is empty
Is_Full	determines if a given bounded list is full, i.e., it contains the maximum number of elements
Append	a given bounded list to the specified bounded list
Break_Up	a given bounded list, at a specified position, into two specified sublists

4.0   State Information

1. The state information for a bounded list is:

    •   The current number of elements contained in the bounded list

    •   Whether a given bounded list is empty

    •   Whether a given bounded list is full

    •   The specific elements stored in a given bounded list

    •   The specific order of the elements stored in a given bounded list

2. Note that while most state information for a given bounded list may be determined via the invocation of a single operation, the specific order of the elements in a given bounded list may require the invocation of many operations to be determined accurately.

5.0   Constants and Exceptions

5.1   Constants

1.   This class will provide the constant "empty list." This constant will be used to perform such operations as list initialization, and comparison operations.

5.2   Exceptions

1.   This class will provide the following exceptions:

   • The exception **Overflow** will be raised if a user tries to: insert an element into a *full* list, copy a list into another list which has a *smaller upper limit* of the number of elements than the former does, append a list into another list whose number of unused spaces is *less* than the current number of elements in the former list, or break up a list into lists whose total maximum lengths are smaller than the current length of the list to be broken up.

   • The exception **Underflow** will be raised if a user tries to remove an element from an *empty* list.

   • The exception **Element_Not_Found** will be raised if a user specifies a *non-existent element* or a *non-existent element location.*

Object and Class Specification

Class: Bid

1.0   Precise and Concise Description

1. A bid represents a document containing all information that a vendor would supply to a customer in response to a request for quote (RFQ). The information supplied by the document includes the following: a list of the items being supplied by the vendor, the location of the buyer, the RFQ number, the vendor number, the date of the bid, FOB, the freight costs for the bid, the estimated lead time required, any special instructions, the vendor's payment terms, and the total weight of the order.

2. The state of a bid is the state of its component parts.

3. The required operations for a bid are: Assign (one Bid Item List to another), Assign (one Buyer Location to another), Assign (one RFQ Number to another), Assign (one Vendor Number to another), Assign (one Bid Date to another), Assign (one FOB to another), Assign (one Freight Cost to another), Assign (one Estimated Lead Time to another), Assign (one Special Instructions to another), Assign (one Vendor Terms to another), and Assign (one Total Weight to another).

4. The suffered operations for a bid are:

   a. Constructor operations are: Set (Bid Item List), Set (Buyer Location), Set (RFQ Number), Set (Vendor Number), Set (Bid Date), Set (FOB), Set (Freight Cost), Set (Estimated Lead Time), Set (Special Instructions), Set (Vendor Terms), and Set (Total Weight).

   b. Selector operations are: Value_Of (Bid Item List), Value_Of (Buyer Location), Value_Of (RFQ Number), Value_Of (Vendor Number), Value_Of (Bid Date), Value_Of (FOB), Value_Of (Freight Cost), Value_Of (Estimated Lead Time), Value_Of (Special Instructions), Value_Of (Vendor Terms), and Value_Of (Total Weight).

   c. Additional operation (for completeness) is Assign (one Bid to another).

5. There are no exceptions associated with a bid.

6. There are no constants associated with a bid.

7. The Bid class is a parameterized class, and requires that eleven classes be imported to correspond to the following: Bid Item List, Buyer Location, RFQ Number, Vendor Number, Bid Date, FOB, Freight Cost, Estimated Lead Time, Special Instructions, Vendor Terms, and Total Weight. There are no restrictions placed on these imported classes.

2.0   Graphical Representations

2.1   Static Representations

2.1.1   Semantic Networks

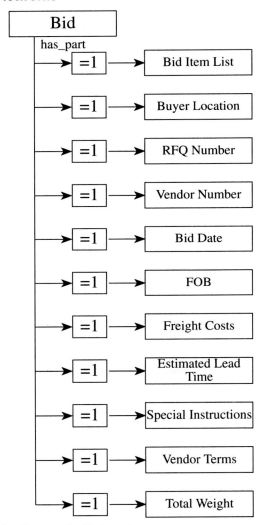

2.1.2   Notes on the Semantic Networks

1. The component parts of the bid are independent, i.e. a change in the state of any component will not change the state of any other component part.

2.2   Dynamic Representations

2.2.1   State Transition Diagrams

2.2.1.1 State Transition Diagrams for Non-Spontaneous State Changes

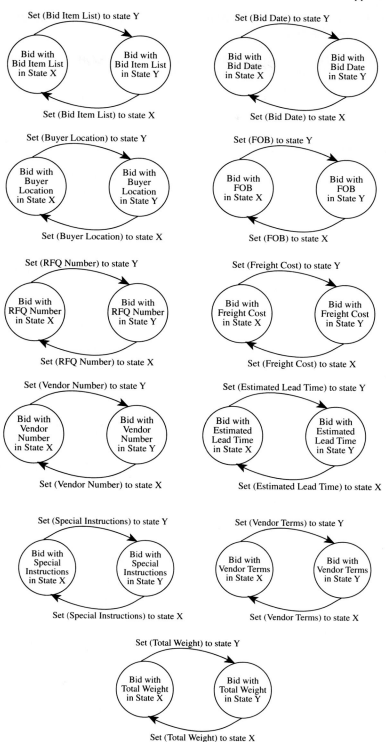

2.2.1.1.1   Notes on the State Transition Diagrams for Non-Spontaneous State Changes

1. There is a selector and a constructor operation provided for each component part of a bid. Each constructor operation changes the state of only one component part.

2. "State X" and "State Y" for each component object can be equal.

3.0   Operations

3.1   Required Operations

Operation	Method
Assign	Copies the state of one Bid Item List object to another.
Assign	Copies the state of one Buyer Location object to another.
Assign	Copies the state of one RFQ Number object to another.
Assign	Copies the state of one Vendor Number object to another.
Assign	Copies the state of one Bid Date object to another.
Assign	Copies the state of one FOB object to another.
Assign	Copies the state of one Freight Cost object to another.
Assign	Copies the state of one Estimated Lead Time object to another.
Assign	Copies the state of one Special Instructions object to another.
Assign	Copies the state of one Vendor Terms object to another.
Assign	Copies the state of one Total Weight object to another.

3.2   Suffered Operations

Operation	Method
Set	Sets the state of the Bid Item List component of a bid.
Set	Sets the state of the Buyer Location component of a bid.

Set	Sets the state of the RFQ Number component of a bid.
Set	Sets the state of the Vendor Number component of a bid.
Set	Sets the state of the Bid Date component of a bid.
Set	Sets the state of the FOB component of a bid.
Set	Sets the state of the Freight Cost component of a bid.
Set	Sets the state of the Estimated Lead Time component of a bid.
Set	Sets the state of the Special Instructions component of a bid.
Set	Sets the state of the Vendor Terms component of a bid.
Set	Sets the state of the Total Weight component of a bid.
Value_Of	Returns the state of the Bid Item List component of a bid.
Value_Of	Returns the state of the Buyer Location component of a bid.
Value_Of	Returns the state of the RFQ Number component of a bid.
Value_Of	Returns the state of the Vendor Number component of a bid.
Value_Of	Returns the state of the Bid Date component of a bid.
Value_Of	Returns the state of the FOB component of a bid.
Value_Of	Returns the state of the Freight Cost component of a bid.
Value_Of	Returns the state of the Estimated Lead Time component of a bid.
Value_Of	Returns the state of the Special Instructions component of a bid.
Value_Of	Returns the state of the Vendor Terms component of a bid.

Value_Of	Returns the state of the Total Weight component of a bid.
Assign	Assigns the state of one Bid object to another.

4.0   State Information

The state of a bid is the sum of the states of all its component parts. Each component part's state is independent of the state of any other component part.

5.0   Constants and Exceptions

5.1   Constants

1.   This class will not provide any constants.

5.2   Exceptions

1.   This class will not provide any exceptions.

Object and Class Specification

Class: Button

1.0 Precise and Concise Description

1. A "real world" button is made of some hard material (usually plastic and metal) and is used to signal the occurrence of some external event (usually by closing a circuit). In most cases, a button is a two-state device (e.g., "pressed" and "not pressed") although it is possible for a button to have more than two states.

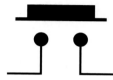

2. A button is an "object with life" which is used by an outside source to request service from the system.

3. The required operations for the button are Signal and Press. Press is the operation which connects an instance of this class with the "outside world" (e.g., with a port) so that it knows that a "real world" button has been pressed. Signal is an operation which allows the button to alert a designated object, or system of objects, that it has been "pressed."

4. Buttons have no suffered operations. [However, hardware ("real world") buttons suffer the operations of being pressed and released.]

5. The states that the button may be in are "pressed" and "not pressed." Neither of these two states is very persistent.

6. There are no constants or exceptions associated with the button.

2.0 Graphical Representations

2.1 Static Representations

2.1.1 Semantic Networks

2.1.2 Notes on the Semantic Networks

1. To the outside world, a button is a simple, monolithic object.

2.2 Dynamic Representations

2.2.1 State Transition Diagrams

2.2.1.1 State Transition Diagrams for Non-Spontaneous State Changes

1. Not Applicable.

2.2.1.1.1   Notes on State Transition Diagrams for Non-Spontaneous State Changes

1.   There are no non-spontaneous state changes for this class.

2.2.1.2 State Transition Diagrams for Spontaneous State Changes

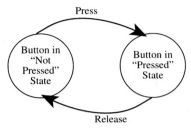

2.2.1.2.1   Notes on State Transition Diagrams for Spontaneous State Changes

1.   The "button abstraction" knows when the "real world" button has been pressed via a required operation, i.e., "Press."

2.   When the "button abstraction" is made aware that the "real world" button has been pressed, it invokes the "Signal" operation.

3.0   Operations

3.1   Required Operations

Operation	Method
Signal	Alerts the button's client that the button has been pressed and returns the buttons identification.
Press	Alerts the button that it has been "pressed."

3.2   Suffered Operations

1.   Buttons have no suffered operations. [However, hardware ("real world") buttons suffer the operations of being pressed and released.]

4.0   State Information

1.   The states that the button may be in are pressed and not pressed.

5.0   Constants and Exceptions

5.1   Constants

1.   This class will neither provide nor require any constants.

5.2   Exceptions

1.   This class will neither provide nor require any exceptions.

Object and Class Specification

Class: Destination_Panel

1.0   Precise and Concise Description

1. Conceptually, a destination panel is a panel containing a number of destination buttons (typically one for each reachable destination), a number of lamps (typically one lamp for each destination button) and, potentially, other devices. The destination panel also contains some computer processing capability. This computer processing capability allows the destination panel to turn particular lamps on and off based on requests, and to inform the outside world when a particular destination button has been pressed.

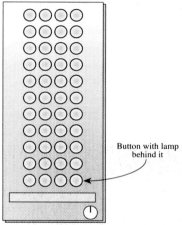

Button with lamp
behind it

2. At any one time, any number of lamps in the destination panel may be lit (i.e., on). A given lamp in the destination panel becomes lit (i.e., is turned on) based on an invocation of the Turn_On_Lamp operation. Once a lamp becomes lit, it stays lit until the destination panel receives a request to turn that lamp off, i.e., via an invocation of the Turn_Off_Lamp operation. Likewise, a lamp remains off until a request is received to turn it on. Once a particular lamp is lit (or turned off), any additional requests for the lamp to be lit (or turned off) are ignored. No facility is provided to determine the state of individual lamps contained in the destination panel.

3. Obviously, any request to turn a given lamp on or off must contain some way of uniquely identifying the specific lamp, and whether that lamp is to be turned on or off. If the lamp identified in the request is not contained in the destination panel, the exception Lamp_Not_Found will be raised.

4. The destination panel must notify the outside world that a particular destination button has been pressed. It does this through a required operation, Signal. Each destination button is associated with a specific lamp, and the panel has the (internal) capability of determining which of its lamps are lit. If someone presses a destination button for which the associated lamp is already lit, no (new) notification is passed to the outside world. No facility is provided to determine the state of individual buttons contained in the destination panel.

5.   Obviously, any notification (to the outside world) that a specific destination button has been pressed (i.e., done through the "Signal" operation) must contain some way of uniquely identifying the specific desired destination.

6.   Since, to all who must deal with the destination panel abstraction, the destination panel appears to be changing its state spontaneously (i.e., specific destinations will be periodically requested), the destination panel is an "object with life."

7.   The required operation for the destination panel is: "Signal" (the user of a destination panel that a button has been pressed).

8.   The suffered operations for the destination panel are "Turn_On_Lamp" (for a given destination), "Turn_Off_Lamp" (for a given destination), and Assign (the state of one destination panel to another destination panel).

9.   Users of the Destination_Panel class must also supply:

     •   a class with discrete scalar values which will be used to uniquely identify destinations, i.e., Destination_ID, and

     •   a value of this class which will represent the largest permissible value for a destination which can be specified by destination panels which are instances of the Destination_Panel class. Valid destinations will be represented by all values of the class Destination_ID from the smallest value up to, and including, the specified largest permissible value for a destination.

10. The state for a destination panel may be defined as:

     •   the sum of the states of the lamps (i.e., on or off) which are associated with destinations (these states are persistent), and

     •   whether a destination button, whose corresponding lamp is not lit, has been pressed (these states are not persistent).

11. The exception Lamp_Not_Found is associated with a destination panel.

2.0   Graphical Representations

2.1   Static Representations

2.1.1   Semantic Networks

Destination Panel

2.1.2   Notes on the Semantic Network

1.   From the outside view, there is no discernible structure or attributes for a destination panel.

2.   Though it seems obvious that the destination panel deals with buttons and lamps, these objects can neither be detected nor affected directly from the "outside." It is for that reason that these objects do not appear on the semantic net.

2.2   Dynamic Representations

2.2.1   State Transition Diagrams

2.2.1.1 State Transition Diagrams for Non-Spontaneous State Changes

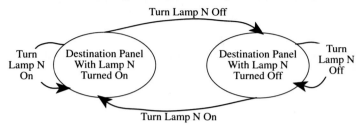

2.2.1.1.1   Notes on State Transition Diagrams for Non-Spontaneous State Changes

1. The states shown in the diagram cannot be interrogated. Specifically, there are no operations provided that will allow a client of the abstraction to determine if a particular destination panel lamp is on or off.

2. A client may not interact *directly* with a specific destination panel lamp. Clients deliver a request to turn a particular destination panel lamp on or off to the "lamp on/off request port." It is the computer circuitry in the destination panel which will actually turn a lamp on or off, or leave a lamp in its particular state.

3. Since a given lamp will only be turned on or off based on a specific request, a destination panel with any given number of lamps lit and not lit represents a persistent state.

4. **Assign**: This constructor operation copies the state of one destination panel object to another instance of the same class. Since the Assign operation produces an exact copy of an existing destination panel, the resulting copy may be in any one of the states shown in the STD. The Petri net graph representation of the Assign operation is:

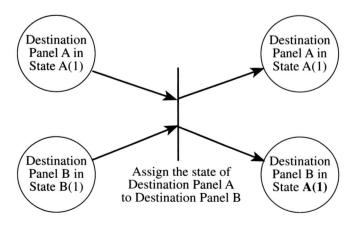

2.2.1.2 State Transition Diagrams for Spontaneous State Changes

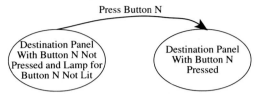

Press Button N

Destination Panel
With Button N Not
Pressed and Lamp for
Button N Not Lit

Destination Panel
With Button N
Pressed

2.2.1.2.1   Notes on State Transition Diagrams for Spontaneous State Changes

1. Clients of the destination panel cannot "press" any of the destination panel buttons.

2. After a button is pressed, the destination panel immediately returns to the state where that button is not pressed, i.e., a destination panel with any given button pressed is a highly non-persistent state.

2. Clients of the destination panel are notified that a particular destination panel button has been pressed via the "Signal" operation. It is the computer circuitry in the destination panel which will actually provide the notification that a particular destination button has been pressed.

3. Pressing a destination button whose corresponding lamp is already lit will have no effect.

4. An attempt to simultaneously press two, or more, destination buttons will result in the following:

    *   All pressings of destination buttons whose corresponding lamps are already lit, will be ignored.

    *   If two, or more, destination buttons, whose corresponding lamps are not lit, are pressed simultaneously, one of the destinations will be picked in a non-deterministic way, and notification of a request for that destination alone will be sent via the "Signal" operation.

3.0   Operations

3.1   Required Operations

Operation	Method
Signal	Alerts the destination panel's client that a button corresponding to a specific destination has been pressed.

3.2   Suffered Operations

Operation	Method
Turn_On_Lamp	Turns on the lamp corresponding to the given destination. If the lamp is already on, then there is no effect.
Turn_Off_Lamp	Turns off the lamp corresponding to the given destination. If the lamp is already off, then there is no effect.

Assign   The state of one instance of this class to
                                          another instance of this class.

4.0   State Information

1.   The state for a destination panel may be defined as:

     •   the sum of the states of the lamps (i.e., on or off) which are associated with
          destinations (these states are persistent), and

     •   whether a destination button, whose corresponding lamp is not lit, has been pressed
          (this state is not persistent).

          Note that there is no way for the client of the destination panel to interrogate these
          states. Note further, that only one button in a given destination panel may be pressed
          at one time. If an attempt is made to press two, or more, destination buttons
          simultaneously, and at least one of the destination buttons has a corresponding lamp
          which is not lit, the destination panel computer circuitry will select a single
          destination which will be transmitted via the "Signal" operation.

5.0   Constants and Exceptions

5.1   Constants

1.   This class will not provide any constants.

5.2   Exceptions

1.   The exception Lamp_Not_Found will be raised if a "lamp on/off request" is received and
     there is no lamp in the panel which corresponds to the specific lamp referred to in the
     request.

Object and Class Specification

Class: Floor_Arrival_Panel

1.0   Precise and Concise Description

1. Conceptually, a floor arrival panel is a panel containing a number of lamps (typically one lamp for each destination (floor)). The floor arrival panel also contains some computer processing capability. This computer processing capability allows the floor arrival panel to turn a particular lamp on, based on a request, and to automatically ensure that all other lamps are off.

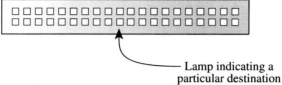

Lamp indicating a
particular destination

2. At any one time, only one lamp in the floor arrival panel may be lit (i.e., on). A given lamp in the floor arrival panel becomes lit (i.e., is turned on) based on an invocation of the Turn_On_Lamp operation. Once a lamp becomes lit, it stays lit until the floor arrival panel receives a request to turn another lamp on. Once a particular lamp is lit, any additional requests for the lamp to be lit are ignored. No facility is provided to determine the state of individual lamps contained in the floor arrival panel.

3. Obviously, any request to turn a given lamp on must contain some way of uniquely identifying the specific lamp. If the lamp identified in the request is not contained in the floor arrival panel, the exception Lamp_Not_Found will be raised.

4. The suffered operation for the floor arrival panel is "Turn_On_Lamp" (for a given destination).

5. Users of the Floor_Arrival_Panel class must also supply:

    *   a class with discrete scalar values which will be used to uniquely identify destinations, i.e., Destination_ID, and

    *   a value of this class which will represent the largest permissible value for a destination which can be specified by floor arrival panels which are instances of the Floor_Arrival_Panel class. Valid destinations will be represented by all values of the class Destination_ID from the smallest value up to, and including, the specified largest permissible value for a destination.

6. The state for a floor arrival panel may be defined as which particular lamp is on.

7. The exception Lamp_Not_Found is associated with a floor arrival panel.

2.0   Graphical Representations

2.1   Static Representations

2.1.1   Semantic Networks

Floor Arrival Panel

2.1.2   Notes on the Semantic Networks

1. From the outside view, there is no discernible structure or attributes for a floor arrival panel.

2. Though it seems obvious that the floor arrival panel deals with lamps, these objects can neither be detected nor affected directly from the "outside". It is for that reason that these objects do not appear on the semantic net.

2.2   Dynamic Representations

2.2.1   State Transition Diagrams

2.2.1.1 State Transition Diagrams for Non-Spontaneous State Changes

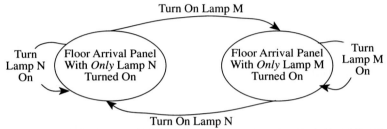

2.2.1.1.1   Notes on State Transition Diagrams for Non-Spontaneous State Changes

1. The states shown in the diagram cannot be interrogated. Specifically, there are no operations provided that will allow a client of the abstraction to determine if a particular floor arrival panel lamp is on or off.

2. A client may not interact *directly* with a specific floor arrival panel lamp. Clients deliver a request to turn a particular floor arrival panel lamp on or off via the Turn_On_Lamp operation. It is the computer circuitry in the floor arrival panel which will actually turn a lamp on or off, or leave a lamp in its particular state.

3. Since a given lamp will only be turned on or off based on a specific request, a floor arrival panel with any given lamp lit, and all others not lit, represents a persistent state.

4. **Assign**: This constructor operation copies the state of one floor arrival panel object to another instance of the same class. Since the Assign operation produces an exact copy of an existing floor arrival panel, the resulting copy may be in any one of the states shown in the STD. The Petri net graph representation of the Assign operation is:

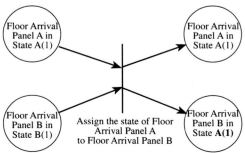

3.0   Operations

3.1   Required Operations

1.   There are no required operations for this class.

3.2   Suffered Operations

Operation	Method
Turn_On_Lamp	Turns on the lamp corresponding to the given destination. If the lamp is already on, then there is no effect. This operation also turns off any other lamp which may be lit.
Assign	The state of one instance of this class to another instance of the same class.

4.0   State Information

1.   The state for a floor arrival panel may be defined as which single lamp (indicating a particular destination (floor)) is on, i.e., all other lamps must, by definition, be off. (Obviously, you cannot be at two different destinations simultaneously.) Note that there is no way for the client of the floor arrival panel to interrogate this state.

5.0   Constants and Exceptions

5.1   Constants

1.   This class will not provide any constants.

5.2   Exceptions

1.   The exception Lamp_Not_Found will be raised if there is a request to turn a specific lamp on, and there is no lamp in the panel which corresponds to the specific lamp referred to in the request.

Object and Class Specification

Class: Lamp

1.0   Precise and Concise Description

1. A lamp is the abstraction of a simple lamp that can either be turned on (illuminated) or turned off (extinguished).

Lamp

2. Instances of this class require two operations, i.e., one which will allow a given lamp to communicate to the "outside world" that it has been "turned on," and one which will allow a given lamp to communicate to the "outside world" that it has been "turned off."

3. The suffered operations for a lamp are: turn the lamp on, turn the lamp off, Assign (the state of one lamp to another), and Is_On (is a given instance of this class in the "on" state). Since a lamp stays either on or off until instructed to change its state, the states of a lamp are persistent.

4. The lamp class will export no constants or exceptions.

2.0   Graphical Representations

2.1   Static Representations

2.1.1   Semantic Networks

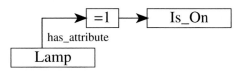

2.1.2   Notes on the Semantic Networks

1. The lamp object "remembers" if it is in the "off" or the "on" state.

2.2   Dynamic Representations

2.2.1   State Transition Diagrams

2.2.1.1 State Transition Diagrams for Non-Spontaneous State Changes

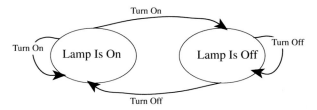

2.2.1.1.1   Notes on State Transition Diagrams for Non-Spontaneous State Changes

1. Note that the operation Turn_On has no effect if the lamp is already on and Turn_Off has no effect if a lamp is already off.

2. The Is_On selector operation can be used to determine the state of a given instance of this class.

3.0   Operations

3.1   Required Operations

Operation	Method
Turn_On	Connects the lamp abstraction with the means of turning the physical lamp on.
Turn_Off	Connects the lamp abstraction with the means of turning the physical lamp off.

3.2   Suffered Operations

Operation	Method
Turn_On	Turn the lamp on.
Turn_Off	Turn the lamp off.
Assign	Assign the state of one instance of this class to another instance of the same class.
Is_On	Returns true if a given instance of this class is in the "on" state.

4.0   State Information

1. The states that the lamp may be in are "on" when the operation Turn_On has been invoked and "off" when the operation Turn_Off has been invoked.

5.0   Constants and Exceptions

5.1   Constants

1. This class will provide no constants.

5.2   Exceptions

1. This class will provide no exceptions.

Object and Class Specification

Class: Read_Only_Port

1.0   Precise and Concise Description

1. A "port" is an abstraction of a highly localized interface between two pieces of hardware in a (potentially embedded) computer system. A port is a place where information can be transferred into, out of, or to and from, a hardware component.

2. A port has several distinguishing characteristics:

    *   an **address**. Every port in a system must be directly, or indirectly, addressable within the "address space" (i.e., the set of all allowable addresses) of the cpu (central processing unit) charged with dealing with the port.

    *   a **width** (measured in bits). The width of a port refers to how many bits may be *simultaneously* read from, or written to, the port. It is assumed that the bits are contiguous.

    *   whether it is **read-only**, **write-only**, or **read-write** (i.e., bi-directional). Often, ports are uni-directional, that is, they can either be read from or written to, but not both.

3. The purpose of the port abstraction is to provide a uniform interface for instances of other classes which use ports. Internally, ports deal with the unique characteristics of the hardware for which they were created. Externally, they present a constant and uniform interface for objects which must deal with ports.

4. A Read_Only_Port is an "object with life," i.e., there is no software mechanism for changing some aspects of the state of the port. Clients of the Read_Only_Port, for example, cannot *force* the Read_Only_Port to provide them with information at any given time. They must wait for the port to provide them with information. Ports do not buffer information, i.e., if the information is not read when it becomes available, the information is lost.

5. Ports view information only as "bit patterns." For example, if a four-bit wide port provides the value 1011_2, it places no special significance, or meaning, on this value. Interpretations of bit patterns are left to the clients of the port.

6. The Read_Only_Port has one *required* operation ("Signal") which contains the actions the client wishes to accomplish when information arrives at the hardware port — usually includes the transference of that information.

7. The *suffered* operations for the Read_Only_Port are Set_Address (dynamically set the address for the port), Address_Of (the specified port), and Assign (the value of one Read_Only_Port to another).

8. In reality, the Read_Only_Port class is a metaclass. Users of the Read_Only_Port class must supply:

    *   a width (i.e., a non-zero, positive integer value) which will be used to set a fixed width (in bits) for all instances of the Read_Only_Port class,

- an integer class which will be used to contain the values read by the port, and

- a system address class, instances of which will be used to dynamically assign a given Read_Only_Port to a specific system address.

9. The Read_Only_Port class will provide no constants.

10. The Read_Only_Port class will provide an exception: Address_Not_Defined.

2.0   Graphical Representations

2.1   Static Representations

2.1.1   Semantic Networks

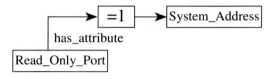

2.1.2   Notes on the Semantic Networks

1. The read only port "remembers" its system address.

2.2   Dynamic Representations

2.2.1   State Transition Diagrams

2.2.1.1 State Transition Diagrams for Non-Spontaneous State Changes

2.2.1.1.1   Notes on State Transition Diagrams for Non-Spontaneous State Changes

1. A given Read_Only_Port object cannot be read from, or queried about its address until it has been assigned an address.

2. The Assign operation requires two instances of the class Read_Only_Port, and therefore cannot be shown on a state transition diagram. The Petri net graph for the Assign operation is:

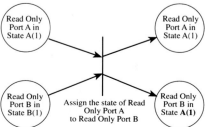

2.2.1.2 State Transition Diagrams for Spontaneous State Changes

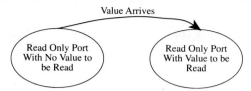

2.2.1.2.1 Notes on State Transition Diagrams for Spontaneous State Changes

1. When information arrives at the hardware port, that information will be transferred to software clients of the port via a Signal operation. Thus, clients of a port will not have to poll the port.

3.0   Operations

3.1   Required Operations

Operation	Method
Signal	The action(s) clients of the Read_Only_Port want the port to take when information arrives at the port. This usually involves the actual transference of the information.

3.2   Suffered Operations

Operation	Method
Set_Address	Dynamically assigns an address to a Read_Only_Port.
Address_Of	Returns the address of a port.
Assign	Assigns the state of one Read_Only_Port object to another.

4.0   State Information

1. The address of a Read_Only_Port object can be changed and queried.

2. A Read_Only_Port is an object with life. Specifically, it periodically and "spontaneously" produces values represented as bit patterns.

5.0   Constants and Exceptions

5.1   Constants

1. This class provides no constants

5.2   Exceptions

1. This class provides an exception Address_Not_Defined which is raised if an attempt is made to read from a port which has not been assigned to an address, or if a port which has not been assigned an address is queried as to its address.

Object and Class Specification

Class: Shared_Motor

1.0   Precise and Concise Description

1. A motor is an abstraction of a physical motor device that converts energy into movement. Movement is delivered in the form of the rotation of the motor's rotor. A rotor may be viewed as a shaft which is part of a motor, and to which varying devices may be attached.

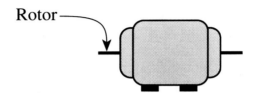

2. "Share semantics" allow for the creation of aliases for an object. This has the advantage of possible increases in time and space efficiency. However, it increases the possibility of actions with unintended results, e.g., unintentional deletion or alteration of an object through operations performed using the alias. (Instances of this class may have more than one alias.)

3. The suffered operations for a motor include movement operations (rotate_clockwise, rotate_counterclockwise, stop), operations for detecting movement (is_rotating_clockwise, is_rotating_counterclockwise, is_stopped), assign (the state of one instance of this class to another instance of the same class), and operations for share semantics (share, is_shared, remove_alias, and clear_aliases).

4. If a motor object is in the "stop" state then either the rotate_clockwise or rotate_counterclockwise operations may be accomplished. If the motor's rotor is rotating clockwise or counterclockwise, and rotation in the opposite direction is desired, the motor must first be stopped. If a motor is in a particular state, and an operation is invoked which would result in the motor maintaining that state, no state changes will occur, i.e., the operation will be ignored.

5. This motor abstraction represents a motor which produces movement of constant speed, i.e., it is incapable of varying speeds of rotation.

6. The motor contains state information about the current direction of rotation, or, more precisely, about the direction of rotation of the motor's rotor. The allowed states for direction of rotation are: clockwise, counterclockwise, and stopped. A second piece of state information is whether a given motor object has aliases, i.e., is shared. Finally, a motor may have mechanical problems, i.e., a motor may be in working condition, or have a mechanical failure.

7. The exceptions for a shared motor object are Not_Stopped and Mechanical_Failure.

8. There are no constants associated with the instances of the Shared_Motor class.

2.0 Graphical Representations

2.1 Static Representations

2.1.1 Semantic Networks

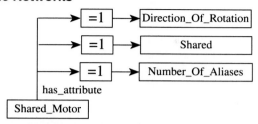

2.1.2 Notes on the Semantic Networks

1. Direction of rotation can only assume one of three values: rotating clockwise, rotating counterclockwise, and stopped.

2. We can determine whether or not a given instance of this class has aliases, and we can determine *how many* aliases it has.

2.2 Dynamic Representations

2.2.1 State Transition Diagrams

2.2.1.1 State Transition Diagrams for Non-Spontaneous State Changes

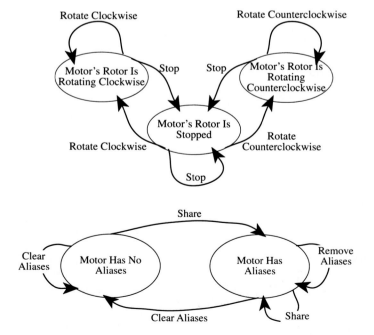

2.2.1.1.1   Notes on State Transition Diagrams for Non-Spontaneous State Changes

1. The operations: Is_Rotating_Clockwise, Is_Rotating_Counterclockwise, and Is_Stopped, are selector operations which can be used to determine if a given motor is in one of the states shown.

2. The operation Is_Shared can be used to determine if a given motor object has aliases. The operation Number_Of_Aliases can be used to determine the number of aliases that an instance of Shared_Motor currently has.

3. The only way it can be determined if a particular motor has a mechanical problem is to detect the raising of the Mechanical_Failure exception upon invocation of the one of rotate_clockwise, rotate_counterclockwise, or stop operations.

4. The operation "assign" requires two instances of this class, and, thus, cannot easily be shown on a simple state transition diagram. Please note that, while a particular shared motor is experiencing mechanical failure is indeed part of the state for that motor, mechanical failure cannot be assigned from one shared motor object to the other. The Petri net graph representation of this operation is:

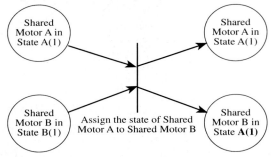

3.0   Operations

3.1   Required Operations

Operation	Method
Rotate_Clockwise	Connects the motor with the necessary operations to rotate clockwise.
Rotate_Counterclockwise	Connects the motor with the necessary operations to rotate counterclockwise.
Stop	Connects the motor with the necessary operations to stop.
Is_Rotating_Clockwise	Connects the motor with the necessary operations to determine if the motor's rotor is rotating clockwise.
Is_Rotating_Counterclockwise	Connects the motor with the necessary operations to determine if the motor's rotor is rotating counterclockwise.

Is_Stopped

Connects the motor with the necessary operations to determine if the motor's rotor is stopped.

3.2   Suffered Operations

Operation

Method

Rotate_Clockwise

Causes the motor's rotor to rotate clockwise.

Rotate_Counterclockwise

Causes the motor's rotor to rotate counterclockwise.

Stop

Causes the motor's rotor to stop rotating.

Is_Rotating_Clockwise

Returns true if the motor's rotor is rotating clockwise.

Is_Rotating_Counterclockwise

Returns true if the motor's rotor is rotating counterclockwise.

Is_Stopped

Returns true if the motor's rotor is not rotating.

Assign

Assigns the state of one instance of this class to another instance of the same class — but, cannot assign a mechanically failed state from one motor object to another.

Share

Allows for share semantics, i.e., allows for the creation of aliases for instances of the motor class.

Is_Shared

Returns true if the given instance of the motor class has an alias.

Number_Of_Aliases

Returns the number of aliases currently assigned to the specified shared motor.

Remove_Alias

Removes a specified alias from a specified shared motor object.

Clear_Aliases

Removes all existing aliases from a given shared motor object.

4.0   State Information

1. The state information for a motor includes the direction of rotation, which typically assumes values of: clockwise, counterclockwise, and stopped.

2. The creation of aliases for instances of this class does change their states, i.e., they now have aliases. Therefore, part of the state information for an instance of this class is whether the instance has aliases.

3. If a shared motor is experiencing mechanical failure, that is also part of the state for that object. However, it is a state which cannot be assigned from one motor object to another.

5.0   Constants and Exceptions

5.1   Constants

1. This class will provide no constants.

5.2   Exceptions

1. This class will provide the following exceptions:

    -   Mechanical_Failure: raised if the motor is not able to respond to a request.

    -   Not_Stopped: raised if the motor's rotor is rotating in a particular direction (e.g., clockwise), and an attempt is made to cause it to rotate in the opposite direction without first stopping the motor.

Object and Class Specification

Class: Write_Only_Port

1.0   Precise and Concise Description

1. A "port" is an abstraction of a highly-localized interface between two pieces of hardware in a (potentially embedded) computer system. A port is a place where information can be transferred into, out of, or to and from, a hardware component.

2. A port has several distinguishing characteristics:

    *   an **address**. Every port in a system must be directly, or indirectly, addressable within the "address space" (i.e., the set of all allowable addresses) of the cpu (central processing unit) charged with dealing with the port.

    *   a **width** (measured in bits). The width of a port refers to how many bits may be *simultaneously* read from, or written to, the port. It is assumed that the bits are contiguous.

    *   whether it is **read-only**, **write-only**, or **read-write** (i.e., bi-directional). Often, ports are uni-directional, that is, they can either be read from or written to, but not both.

3. The purpose of the port abstraction is to provide a uniform interface for instances of other classes which use ports. Internally, ports deal with the unique characteristics of the hardware for which they were created. Externally, they present a constant and uniform interface for objects which must deal with ports.

4. Ports view information only as "bit patterns." For example, if a four-bit wide port provides the value 1011_2, it places no special significance, or meaning, on this value. Interpretations of bit patterns are left to the clients of the port.

5. In reality, the Write_Only_Port class is a metaclass. Users of the Write_Only_Port class must supply:

    *   a width (i.e., a non-zero, positive integer value) which will be used to set a fixed width (in bits) for all instances of the Write_Only_Port class,

    *   an integer class which will be used to contain the values written by the port, and

    *   a system address class, instances of which will be used to dynamically assign a given Write_Only_Port to a specific system address.

6. The *suffered* operations for the Write_Only_Port are Set_Address (dynamically set the address for the port), Address_Of (the specified port), Assign (the value of one Write_Only_Port to another), and Write (a specified bit pattern to a given Write_Only_Port).

7. The Write_Only_Port class will provide no constants.

8. The Write_Only_Port class will provide an exception: Address_Not_Defined.

2.0   Graphical Representations

2.1   Static Representations

2.1.1   Semantic Networks

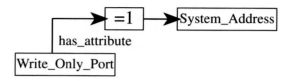

2.1.2   Notes on the Semantic Networks

1.   The write only port "remembers" its system address.

2.2   Dynamic Representations

2.2.1   State Transition Diagrams

2.2.1.1 State Transition Diagrams for Non-Spontaneous State Changes

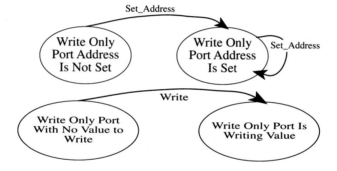

2.2.1.1.1   Notes on State Transition Diagrams for Non-Spontaneous State Changes

1.   A given Write_Only_Port object cannot be read from, or queried about its address until it has been assigned an address.

2.   After writing a value, the Write_Only_Port immediately returns to an inactive state.

3.   The Assign operation requires two instances of the class Write_Only_Port, and therefore cannot be shown on a state transition diagram. The Petri net graph for the Assign operation is:

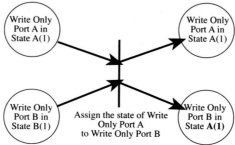

3.0   Operations

3.1   Required Operations

1.   The Write_Only_Port class has no required operations.

3.2   Suffered Operations

Operation	Method
Set_Address	Dynamically assigns an address to a Write_Only_Port.
Address_Of	Returns the address of a port.
Assign	Assigns the state of one Write_Only_Port object to another.
Write	A value of the given integer class to a given Write_Only_Port.

4.0   State Information

1.   The address of a Write_Only_Port object can be changed and queried.

2.   A Write_Only_Port is momentarily in a different state when it is writing values represented as bit patterns.

5.0   Constants and Exceptions

5.1   Constants

1.   This class provides no constants

5.2   Exceptions

1.   This class provides an exception Address_Not_Defined which is raised if an attempt is made to read from a port which has not been assigned to an address, or if a port which has not been assigned an address is queried as to its address.

Glossary

abstract class   a **class** which represents an incomplete definition for a category of objects. The usual connotation is that an abstract class encapsulates a set of characteristics that are common to the specializations of the abstract class. However, these common characteristics alone are not sufficient to fully define a class. Abstract classes are sometimes referred to as "partial types" and "hyperclasses."

abstraction   *as a process*, denotes the extracting of the essential details about an item, or a group of items, while ignoring the inessential details. Abstraction, *as an entity,* denotes a model, a view, or some other focused representation for an actual item. Abstraction is most often used as a complexity mastering technique. Abstractions can exist at many different levels: at higher levels of abstraction we emphasize the more essential and general characteristics of something, and at lower levels of abstraction more details are revealed. Four types of abstraction which are important in object-oriented technology are *functional abstraction*, *data abstraction*, *process abstraction,* and *object abstraction*.

active iterator   (sometimes referred to as an "open **iterator**") a capability which allows systematic traversal over a **homogeneous composite object** by means of several low-level methods, i.e., the iteration itself is *not* atomic. Further, the same method need not be performed at each node, i.e., the user has the ability to decide which method(s) are to be performed at each node. Users of active iterators have a great deal of control, but must be careful to avoid unwanted changes in the object during iteration, and must constantly check to see if all nodes in the homogeneous composite object have been visited.

active object   an object which is capable of spontaneously changing its own state. By "spontaneously" we mean that the changes in the object's state are accomplished via some means *other than through the operations in the interface to the object*. Active objects (sometimes called "actors" or "objects with life") have their own, *internal, independently executing thread of control*.

agency   1.   "any assembly of parts considered in terms of what it can accomplish as a unit, without regard to what each of its parts does by itself." (A definition supplied by Marvin Minsky.)

2.   a collection of one or more **agents** which is used to represent some large behavioral characteristic. Within an agency, agents may collaborate in much the same way as a group of consultants providing information to a client. One or more agencies may be assigned to a given object.

agent

1.   "any part of a process of the mind that by itself is simple enough to understand, even though the interactions among groups of such agents may produce phenomena that are much harder to understand." (A definition supplied by Marvin Minsky.)

2.   a collection of one or more **(agent) rules** which is used to represent some behavioral characteristic, e.g., self preservation, aggression, or wandering. One or more agents may be assigned to a given object, and are used to provide "behavioral characteristics" to the object. Within an agent, rules run in parallel. Further, the importance of each rule in an agent, and hence its impact on the overall behavior, can be separately attenuated.

agent rules

an active object that is sensitive to changes in its environment. Although agent rules can exist (and execute) in parallel, they need not be atomic, i.e., they can yield control at any point, based on some pre-determined condition or conditions. As with **agents**, one or more rules may be associated with a given object. The composition of agent rules is usually programming language specific, i.e., the implementation of a rule varies depending on its environment.

aggregation

the process of combining two, or more, items to make a composite item (i.e., an aggregate). In object-oriented systems, we refer to aggregations as **composite objects**, and to the individual objects which make up the aggregation as **component objects**.

algorithm

a step-by-step description of a method for solving a problem. Algorithms need not be strictly sequential, i.e., some, or all, of the steps in an algorithm may occur concurrently.

attribute

a metric for, a characteristic of, or piece of (state) information about, an **object**. Attributes themselves are objects.

binding the association of one item with another, e.g., the association of a name with a given method, the assignment of a value to a variable, and the association of a name with an object. Binding can be static (early) or dynamic (late)

class an object which is used to create **instances**, i.e., a template, description, pattern, or "blueprint" of a category or collection of very similar items. Among other things, a class describes the interface these items will present to the outside world, i.e., the available and appropriate methods, constants and exceptions. A class represents an abstraction of the items. A class may itself be parameterized (i.e., it actually represents a family of very closely related classes), in which case we refer to it as a **parameterized class. Class** is a recursive concept. Specifically, we may define classes as being composed of other classes (i.e., heterogeneous composite classes and homogeneous composite classes), in terms of itself (a recursively defined class), as inheriting characteristics from one or more other classes (i.e., the superclasses of the class), and as providing characteristics to other classes (i.e., the subclasses of the class). In some places, classes are defined as "the set of all instances of a type," and the term "type" is given the above definition for class.

class variables [in some object-oriented programming languages] a set of variables which is common among all instances of the **class**. In some object-oriented programming languages, class variables are used to represent "the state of the class."

complete [in the context of describing a set of primitive methods for an object] denotes that we have not only the minimally complete set of primitive methods for the object (i.e., a sufficient set), but also that we have a set of primitive methods "that covers all [useful] aspects of the underlying abstraction." This set of methods includes all those primitive methods which are commonly associated with the abstraction. We may also speak of a complete set of all methods, including composite (i.e., non-primitive) methods, in the context of a **kit** based on an **object**.

completeness ensuring that all essential details have been addressed; all details need not be shown, but all aspects of an item must be covered.

component object	an **object** which is part of a **composite object**. A component object is an object which, from an *external* viewpoint, is *conceptually* a component of a composite object.
composite method	a method that is composed of two or more **primitive methods**.
composite object	an **object** which, from an *external* viewpoint, is *conceptually* composed of other objects. These "other objects" are referred to as **component objects**.
confirmability	the degree to which a system can be verified and validated.
constant	an object whose state or value never varies.
constructive iterator	a passive **iterator** that allows changes in the state of the **homogeneous composite object** over which it iterates.
constructor	a **method** that can (and often does) change the state of the **object** upon which it operates. Although a constructor method may return state information about the object upon which it operates, this is *not* the primary function of a constructor method. In some object-oriented programming languages (e.g., C++), "constructor" is more narrowly defined to refer to the specific method, defined in a class, which is used to create instances of the class.
constructor decoupling	a way of eliminating **interface object coupling** in which an encapsulated *composite* method, which originally directly referenced the state information in an instance of a different class, is replaced by a *primitive* constructor method for the encapsulating class. Outside of the encapsulating class, this constructor method may be used to (re)create the composite method which couples objects of differing classes.
container object	a synonym for **homogeneous composite object**.
copy semantics	semantics where **methods** produce one or more "copies" of an **object**, or where some, or all, methods are accomplished on a copy of the original object.
coupling from the side	object coupling in which an object that is *not* a specialization of another object has access to the underlying implementation of that other object (for example, the first object is not a subclass, a derived class, nor an extension of the other object).

coupling from underneath   object coupling in which an object that is a specialization of another object (e.g., the object is a subclass, a derived class, or an extension of the other object) has access to the underlying implementation(s) of one or more of its less specialized predecessors (e.g., its superclasses, base classes, or prototypes).

currying   a technique for reorganizing an method that requires multiple objects into a series of methods, each of which requires only one object.

data abstraction   a type of abstraction that extends the concept of functional abstraction, i.e., not only are the details of the how the function is accomplished ignored, but the details of the structure and underlying implementation of the data are ignored as well. Specifically, the data itself is treated as an abstraction, or high-level concept.

delegation   [in systems where new objects are created via prototyping] a mechanism whereby an method is not accomplished *directly* by an object, but is instead directed to (one of) the prototypical object(s) which was used to create the object, and it is the prototypical object which actually accomplishes the method. Alternatively, delegation has been defined as the creation or designation of an object to handle (supervise) a number of other objects in the accomplishment of an method.

deobjectification   the process of decomposing an object into smaller (typically low-level, primitive) objects, usually for the purposes of object storage, or object transmission (e.g., over a network). (See **objectification**.)

destructor   a specific **method**, defined in an **object** which is used to destroy, or remove, instances of that object. In some object-oriented programming languages, this is the only way in which an instance of a class can be removed.

empathy   allows one object to share the behavior of another object without explicitly redefining the behavior.

encapsulation   *as a process*, encapsulation means the act of enclosing one or more items within a (physical or logical) container. Encapsulation, *as an entity*, refers to a package or an enclosure that holds (contains, encloses) one or more items.

exception   a term used to indicate both "an abnormal condition" and "the mechanism for notifying the system that an abnormal condition has occurred."

exception handler   a specific sequence of instructions that handles a raised exception.

first class objects   objects that can be treated as variables within a program, e.g., they can be used in the assignment of values, passed as parameters, and used directly in aggregations.

functional abstraction   a type of **abstraction** where the details of how a function is accomplished are ignored and the function becomes a high-level concept. We may know a great deal about the interface to the function (e.g., the names, numbers, and ordering of the parameters, and the specific type of data required), but we know little about the specific algorithm(s) used to implement the function.

functional decomposition   the process of breaking a larger concept into components based primarily on the functional nature of both the larger concept and its components.

generalization   the process of taking an object, concept, or phenomenon to a higher level of abstraction. Specifically, we restrict our attention to the larger and more important details, and remove the smaller and less important details.

genericity   the ability to parameterize items, or create templates.

GIGO   Garbage In, Garbage Out.

handling an exception   executing a sequence of statement as a direct result of a specific exception being raised.

heterogeneous composite object   a **composite object** that is *conceptually* composed from objects which are not all *conceptually* the same.

homogeneous composite object   a **composite object** that is *conceptually* composed of component objects which are all *conceptually* the same.

identity   that property of an object which uniquely specifies the object, or distinguishes it from all other objects.

information hiding   making certain details of an item inaccessible.

inheritance   the process by which one object acquires (gets, receives) characteristics from another objects. "Characteristics" include such things as operations (and their corresponding methods), knowledge of state, exceptions, and constants. Inheritance is subject to some rules. The object receiving the characteristics may add additional characteristics to those which it inherits, modify some, or all, of the inherited characteristics, and delete (cover up) some, or all, of the inherited characteristics. Therefore, the characteristics for a given object are not necessarily the *sum* of all the characteristics of all of its antecedent objects.

inside internal coupling   occurs when: the methods for an object are coupled to the encapsulated state information for the object, and/or, the component objects that make up a composite object are coupled with the overall composite object and/or with each other. All objects will exhibit one or both of these forms of inside internal object coupling. However, there are varying degrees of tightness for this form of coupling, and software engineers should strive to keep this variety of coupling as loose as possible.

instance   an **object** which represents a specific thing, as opposed to a pattern for a (potentially broad) category of things. The usual connotation is that an instance is an item created using a pattern, e.g., a **class**.

instance variables   [in some object-oriented programming languages (e.g., C++ and Smalltalk)] are a means for maintaining all, or part of, the state for a given **object**. The **class** defines what the instance variables are, and each instance of the class (i.e., each object) has its own set of instance variables.

instantiation   the process of creating an **instance**.

interface coupling   a type of coupling that occurs when one object refers to another *specific* object, and the original object makes direct references to one or more items contained in the specific object's public interface. We further stipulate that items other than operations (method selectors), e.g., constants, variables, exportable definitions, and exceptions, may be found in the public interface of an object. Of course, the exact form and nature of any items that may be present in an object's public interface is dictated by the syntax and semantics of the implementation language.

internal coupling   occurs when one object has direct access to the underlying implementation of another object.

interoperability   given a computer network with potentially dissimilar nodes, and given that each node is viewed as a collection of (hardware and software) resources — interoperability is the degree to which an application, or part of an application, which is executing on one node on the network can use any of the (hardware and software) resources on any other node on the same network.

iterative approach

an iterative approach to (software) design stipulates that the design proceeds in steps (stages), and that, *at any time*, the designer(s) may return to some previous step, introduce a change, and then propagate the affects of that change (if any) through the design. Virtually every software design approach, with the possible exception of some rapid prototyping approaches, is iterative.

iterator

a capability that allows a user to traverse the nodes of a **homogeneous composite object**. Specifically, it allows a user to visit some, or all, of the nodes in a homogeneous composite object and perform some method (most often a selector) at each node. There are several types of iterators, e.g., selective, constructive, active, and passive.

JSD

Jackson System Development; a software design methodology developed at Michael Jackson Systems Limited and identified in the first Methodman study as a candidate for further consideration for use in the development of Ada software.

kit

a collection of objects (e.g., classes, metaclasses, non-class instances, unencapsulated composite operations, other kits, and systems of interacting objects) all of which support a single, large, coherent, object-oriented concept, e.g., windows, switches, and insurance policies. There may indeed be some physical connection among some of the members of a given kit. However, kits are "granular," i.e., while all the components of a kit are logically related, there are very few physical connections that bind them together.

life-cycle

[for a particular piece of software] the process that begins with the recognition of the need or desire for that particular piece of software, and terminates when the software is discarded or retired from use

localization

the process of placing items in close physical proximity to each other, usually with the connotation of having some mechanism for precisely defining the boundaries of the "area" into which the items are being gathered. In object-oriented approaches the localization is object-based, and in functional decomposition approaches the localization is function-based.

maintainability

the degree of ease with which a software product can be adapted, perfected, and corrected.

message

[in some object-oriented programming languages and systems] a means by which **objects** communicate.

Messages request an method on the part of the receiver and contain any additional information (i.e., other objects) needed to accomplish the method.

metaclass

[in structurally reflective systems] a **class** whose instances are themselves classes.

metaobject

[in reflexive systems] an **object** which parallels (i.e., "reflects") a computational object (i.e., the metaobject's referent object) and knows about the computational object as a computational entity.

method

the actual mechanism (algorithm) by which an **operation** is accomplished. Operations exist in the interface to an **object** and advertise a capability. Methods are internal to an object, i.e., they are not visible to those outside of the object.

mixins

In a **multiple inheritance** scheme, mixins are classes that embody "small," but highly-important characteristics of (potentially many different categories of) objects. (A mixin does not capture the essence of any one object, but rather the essence of a characteristic that may be found in several different objects.) The characteristics embodied in mixins are provided via inheritance. Mixins may be totally disjoint, or mixins may have overlapping subcharacteristics. Mixins are themselves objects. Mixins may be primitive or composite, i.e., a composite mixin may be decomposed into two, or more, primitive mixins. Mixins are sometimes referred to as "traits."

Methodman

a study conducted by the U.S. Department of Defense to identify methodologies which may be used during the software life-cycle. (*Note*: These studies focused on the development part of the software life-cycle.)

methodology

an organized collection of algorithms, rules, techniques, tools, procedures, and guidelines used to solve a problem.

modularity

the extent to which a larger system is broken into smaller, easily integrated, easily maintained, easily tested, easily reused, components; purposeful structuring. Modularity varies with the approach taken in the design of a system. In functionally decomposed systems, each module usually represents a functional capability or concept. In object-oriented systems each module represents an object-oriented concept or capability.

module cohesion

a measure of how logically related the parts of a module are to each other.

module coupling

a measure of the strength of the physical connection between two modules.

monolithic object

a *non-primitive* **object** that conceptually has no *externally* discernible structure. Monolithic objects may be implemented *internally* using any appropriate objects, but appear as monolithic entities to the outside world.

multiple inheritance

a concept whereby an object acquires characteristics directly from more than one other object.

non-class instance

an instance which is not a class. The usual connotation is that a non-class instance cannot be used directly as the basis for creating additional instances.

object

Objects are the physical and conceptual things we find in the world around us. An object may be hardware, software, a concept (e.g., velocity), or even "flesh and blood." Objects are complete entities, i.e., they are not "simply information" or "simply information and actions." Software objects strive to capture as completely as possible the characteristics of the "real world" objects which they represent. Finally, objects are "black boxes," i.e., their internal implementations are hidden from the outside world, and all interactions with an object take place via a well-defined interface.

object abstraction

the process of dealing with objects without regard to their underlying implementation. When we deal with an object as an abstraction, we may know a great deal about its externally discernible characteristics (e.g., what operations are available in its interface), but virtually nothing about its internal implementation.

object abstraction decoupling

a means of eliminating interface coupling by replacing references to specific different objects within an object with parameters, i.e., using data abstraction techniques to allow creation of objects using these parameters.

object cohesion

a measure of how logically related the components of the *external* view of an object are to each other. Additionally, and less importantly, object cohesion is a measure of how tightly bound or related the *internal* elements of an object are to each other. An intuitive measure of object cohesion is "how much sense the object makes" when viewed in isolation.

object coupling

describes the degree of inter-relationships among objects. It is important both to keep these inter-relationships as tenuous as possible, and to avoid *unnecessary* object coupling. There are two major types of object coupling: interface object coupling and internal object coupling. If the only other objects referred to by a specific object are primitive objects, we generally refer to the specific object as being "non-coupled."

object-based concurrency
a form of **process abstraction** where the protection (or the responsibility for protection, or the capability of protection) of an **object** in a concurrent system is localized on each instance of a **class**, and is independent of other instances of the same class.

object-oriented decomposition
a method of breaking down an item in such a way that its components correspond only to **objects**. Specifically, one views the item as a **system of objects** (and/or as a **composite object**) and identifies its **component objects** and their interactions and interrelationships, if any.

objectification
the process of re-constructing an **object** from smaller (typically low-level, primitive) objects after the original has been reduced to these smaller objects — usually to facilitate some form of transmission of the object over a communications link, or to facilitate persistent storage of the object

operation
an action which is suffered by, or required of, an **object**. Operations may be *selectors*, *constructors*, or *iterators*. An operation is contained in an object's interface and has its details described in a corresponding **method.** **Operations** may be composite, i.e., composed of other operations. However, encapsulation of composite operations within the interface to an object is not encouraged.

operation-based concurrency
(sometimes called "class-based concurrency") a form of **process abstraction** where the protection (or the responsibility for protection, or the capability of protection) of an **object** in a concurrent system is localized in the **class** itself, *not* in each instance of the class.

outside internal coupling
occurs if an object external to another object has access to, or knowledge of, the underlying implementation of the other object, i.e., that part of an object that we normally consider hidden to those outside of the object.

parameterized class
(also known as a generic class) a class that serves as a template for other classes — a template that may be parameterized by other classes, objects, and/or methods.

passive iterator (sometimes referred to as an "closed iterator") a capability which allows iteration over a **homogeneous composite object** by means of a single atomic **method**. Once set in motion, iteration continues until every node in the composite object has been visited, or until some pre-determined conditions have been met. Further, the *same* method(s) is performed at each node. Users of passive iterators have less control than users of **active iterators**, but do not have to concern themselves with the low-level methods necessary to accomplish the iteration.

PDL [originally] Program Design Language; [alternately] Process Description Language; a tool used to provide a high-level description of the logic, interfaces, and data of a proposed piece of software. In the object-oriented design process, software engineers may use the implementation language as a PDL

persistence a measure of the volatility of the state of an **object.** The usual connotation is that persistent objects remain (i.e., their states are preserved) after the execution of a program terminates, and are thus available for other applications (in the states which they were last left in by the previous application).

perspective different views of the same **object**. A perspective may be viewed as a specific instance of a **property** class.

polymorphism a measure of the degree of difference in how each item in a specified collection of items must be treated at a given level of abstraction. Polymorphism is increased when any *unnecessary* differences, at any level of abstraction, within a collection of items are eliminated. For example, if two, or more, **objects**, each an instance of a different *class*, exhibit the same general behavior when they suffer an operation with the same name in each of the classes, then the objects are said to be polymorphic with respect to that suffered operation.

portability the degree of ease with which a software product may be moved (re-hosted, re-targeted) to a different environment.

predicate a test which has a discrete (as opposed to continuous) result, e.g., true or false (although predicates are not restricted to binary results).

primitive object an **object** that is provided by the environment, most typically by the programming language. Primitive objects have two main uses: providing a basis for the construction of other, non-primitive objects, and as mechanism for communication among otherwise uncoupled objects.

primitive method

a method which *cannot* be accomplished simply, reliably, and efficiently without knowledge of the underlying implementation of the object, or class of objects, e.g., "adding an item to a list."

problem space

the name given to all "real world" items (e.g., "real world" objects and "real world" algorithms) used to describe our problem.

process

[in the "process paradigm" — a paradigm closely related to the object-oriented paradigm] an active entity the behaves just like a real world entity and communicates with the outside world usually by passing and receiving messages via ports.

process abstraction

a type of abstraction which is built "on top of" data abstraction, i.e., both the details of how a function is accomplished and the details of the structure and underlying implementation of the data are suppressed. Further, the specific details of how something will behave, or protect itself, in the presence of multiple threads of control (i.e., in a concurrent environment) are also suppressed.

property

a description of a relationship, specifically an encapsulation of those things which comes into existence when one **object** is placed in the context of another. Said another way, a property is a set of characteristics which are *not* characteristics of any of the individual objects involved in the relationship, but rather are characteristics of the relationship itself. Properties are themselves objects.

protocol

[in Smalltalk] the set of all types of **messages** which may be received by an **object**. A protocol description describes not only the types of messages which an object may receive, but also the operations which will be taken for each type of message. Alternatively: the set of all **operations** in the interface of an object.

prototype

[in some object-oriented systems] an **object** from which new objects with different characteristics can be created. Specifically, prototyping is a means of creating a different type of object without creating a **class** for that object.

rapid prototyping	an approach to software development which allows a user to rapidly create a "mock up," a complete working version of a software product, or a nearly complete working version of a software product. Rapid prototyping today is most often accomplished via a software tool, and less often via a library of reusable modules.
recursive approach	an approach which can be (re)applied to the end products of a usage of the approach.
referent object	[in reflexive systems] the computational object which is referred to (i.e., reflected by) a corresponding **metaobject**.
reflection	a process whereby a system knows about itself as a computational, or structural, entity and has the capability to act on this knowledge. There are two main types of reflection: *structural reflection* which involves the reflective use of classes and metaclasses for implementing objects, i.e., this is a static model of reflection, and *computational reflection* which dictates that each object in an object-oriented system has a **metaobject** counterpart (i.e., a reflection), and that this metaobject knows about its **referent object** as a computational entity and can interact dynamically with this object and any other object or metaobject in the system.
reification	the process of transforming an entity into something which can be manipulated at the meta level in a reflexive system.
required operation	an operation for a *different* **object** which is needed (required) by an object to ensure the proper and desired characteristics for the object.
resilient object	[in networking applications] an **object** whose state is simultaneously maintained on several different nodes on the network, specifically with the intention of continuing processing with the preserved state should a node containing the object become unavailable for any reason.
reusability	the degree to which a piece of software can be used for more than one application or in more than one place in the same application.
SADT	**Structured Analysis and Design** Technique; a **functional decomposition** software design methodology developed at SofTech

SASD

Structured Analysis and Structured Design. SASD is a functional decomposition approach to software analysis and design.

selective iterator

a passive **iterator** that does not allow changes in state in the **homogeneous composite object** over which it traverses.

selector

a **method** that returns state information about the **object** in which it is encapsulated, and cannot (by definition) change the state of that object. In Smalltalk-80 a selector is the symbolic name of "the type of operation a message requests of its receiver."

selector decoupling

a way of eliminating interface object coupling in which an encapsulated method, which originally directly referenced the state information in a different **object**, is replaced by a selector method which returns state information about an object which may be used by methods of different objects.

sequential approach

an approach which stipulates that once a particular part of the approach is completed, it can never be altered, i.e., the only way to change the results of the approach is to completely redo the approach. Sequential approaches are only practical for very small problems, or where rapid prototyping techniques make the re-application of the approach trivial.

share semantics

semantics where **methods** may produce multiple names (aliases) for the same **object** (as opposed to multiple copies of the same object), or where some, or all, methods may use multiple names for the same object (thus all methods anywhere, regardless of which name (alias) is used, are accomplished on the *same* object).

signature

the precise description of the interface to an **operation**. This usually includes: the precise name of the operation, and the number, order, names, and types of the operands. Depending on the implementation environment, some of these aspects of a signature may not be present, or others may be added.

slot

often used as a synonym for **instance or class variables**. Sometimes the definition is expanded to include all externally definable characteristics of an object.

solution space

those software items which are used to solve (model) the "real world" problems, e.g., programming language objects.

specialization the process of modifying an item for a more specific purpose. In object-oriented systems there are two main forms of specialization: **inheritance** and **delegation**.

state a set of circumstances or attributes characterizing an object at a given time; the condition of an object. Normally, when we refer to the state of an object, we are referring to its own (self-contained), externally-discernible state, and not to the state of the system that contains the object.

subclass a class which has inherited characteristics from one (or more) specified classes (i.e., its **superclasses**), and has added to, removed, or modified some, or all, of these inherited characteristics, i.e., a subclass is supposed to be different from its superclass(es). Some refer to "subclass" as the Smalltalk-specific way of denoting a specialization.

subtype a further refinement (specialization) of a **type**. The usual connotation is that a subtype is more restrictive than a type, and that objects that participate in methods defined by a subtype, may also participate in methods defined by the parent type from which the subtype was derived.

suffered operation an **operation** which is provided (advertised, exported) in the public interface of an **object**, i.e., those operations made available to those outside of an object, and allow the state of the encapsulating object to be changed or queried.

sufficient [in the context of describing a set of **methods** for an object] denotes a *minimal* set of **primitive methods** necessary to accomplish any desired behavior for an object.

superclass a **class** which *directly* provides characteristics for a specified class (i.e., the **subclass**). We say that a subclass inherits characteristics from its superclass(es). Since **class** is a recursively defined concept, a superclass may itself be a subclass of some other class. Some refer to "superclass" as the Smalltalk-specific way of denoting a generalization.

swizzling [most commonly used in object-oriented database systems] the process whereby non-persistent computational links, which are used to bind together a composite object, are converted into persistent links within a persistent storage medium (e.g., an object-oriented database management system). This is also the name given to the reverse process.

system of interacting objects a collection of objects (e.g., classes, metaclasses, non-class instances, unencapsulated composite operations, kits, and other systems of interacting objects) all of which support a single, large, coherent, object-oriented concept, and in which there must be a direct or indirect physical connection between any two arbitrary objects within the collection. Further, systems of interacting objects have at least one internal, independently executing thread of control. Lastly, systems of interacting objects may exhibit multiple, completely disjoint public interfaces.

testability the degree of ease with which a software product can be examined with the intention of finding errors.

tool [in the software engineering sense] usually an automated (i.e., executable on a computer) technique used at some point during the software life-cycle.

traceability the degree of ease with which a concept, idea, or other item may be followed from one point in a process to either a succeeding, or preceding, point in the same process. For example, one may wish to trace a requirement through the software engineering process to identify the delivered source code which specifically addresses that requirement.

type something which defines the **methods** in which a given **object** may participate. Whereas **classes** define the structure, appearance, and behavior of objects, types merely define sets of legal methods for given objects.

uniformity the absence of confusing (and costly) inconsistencies in a product.

value the unambiguously defined state, or partial state, of an object. While some use the terms "state" and "value" interchangeably, others place special, and different, connotations with each term.

VDM **Vienna Development Method.** A formal approach to software development that has two principle components: a description of the abstract data structures that comprise the internal state of a system, and the definitions of the operations that are used to manipulate the state.

Index